Praise for *Fine-Tuning AI*

This book is a definitive masterclass for any engineer transitioning from fragile API prototypes to robust, edge-deployed services. The practical deep dives into parameter-efficient fine-tuning make production-grade AI genuinely accessible.

—*Vishwesh Ravi Shrimali, AI engineer, automotive industry*

Laurence has written a book that goes well beyond teaching how to fine-tune AI models. He connects fine-tuning, evaluation, quantization, optimization, and deployment into a practical engineering journey, making the tradeoffs and decisions behind production AI easy to understand. I would confidently recommend this book to any AI engineer looking to build systems that go beyond prototypes.

—*Aditya Goel, independent AI consultant, GenAI & AI products*

Fine-Tuning AI is a rare book that makes modern fine-tuning approachable without sacrificing technical rigor. From LoRA to multimodal and diffusion models, it builds intuition first and equips readers with practical skills they can immediately apply. Small, personalized models are coming for the world!

—*Lipi Deepaakshi Patnaik, software development engineer, Uber Technologies*

What sets this book apart is its scope: it doesn't stop at LoRA and training loops, but pushes into alignment, multimodal models, and production serving. It's the book I wish I'd had when I started fine-tuning models myself.

—*Gourav Singh Bais, lead AI engineer*

Fine-Tuning AI

Customizing Large Language Models

Laurence Moroney

O'REILLY®

Fine-Tuning AI
by Laurence Moroney

Published by O'Reilly Media, Inc., 141 Stony Circle, Suite 195, Santa Rosa, CA 95401.

O'Reilly books may be purchased for educational, business, or sales promotional use. Online editions are also available for most titles (*https://oreilly.com*). For more information, contact our corporate/institutional sales department: 800-998-9938 or *corporate@oreilly.com*.

Acquisitions Editor: Nicole Butterfield
Development Editor: Michele Cronin
Production Editor: Ashley Stussy
Copyeditor: Vanessa Moore
Proofreader: Krsta Technology Solutions
Indexer: Sue Klefstad
Cover Designer: Susan Brown
Cover Illustrator: Monica Kamsvaag
Interior Designer: David Futato
Interior Illustrator: Kate Dullea

October 2026: First Edition

Revision History for the First Edition
2026-10-21: First Release

See *https://oreilly.com/catalog/errata.csp?isbn=9798341673373* for release details.

979-8-341-67337-3

[LSI]

Table of Contents

Preface

I want to make a simple case to you. In the age of AI, and in particular code generation and vibe coding, the greatest opportunity for you as a software developer is in fine-tuning small models.

Consider where we are. The last few years have been full of releases of enormous, generalist models that are genuinely astonishing. They can do everything from writing poetry to generating code to explaining quantum mechanics. But, when you build software on top of them, you'll soon hit a wall. With them, you *rent* intelligence, paying by the token. You send data (sometimes critical private data!) to another person's servers. There, it will be handled by a very smart model that doesn't really know anything specific about *your* domain beyond its public training data. So your protocols, your codebase, your customers, and your visual style will at best be guessed at.

That's the wall.

The door: you don't need a massive model to be excellent at a single thing. Smaller models, themselves excellent generalists, can be fine-tuned on *your* data. Also, they can be deployed in *your* data center, or even on your desktop! With a few examples, and techniques such as LoRA, you can have a model that's as good as, or better than, the giant generalist. And importantly, you own it. You run it where you want it. No more *rented* intelligence.

And what makes this an opportunity for you as a developer? The collapse in the barrier to entry. You don't need to be a frontier lab. It's a laptop, plus a few hours of learning and work.

I foresee a future where *most* intelligence is local. Where most users and producers of intelligent solutions will run them on laptops and phones. That's the opportunity for you as a software developer: to build that future.

And this book gives you the skills to do exactly that!

Intended Audience

I wrote this book for anybody who's interested in building. While it might say "AI" on the cover, that doesn't mean it's meant for an exclusive group of mathematicians or research scientists.

All you need is a bit of curiosity, a sprinkle of data, and a willingness to learn, and you can get involved in the creation of specialized intelligent models. The only code I'll use in the book is simple-to-learn Python.

Prerequisite Knowledge

It would be good to understand a little Python code, as well as the mechanics of calling applications over the internet with requests and responses.

Hardware and Software Dependencies

There are no particular hardware or software dependencies. Indeed, all of the work you do in this book can be achieved using Google Colab's free tier.

Book Structure

This book is made up of four core parts, each aligned with the skills that you'll learn.

The first part, Chapters 1–3, sets the table, showing you the core ideas of moving from generalist models to specialist ones, and explaining the core architectures of language models and how they can be fine-tuned.

Next, in Chapters 4–10, you'll get the core loop of fine-tuning a model. Everything from data collection to preparation, the mechanics of adaptation, tuning, alignment and preference optimization.

We'll take a side tour into tuning image-based models in Chapters 11–13, where you'll learn about vision language models, and how they can be tuned to add specific subjects and styles.

Then, we'll wrap up the book by showing how you can ship and manage your new expert models in Chapters 14 and 15.

Conventions Used in This Book

The following typographical conventions are used in this book:

Italic
: Indicates new terms, URLs, email addresses, filenames, and file extensions.

`Constant width`
: Used for program listings, as well as within paragraphs to refer to program elements such as variable or function names, databases, data types, environment variables, statements, and keywords.

`Constant width italic`
: Shows text that should be replaced with user-supplied values or by values determined by context.

> This element signifies a tip or suggestion.

> This element signifies a general note.

> This element indicates a warning or caution.

Using Code Examples

Supplemental material (code examples, exercises, etc.) is available for download at *https://github.com/lmoroney/fine-tuning-book*.

If you have a technical question or a problem using the code examples, please send email to *support@oreilly.com*.

This book is here to help you get your job done. In general, if example code is offered with this book, you may use it in your programs and documentation. You do not need to contact us for permission unless you're reproducing a significant portion of the code. For example, writing a program that uses several chunks of code from this book does not require permission. Selling or distributing examples from O'Reilly books does require permission. Answering a question by citing this book and quoting example code does not require permission. Incorporating a significant amount of example code from this book into your product's documentation does require permission.

We appreciate, but generally do not require, attribution. An attribution usually includes the title, author, publisher, and ISBN. For example: "*Fine-Tuning AI* by Laurence Moroney (O'Reilly). Copyright 2027 Laurence Moroney, 979-8-341-67337-3."

If you feel your use of code examples falls outside fair use or the permission given above, feel free to contact us at *permissions@oreilly.com*.

O'Reilly Online Learning

For more than 40 years, O'Reilly Media has provided technology and business training, knowledge, and insight to help companies succeed.

Our unique network of experts and innovators share their knowledge and expertise through books, articles, and our online learning platform. O'Reilly's online learning platform gives you on-demand access to live training courses, in-depth learning paths, interactive coding environments, and a vast collection of text and video from O'Reilly and 200+ other publishers. For more information, visit *https://oreilly.com*.

How to Contact Us

Please address comments and questions concerning this book to the publisher:

O'Reilly Media, Inc.
141 Stony Circle, Suite 195
Santa Rosa, CA 95401
800-889-8969 (in the United States or Canada)
707-827-7019 (international or local)
707-829-0104 (fax)
support@oreilly.com
https://oreilly.com/about/contact.html

We have a web page for this book, where we list errata and any additional information. You can access this page at *https://oreil.ly/fine-tuning-ai-1e*.

For news and information about our books and courses, visit *https://oreilly.com*.

Find us on LinkedIn: *https://linkedin.com/company/oreilly*.

Watch us on YouTube: *https://youtube.com/oreillymedia*.

Acknowledgments

It takes a village to ship a book like this.

First of all, everyone on the O'Reilly team: Nicole Butterfield, who believed in my vision and helped me bring it to reality; Michele Cronin, who took my poorly written words and honed them into clear prose; Kate Dullea, for taking my crude, and often AI-generated, images and making them shine; and Vanessa Moore, Ayisha Mohamad, Sue Klefstad, and Ashley Stussy with their magic post-production skills to get it across the finish line!

A book like this also isn't possible without the contributions of technical reviewers who find bugs, fix issues, help guide direction, and give inspiration at all stages. The team behind this book is among the best I've ever worked with: Gourav Singh Bais, Aditya Goel, Lipi Deepaakshi Patnaik, and Vishwesh Ravi Shrimali.

But most of all I'd like to thank my family for their infinite patience with me while I was working on this. To Rebecca, my wife, who is the light of my life, and the greatest blessing imaginable. To my son, Chris, who is taking his steps into the world of software engineering at an exciting time, and who will thrive at it. And to my daughter, Claudia, and son-in-law, Ben, who never fail to inspire me. I thank God for you all!

Acknowledgment

CHAPTER 1

From Generalist to Specialist

The honeymoon is over.

Like me, you've probably already built prototypes using large language models (LLMs) as the backend. You've felt that initial rush when your complex query, expressed as a prompt, returns a perfect, coherent response. Design that "surprises and delights" is a desirable goal, and the response from the LLM attains that. For a moment, you feel that the future of software is infinite, and that prompting is the new programming language. You just need to come up with clever ones.

Since the emergence of LLMs, popularized by ChatGPT, we've been in the era of the *generalist*. We've been awed by LLMs that have been trained on the entire internet and beyond. They can do everything from writing haiku poetry to optimizing Rust functions. They are technological marvels.

But what if you want to ship a *real* product? When using these models, you'll often find that, for various reasons, despite the initial euphoria, they could be the wrong tool for the job. While its ability to rhyme is impressive, you really want it not to hallucinate nonexistent tables while querying your legacy SQL database!

And this is what's emerging as the "API wall." It's that invisible barrier that separates a cool hackathon demo from a profitable business, and that separates successful startups from buzzworthy ones. There are hard realities in overcoming that wall: the potentially crushing cost of scale, unpredictable latency, and, of course, the terrified look on the face of your chief information security officer (CISO) when you mention that you'll be sharing customer data with a third party.

This book is ultimately about breaking through that wall. It's about moving from *renting* intelligence to *owning* it. It will have you replace the massive generalists with agile, hypercompetent specialists: fine-tuned AI that knows your business better than any trillion-parameter giant ever could. You're going to dismantle the "prompt engineering" paradigm.

In this chapter, we'll look at the brutal "unit economics" that has killed many AI startups. And we'll see why a small, open source model running on a single GPU can and should beat the world's smartest AI in *your* specific domain.

The Cost of Renting Intelligence

Every project starts innocently. You get an API key and start coding. You craft a system prompt honed from lots of experimentation. It works. You deploy to beta.

And then you look at the costs. Your eyes go wide. You think about what it would look like. They go even wider! We'll explore those costs in this section.

The Token Tax

In the prototyping phase, inference costs feel negligible. A fraction of a cent per request is basically free. But when you move from "chatting" to automation, the math turns against you.

Most providers charge by the token (where a token is roughly 0.75 words), so you have to consider per-token costs when projecting your system costs.

Table 1-1 shows the costs (at the time of writing) per million tokens for major models.

Table 1-1. Cost per million tokens for major models

Model	Input $/M	Output $/M	Per doc (no reasoning)	Per doc (reasoning, +5k thinking)	Daily (5,000 docs)
GPT-5.5 Pro	$30.00	$180.00	$0.69	$1.59	$7,950.00
Claude Fable 5	$10.00	$50.00	$0.22	$0.47	$2,350.00
GPT-5.5	$5.00	$30.00	$0.12	$0.27	$1,325.00
Claude Opus 4.8	$5.00	$25.00	$0.11	$0.24	$1,175.00
Claude Sonnet 4.6	$3.00	$15.00	$0.07	$0.14	$705.00
GPT-5.4	$2.50	$15.00	$0.06	$0.13	$665.00
Gemini 3.1 Pro	$2.00	$12.00	$0.05	$0.11	$530.00
Claude Haiku 4.5	$1.00	$5.00	$0.02	$0.05	$235.00
DeepSeek V4 Pro	$0.44	$0.87	$0.008	$0.013	$63.00
DeepSeek V4 Flash	$0.14	$0.28	$0.003	$0.004	$21.00

So, for a high-end reasoning model, if you're building a system that processes documents, your costs could be from $21 to $7,950 per day, depending on the model used. And while those prices are coming down over time, it's still very expensive!

Let's play that out with a scenario. Consider a "legal contract analyzer" app. Your users upload documents, and your app will extract summaries of potential issues or risks in the contracts.

The architecture might look like Figure 1-1.

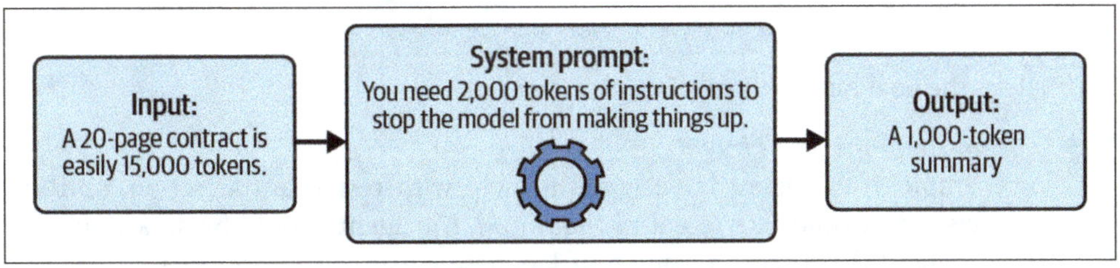

Figure 1-1. A simple LLM-based architecture for a legal contract analyzer

Your input is your prompt plus the contract. A typical contract with lots of legalese can be about 15,000 tokens. Your system prompt is something you've carefully crafted with lots of instructions to avoid hallucinations, and to structure your output exactly the way the rest of the system needs it, maybe as JSON or other structured files. This takes tokens. And of course your output is yet more tokens.

So, let's say, 17,000 tokens in, and 1,000 tokens out. Given the costs just outlined, that could be 20 cents per document. If you have 1,000 users each analyzing 5 documents per day, that's the costs shown in Table 1-1—anything from $21 per day to almost $8,000 depending on the model and service!

That's the money you have to spend just to *operate* the model in this system. You, of course, also have to invest in the infrastructure. And you *own* none of the intelligence at the end of it; you're only *renting* intelligence. If you charge your users a monthly fee, say $20 per month, they can become a net loss very quickly. You have very risky margins.

The Agentic Multiplier

Now consider the impact of agents. They've been the darling of the tech industry since about mid-2024, and for good reason. They're an excellent design pattern to get the most out of LLMs by moving beyond just getting an answer for a question. To understand their explosive growth, less than 1% of enterprise software included agentic AI in 2024, but Gartner (*https://oreil.ly/RTVLe*) predicts that over 40% will by the end of 2026. That's a 40-fold increase in less than 2 years!

But what *are* they? I usually like to think of agents as following the pattern shown in Figure 1-2.

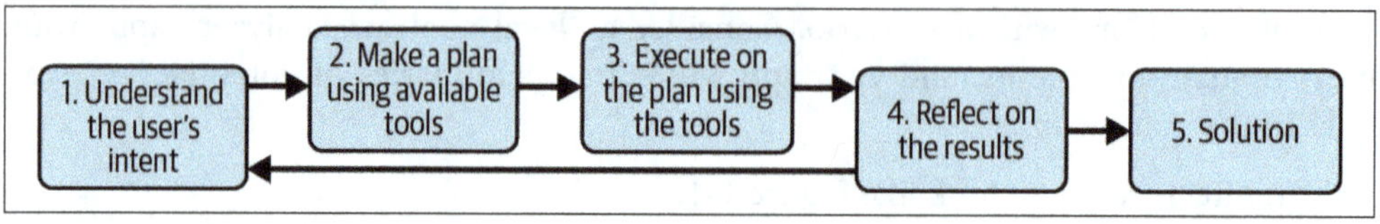

Figure 1-2. An agentic workflow

Ultimately, the goal here is to follow these steps:

Step 1: Understand the user's intent.
: For example, if the agent is designed to help with restaurant selection, and the user says they would like to eat *okonomiyaki*, the agent should be smart enough to understand that this is a branch of Japanese cuisine. The user doesn't need to specify this.

Step 2: Make a plan to solve the problem with the available tools.
: If the agent knows that its tools are Google Search, Google Maps, and web browsers, it can make a plan to search for Japanese restaurants near the current location. For each of these, it can then browse their websites to find their menus. It can then search the menus for *okonomiyaki*.

Step 3: Execute the plan using the tools.
: It then follows the plan, using LLMs as appropriate; for example, generating code to call the Google Maps APIs, or parsing downloaded HTML to find the desired dish.

Step 4: Reflect on the results.
: After it's done all this, it should then match its results with the user's requirements. Did it find restaurants serving this specific dish, or just generic Japanese ones, and so on. If it did, great, it can move on to step 5 and present the solution. Otherwise, it'll have to go back to steps 1 and 2.

Step 5: Present the solution.
: Finally, it presents the solution to the user, and possibly offers the user access to other agents, such as one that can handle making a reservation at the desired restaurant.

This workflow, with a dedicated chain of thought, is the simplest DNA of an agent. But when it comes to token usage, you can see that it can use significantly more tokens than a simple prompt → result scenario. So those costs we predicted earlier based on different models could be multiplied by five to ten times when using an agentic workflow like this.

No wonder companies are investing billions of dollars in data centers!

The Instruction Tax

There's also a more subtle inefficiency when using large hosted models. The generalist model doesn't understand anything about your specific task until you tell it. To make it useful, you have to paste your rules, formatting guides, and how to handle edge cases into the system prompt on *every single request*!

"You are an expert at understanding a variety of dishes and where to find them. Understand the user's request, and map it to one or more popular cuisines. If there isn't a direct match, find other restaurant types that might serve this dish. Output your results as JSON structured in this way {...}"

You're paying to send this instruction manual, and all of its tokens, to the server over and over again. It's extremely wasteful.

And, context window pollution is something to consider. Research has shown that as you stuff the context window with instructions, the model's performance will degrade. This is known as the "lost in the middle" (*https://oreil.ly/EVtK3*) phenomenon. I've seen so many examples where strict instructions (usually in ALL CAPS for emphasis) have to be entered to get the model to pay attention to a particular part of the prompt. And this, of course, consumes more tokens.

Fine-tuning moves these instructions from the context window (which you pay for) into the model weights (which are permanent). The model doesn't need to be told how to behave, as it's already baked in.

The Latency Killer

Costs are a business problem. Latency is a user experience problem. And if your users have a poor experience, they won't pay the costs.

Consider a massive foundation model with hundreds of billions of parameters. The physics of inference on this model is inescapable. Even with state-of-the-art GPUs, moving terabytes of weights through memory takes time and power. An important metric: time to first token (TTFT) can sit anywhere from 500 ms to several seconds. The next metric, tokens per second (TPS), then measures how frequently tokens appear after the first one.

Think of this as you build a chatbot. If it takes 500 ms to produce the first token (TTFT) and then 50 tokens per second (TPS), your user experience will be fine. Your tolerance to higher TTFT and less TPS is probably okay because you are used to people thinking before they respond.

But what about other scenarios? For example, coding with intelligent autocomplete. Developers typically need suggestions *quickly*. If the TTFT is very high, they can probably just type it quicker themselves. Or with *voice* applications? If there's a multisecond lag, then conversations might feel broken. As such, depending on your application type, the quality of response is important.

And moving tokens through a behemoth is slower due to the size of the model. Faster, better machines with dedicated hardware are, at best, a patch for this problem.

And, of course, if that machine is shared with millions of other customers, you face the possibility of different TTFT and TPS, because your query just has to get in line alongside others. It's not a good look if your enterprise customer's dashboard is slow, because your system is competing with high schoolers using ChatGPT to write their essays!

Thus, if you consider an on-premise model that's fine-tuned to the specific need, you'll see that it's generally smaller, so it doesn't need the dedicated high-cost hardware to manage syncing the model across many machines. There's less latency, no round-tripping to the cloud or getting in line behind other models. You can scale your hardware investments to your needs. And, of course, you can tune the model yourself to optimize it for your particular workload.

I've seen applications that were sluggish and brittle on a hosted model, but they become instant and snappy when moved to a local model. The problem then shifts from mitigating failures due to others hosting the model, toward adding business value by fine-tuning the local one. Ultimately this adds to the value of your business, instead of flowing operating expenses to a third party.

The Data Firewall

If cost and latency weren't enough to make you rethink, the enterprise sales cycle, and necessary compliance when working with them should.

True story: I once sat in on a meeting for a potential investment on a very hot startup that was pitching AI to solve a common problem in hospitals. It used computer vision with vision language models. I can't go into the specifics, of course, but ultimately it would save hospitals a lot of time and money, as well as helping them improve quality of care. But, being vision based, it involved putting cameras in common places, including the hospital ward.

Given the requirements for *flexibility*, where one day they might want to be able to spot a particular issue, but another day they might want to see something different, the idea of vision language models (VLMs) was appealing. One can train a nontransformer-based model for computer vision, but then it becomes static. It's good at spotting X or Y, but if you then want to see Z, you need a whole new model. With a VLM, it's just a prompt: "What's in this picture?" or "Tell me if you see violation (X) in this image" etc.

The startup demonstrated how they would do this. The demo was amazing. It did everything that the customers thought hospitals would need. There was a lot of excitement. Then, someone asked about the architecture. The VLM was a hosted giant model.

"Wait," the CISO asked. "You're sending images to <Company Name>?"

The CEO of the startup nodded slowly. "Yes," she replied. She then held up documents showing how <Company Name> manages privacy, guarantees anonymity, and everything else to ensure that their system had integrity.

But that wasn't enough. They would have to go to the hospital with a "trust me, bro" attitude around a very large third party, who themselves weren't at the table. Naturally, despite the optimism, the deal died at that table (and hospitals aren't nearly as secure today as they could be, had this system come to fruition).

And that's a good thing, at least until now. Now there's an alternative path forward. I hope that the startup has moved into the space of local VLMs so they can get to the best of both worlds. If you are part of this startup and happen to be reading this, please reach out and let me know!

The Metadata Leak

The preceding story is an example of where the *data* that belongs to the customer was a showstopper, but the design of the product was, to its disadvantage, shared with a third party.

But it's not just the data or the prompt content that can be a risk. It's also the metadata. Do note that an API provider, even if they don't look at or leak your data, still knows who you are when you send requests, how big the requests are, and what you might be working on.

In high-stakes businesses like financial investment, a leak about the things you are researching could tip the hands of your competition. For example, in businesses that are considering mergers and acquisition (M&A), if it leaked that Company A is spending a lot of time looking at the fundamentals of Company B, it could be inferred that they're considering acquiring them. Knowledge of this could lead third parties to purchase shares in Company B and drive up the eventual acquisition price. This could easily become a new form of insider trading.

Compliance Issues

Frameworks like General Data Protection Regulation (GDPR) can also make this much stickier. If a user demands their data to be deleted, you can remove it from your infrastructure, but what if you used it to prompt a third-party model? How can you guarantee that it's deleted from their servers?

When you own the model, you have full provenance. You can show exactly what data you used to fine-tune. You can keep logs of all data that's passed into your model for inference and delete as necessary. You can retrain from a clean dataset if you need to.

Ultimately, you have control.

Model Drift

I've personally been very surprised by how many times I've spoken with companies that had an "it worked yesterday, it fails today" problem. They didn't understand why. And the explanation was simple: API providers update their models constantly. So, all the effort that goes into prompt engineering (in particular, injecting commands into the context window) can evaporate overnight. The only solution, which is to reengineer the prompts and hope the vendor doesn't introduce breaking changes to *your* prompt, isn't exactly the most inspiring!

But, of course, owning your own fine-tuned model creates that static artifact that *you* control. It won't change unless *you* want it to. And if you do change it, you still hold the older versions, so you can introduce regression and gradually update your apps that use it.

The Specialist Revolution

For a long time, scaling laws were the vectors that pointed to a better future. Bigger, more data, more layers, more transformers, more parameters was always better. The direction of innovation followed this.

Once models reached a certain size, it became infeasible to host them yourself, and you had to depend on the giants with the billion-dollar data centers to host them for you, and you paid by the token.

But that's no longer strictly true. We are well into the transition toward a bifurcation with the era of LLMs being small enough to self-host, licenses that allow for this, and open source pretrained models being freely shared. With the ability to further fine-tune those models on your downstream tasks, and your particular data, you now have a viable alternative.

In early 2023, the release of LLaMA started this ball rolling. And, it proved that well-engineered models, despite their much smaller size, could punch way above their weight. It also started massive innovation in research where new optimizations drove better quality of model, instead of just throwing scale at the problem.

And that's the spirit of this book. The generalist is still alive and well and able to do amazing work with its vast knowledge.

But maybe it's time for more specialists in our lives. And that's what I think is a very bright future for developers like you: building specialists.

Hardware Is No Longer the Blocker

I once spoke at a conference in Wales. The speaker before me was a medical researcher using AI to detect brain disease. Over a beer later, I asked him what his biggest bottleneck was. I expected him to say data.

"Compute," he said. "We have ten researchers and only enough budget for one GPU. My slot is Tuesday afternoon. The rest of the week, I just have to theorize."

That was only a few years ago. Today, the laptop I'm writing this on—a standard MacBook Pro—can fine-tune a model that is orders of magnitude more powerful than what he was using.

The shift to *Unified Memory* (in Apple Silicon and newer chips) means we don't need massive industrial server farms to build AI. We can load 70B parameter models into system RAM. We can build and test locally. The AI R&D lab now fits in a backpack.

The Spectrum of Customization

There are many ways that you can customize your model, which fall into three broad areas:

Using prompts
: Within the prompt you can "teach" the model how to do things by sharing examples. This can include more advanced criteria, such as soft-prompting.

Using RAG
: Retrieval-augmented generation (RAG) is a way of embedding "new" knowledge by having an automated system add related content to your prompt to give your model extra context.

Fine-tuning
: Here's where you will burn new patterns into the model's brain so it does them without extra prompting. It's the hardest to do, but the most valuable in the long run.

I'm not going to cover the first two in this book, as they've extensively been covered, and ultimately don't change the model; they are just smarter ways of prompting.

Instead, this book is for the hard part—the fine-tuning of models. We won't just talk theory; we're going to calculate VRAM requirements, scrape and clean messy data, and debug training loops that refuse to converge.

The API wall is very high, but now, more than ever, there's an alternative. And I do believe the high-value skill of tomorrow lies with the developers that can overcome that, and build an AI that you own completely.

In Chapter 2, you'll begin that journey by looking at a few of the more popular models and how they're built. That will hopefully help you choose the best one for your task.

CHAPTER 2

Model Architectures: The DNA of AI

In Chapter 1, we explored that the era of "one giant model fits all" is evolving, and why fine-tuning smaller, more specialized models represents a strong future of practical AI deployment. The opportunity is in front of you to expand your skills to be a model customizer. But before you can do this, you need to understand *what* you are customizing. To use an analogy: a mechanic who doesn't understand how an engine works may be able to change the oil, but they cannot rebuild the transmission. Similarly, if you're a fine-tuning practitioner, you need to grasp the fundamentals of how transformer models work. That way, you won't be limited to surface-level adjustments, and you'll be able to make the deep, strategic decisions that separate a mediocre fine-tuned model from an exceptional one.

So, in this chapter, we're going to do an anatomy lesson. The goal is to dissect the architecture that powers every major language model today. You'll examine the key innovations that differentiate the leading open source model families, and understand how they convert raw text into the mathematical representations that make "understanding" possible. It will be a very high-level look, as one could write several whole books on how transformers work under the hood, so we'll just be hitting the highlights.

By the end, you'll have the foundation you need to make informed decisions about which base model to choose for your specific fine-tuning project.

The Flow of Information: How Transformers Work

Before going into the details, it's good to get a high-level mental model for how a transformer-based language model deals with text.

You can see this in Figure 2-1.

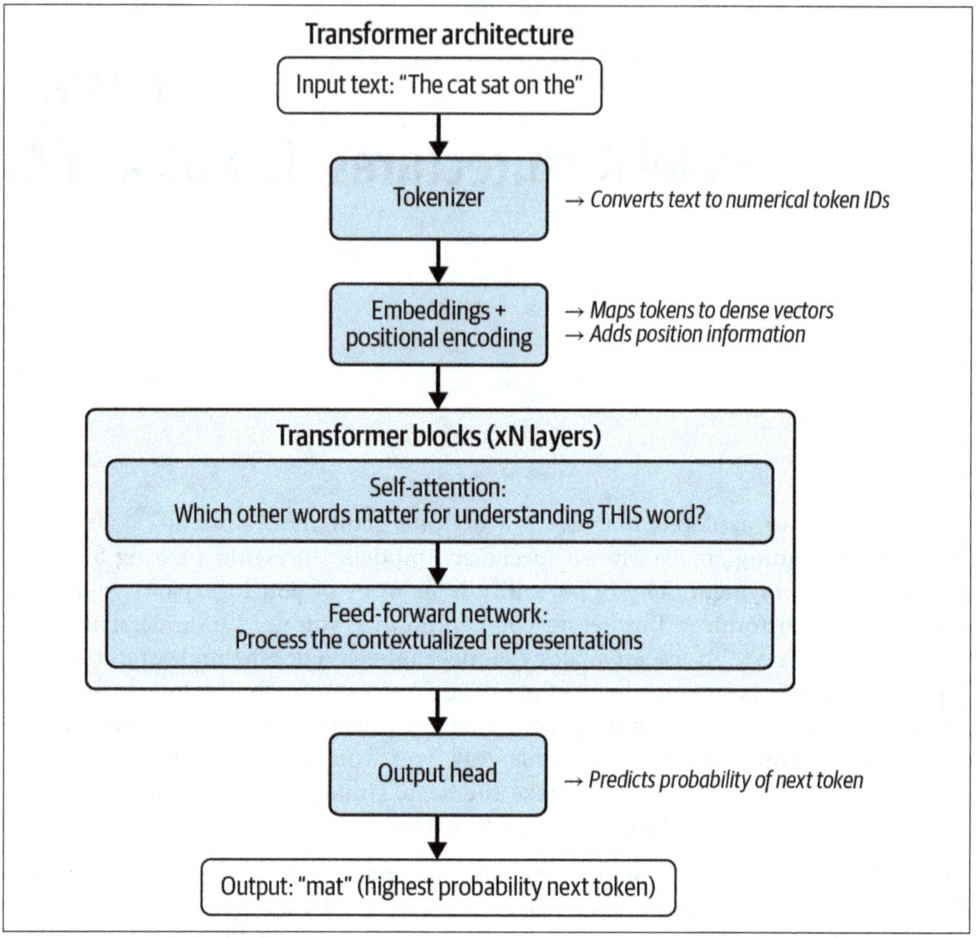

Figure 2-1. High-level transformer architecture

The key insight is that text enters the model as a sequence of discrete symbols. Usually, these are character encodings like ASCII or Unicode for the letters "T," "h," and "e" or innovative calculated encodings based on the body of text, such as byte pair encoding (BPE), commonly used by OpenAI models. Words are then converted into tokens using a tokenizer. These tokens are mere numerical representations of words or subwords.

There's no inherent "meaning" intrinsically encoded in the token values. That's where the second box in Figure 2-1—the embeddings—comes in. An *embedding* is a vector that represents the meaning of the word. Think of an embedding as an arrow in a higher-dimensional space. The direction it points in represents the meaning. For example, words that are similar in meaning, like "King" or "Prince," would point in roughly the same direction.

In a transformer, *positional* encoding is also added to the vector. This positional encoding represents the location of the word in the expression, on the theory that word location can impact its semantics. For example, consider the sentences "The man bit the dog." and "The dog bit the man." For these sentences, the token values remain the same, but the semantics of the word vary wildly based on the positions of the words in the sentence.

All this happens *before* the tokens flow into the transformer blocks, and here is where the innovation that led to the current explosion in AI technology lies.

Attention Mechanisms

This is the heart of the transformer. I like to think of them using this analogy: imagine you are reading a document while you hold a highlighter in your hand. As you read each paragraph, you might highlight certain words or phrases because they'll help you understand the current sentence. Maybe it's a piece of fiction, and the character is eating a certain food that you've never heard of. You look back and you see that the events take place in a particular location. This can help you understand, or at least make an educated guess, about the piece of food in relation to its physical environment.

The attention mechanism artificially does the same type of process. For each position in the sequence, it will calculate how much "attention" should be paid to every other position.

Let's consider this sentence: "The cat sat on the mat because it was tired."

When processing the word "it," you would need to infer what "it" refers to. As a human, reading that passage, you know *it* refers to the *cat*. But technically, *it* could also refer to the *mat*. And with strict grammatical rules, and not semantics, one might argue that it does!

The attention mechanism calculates attention scores for the word "it," to see what it refers to. Ultimately, based on lots of training data, it likely makes a stronger connection between the words "it" and "cat," instead of "it" and "mat."

Note that in a multilayered, multihead model, depending on where this attention mechanism is, deeper meanings can be learned, so it may go a lot deeper than "it" and "cat" in other layers or other heads.

This works through an elegant mathematical operation. It does this through calculation of three vectors:

- The query (Q): "What am I looking for?"
- The key (K): "What do I contain?"
- The value (V): "What information do I provide?"

They are calculated by multiplying the embedding vector for the word (as discussed earlier in this chapter) with weight matrices that will be learned over time.

You can see this demonstrated in Figure 2-2.

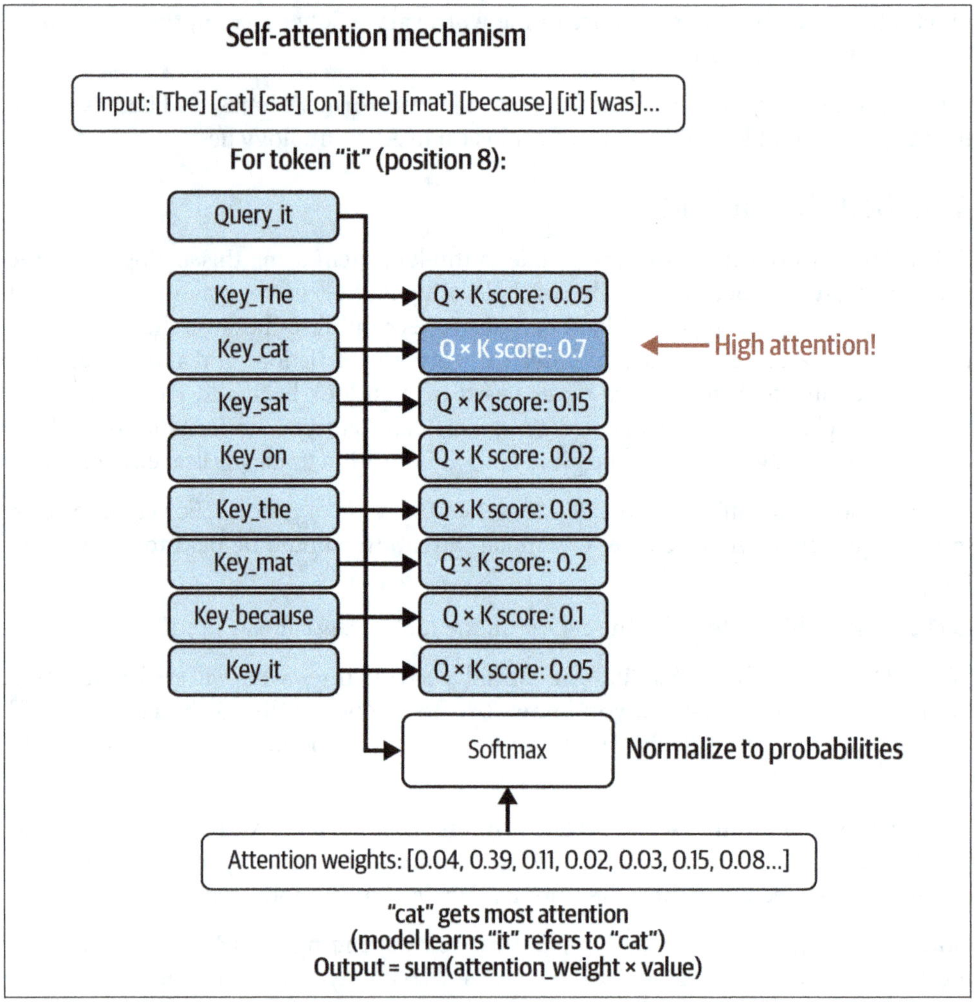

Figure 2-2. Understanding the attention mechanism

In this case, we explore the input tokens, and focus on the token for "it," which is at position 8.

Then, we look at the keys for each of the words, and examine their values. They have a score, and we multiply the Q for "it" by the K for each of these words. We'll take the results and softmax them to get probabilities to have a resulting set of attention weights.

These weights are the probabilities of attention that should be applied to the word. So, for the word "it," the highest probability word that is most closely associated with it is "cat." To calculate the output, and the final attention, we then multiply out the weights by the values.

This whole process is captured in a single formula, which comes from the original transformer paper (*https://oreil.ly/UbAUe*):

$$\text{Attention}(Q, K, V) = \text{softmax}\left(\frac{QK^T}{\sqrt{d_k}}\right)V$$

The beauty of this mechanism is that it is entirely *learned*. You might wonder where those values in the equation come from, and without a good set of K values to begin with, all this will be nonsense. Realize the vast amounts of text that models are trained on; it is from this, over time, that useful patterns get learned.

How that works is worth a quick look. During training, the model repeatedly tries to predict the next token in a passage, and a loss function (typically cross-entropy) measures how wrong it was. Backpropagation then traces that error backward through the network to work out how much each weight—including those Q, K, and V matrices—contributed to the mistake; and then, gradient descent nudges each weight in the direction that reduces the error. In practice, an optimizer such as Adam or AdamW handles the nudging, adapting the step size for each weight individually. Repeat this many times over the training data, and those attention matrices gradually converge on the useful patterns we saw earlier.

These "chunks" of Q, K, V are often referred to as "heads." When multiple heads are used, we've learned that some will end up tracking semantic relationships, some grammatical, and some will capture relationship patterns for words that we don't even have names for.

Typically, when there are multiple layers of heads, then the earlier heads in the sequence will learn the more obvious connections like syntax or grammar, and the later heads will capture the more complex, semantic relationships.

Multihead Attention

A single attention operation captures one type of relationship type between the tokens. Language is rich with multiple, simultaneous relationship types. And different languages can have different relation types that don't exist in English. To capture this richness, the idea of multihead attention (MHA), which runs multiple attention operations in parallel, each with their own learned Q, K, V matrices is useful.

You can see this in Figure 2-3.

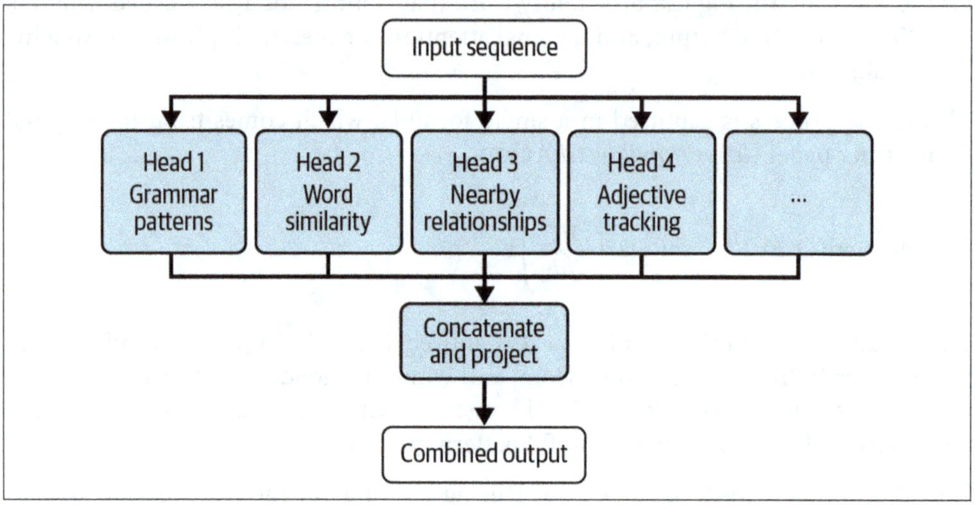

Figure 2-3. Multihead attention

Early open weights models like Llama 3 8B, for example, were designed with this architecture. In that case, the model had 32 attention heads per layer, across 32 layers. Later models added new innovations to that. For example, Gemma 4, which we'll be mostly covering in this book, shows how the structure has evolved. In the case of the Gemma E4B variant, 8 attention heads per layer are used across 42 layers, but the layers themselves use different forms of attention, and many of the heads share KV to save memory. But the overall idea remains the same.

Each layer's heads will operate at different levels of abstraction—early layers tend to learn syntactic patterns, while later ones get into semantics.

Reducing dimensions in MHA

These layers will reduce dimensions per head in order to save computation costs.

The *hidden* dimension is 4,096, which is the size of the vector representing each token as it flows through the network. Rather than running the attention operation on all 4,096 dimensions, the model will split this into the 32 parallel heads, where each will work on 128 dimensions (4,096 / 32 = 128).

Thus, each head will compute its own attention scores and produce output in 128 dimensions. These 32 outputs will then be concatenated back together and passed through one more learned weight matrix, often called the "output projection." This serves an important purpose: it allows the model to mix information across heads. Without it, the heads would be completely independent (i.e., head 1 has the first 128 dimensions, head 2 has the next 128, and so on), and as a result the learned meanings would not be "mixed" between dimensions, and the model may not effectively understand the text. With this output projection, the model learns how to combine the different perspectives from different heads into a unified representation for the next layer.

This keeps the total computation roughly similar to a single large attention operation, but it gives the model much more flexibility to learn diverse patterns.

> It's tempting to imagine that different heads neatly divide labor, and visualizations like Figure 2-3 tend to represent this because it's easier for us to grasp things like "head 1 does grammar, head 2 does semantics, and so on," but reality is much messier. Research into transformer interpretability has shown that specialization tends to happen more *across* (*https://oreil.ly/wahOj*) layers than *within* (*https://oreil.ly/M1UiR*) them. Earlier layers (closer to the input) tend to capture local syntactic patterns: which words are adjacent, basic grammatical relationships, positional information, etc. Deeper layers progressively build more abstract, semantic relationships: what the sentence means, how concepts relate, what an appropriate response to a question might be, and other more complex determinations.

Within any single layer, multiple heads do learn different patterns, but in reality they do not map to human-interpretable categories. The power of MHA comes from this redundancy and diversity—the model figures out what's useful for its corpus while training, and not through an engineered direction by a human.

Self-attention versus cross-attention

There are two main types of attention in transformer architectures you should consider.

What we've been discussing so far is *self-attention*, where a sequence attends to itself. The queries, keys, and values all come from the same sentence. In our hypothetical scenario of reading a fiction book, we have a paragraph in which a location is mentioned and a food type is mentioned; our attention is *only* on that paragraph.

Cross-attention extends this, and considers where one sequence can attend to a different one. In the hypothetical example, we might have learned in an earlier chapter that the character is vegetarian, which would give us a clue about what the unknown food might be. In ML terms, ultimately what's happening here is that the Q values could come from one sequence, while the K and V values come from another.

Figure 2-4 demonstrates the differences between the two attention types.

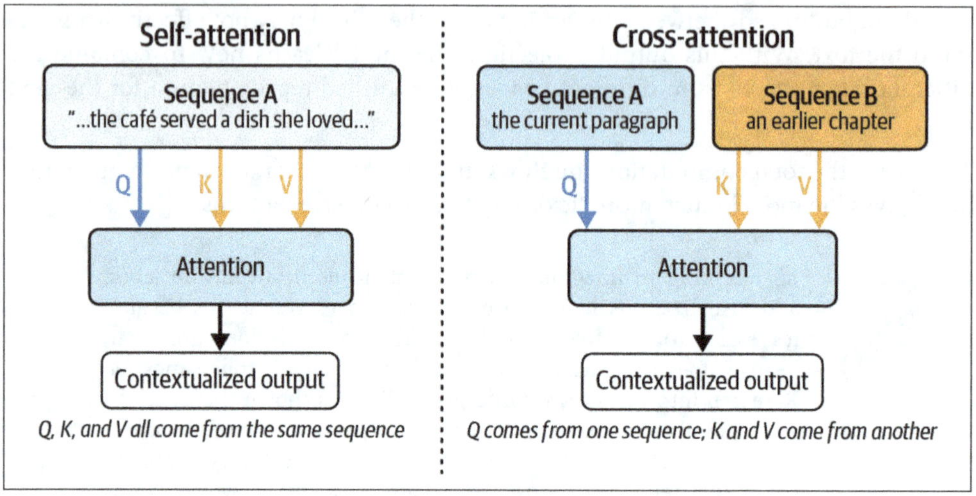

Figure 2-4. Self-attention versus cross-attention

For *most* attention models, including all the ones you're likely to fine-tune, self-attention is the dominant mechanism. Cross-attention appears in encoder-decoder type architectures, and in multimodal models, where the model might need to attend to image, voice, and video features as well as text.

The Feed-Forward Network

Once the attention mechanism has done its thing, and allowed tokens to gather context from other ones, each position will pass through a feed-forward network (FFN). This is a simple, but powerful two-layer neural network that is applied independently to each position.

You can see it demonstrated in Figure 2-5.

Its purpose is ultimately to store the "knowledge" of the model, or how it effectively understands the data it was trained on. Think of the attention mechanism as gathering *context*, where after attention is applied, each token's representation is enriched with information for other tokens that it attended to. The FFN will then process this contextualized representation, extract useful features, and transform it for the next layer.

This expand-then-contract structure is ultimately the key to learning and understanding the complex patterns within the data. The first layer will expand the dimensionality of the embedding from 4,096 to 14,336 dimensions. This larger space allows the network to represent more complex patterns. It does this with that number of neurons, and each could be thought of as a "pattern detector." When the input matches a pattern that the neuron has learned to recognize, it will activate strongly.

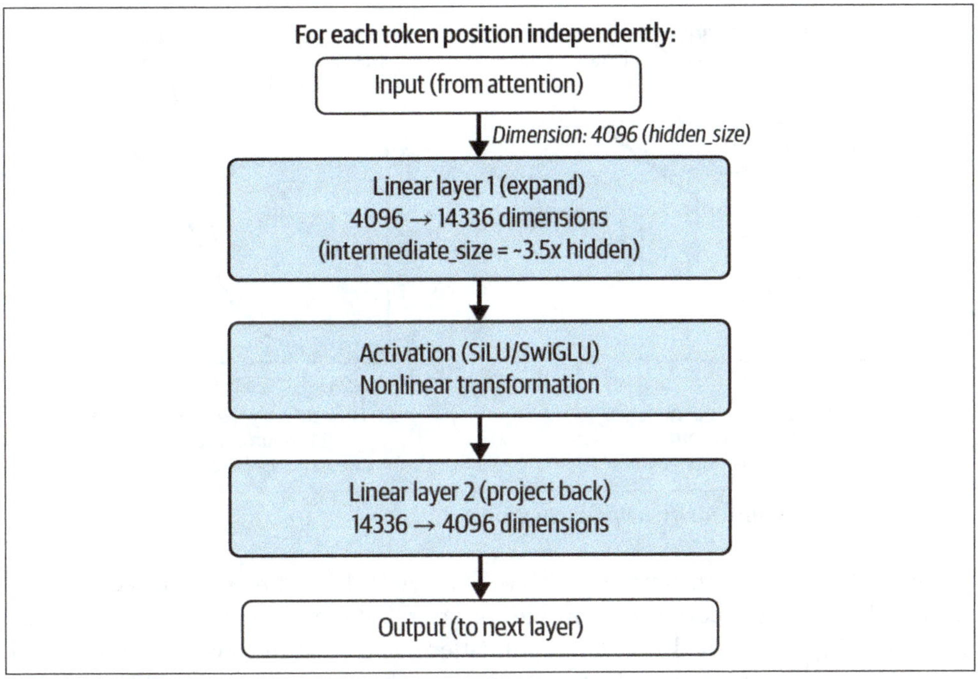

Figure 2-5. The feed-forward network

Once you've heightened the dimension, then the *nonlinear* activation function, such as SiLU (*https://oreil.ly/qV1pK*) or SwiGLU (*https://oreil.ly/BiZaS*), is applied. I'm emphasizing *nonlinear*, because if you think about a linear transformation, it's just a matrix multiplication that scales or rotates vectors, but doesn't handle curves or thresholds. So, if you stack two linear layers, you're effectively multiplying by Matrix A and then again by B, but that's mathematically equivalent to multiplying by a single matrix BA. No matter how many you stack, they still effectively collapse into one—and you get nothing from the additional depth.

But if you use a nonlinear activation function, the neurons get more selective. Imagine one of them, where its weights in the first layer compute a high value when the input looks like "question about cuisine," and a low or negative one otherwise. The activation function, if nonlinear, will be curved—thus strengthening the activation for cuisine questions, and staying near zero for everything else. Without the nonlinearity, the neuron would respond proportionally for *everything*, and wouldn't learn to trigger on specific relevant patterns, and ignore the others.

You can see this core idea in Figure 2-6.

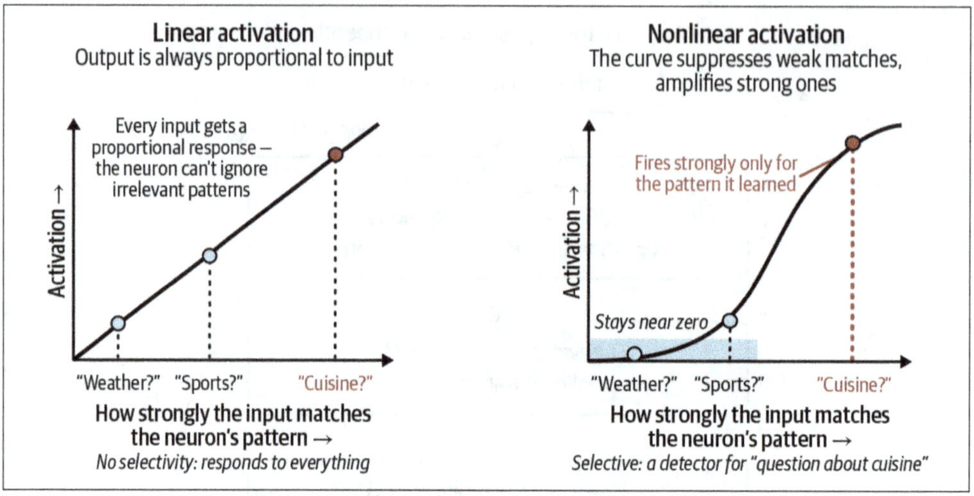

Figure 2-6. How nonlinearity helps activation

The second linear layer then projects this back down to 4,096 dimensions. Each neuron in layer 1 now has a corresponding one in layer 2. Often, this is considered to be the "knowledge" associated with the input pattern, and what the model should output when that pattern is detected. This is why researchers often describe FFN layers as functioning like key-value *memory*. The first layer's weights are the keys that match input values, and the second layer's are values that get retrieved when a key matches.

For example, a neuron on the first layer might activate when the input represents "food from Nagasaki," and the corresponding output one might push the representation toward the tokens for "okonomiyaki." This is an oversimplified abstraction; the real ones don't map nearly as closely to human-understandable concepts as this, but it does capture the basic mechanism of how factual knowledge from the text corpus gets encoded.

For fine-tuning, this really matters, as the FFN layers capture a significant portion of the model's deep knowledge. In techniques like LoRA (Low-Rank Adaptation, which we'll explore in Chapter 7), we can inject knowledge to this layer. Ultimately, if you can build the mental model of the attention layers focusing on "what to look at," while the FFN handles "what to do with it," you'll have a huge head start in understanding how and where to apply custom adaptation.

Layer Normalization and Residual Connections

Two additional components that are crucial but often overlooked are *layer normalization* and *residual connections*. You'll often find these components mentioned in any discussion of transformers, as they are key to enabling stable training of deep networks:

Residual connections
: Also called skip connections, these add the input of each sublayer to its output. This allows gradients to flow more easily during training and lets the model learn to make incremental refinements at each layer rather than complete transformations. They also help prevent gradients from exploding (growing too large as to be meaningless) or vanishing (approaching zero, so they lose information).

Layer normalization
: These normalize the activations across the feature dimension, stabilizing the distribution of values as they pass through the network. Noting that the ultimate value of a vector is relatively meaningless, and that its distributions for probabilities can be more important, the idea of normalization means that values are generally distributed between 0 and 1, avoiding clustering of values and loss of information. Modern models like Llama use RMSNorm (root mean square normalization), which is computationally simpler.

Decoder-Only Dominance

The original transformer paper (*https://oreil.ly/mbXkw*) described an "encoder-decoder" architecture designed for machine translation. The encoder processes the input sequence (source language), and the decoder generates the output sequence (target language), attending to the encoder's representations via cross-attention. Figure 2-7 shows a representation of this.

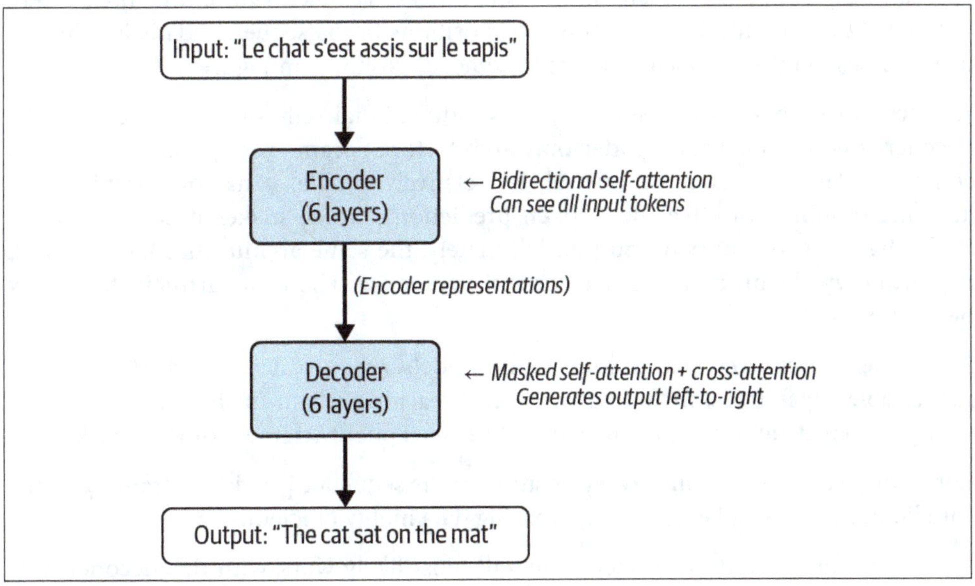

Figure 2-7. Encoder-decoder transformer

For *language translation* this was essential, because languages don't map word-for-word and order-for-order. To translate effectively, an encoder must read the entire input sentence, looking ahead and behind to capture the full context, and then compress it into a unified meaning. Then, the decoder takes that meaning and generates the translation in the new language.

For example, consider this English sentence: "The cat sat on the mat."

In French, this would be: "Le chat s'est assis sur le tapis."

While the words are very close to each other making for a relatively easy translation, the fact that the French version has one more word might confuse other systems.

Then consider the Gaelic translation: "Shuigh an cat ar an mata."

Even if you don't understand Gaelic, you can see the words "cat" and "mata" and guess that they're similar to the English words "cat" and "mat." But look at the order. In English and French, the verb follows the words "The cat" and "Le chat," respectively; however, in Gaelic, the sentence *begins* with the verb "Shuigh," which translates to "sat"!

Thus, the full sentence has to be understood, by looking forward and backward to capture the full context.

But for *generation* purposes, one cannot pay attention to words that are ahead, because they don't exist yet. If you have a sequence of tokens like "The cat sat," then you can only look back for attention. This process is called *causal attention*, where each position will only attend to previous positions in the sequence. This is achieved using a mask on the tokens to prevent lookahead, as shown in Figure 2-8.

As such, an encoder isn't needed with its bidirectional self-attention, and only the decoder is necessary. This decoder-only architecture became very popular with open source models like Llama or Mistral. It's relatively simple: it has one architecture, and one training objective (next token prediction), which makes it easier to scale. It also has unified input and output. Ultimately, the same architecture handles both *understanding* the prompt and *generating* the response. There's no artificial boundary between input and output.

Researchers discovered that decoder-only models, when scaled sufficiently, develop remarkable capabilities, including in-context learning, chain-of-thought (CoT) reasoning, and instruction following, without being explicitly trained for these tasks.

For training and fine-tuning, every position in the sequence provides a training signal (predicting the next token), making training data highly efficient.

When you fine-tune these models, you will most likely work with this decoder-only architecture. The training process adjusts the model's weights so that given your specific prompts and contexts, it can predict the next token in a way that matches your desired outputs.

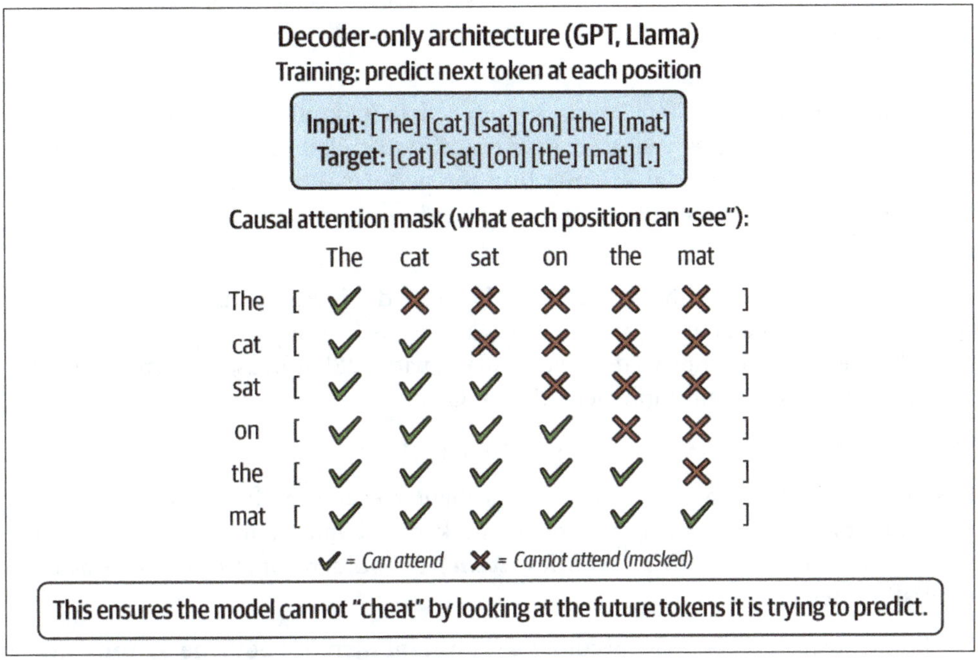

Figure 2-8. Decoder and causal attention

Grouped Query Attention

To understand grouped query attention, it's good to look at the early history of Llama. Open, tunable models are pretty much synonymous with this model. Additionally, access to pretrained weights of the model is available under various open source licenses so we can modify it, and papers are available describing the architecture.

The first version of this was released in February 2023 with a relatively standard transformers implementation. Its overall significance was to demonstrate that smaller, well-trained models were in the game—at least when comparing with larger models using standard benchmarks. It should be noted that many benchmarks were invented with larger models in mind, so the idea of benchmarks will need to evolve as more smaller models come online. Similarly, while the performance against benchmarks might have been equivalent, the context window size was the biggest notable difference between smaller and larger models. Llama had a context window of only 2,048 tokens.

My favorite model-to-model analysis tool is Artificial Analysis (*https://oreil.ly/aKODE*) where you can check the performance of models against each other with various tests of efficacy and cost.

A few months later, version 2 was introduced that doubled the context window size (to 4,096 tokens), as well as a new innovation called grouped query attention (GQA), which was a crucial optimization for performance. You'll also see that it's the constraints of going smaller that has driven innovation, and GQA is an excellent example of that.

A little over a year after the first release, Llama 3 doubled the context window size again—to 8,192 tokens in the small model, as well as a family of larger ones with up to 128k tokens. It also improved the vocabulary, with 128k tokens, a 4× improvement, as well as updates to their implementation of GQA.

So let's explore what GQA is, and why it's so important.

In standard MHA, as you saw earlier in this chapter, each head has its own query, key, and value projections. During inference, the key and value tensors for all previous tokens must be cached (this is the *KV cache*) to avoid recomputing them at each generation step.

For long sequences, this cache becomes a significant memory bottleneck. You can see this in Figure 2-9.

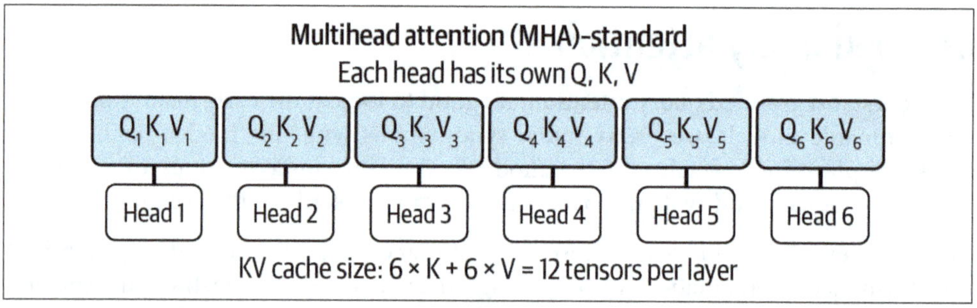

Figure 2-9. Multihead attention and KV cache size

The idea of GQA is to strike a balance here by grouping query heads, with each group sharing K and V projections. You can see this in Figure 2-10.

In this simple example, where there are 6 heads, instead of each Q having its own dedicated KV, we have a situation where Q1 and Q2 share a KV, Q3 and Q4 share one, and so on. This gives us a 50% reduction in KV cache size.

In Llama 3 8B, there are 32 query heads grouped into 8 groups of 4. Each group shared a key-value head, so there are only 8, reducing the size of the KV cache by 75% compared to standard MHA, dramatically improving inference speed and reducing memory requirements—especially for long contexts. Of course this comes with downsides, and you have to trade off against them when choosing a model. The chief cost is that when multiple heads attend to different things, they're all looking at the same "view" of the context, but their attention is diversified. They lose some of their specialist value. It's like being able to ask different questions, but the answers are all the same. Thus, it can lose nuance.

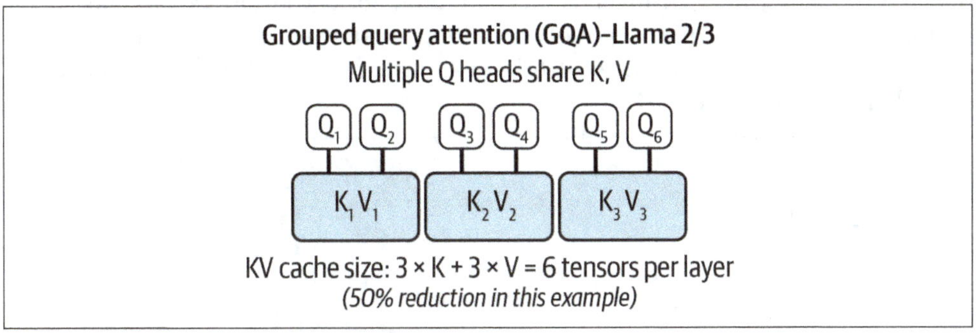

Figure 2-10. Grouped query attention

So, when it comes to fine-tuning, it's good to consider models that use GQA because they can give you better inference performance without sacrificing much quality.

Mistral and Mixtral

Continuing the story of innovation being driven by smaller models, and the need for efficiency that can be generally forgotten in larger models, let's now explore Mistral and Mixtral.

Mistral 7B, introduced in September 2023, demonstrated that a relatively small model—only 7B—could compete (*https://oreil.ly/AxY4V*) with much larger models on benchmarks. It did so with several key innovations.

Sliding Window Attention

As we pay attention to previous tokens, the longer the sequence of tokens becomes—and the computational cost of managing that sequence rises quadratically. So, if every token has to look at every other token, including itself, we end up with a quadratic number of lookups. For 2 tokens, there would be 2 comparisons of 2 tokens each, so 4 lookups. With 10 tokens, this becomes 100. With 1,000 tokens we now have 1 million lookups! How large would this get for a context window of 128k tokens?

Mistral introduced a sliding window, where each token only directly attends to the previous 4,096 tokens. Your initial thoughts on this might be that information outside the context window might be lost, but think about it a little.

If the context is 128k tokens, and you are using a sliding window of only 4k, it may feel like the majority of tokens are ignored. But in a multilayer model, this isn't necessarily true. Let's explore this.

Imagine 10 tokens, with a 4-token context window. So, as you can see in Figure 2-11, for tokens 7 through 10, the output of our sliding window will be the rightmost token in layer 2. Similarly, the window of tokens 4 through 7 will have an output at an equivalent position for token 7.

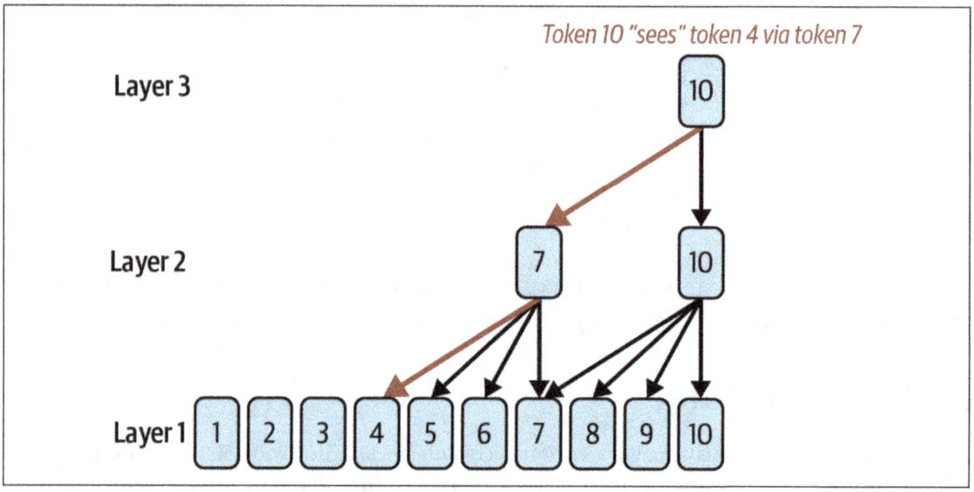

Figure 2-11. Sliding window context movement

You can see that tokens 5 through 8 will output at position 8, and tokens 6 through 9 will output at position 9 (though these aren't drawn in the figure).

Then, when you get to layer 3, the token at position 10 is actually receiving context from all the way at position 4 because of the "pyramid" effect with the context being fed through the layers.

The receptive field grows linearly with depth, and the result is that the amount of processing required for tokens loses the quadratic explosion of processing. Amazingly enough, the model performed equivalently to many larger models that didn't innovate on managing the processing of the attention! They simply brute forced it!

Mixture of Experts and Sparseness

While Llama 4 may have been the most famous model to broadly use mixture of experts (MoE), Mixtral introduced a transformative version of this—a sparse mixture of experts (SMoE). It's a fundamentally different approach to scaling. Let's look at this, starting with understanding what an MoE model does.

In a standard transformer, every token passes through every parameter of the model, as shown in Figure 2-12.

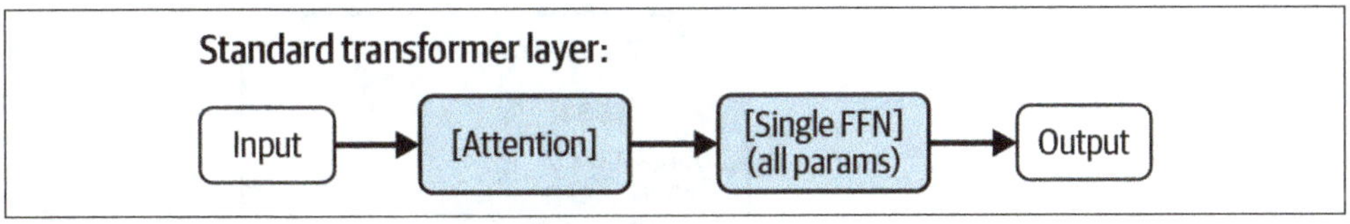

Figure 2-12. Feed-forward in a standard transformer

In an MoE model, the FFN layer is replaced by multiple "expert" FFNs, and a routing/gating network decides which experts to use for each token.

How an FFN becomes an "expert" is a detail from training, where the training code has a "router" that learns to divide tokens between FFNs that handle a particular subdivision of tokens well. They start out identical, but diverge over time, and together with the router, end up becoming experts in particular sets of tokens. It's explained in detail in the Mixtral paper (*https://oreil.ly/TurzK*). While I use code, math, and language as examples here, research has found that the "experts" aren't typically as high level and human legible as those examples, but they do work! You can see this in Figure 2-13.

In this case, the input is passed through the attention layers, and the router/gate chooses which FFN to use. So, for example if the token is code, the top two experts that are appropriate may be one that's dedicated to coding, and another that's dedicated to math. The data is routed to these FFNs, and a weighted combination forms the output.

This is what makes the Mixtral model a "sparse" MoE. Instead of passing the tokens through *every* expert, and then weighting the output, it simply selects two and then weights the output.

With a model like Mixtral 8x7B, the name may suggest it's a 7B model, but it isn't—the 8x7 refers to 8 experts, each of which is close to 7B parameters, and as such the model has 46.7B parameters! So the sparsity isn't about the model memory being smaller, it's about how the tokens flow through the model—they're routed through a subset of the model. The entire model is in memory, but you're only doing computation on a subset of the weights.

So, for each token, the router will select the top two experts, as shown, and for any given inference, only two experts are used, so 12.9B parameters are used. Thus, you get the capacity of a much larger model, while paying the computational cost of a smaller one at inference time.

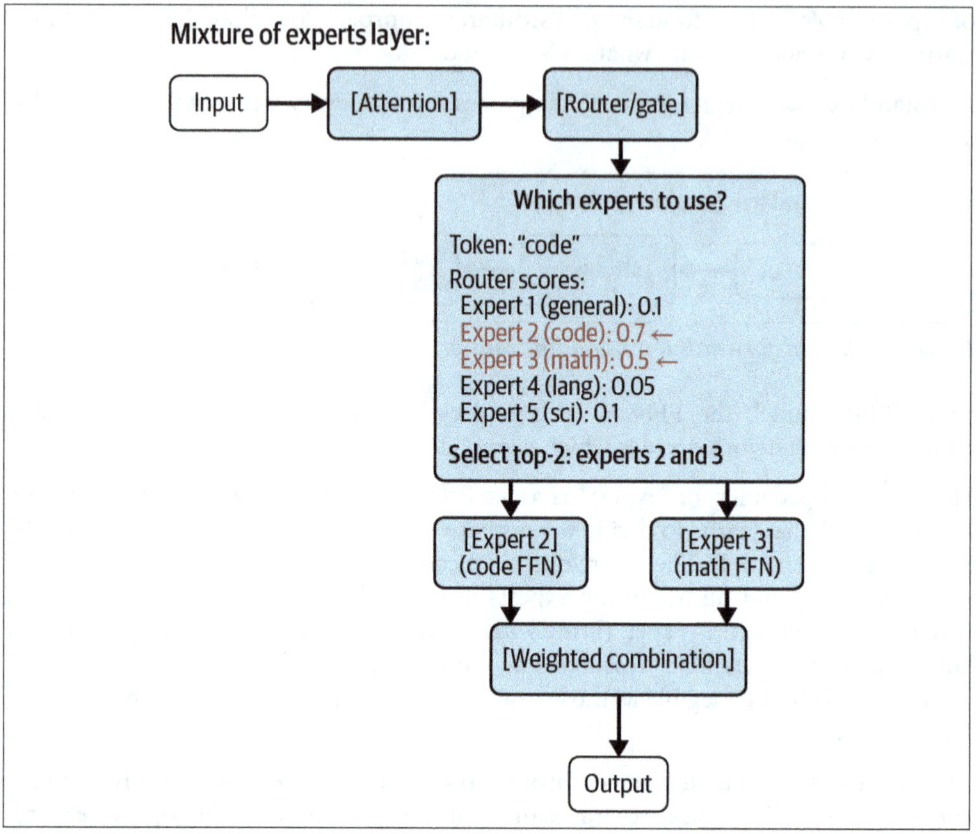

Figure 2-13. Mixture of experts

When it comes to fine-tuning, MoE models are trickier to deal with. You might want to only fine-tune selected experts, or perhaps the routing model. The training dynamics are far more complex, and you need much more VRAM to hold all the parameters, even if the inference is efficient. For many fine-tuning projects, a non-MoE may be an easier approach.

Gemma: Google's Open Approach

Google entered the open weights space with a variety of models over the years, but the most recent, at the time of writing, is called *Gemma*. Based on the same research (*https://oreil.ly/PocWV*) performed to create the giant *hosted* Gemini models, Gemma comes in a variety of smaller sizes that you can self-host. The most recent version (at the time of writing), Gemma 4, comes in variations from 2B parameters up to 31B.

One key characteristic of Gemma is that many of the variations of Gemma are *instruction tuned* from the start. This means that they are already aligned to follow instructions, making them ready for many tasks out of the box. When you inspect the list of Gemma models on a hub like Hugging Face (*https://oreil.ly/1SI9e*), you'll see all of them listed, which for Gemma 4 will look much like Figure 2-14.

Figure 2-14. Gemma on Hugging Face

You'll see some models with the suffix "-it" for "instruction tuned," and "-pt" for "pretrained." The latter hasn't had additional alignment to make it useful for chat scenarios, and instead is just raw tokens in and tokens out. This is pretty powerful for you to be able to create your own instruction tuning, without needing to work around Google's work here.

Given the variety of sizes, there are slightly different architectures with Gemma 4 when it comes to managing the KV cache.

It applies a hybrid attention scheme across the entire family, where layers will alternate between sliding window attention and global attention. The final layers are always global. The inner local layers keep the KV cache size under control, where each token only caches keys and values for a small window of neighbors—with 512 tokens in the smaller edge models (E2B and E4B) and 1,024 in the larger ones (12B, 26B, and 31B). These interleaved global layers are the engine to provide long-range awareness that a pure sliding window would lose.

Two further efficiency moves show up in the Gemma 4 architecture. In the larger models, the global attention layers reuse the keys as the values, so a single tensor does both jobs and the global KV cache shrinks accordingly. The edge models (E2B and E4B) take a different route: roughly half their layers don't compute their own key and value projections at all, instead reusing the tensors from the most recent layer that did—20 of 35 layers in E2B, 18 of 42 in E4B. Head-sharing follows the GQA pattern you saw earlier, pushed further in the global layers, where as many as eight query heads can share a single KV head. Positions are encoded using a variant of RoPE (we'll explore this later) to stretch across long inputs. Together, this is how the small models support a context window of up to 128k tokens, and the larger ones up to 256k, without the memory requirements exploding!

Tokenizers and Embeddings

In the discussion on architectures, it's also important to think about different methods for tokenization (conversion of the human-language words into numbers that represent them), embeddings (giving a high-dimensional vector representation for a token to try to capture context), and methodologies to use these efficiently.

Tokenization

When we look in detail at tokenization, and define it as the process of breaking text into discrete units that the model can process, we can see that it is more complex than simply splitting on words.

Some reasons for this may be situations such as:

- Rare words would require enormous vocabulary. Is it worth having a token dedicated to the word "antidisestablishmentarianism"?
- Non-English languages may handle spacing between words differently.

- Typos, new or slang words, and code would be very difficult to handle.
- Variants of a word (e.g., run, running, runs) would be completely separate from each other, potentially losing their semantic similarity.

To overcome this, most modern LLMs use *subword* tokenization, where the vocabulary consists of common words, or pieces of them. It gives a balance—common words like "the" will be single tokens, which is efficient, while more rare words will be broken down into multiple tokens like "anti," "dis," "esta," "blish," and so on. Note that the makeup of how tokenizers will split words is more likely to be frequency and statistically driven. So, depending on the scheme used, they may not look as intuitive as the syllable-based ones demonstrated here.

The tokenizer choice matters because different models use different tokenizers, trained on different data. The tokenizer will have a vocabulary of tokens that it works with, and this affects efficiency. Models like Llama 2 have 32,000 tokens, and Llama 3 has over 128,000. A larger vocab means common words and phrases are more likely to be single tokens—which will reduce sequence length, giving you more information within the context window. But it also means bigger embedding matrices, giving you a trade-off.

Understanding Language and Tokenization

If you are working with models for code or special characters, the tokenizers will vary widely. Many are trained primarily on *English* text, and won't be optimized for code, where some structures (e.g., curly braces { }) or some punctuation (e.g., a semicolon ;) are used differently than they may be in common language. Others will have programming languages in their training data—and most notably, the tokenizers used will be "code friendly" in their vocab.

Additionally, when it comes to multilingual coverage, a tokenizer that is trained on English will likely fragment non-English text into many smaller tokens.

Consider the phrase "你好世界," which is "Hello World" in Chinese. If this uses a tokenizer trained on English text, it will encode this into four separate tokens, representing the Unicode characters for the Chinese text [你][好][世][界].

A multilingual tokenizer that understands Chinese characters, and how they are grouped into words would be more efficient, and split it appropriately into the "words" for "Hello" and "World" [你好][世界].

This, as you can see, will greatly affect both efficiency and quality. More tokens means longer sequences that are slower and carry less context, and the performance can be negatively impacted.

Ultimately you need to consider the tokenizer when fine-tuning. You cannot change a model's tokenizer without retraining from scratch. When selecting a base model, check that its tokenizer handles your domain's text efficiently. If you are fine-tuning for a specific programming language or a non-English language, you have to verify that the tokenizer doesn't produce excessively long sequences.

Byte Pair Encoding

The most common algorithm to perform tokenization is byte pair encoding (BPE), a methodology that was originally developed for data compression.

The process of BPE follows this workflow:

1. Start with a vocabulary of individual characters, each represented by a byte.
2. Count all adjacent pairs in the training corpus.
3. Merge the most frequent pair into a new token.
4. Repeat the process until the vocab reaches the desired size.

For example, imagine a corpus of only three words: "low," "lower," and "lowest."

We would start with the full vocab of individual characters:

[l], [o], [w], [e], [r], [s], [t]

Then, we would look at the tokenization of each word (where I am representing a space with the [*]):

[l], [o], [w], [*], [l], [o], [w], [e], [r], [*], [l], [o], [w], [e], [s], [t]

From this we can see that [l] followed by [o] is the most frequent pairing, so we reencode to have an [lo] character instead of [l] and [o]:

[lo], [w], [*], [lo], [w], [e], [r], [*], [lo], [w], [e], [s], [t]

Now we can see that [lo] followed by [w] is the most common, so we reencode to:

[low], [*], [low], [e], [r], [*], [low], [e], [s], [t]

And we would continue until we have the desired number of tokens.

Embeddings

Once text is tokenized, each token ID is mapped to an embedding vector. This is a representation of the token in a higher dimensional space. Let's explore what that means. Let's use Llama 3 8B, where the embedding dimension is 4,096. In other words, the vector representing the semantics for a token is a direction in a space of 4,096 dimensions.

While this is hard to visualize, consider that the goal here is to encode semantic relationships. Tokens with similar meanings tend to have similar embeddings after training. Similar embeddings are close together in vector space, where their vectors are "pointing" in similar directions.

A good way to understand this is to consider it in only two dimensions. For example, suppose we were to look at characters from the Jane Austen novel *Pride and Prejudice*, considering the dimensions of gender and nobility. We could plot the former on the x-axis and the latter on the y-axis, with the length of the vector denoting each character's wealth (see Figure 2-15).[1]

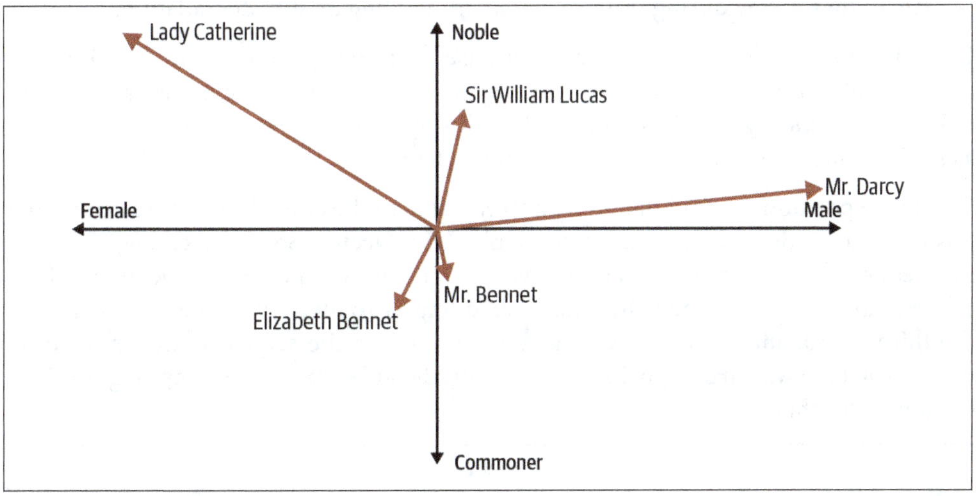

Figure 2-15. Characters in Pride and Prejudice *as vectors*

From an inspection of the graph, you can derive a fair amount of information about each character. Three of them are male. Mr. Darcy is extremely wealthy, but his nobility isn't clear (he's called "Mister," unlike the less wealthy but apparently more noble Sir William Lucas). The other "Mister," Mr. Bennet, is clearly not nobility and is struggling financially. Elizabeth Bennet, his daughter, is similar to him, but female. Lady Catherine, the other female character in our example, is nobility and incredibly wealthy. The romance between Mr. Darcy and Elizabeth causes tension—*prejudice* coming from the noble side of the vectors toward the less noble.

1 Example adapted from Laurence Moroney, *AI and Machine Learning for Coders* (Sebastopol, CA: O'Reilly Media, 2020).

As this example shows, by considering multiple dimensions we can begin to see real meaning in the words (here, character names). Again, we're not talking about concrete definitions, but more a *relative* meaning based on the axes and the relation between the vector for one word and the other vectors.

Understanding Positional Embeddings with RoPE

Transformers process all tokens in parallel, so they have no inherent sense of order. To inject positional information, we add positional embeddings to the token embeddings.

Modern models like Llama use rotary position embeddings (RoPE), which encode position through an innovative technique involving rotation in the embedding space. The key advantage of RoPE is that it allows the model to generalize to longer sequences than it saw during training while minimizing quality degradation.

Consider the sentence "The cat ate the mouse." Without positional information, the model would find the sentences "The cat ate the mouse." and "The mouse ate the cat." to be *mathematically* identical. RoPE solves this by treating word embeddings not just as static points in space, but as vectors that can be *rotated*.

To encode position, instead of adding a fixed value to the embedding representing the position, RoPE does it by rotating the embedding vector. So, for each step forward in a sequence, the idea is to rotate the vector for that word by a specific angle. If we call that angle theta θ, then the first embedding is rotated by θ, the second by 2θ, the third by 3θ, and so on. As we move further down the sequence, the embedding vector rotates away from position 0 in a predictable, calculable way. Figure 2-16 demonstrates this.

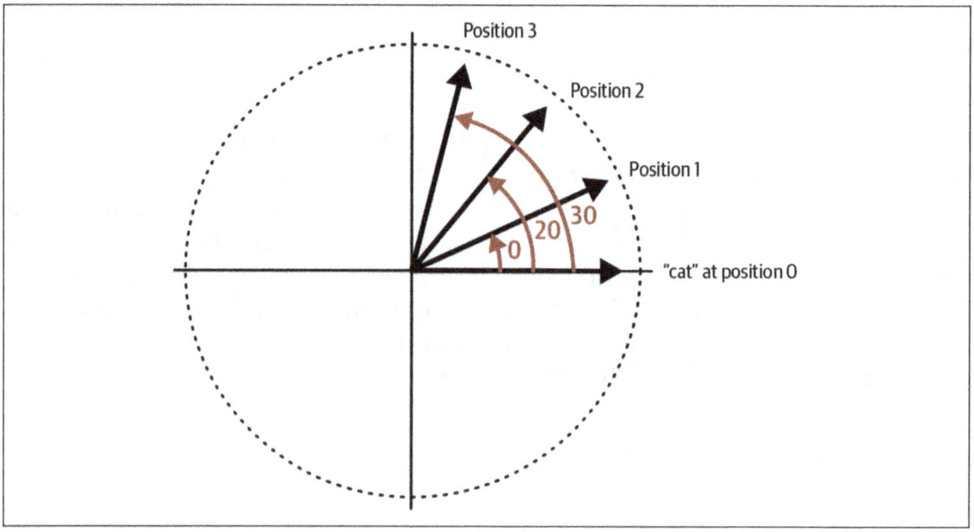

Figure 2-16. How RoPE works

The idea now is that as well as the semantics of the words being encoded in the embedding, as we saw in the previous section, the *position* of the word can also be encoded, so when the model calculates the attention scores it can keep both in mind. So, recalling that the embeddings are vectors, and the relative *meanings* between words (like we saw with characters in *Pride and Prejudice*) can be encoded in the relationships between those vectors, we can evaluate this in mathematics using a dot product (*https://oreil.ly/Je-QZ*). When words are semantically similar, their dot product is high because their vectors are similar. Otherwise the dot product is low. Models use this to pay attention based on relevance.

But, without positional encoding, the model may think that, for example, the word "cat" at the beginning of a story is the exact same "cat" that shows up at the end of the story (which may not be the case). It can see the meaning of a cat, but is blind to the order in which the cat appears.

Using RoPE, you don't destroy this semantic; you just *twist* it by rotating it through an angle. Now, words that are closer together in a sentence have similar rotations, and as such a similarity of *position* is encoded into the vector also (see Figure 2-17). It's complex math that gives a simple solution.

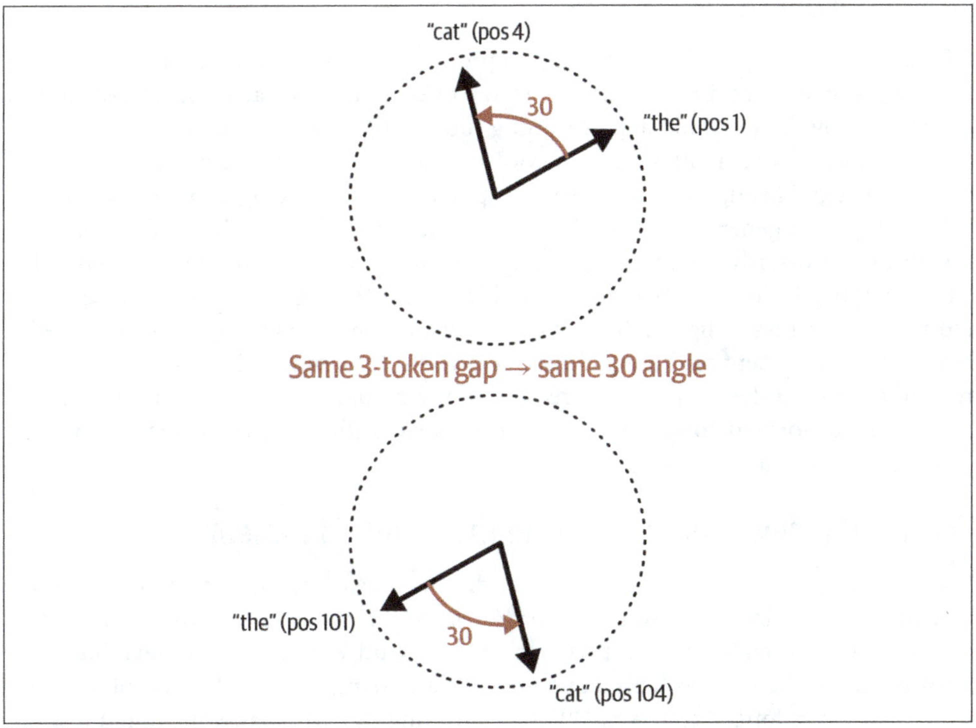

Figure 2-17. Position via rotation

Other Considerations

Beyond the architecture, there are several other model capabilities you should keep in mind. We'll discuss them in this section.

Instruction Following

Some models are better at following complex, multistep instructions. This emerges from instruction-tuning during post-training. This means that data used to post-train or fine-tune the model was explicity done as question-answer pairs to look more like real-world usage. This makes the model better at generalizing for conversations where the user typically asks a question, and the model answers.

Models labeled "Instruct" or "Chat" have been specifically trained for this. We saw this previously when looking at Gemma, when the models are helpfully named with an "-it" at the end when instruction-tuned. Do note that if your task requires precise instruction following, starting from an instruction-tuned base is usually better than starting from a base model.

Reasoning Depth

Often, reasoning is just the model "talking to itself." It looks at the user's query, then looks at its answer, and then uses that to try to drive a better answer. Larger models generally show better multistep reasoning, but architectural choices, particularly in smaller models, also matter greatly. MoE models like Mixtral can route different reasoning steps through different experts, potentially improving complex reasoning, and giving you a generalized overview of the solution. While this is usually a plus, it's not always necessarily the case. For example, a single step through the code expert for a code solution, may work better than multiple steps through other experts. For tasks requiring deep reasoning (mathematical proofs, complex analysis), you may need a larger model or accept multiple inference calls with CoT prompting where, instead of relying on the model to internally reason, you can just prompt it again (and again, and again) to force it to reason. This can be very difficult to fine-tune, so manage your expectations accordingly!

Context Windows and the "Lost in the Middle" Problem

Just because a model has a large context window doesn't mean it uses long contexts effectively. "Lost in the middle" (*https://oreil.ly/HM7Ih*) is a known phenomenon where models attend strongly to the beginning and end of the context but miss information in the middle. This can be particularly dangerous in the case of a sliding window to drive longer contexts. When fine-tuning in particular, you should test the base model's ability to recall information from various positions in the document to see if it has this problem, before committing to the significant investment of fine-tuning it.

Considerations for Choosing a Model

As you can see, deciding which model to use relies on a variety of factors. Personally, I like to use the following questions and notes, in no particular order of priority:

- What tokenizer does the model use? Will it encode *my* data accurately and meaningfully?
- How large is the context window? How large is it in reality, and how large is it because of neat tricks in the KV cache? Does the context window meet the expected demands of my users?
- How big is the model? Will it fit into the available memory I have in order to host it where I want? Can it be quantized? What will the impact of quantizing be?
- If I am retraining, what are the memory constraints of my training system? Will it work with the number of parameters, the context window size, and the memory available to me?
- When it comes to attention type, models that use GQA generally offer high inference efficiency.
- Dense models like Llama and Mistral are usually easier to fine-tune. MoE models offer more capacity but are more difficult to change.
- Tokenizer efficiency can have a huge impact on the time it takes to retrain or fine-tune a model.
- The context window size should accommodate your longest training examples and expected inference inputs.
- Typically base models are better to give you the control you want over the final behavior, but if your scenario is an instruction-based one (like chat), you might be better off using an instruction-tuned variant of the model.
- What hardware do I need? Remember that *training* takes significantly more resources than inference. Make sure that your model isn't just suited to your end users' inference needs, but also that you can think about the training needs and costs, which can be significant!

You shouldn't limit yourself to these questions, of course, but I hope they'll provide you with a good starting point as you think about what model to use when fine-tuning. For the rest of this book, I'll be using the Gemma 4 family, as it gave me the best answers to these questions for my needs.

Summary

In this chapter, you looked at the architecture of modern language models, giving you the foundation for choosing which one to fine-tune. You saw how a transformer processes information: tokens become embeddings, attention mechanisms let each token gather context from the others (using query, key, and value vectors across multiple heads), and how FFNs store the knowledge, with nonlinear activations making individual neurons selective pattern detectors.

You then saw how open models drove efficiency innovations. Llama popularized well-trained small models and GQA, which shrinks the KV cache that dominates inference memory. Mistral added sliding window attention, and Mixtral introduced the SMoE, which gives large-model capacity at small-model compute cost. Gemma brought these ideas to Google's open lineup.

You then explored how tokenizers, embeddings, and RoPE positional encoding make text become something a model can reason about.

Finally, you saw some practical selection criteria: attention type, dense versus MoE, tokenizer efficiency, context window, base versus instruction-tuned variants, and hardware budget.

Understanding these architectural foundations will serve you throughout your fine-tuning journey. In the next chapter, we'll translate this theoretical knowledge into practical hardware and software setup—the fine-tuner's workshop, where you'll start building your expert models.

CHAPTER 3

The Fine-Tuner's Workshop

Have you ever tried to assemble furniture with the wrong tools? Thankfully, the Ikeas of the world include the necessary Allen keys and screwdrivers. But before manufacturers started providing those tools, you usually, at best, ended up with a wobbly desk. And that's *after* fighting with your equipment before you actually put anything together.

Fine-tuning a model is no different. The right hardware and software setup is critical, and the perfect investment to prevent frustrating long nights full of cryptic error messages.

In this chapter, we'll talk about that workbench. The search space for the correct hardware is near infinite, so I'll be opinionated about what I think is a good set to begin with. You don't have to go with my suggestions, of course, but I *will* be using them through all the examples in this book.

Why Setup Matters

When you run inference on a model, feed a prompt and get a response, you're doing relatively lightweight work. The model's weights sit in memory, data flows through the network and causes a bunch of calculations. The tensors get collapsed into output tokens that get decoded into words. A decent laptop can handle inference on a 7B-sized model.

But fine-tuning is fundamentally different. You're not just running data through the model; you're updating the parameters within the model itself. So, every training step requires you not just to store the weights and biases, but also the gradients—the direction each weight should move to get your desired goals. Additionally the optimizer keeps states, which are momentum and variance history that is tracked for every parameter. Some common optimizers, like the famous Adam (*https://oreil.ly/Dm7OQ*), may have double the storage of the weights and biases.

A rough calculation is that a 7B-parameter model with 16-bit precision takes about 14 GB of memory to handle the parameters. But there's much more to it than just the parameters. Add the gradients, optimizer states, activations, and so on and you're pushing 70–80 GB, which is way beyond consumer GPUs at reasonable price points, likely setting you back five figures for a workstation. You'll see that calculation in more detail later in this chapter.

If you've tried doing anything with fine-tuning models you've probably seen a "CUDA out of memory" message. It worked yesterday when you did inference, but now you're asking a lot more of that memory!

So, if you get nothing else from this chapter, please realize that measuring the size of the model is just the first step in understanding your needs for tuning that model.

After memory, the next important thing to consider is your software environment. For fine-tuning, the ecosystem is constantly evolving, but consider it to sit at the intersection of PyTorch, CUDA, Hugging Face, and quantization tools. Each has their own version requirements and interdependencies. For example, version mismatching between CUDA and PyTorch will often give you a silent failure—your code works, but it won't take advantage of the GPU, greatly increasing the training time!

There are many other tools that you may need, such as the bitsandbytes library for quantization (we'll see more on this in Chapter 14). And, of course a mismatch between these tools and your CUDA version can give you a load failure or a compilation error that sends you down a Stack Overflow rabbit hole or a very long conversation with your LLM of choice.

> *Vibe coding* is awesome, but it is prone to issues like this. Training sets used to train models to understand and generate code don't have errors like this; they're based on reference implementations that just work. So the code the LLM spits out might be factually correct, but it still has problems because your environment isn't correctly set up for it. And when you ask the LLM to fix the problem, it will likely try to fix the code, but the code wasn't broken to begin with! The bottom line: you have to understand your environment, and you have to ensure that it works! Indeed, often it may not even *look* like it's broken, and you end up with the issue of "silent decay" where the model appears to be training, but doesn't perform as well as it should because of inconsistencies in your environment.

The good news: these problems aren't insurmountable. When you know what to look for, you'll know how to solve them. This chapter will give you the map to that hidden treasure.

One thing to keep in mind is that there are many options for the environment, not least the GPU—AMD's ROCm (*https://oreil.ly/tXWhJ*) or Apple's Metal (*https://oreil.ly/K3TuB*) are valid competitors to CUDA. For the most part, in this book, I'll follow the most common path (NVIDIA's CUDA (*https://oreil.ly/5z5It*)).

The GPU: Your First Decision

Modern language models are typically built on transformer (or transformer-derivative) architectures and these function primarily using matrix multiplications. A single forward pass through a model will involve many thousands of large matrix operations. Recall from Chapter 2, where we saw how we multiply weight matrices against input vectors, computing attention scores across sequences of tokens, and projecting values through feed-forward layers.

A CPU is designed for sequential logic—branching decisions, routing control flow, and threading output. Generally it has a handful of very powerful cores, each of which can do one thing very, very fast.

A GPU, on the other hand, can have many thousands of smaller cores. For example, an NVIDIA A100 has almost 7,000, and an H100 can have more than 15,000! (Both of these GPUs are available in Colab in the low-cost tier.)

GPUs are designed to do the same operation on many pieces of data simultaneously. Despite being designed for graphics (that's the G in GPU!), this also perfectly suits AI's hunger for matrix multiplication. The architecture of the GPU allows you to do thousands of them *in parallel*.

The result is that AI workloads can be orders of magnitude faster on a GPU than on a CPU. So they're not optional. Don't worry if you don't own a setup with GPUs; many cloud platforms offer access to GPUs by the hour, or tools like Google's Colab will give you GPU access for free. Do note that the free tier is limited, and if the servers are busy, Google will prioritize paid users. Free users may be queued up or temporarily restricted to CPU-only instances. We'll explore the options later.

VRAM: One Number to Rule Them All

Given that GPUs aren't optional, we now have to explore the memory that's available to the GPU, and that's VRAM (Video RAM). Why "video"? Well, it's another holdover from video games and GPUs. In our case, it has nothing to do with video or games, but the important point is that it's the memory that is *directly* accessible to the GPU. Many computers have a motherboard and a CPU with RAM, and then a card with the GPU on it as a separate plug-in device. As the GPU needs to work with numbers, those numbers have to be in memory—and transferring to and from the system RAM through the card slot slows things down. The obvious solution: give the GPU card its own dedicated memory. And that's VRAM.

It is a hard constraint that determines what you can and cannot fine-tune effectively. If the combined footprint of your model, gradients, optimizer states, activations, and other overhead exceeds the available VRAM, training will at best be very slow (because of all the memory swapping across the card interface and the motherboard), or at worst, crash completely. My experience has been that if it doesn't fit in VRAM, don't bother—you'll be setting yourself up for a world of pain. In that case, you should choose a different model that *does* fit.

A drawback: VRAM is very expensive. It's rare to find GPUs with more than 32 GB of VRAM without breaking several banks. The solution is *distributed* training, where multiple GPUs work in tandem *sharing* their VRAM. Two GPUs with 32 GB each are a lot cheaper than one GPU with 64 GB. Of course, distributed training can have its own complexities, not least of which is managing the weights and data across the different devices.

Let's now get a little deeper into VRAM requirements and take a look at how it can and will impact your decisions.

To fine-tune a 7B model, we need to calculate how much VRAM we will use during training, and this will start with the *model weights*. As there are seven billion of them, they'll have an immediate impact. The first thing we need to figure out is how much they store based on their precision. You'll see several methods of precision in technical documentation, but the most common ones are:

- FP32 (32-bit floating point) = 4 bytes per parameter, so 28B bytes
- FP16 (16-bit floating point) = 2 bytes per parameter, so 14B bytes
- BF16 (16-bit floating point) = 2 bytes per parameter, so 14B bytes
- INT8 (8-bit quantized) = 1 byte per parameter, so 7B bytes
- INT4 (4-bit quantized) = 0.5 bytes per parameter, so 3.5B bytes

> While FP16 and BF16 are similar in size, they vary in the range of data they can cover. The modern NVIDIA stack tends to prefer BF16.

There are other areas in research looking at different levels of precisions; for example, FP8 is becoming popular, as are much smaller ones like 2-bit encoding. As you can probably guess, the lower the memory, the lower the precision; however, for tasks that language models perform, you really don't need 32-bit precision. Think about it, when predicting the next token, you don't gain anything from being 99.0000234023523% accurate as opposed to 99.00002% accurate!

So ultimately there's a trade-off, but fine-tuners will typically begin with FP16 or BF16, costing 14B bytes off the bat. You can experiment with INT8 and INT4, which I would definitely recommend at least to begin with, if you're hitting memory constraints.

Next up is the *gradients*. While this book won't go into depth on the machine learning (ML) process, an important part of it is called *backpropagation*, where, in order to adjust parameters, and by definition "learn," the algorithm has a gradient that it calculates for the *direction* in which it should adjust a parameter. In simplistic terms, that means *up* or *down* and by *how much*. Each gradient is the *same size* as its associated parameter. The previous calculations hold true, effectively doubling the amount of memory. So, at 16-bit precision, you need 14B bytes for the parameters, and another 14B bytes for the gradients.

> A fine-tuning technique called *LoRA* which we will explore in Chapter 7 doesn't use *all* the parameters, just a very small subset of them. So for example, if it only uses 1% of the parameters, that's 0.14B for the parameters and another 0.14B for the gradients. That's very little, and possible to do on a GPU with only 8 GB of memory. As a result, you can see why it's very popular!

A necessary part of ML and fine-tuning is to use an *optimizer*. A very common one in fine-tuning is Adam. The goal of the optimizer is to take the gradients we mentioned previously and use them to update the parameters, determining the direction and quantity they need to move in order to become more effective at their job (aka "learning"). The Adam optimizer needs *two* additional values per parameter: a running mean and a running variance. These should be stored at least the same precision as the weights being trained. For a full fine-tune at 16-bit precision, that means each of them needs 2 bytes to store, and as a result, they take up 4 bytes per trainable parameter. So, for a full fine-tune of a 7B model, that's 28 GB extra just for the optimizer! Should you use the full 32-bit precision, that would be 56 GB!

LoRA is different: the small set of adapter weights it trains is kept in FP32, so the optimizer needs 8 bytes for each of them. But if that's only 1% of the parameters, it comes to 0.56 GB, which is much more palatable.

One part of ML that is often forgotten about storage-wise is *activations*, where the output of each layer is stored, so it can be used in the backward pass to compute the gradients. The memory here depends on the model architecture for things like batch size, sequence length, and so on. For a 7B model with a batch size of 1, and a sequence of 2,048 tokens, the activations might consume 2–4 GB. Again it depends very much on the model architecture, but it's important to note that it will scale linearly with batch size, so that will double for a batch size of 2, and so on. So when it comes to fine-tuning, the memory requirements might constrain your batch sizes. Less memory, and you can only do the smallest batch (1), more memory and you can do more batches. Another reason why VRAM is important: the more data you can move in a single pass by batching it, the faster your training or retraining will move.

So let's add these numbers up.

For full fine-tuning at FP16, see the requirements in Table 3-1.

Table 3-1. Memory usage by component

Component	Memory (approximate)
Model weights (FP16)	14 GB
Gradients (FP16)	14 GB
Optimizer states (FP32)	56 GB
Activations	2 GB
Total	86 GB

That's more than any single consumer GPU can hold. Even the 80 GB A100 (the superstar workhorse for ML) would struggle without aggressive optimization. At the time of writing, these GPUs cost about $14,000 each.

If, instead of full fine-tuning, you were to do a LoRA at FP16, it would look like what we see in Table 3-2.

Table 3-2. Memory usage by component with LoRA

Component	Memory (approximate)
Model weights (FP16)	14 GB
LoRA adapter weights	0.14 GB
Gradients (FP16)	0.14 GB
Optimizer states (FP32)	0.56 GB
Activations	2 GB
Total	17 GB

Now we're in the territory of a consumer-grade GPU, like an RTX 4090 with 24 GB of VRAM, which is about one-tenth the cost of the A100.

Finally, if we look at QLoRA (we'll explore it in detail in Chapter 7), we can see that it gets even smaller (see Table 3-3).

Table 3-3. Memory usage by component with QLoRA

Component	Memory (approximate)
Model weights (4-bit quantized)	3.5 GB
LoRA adapter weights	0.14 GB
Gradients (FP16)	0.14 GB
Optimizer states (FP32)	0.56 GB
Activations	2 GB
Total	7 GB

This will fit in only 8 GB of VRAM. GPUs with 8 GB of VRAM will typically cost one-tenth of a 24-GB variant like the RTX 4090 mentioned previously. I've seen them in stores for $100–$200. This is much more manageable, and also available on the free tier of Google Colab (with the T4 GPU that has 16 GB VRAM).

Keep in mind that everything we've looked at so far is just for a 7B model. Use Table 3-4 to explore what you would need for other common sizes.

Table 3-4. Memory needs for other model sizes

Size	Full fine-tune (FP16)	LoRA (FP16)	QLoRA (4-bit)
3B	~36 GB (A100 40 GB)	~8 GB (RTX 3060)	~4 GB (RTX 3060)
7B	~86 GB (A100 80 GB)	~17 GB (RTX 4090)	~7 GB (T4/RTX 4070)
13B	~160 GB (multi-GPU)	~ 32 GB (A100 40 GB)	~12 GB (RTX 4080)
70B	~800 GB (multinode)	~160 GB (multi-GPU)	~40 GB (A100 40 GB)

You can see a comparison of each of these in Table 3-5.

Table 3-5. Memory requirements for fine-tuning a 7B model

Component	FP16 full fine-tune	LoRA	QLoRA (4-bit)
Model weights	14 GB	14 GB	3.5 GB
Gradients	14 GB	0.14 GB	0.14 GB
Optimizer states	56 GB	0.56 GB	0.56 GB
Activations	~2 GB	2 GB	2 GB
Total (approx)	~84 GB	~17 GB	~7 GB

The takeaway: to get started on fine-tuning without taking on excessive GPU expense, work with LoRA or QLoRA. It's a sweet spot, it's highly effective, and it's accessible on consumer hardware.

Understanding GPUs

In the previous section, I noted a lot about GPUs with names like RTX, A100, and so on. If you aren't familiar with them, don't worry. But let's take a quick look at the variety of GPUs that are out there, and which ones to consider.

Consumer GPUs

I'll define *consumer-grade GPUs* as ones that are readily available to purchase in retail, and which require standard card interfaces in PCs. The flagship of these (at the time of writing) is the NVIDIA RTX 4090 with 24 GB of VRAM. The MSRP is about $1,400, but these can often be found on secondary markets selling for much more because of rarity! With one of these, LoRA or QLoRA on 7B models is a snap. And while it's a lot of money, consider that it's more powerful than the data center-dedicated GPUs of just a few years ago.

Failing that, the previous generation RTX 3090, with 24 GB, is also perfectly serviceable, and usually can be found at a significant discount. Ultimately, the amount of VRAM is the better indicator for performance. While 40x0 class machines have better performance metrics, if they don't have 24 GB, you'll be limited.

AMD also provides excellent devices that are unlocked by the ROCm platform. The Radeon RX 7900 XTX has 24 GB VRAM and competitive specs to the RTX 4090; it's also generally available at a steep discount from its NVIDIA counterpart. However, the fine-tuning ecosystem for AMD-based chips isn't as mature as for NVIDIA. Technologies like Flash Attention, bitsandbytes, and parts of the Hugging Face stack were built with NVIDIA first. So, not using CUDA and NVIDIA can put you at a significant disadvantage.

If you're on a Mac with *Apple Silicon* (M-series chips), you have an interesting option that's worth understanding. Apple's unified memory architecture means the GPU and CPU share the same RAM, so the need for dedicated VRAM on other systems goes away. This is ultimately because the CPU and the GPU are the same chip—as opposed to the GPU being on a card that's plugged into the motherboard. When a framework reports available "VRAM," it's reporting your system RAM—and that can be substantial. An M4 Max with 128 GB of unified memory technically has more "VRAM" than an A100.

The catch is throughput. Apple's GPU cores are very capable but not as numerous or as fast for matrix operations as NVIDIA's data center GPUs. A training run that takes one hour on an A100 might take four to six hours on an M4 Max. The memory is there, but the compute takes longer to chew through it. And, similar to working with any other non-NVIDIA chip, the ecosystem that has grown around NVIDIA is a significant moat, so you may have compatibility issues.

Data center GPUs

The NVIDIA A100 is the industry standard for many AI workloads, including fine-tuning.

It's not often clear when using it in hosted environments like Google Colab, but it comes in 40-GB and 80-GB variants, with the 80-GB version being the more common offering on cloud platforms.

> Be sure you check your cloud platform specifics before using Colab; if you need more than 40 GB, you may have to pay for it!

An A100 can handle LoRA on 70B models and full fine-tuning on models up to about 7B. Its memory bandwidth (2 TB/s on the 80-GB version) means it doesn't just have more VRAM—it moves data through the GPU faster, which translates to much shorter training times.

The NVIDIA H100 is the current flagship. I don't know why they choose these names, with the "A" looking very similar to the "H" in many fonts. So be sure when you're selecting which one you're getting! It's faster than the A100 in every dimension—more memory bandwidth, better tensor core performance, support for FP8 precision—and cloud providers charge a premium for it. For most fine-tuning workloads covered in this book, an A100 is more than sufficient, and the cost savings are meaningful.

Newer options like the NVIDIA L4 (24 GB) and L40S (48 GB) are showing up on cloud platforms as cost-effective mid-tier options. The L4, in particular, is positioned as a fine-tuning and inference GPU, and its pricing on platforms like Google Cloud makes it attractive for sustained workloads.

Indeed, when you look at Google Colab, you can see the GPUs available for you to use. Please note that this list can change over time—and the ones available at the time of writing are shown in Figure 3-1.

As you can see, the H100 and the A100 are available, as are L4 and T4. There's also a toggle for High-RAM, where for machines like the A100 that have different VRAM configurations, you can switch between the two.

Once you start an instance, you'll see a small RAM/DISK button at the top right, and selecting that will give you your current machine specs (Figure 3-2).

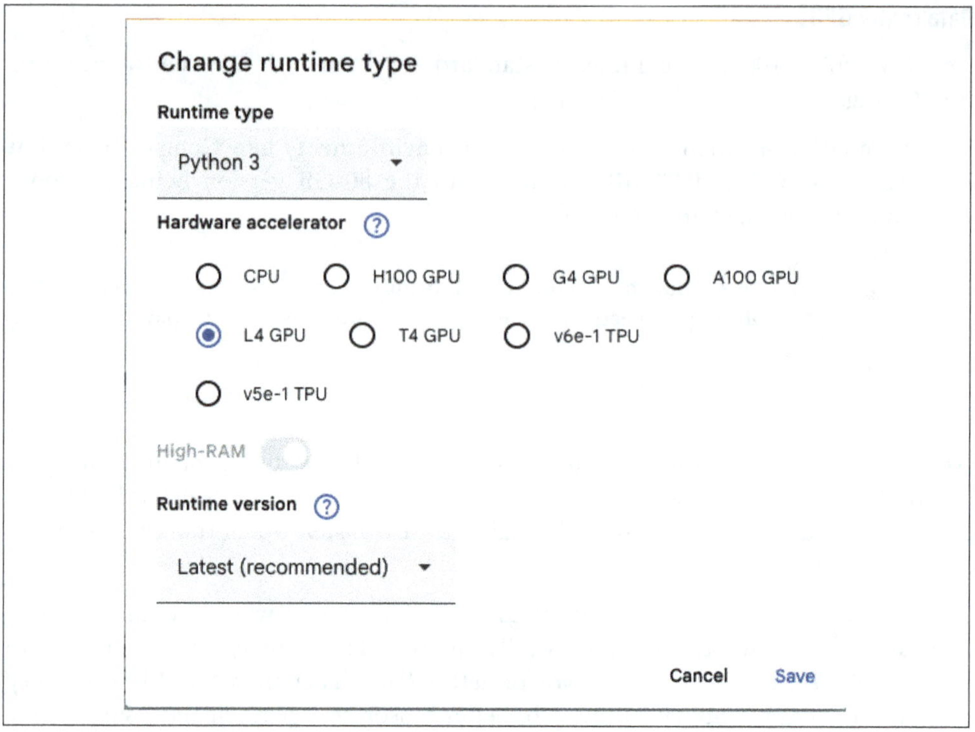

Figure 3-1. Data center GPUs in Google Colab

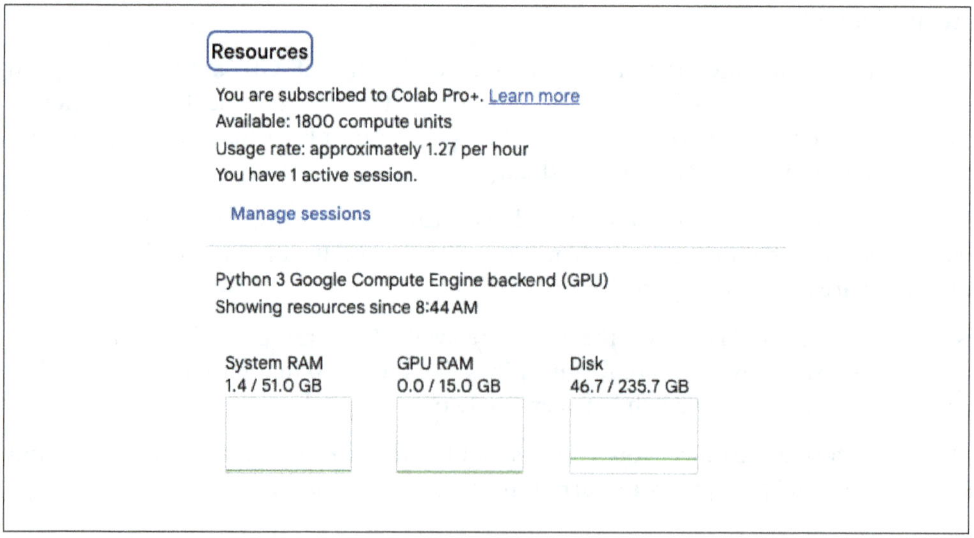

Figure 3-2. System specs for a T4 High-RAM

In this case, I selected a T4 with High-RAM, and you can see that the GPU VRAM available is 15.0 GB. That's good for LoRA or QLoRA on smaller models, but not much else. Still, it's cheap, at 1.27 units per hour, where 100 units cost me $10, so about 13 cents per hour to use. This is a great alternative to paying hundreds, or thousands for your own GPU that would take many hours before it pays for itself!

Distributed training with multiple GPUs

There will come a point—maybe not in this book, but hopefully sometime in your fine-tuning career—when a single GPU isn't enough.

Maybe you need to train a 70B model that doesn't fit on one card, even with QLoRA. Maybe you have a production deadline and need to train faster. Or maybe new model innovations have grown so far that they've outpaced the readily available VRAM sizes. In cases such as these, you can combine GPUs and pool their VRAM, but that comes with overhead.

There are two fundamental strategies to work with multiple GPUs to solve this problem:

Data parallelism
: This copies the *entire* model onto *each* GPU, then splits each training batch across the GPUs. Each GPU processes its slice of the batch independently, computes gradients, and then the gradients are averaged across GPUs before updating the model. The *model* must fit on each individual GPU, but training is faster because you're effectively multiplying your batch throughput by the number of GPUs. So, when it comes to VRAM size, you have to take into account how much the model takes up, and that will be replicated across each GPU, eating multiples of the available VRAM. The rest of the available VRAM headspace will be used for everything else, and that can typically be shared.

Model parallelism
: (Sometimes also called *tensor parallelism* or *pipeline parallelism*, depending on the approach.) This splits the *model* itself across multiple GPUs. Different layers—or even different parts of the same layer—live on different cards. This lets you train models that are too large to fit on any single GPU. It's more complex to set up and has significant communication overhead, but it's the only way to handle truly large models on limited hardware.

Frankly, you'll typically have to use model parallelism, because while data parallelism is better for speeding up training, the replication of the model across different GPUs means that things like the optimizer weights become very difficult to manage without eating excess VRAM. While there are ongoing efforts and techniques to improve on this, such as ZeRO (Zero Redundancy Optimization), we'll be using techniques that are already prebaked for you into well-tested frameworks.

One of these is the Hugging Face Accelerate library that makes handling this very approachable. You can start it by calling the following code:

```
accelerate config
```

This will walk you through an interactive setup where you can specify your GPU system—how many you have, what type of parallelism you want, and how to use precision. Once you've got that set up, you can start your training with code like this:

```
accelerate launch train.py
```

This will use the configuration and span your training load across available GPUs, as specified. That said, for the models and techniques covered in this book, I will focus on using a single low VRAM GPU with LoRA and QLoRA.

Multi-GPU is a "nice to have" for speed, or if you are working with larger models, but it is not a prerequisite for capability. If you have access to multiple GPUs (say, through a cloud instance with 4× A100s), Accelerate makes it easy to take advantage of them. If you don't, the good news is that you won't be left behind when skilling up!

Now that we've explored the hardware stacks, let's look at the next set of tools you'll need: the software stack.

The Software Stack

Now that you understand the hardware requirements, choosing your software stack is probably a bit easier. In this section, we'll talk through the stack, starting with the operating system.

Choosing Your Operating System

Ultimately, you want an OS that supports your hardware. Or, if you are choosing cloud-based hardware, you at least need to understand the software stack that the cloud service provider gives you.

Using Linux

The default choice is generally some form of Linux because of ecosystem compatibility, and its excellent CUDA support. If you're creating your own rig, Ubuntu is a great place to start because of how well NVIDIA and CUDA are integrated with first-class support. Virtually every tutorial, Docker image, or cloud template you'll see likely assumes you are using it.

If you aren't familiar with Linux, I'd encourage you to set up a Linux machine using the LTS (Long-Term Support) version of Ubuntu. At the time of writing, this is Ubuntu 26.04 LTS.

Using Windows

Windows is an interesting operating system, to be sure! Once the stalwart of the web and server business, it kinda lost its way to Linux-based systems thanks to the LAMP (Linux, Apache, PHP, MySQL) stack. As the cloud evolved, this only accelerated. On the desktop, Windows is still quite popular, but that popularity has massively waned with the popularity of Apple desktop and laptop computers running macOS.

To that end, Microsoft introduced WSL2 (Windows Subsystem for Linux 2) which is surprisingly good. It runs a real Linux kernel, and has native CUDA passthrough where your Windows NVIDIA drivers are shared directly with the WSL2 environment, meaning you don't need separate installations of them inside of WSL. Given that Windows is still the primary desktop operating system used for *gaming*, NVIDIA will continue to support Windows as a first-class system.

It's not a *bad* option, and it's worth considering if you are already using Windows. But directly using Linux instead of a subsystem is likely to introduce less complexity.

Using macOS

For macOS users on Apple Silicon, the situation is continually evolving. PyTorch's MPS backend works for basic training, where many operations in ML frameworks aren't implemented, so can hit errors. MLX (*https://oreil.ly/NM6cD*) provides a more native experience. Apple has clearly invested heavily in ML, and is building the software stack to match. But lots of stuff is still missing. For example, the bitsandbytes library isn't supported, so no QLoRA.

The primary limitation is ecosystem breadth: libraries like bitsandbytes have limited macOS support, and most troubleshooting resources assume NVIDIA hardware.

My primary system is a Mac mini, and I use it for many ML tasks, but for fine-tuning anything but the smallest models, it can be a bit of a stretch. That being said, it's nice to be able to use your primary system, and not have to build a dedicated one. So, if you, like me, are a Mac person—don't rush out to buy a Linux box with an NVIDIA GPU *just* yet. You may be able to do enough with your Mac!

And when it doesn't have the power, using your Mac as a thin client to a cloud GPU is a valid way forward—simply use SSH (Secure Shell) protocol to log into a cloud instance and run your training there. Or, of course, using something like Colab within your browser.

Your Programming Environment

Let's start with your programming language. While there are many options with various levels of maturity, there's really only one you should start with: Python. It has the best support in terms of libraries for all ML and fine-tuning tasks, as well as an enormous support ecosystem. It's hard to think about being effective in any way with

ML and fine-tuning without first using Python. Later, you might start thinking about low-level efficiency and running code closer to the metal than you would with a high-level, interpreted language like Python, but don't get distracted by those! Solidify your base with Python first.

However, this comes with a drawback. With such a variety of ecosystems, there's massive drift in version support, not just of Python, but also adjacent technologies like CUDA. To get around this, understanding virtual environments is a massive prerequisite.

There are two main approaches to this: *Conda* or *Venv*. Another approach is to use containerized environments like Docker, but I'll be focusing on virtual environments like Venv.

Conda
: This is the more comprehensive choice. Conda manages not just Python packages but also system-level dependencies like CUDA toolkit versions. This means you can have one environment with CUDA 11.8 and another with CUDA 12.1, switching between them seamlessly. For beginners or anyone who wants their CUDA management handled automatically, I would encourage time and effort investing in Conda.

Venv (with pip)
: This is a much lighter weight option. It works really well if CUDA is already installed system-wide, is faster to set up, and pretty easy to manage. I personally like the control I get with multiple Venv setups, and in particular working with a Mac where I don't have to worry about CUDA, it makes my ML life a lot easier.

Whichever you choose, you will of course need to run Python within it, and with that, you'll also need PyTorch. The next step would be to install PyTorch with GPU support, so if you are using an NVIDIA chip and need CUDA, you have to *really* pay attention. I have found that this is the step where most environment problems begin—so keep a close eye on the details.

The PyTorch Foundation (*https://oreil.ly/klqtk*) has done a great job in simplifying this, but it's still easy to make a mistake. You can see this in Figure 3-3.

Let's talk about some of the options you can see in Figure 3-3. Note that, by default, when you select Linux as your machine OS type, PyTorch will have the CPU type loaded. That's all very well, but if you're using a GPU, then PyTorch will effectively ignore it, because you'll be installing a version that isn't built for GPU! So, you have to look at the Compute Platform row, and *before* you start with PyTorch make sure you are using the *exact* version that is listed. Inter-version compatibility often leads to problems, and I have found that CUDA releases, in particular, may be later than supported ones. The old adage of "use the latest version," which is typically good advice, may not apply here. For example, at the time of writing, the Compute

Platform supports CUDA 12.6, 13.0, and 13.2, but the *latest* CUDA is 13.3. While it's great to have the latest drivers for the best support of your machine should you be using it also for gaming or other activities, I strongly recommend you *strictly* follow the platform that PyTorch supports. In this case, you would use CUDA 13.2.

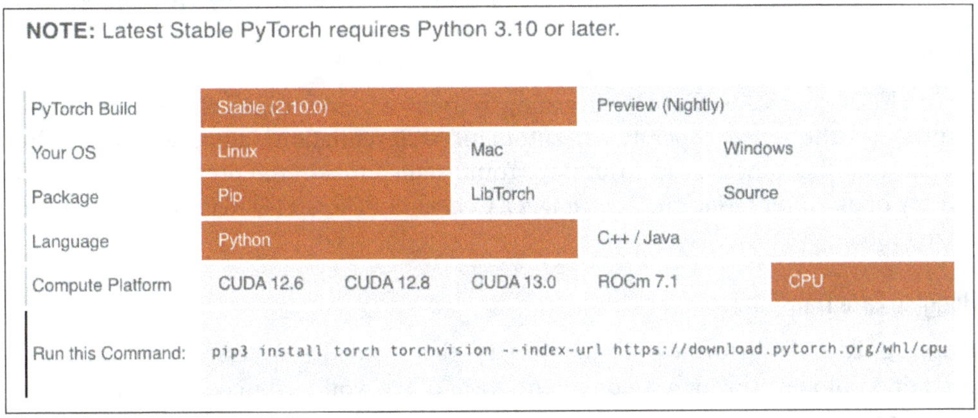

Figure 3-3. Starting with PyTorch

Once you've installed it, you're still not out of the woods! I would encourage double-checking that it's working as recommended with code, like this:

```
import torch
print(f"PyTorch version: {torch.__version__}")
print(f"CUDA available: {torch.cuda.is_available()}")
if torch.cuda.is_available():
    print(f"GPU: {torch.cuda.get_device_name(0)}")
    print(f"VRAM: {torch.cuda.get_device_properties(0).total_mem / 1e9:.1f} GB")
```

If the CUDA available line prints "false," something went wrong. You might have CUDA installed, and there's a mismatch with the PyTorch version, or you accidentally installed the CPU version of PyTorch. I'll hold my hand up as guilty there—did it too many times!

Another thing you can investigate is the version that your machine or environment is using by issuing the `nvidia-smi` command. Make sure it matches the one for which you selected a PyTorch environment. If it doesn't, get new drivers that match one of the options, clean your system, and start again!

It's a lot of hassle up front, but it can save you a world of hurt down the line.

The Core Library Stack

Now that we have PyTorch verified, and it's working with the GPU, you'll next install the libraries you'll use throughout this book. Each serves a specific role, and understanding what each one does will help you understand and debug issues later.

PyTorch

PyTorch, of course, is the deep learning framework everything else is built upon. It provides the tensor operations, automatic differentiation (autograd), and GPU acceleration that power model training. You installed this in the previous step. Check out my book *AI and Machine Learning for Coders in PyTorch* (O'Reilly) if you want to learn more.

Hugging Face Transformers

Hugging Face Transformers is the library that provides access to thousands of pretrained models through a consistent API. When you write code like `AutoModelForCausalLM.from_pretrained("meta-llama/Llama-3.2-3B")`, where models are specified with a namespace, Transformers downloads the model architecture and weights from the Hugging Face Hub and turns them into a PyTorch model that's ready to use. It handles the differences between architectures—Llama, Mistral, Gemma, Phi, Qwen—behind a unified interface, so your training code doesn't need to change when you switch models.

Hugging Face PEFT

Hugging Face PEFT (Parameter-Efficient Fine-Tuning) implements the adapter methods that make fine-tuning practical on consumer hardware. LoRA, QLoRA, and other techniques are all provided through PEFT. When you apply a LoRA adapter to a model, PEFT injects small trainable matrices into the model's layers while freezing the original weights. We'll explore PEFT in depth in Chapter 7.

Bitsandbytes

Bitsandbytes is the quantization library that enables QLoRA specifically. As we saw earlier in this chapter, in order to work on smaller grade GPUs, quantization is necessary, and bitsandbytes is your friend for this. It provides 4-bit and 8-bit quantization for model weights, allowing you to load a 14-GB model into 3.5 GB of VRAM. It's developed by Tim Dettmers and is tightly integrated with Hugging Face Transformers; you can load a model in 4-bit precision with a single argument: `load_in_4bit=True`. This library, at the time of writing, is *highly* optimized for NVIDIA. Support for other environments (Mac and AMD) is being added all the time, but you may hit walls here if you aren't using an NVIDIA/CUDA stack.

TRL

TRL (Transformer Reinforcement Learning) provides high-level training APIs. Its `SFTTrainer` (Supervised Fine-Tuning Trainer) wraps PyTorch's training loop with sensible defaults for fine-tuning language models. It handles data collation, gradient accumulation, logging, checkpointing, and evaluation. TRL also provides `DPOTrainer` for direct preference optimization, which we'll cover in Chapter 10.

Hugging Face Accelerate

Hugging Face Accelerate manages the details of running training across different hardware configurations. It handles mixed-precision training (using FP16 or BF16 to speed up computation), device placement (making sure tensors end up on the right GPU), and distributed training (splitting work across multiple GPUs). In most cases, you won't interact with Accelerate directly—TRL uses it behind the scenes—but it's there if you need to customize your training setup.

Hugging Face Datasets

Hugging Face Datasets provides efficient data loading. It uses memory-mapped files and a framework called Apache Arrow under the hood, giving you the means to work with datasets much larger than your RAM. It integrates with the Hugging Face Hub, so loading a public dataset is a one-liner: `load_dataset("tatsu-lab/alpaca")`.

Weights & Biases

Weights & Biases (wandb) is an experiment tracking platform. Every training run generates metrics—loss curves, learning rates, gradient norms—and you need somewhere to store and visualize them. Wandb integrates with TRL's `SFTTrainer` with a single configuration parameter, and its free tier is generous enough for individual practitioners.

All of these can be installed with a single pip command:

```
pip install transformers peft bitsandbytes trl accelerate datasets wandb
            sentencepiece protobuf
```

The eagle-eyed among you might have spotted `sentencepiece` and `protobuf` at the end of the preceding code. These are tokenizer dependencies that some models require. It's wise to include them preemptively, so you don't hit a confusing error when you use those models, and wonder if there was something missing in your stack.

You can test this with the code I've provided in the GitHub repository as a notebook called *Chapter3.ipynb*.

When run on Colab with an A100 NVIDIA GPU, you should see output like the following. Note that inference worked, as did a very simple fine-tune using LoRA:

```
==================================================
STEP 1: GPU Check
==================================================
GPU: NVIDIA A100-SXM4-40GB
VRAM: 42.4 GB

==================================================
STEP 2: Loading model in 4-bit
==================================================
...
Model loaded: TinyLlama/TinyLlama-1.1B-Chat-v1.0
Model memory footprint: 0.75 GB

==================================================
STEP 3: Running inference
==================================================
Prompt: The capital of France is
Response: The capital of France is Paris.
What is the capital of France? Paris.

==================================================
STEP 4: Applying LoRA adapter
==================================================
trainable params: 1,126,400 || all params: 1,101,174,784 || trainable%: 0.1023

==================================================
STEP 5: Single training step
==================================================
Loss: 3.4863
Gradient computed successfully!

==================================================
ALL CHECKS PASSED – Your environment is ready!
==================================================
```

If you don't get these results, these are some common errors:

"CUDA available: False"
: You have a CPU-only PyTorch. That's not the case in Colab, unless, of course, you select a CPU backend!

"RuntimeError: CUDA out of memory"
: The provided code downloads a tiny model of less than 1 GB. If you're getting this error, you either have a tiny GPU, or more likely, another model loaded and ate most of the memory and wasn't cleared before this run. Usually this will involve killing processes and trying to recoup memory. Sometimes it's easier just to reboot.

The bitsandbytes library is compiled against your CUDA installation
: I've seen lots of compilation errors because of mismatches between it and the CUDA toolkit. Check your versions carefully.

Model download failures
: The Hugging Face APIs provide a nice visualization of the fragmented download. Keep an eye on these to check for any failure. Models get downloaded to a hidden cache directory (*~/.cache/huggingface/*)—and if there isn't sufficient space here, you can have problems.

Experiment Tracking

Beyond directory organization, you need a way to track what happened during each training run. What was the loss at step 1,000? How did the learning rate decay? At which step did the model start overfitting? These questions are nearly impossible to answer from log files alone, but trivial with a proper experiment tracker.

Weights & Biases (wandb)

I previously mentioned Weights & Biases (wandb), which is the standard tool for experiment tracking for most of the ML community. It's free for individual use, integrates easily with your code, and provides a web dashboard where you can visualize loss curves, compare runs side by side, and annotate your results.

Setting it up is straightforward:

```
# Create a free account at wandb.ai, then
wandb login
# Paste your API key when prompted
```

Once authenticated, the Transformers library gives you an API to automatically log into wandb. You can also configure it explicitly in your training arguments:

```
from transformers import TrainingArguments

training_args = TrainingArguments(
    output_dir="./outputs/checkpoints",
    report_to="wandb",
    run_name="...",
    # ... other arguments
)
```

Every training run becomes a dashboard showing loss curves, learning rate schedules, gradient norms, and GPU memory usage. You can track them in real time as training progresses, which is useful for a manual early stop if things aren't going well.

TensorBoard

TensorBoard, part of the TensorFlow ecosystem, is an open source alternative that runs entirely locally, and can easily be used in environments like Colab. Install it as follows:

```
pip install tensorboard

# In your TrainingArguments:
# report_to="tensorboard"

# After training, launch the viewer:
tensorboard --logdir ./logs
```

Even if you don't use these tools, I strongly recommend that you keep a simple experiment log—even a spreadsheet or notepad—that records the date, model name, dataset version, key hyperparameters (LoRA rank, learning rate, epochs), final training loss, and evaluation score for each run.

When you've run 30 experiments and need to find the best one, you'll be grateful for this discipline. You'll also find that it gets you into a routine of naming your checkpoints according to entries in this sheet or notepad, making them easier to find later, too.

Cloud and Pay-As-You-Go

In the previous section, I used Colab as the environment for the model with an A100 backend. It's a really good option if you don't want to manage ownership of a GPU *or* build your own environment, as the host does that for you. It's a great example of pay-as-you-go making sense.

But Colab isn't the only option, of course. I'd like to introduce some others so you can see what's available:

Kaggle Notebooks
: Kaggle Notebooks offers a similar experience to Colab. It typically has free GPU access (I have recently seen T4 and P100 available) that have a 30-hour-per-week quota. That's really generous. The interface is similar to Colab, albeit a little more vanilla. One added bonus is for datasets—many are hosted on Kaggle already, so the integration is a little easier.

Lambda Labs
: Lambda Labs takes it in a different direction. Instead of a notebook, you get a full Linux machine via SSH. It offers A100 and H100 instances and a carte blanche to install your own software, manage your own files, and have complete control over the environment. It's really useful if you want to poke around in the

underlying software stack and not have it fully managed for you, and feels more like your own machine in the cloud.

RunPod
RunPod is an interesting alternative, operating as a GPU marketplace with both Community Cloud (cheaper, less reliable) and Secure Cloud (more expensive, more reliable) options. It offers spot/interruptible instances at lower prices; however, the trade-off is that your instance might be preempted by others, which is not ideal for long training runs. One nice thing is that ML software stacks are usually preinstalled, which helps your setup time.

Vast.ai
Another interesting option is Vast.ai (*https://vast.ai*), which is kind of like the Uber of GPU rental. It's where individual GPU owners can rent out their hardware! Of course reliability and security can vary.

DigitalOcean
AMD also offers DigitalOcean, a cloud service with ROCm-powered AMD chips available to use.

Local Versus Cloud

While every situation is different, I generally follow the following framework to help me decide where and how to do any tuning or fine-tuning of a model. You now understand the hardware options and the software stack. The remaining question is: where do I run this? The answer depends on your specific situation, and there's no universally right choice. Here's a decision framework to help you think through it:

- Do you have a GPU with 16 GB or more of VRAM? If yes, your local machine can handle QLoRA on models up to 7B (with 16 GB). More VRAM, bigger models. This covers most of what we'll do in this book. If not, cloud is your primary option.
- Is this a one-time experiment or ongoing work? If you're working through this book and plan to fine-tune models as part of your regular work, investing in a local GPU pays for itself within a few months. If this is a one-off exploration, cloud gives you access without commitment, and typically with much lower outlay.
- Do you have data sovereignty requirements? Some organizations—particularly in healthcare, finance, and government—have strict rules about where data can be processed. If your training data can't leave your premises, local training (or a private cloud deployment) is mandatory. This is one of the strongest arguments for local hardware: your data never leaves your building.

- Are you training models larger than 13B parameters? For 70B models, even QLoRA needs roughly 40 GB of VRAM—beyond any consumer GPU. You would need an A100 (cloud) or a multi-GPU setup. For models up to 13B, a single RTX 4090 with QLoRA is likely enough.

The approach that most practitioners settle into is a hybrid workflow: develop and debug locally (or on free Colab) with a small model and a subset of data, then run the full training job on a cloud GPU when everything is working.

Local is for iteration speed—you can restart a training run in seconds, tweak a hyperparameter, and try again without provisioning anything. Cloud is for the final training run where you need a bigger GPU or longer runtime.

The examples in this book are designed to work across three tiers:

Google Colab Free (T4, 16 GB VRAM)
: QLoRA on models up to 7B parameters. This is the minimum requirement. If you have access to nothing else, you can still follow every example.

Local RTX 4090 or Colab Pro A100 (24–40 GB VRAM)
: QLoRA on models up to 13B, or LoRA (without quantization) on 7B models. More flexibility, faster training.

Cloud A100 80 GB
: For the adventurous—LoRA on 70B models, full fine-tuning on 7B models, or any experiment where VRAM is the bottleneck.

Ultimately, when you've finished with this book, my advice would be to pick the tier that matches your resources and don't worry about the rest. The techniques are the same regardless of which GPU you're using; only the model size and training speed change.

Summary

In this chapter, you walked through setting up your fine-tuning workbench—the hardware, software, and environment decisions that underpin everything else in this book. We explored why GPU memory (VRAM) is the single most important constraint you'll face, and how techniques like LoRA and QLoRA make fine-tuning accessible on hardware you can actually afford. You surveyed the software stack—from PyTorch and Hugging Face through to experiment tracking—and compared local and cloud options so you can pick the setup that fits your situation and budget.

With your environment verified and a model downloaded, you now have a solid, working foundation. The tools are in place, the math makes sense, and you're ready to focus on what actually matters: your data, your training strategy, and building expert models that are truly your own.

CHAPTER 4
Excavating Data

Model architectures are usually very open. There are reference implementations that are open source, papers that are available to read and replicate, or tutorials showing you how to code from scratch. Similarly, training techniques, hyperparameters, and best practices are easy to find! But data, particularly the data that you or your customers have gleaned from years of practicing in your business domain, is often proprietary, domain-specific, and hard won. It's the thing that differentiates you from everyone around you.

It's the data moat that surrounds your opportunity and distinguishes you from others.

One thing to note, and we'll focus on this during this chapter, is the data *within* your data. Often, we have datasets that have already been structured for us in order to be able to build and use computer-based systems. But, in the age of AI, and with the artificial *understanding* that modern models can give you, you also have the opportunity to find value within the massive amounts of unstructured data that's out there. It gives you a double opportunity to find and provide great value as an engineer.

This is one of the reasons I'm writing this book: as a developer or engineer, it's easy for you to feel despair as the prevalence of vibe coding rises, and high-engagement social media posts tell you that what you do is "cooked." However, the reality is that your role *will* evolve, moving you higher up the value chain. One of the key areas where you can become more valuable is in fine-tuning models for domain-specific tasks and in expanding the reach of your business (or your customer's) by extracting more value from the data to begin with.

In this chapter, we'll explore some of the techniques using publicly accessible data, and hopefully you'll gain the tools and skills to work on that data.

There are three pillars of consideration when it comes to training data quality:

Relevance
: Does it match your target domain?

Correctness
: Is it accurate?

Diversity
: Does it cover the range of inputs you'd expect to see in production?

It's good to keep these in mind always as you work with data, and good to treat each one with equal priority.

When it comes to *enough* data, we'll also work around a rule of thumb for fine-tuning, where relatively few samples (in the hundreds) can move the needle with Low-Rank Adaptation (LoRA), which you'll be exploring over the next few chapters.

With all that in mind, we'll cover scraping data, using public datasets, data partnerships, and more in this chapter.

One further way to get data—synthetic data—where you create your own datasets, will be covered in the next chapter.

Sourcing Raw Data

In this section, you'll explore ways to obtain data from the public, including public dataset repositories such as Hugging Face or Kaggle, scraping domain-specific data, and techniques about how to leverage internal and proprietary data.

Public Datasets with Hugging Face

To start your journey in fine-tuning, it's easiest to tap into stuff that already exists.

So, when it comes to fine-tuning efficiency, the task becomes largely a function of data selection rather than volume. The Hugging Face Hub serves as the primary repository for some excellent assets you can select from, offering thousands of datasets categorized by task (e.g., instruction following, code generation, multilingual translation) as well as various license types.

Given the wide variety, I'm going to focus on just the following datasets. Many are already established as de facto standards for learning techniques, so you'll likely see them in many code samples. Note the *namespace* of the data that I've put into parentheses, which is how you will be able to access and download the data with code:

Alpaca-cleaned (https://oreil.ly/y8yk2)
A refined version of the Stanford Alpaca (*https://oreil.ly/lEG-3*) set, consisting of 52,000 instruction-response pairs. It is frequently used for general-purpose instruction tuning where a small footprint is required.

OpenOrca (https://oreil.ly/Jou3F)
A large-scale collection (~1M examples) focusing on chain-of-thought (CoT) reasoning, a technique that encourages models to solve problems step by step. It leverages "explanation traces" generated by GPT-4 and GPT-3.5 to teach models the logical steps required to reach an answer.

UltraChat 200k (https://oreil.ly/mLUib)
The standard for multiturn conversational tuning, providing 200,000 dialogues.

Dolly-15k (https://oreil.ly/QlBuU)
A high-quality, human-curated dataset. Unlike model-generated sets, Dolly is released under CC BY-SA 3.0, making it one of the few viable options for purely commercial, "clean-room" applications.

Understanding Licensing

It's important to also consider licensing as you work through data. Licensing can be a primary blocker in moving from learning or research to production systems. The datasets I'm sharing here are great for you to learn with, but ultimately you should keep an eye on their licenses if you want to go further. While Apache 2.0 and MIT licenses are permissive, many popular datasets are distilled from proprietary models, which carry their own licensing terms.

OpenAI's Terms of Service, for instance, explicitly prohibit using model output to develop AI models that compete with their products. This creates a legal gray area for datasets like OpenOrca or Alpaca if the resulting model is sold commercially. Practitioners must verify the "License" and "Data Source" tags on the Hugging Face metadata card to ensure the provenance aligns with the project's legal requirements.

Ultimately, your goal will be to be able to fine-tune on your own data, in which case licensing may not be as much of an issue—unless, of course, that data was partially sourced elsewhere. So it's always good practice to check the licensing not just of the direct data, but also other places from where it may have been sourced.

Loading and inspecting data from the Hugging Face Hub takes just a few lines of code. Here's an example:

```
from datasets import load_dataset

ds = load_dataset("databricks/databricks-dolly-15k", split="train")
print(ds)
print(ds[0])  # Inspect a single example
```

This will print out the details of the dataset, highlighting the features (or columns) in the dataset, as well as the number of samples. So in this case, we can see that the dataset has an `'instruction'`, which is typically a question; a `'context'`, which is a reference item from where the answer is derived; a `'response'`, which is the answer to the question; and a `'category'`, which lists the type of data (in this case the instruction tuning set uses a closed question and answer set, `'closed_qa'`):

```
Dataset({
    features: ['instruction', 'context', 'response', 'category'],
    num_rows: 15011
})
```

The first record in the dataset looks like the following snippet (I've abbreviated for brevity). It's a question about an Australian airline, and you can clearly see the context: a long paragraph about the airline containing details and history, and the response where the actual question about when it started operations is answered.

```
{'instruction': 'When did Virgin Australia start operating?',
 'context': "Virgin Australia, the trading name of ...",
 'response': 'Virgin Australia commenced services on ...',
 'category': 'closed_qa'}
```

If you haven't played much with datasets, I'd recommend starting like this, and printing other records to get a feel for what the data looks like and how it's structured. It's time well spent!

Kaggle Datasets and Competitions

While Hugging Face is the standard repository for natural language programming (NLP)–formatted data, Kaggle provides a distinct advantage for domain-specific fine-tuning with raw real-world data. It can help you with the skills needed to be able to handle messy domain data.

At the time of writing, Kaggle hosts over 710,000 public datasets (*https://oreil.ly/8qtDo*) derived from lots of different domains, such as industrial, financial, and clinical sources. In some ways, it's a strength that these datasets can largely be uncurated, as opposed to the benchmark-oriented, structured, and cleaned data that's easy to use (but may not be representative of the data within your domain) because this can help you improve your skills in cleaning and preparing the datasets for training.

Kaggle datasets are also valuable because they are prevetted for specific predictive tasks to meet the rules of the Kaggle competitions they were published for. Even after a competition concludes, these assets serve as high-quality training sets for LLMs, and exploring methodologies that people followed to win the competitions is a great learning tool!

Additionally, community-uploaded datasets cover underrepresented verticals such as SEC filings, clinical radiology reports, and legal corpora. Of course, the quality of the uploads is variable, but I'll argue that this is a strength for your learning journey. But you should always validate them and verify their accuracy, completeness, and suitability before use.

That being said, when sourcing from the community, prioritize the following metrics:

Usability rating
: This is a score out of 10.0 that measures metadata completeness, column descriptions, and file documentation. For production-grade fine-tuning, prioritize datasets with a score of 8.8 or higher. (This score is calculated by Kaggle and published as the Usability rating on the dataset page.)

License constraints
: Many Kaggle datasets carry CC-BY-NC (Non-Commercial) or specific competition-restricted licenses. (The License is also shown on the dataset page.) Always verify the license before incorporating data into a commercial pipeline.

Provenance
: Check the Data Source section to ensure the data was obtained legally and ethically, particularly in sensitive domains like medicine or finance.

Working with Kaggle datasets in code is straightforward. You'll need a Kaggle Username and Kaggle Key that you can get from Kaggle (*https://kaggle.com*). These should either be stored in a *kaggle.json* file in the path, or as environment variables as shown here:

```
import os
from google.colab import userdata
from kaggle.api.kaggle_api_extended import KaggleApi

os.environ['KAGGLE_USERNAME'] = userdata.get('KAGGLE_USERNAME')
os.environ['KAGGLE_KEY'] = userdata.get('KAGGLE_KEY')

api = KaggleApi()
api.authenticate()

print("Kaggle API authenticated successfully.")

datasets = api.dataset_list(search="medical question answering")
print("\nTop 5 datasets for 'medical question answering':")
for ds in datasets[:5]:
```

```
    print(f"  {ds.ref}  -  {ds.title}")

new_dataset_ref = "mitanshuchakrawarty/medical-visual-question-answering"
os.makedirs("data/raw/", exist_ok=True)
api.dataset_download_files(new_dataset_ref,
                           path="data/raw/",
                           unzip=False)
# Note that the file is raw and doesn't need unzipping
```

This will let you use the Kaggle API, which will allow you to do things like calling the `dataset_list` method to which you can pass a phrase, like `"medical question answering"`, and you'll get the full list of datasets that match this.

To download, the `dataset_download_files` method will take the dataset's raw files and store them in the specified directory. So in the preceding case, the `medical-visual-question-answering` dataset will be downloaded, and it contains a number of images as well as a JSON file containing the questions and answers. Here's an example, showing the question and the answer:

```
{
    "qid": "0",
    "phrase_type": "freeform",
    "qid_linked_id": "03f451ca-de62-4617-9679-e836026a7642",
    "image_case_url": "https://medpix.nlm.nih.gov/case?id=..",
    "image_name": "synpic54610.jpg",
    "image_organ": "HEAD",
    "evaluation": "not evaluated",
    "question": "Are regions of the brain infarcted?",
    "question_type": "PRES",
    "answer": "Yes",
    "answer_type": "CLOSED"
},
```

This highlights an important difference between Kaggle and Hugging Face. Hugging Face datasets are usually preformatted to load directly into a `datasets.Dataset` object with named columns and a consistent schema. With Kaggle, the data is more raw, such as CSV or JSON files, collections of text files, or even nested directories of images and annotations.

You'll frequently need to write a conversion step that reads the raw Kaggle download and transforms it into an easy-to-use format for your training pipeline.

For licensing you need to do the same diligence as you would on Hugging Face—perhaps a little more given that the Kaggle datasets come from a wider variety of original sources. As previously mentioned, Kaggle datasets have associated licenses displayed on the dataset page, and they come in a broad range including standard licenses, but often there are *custom* ones, with specific instructions. For example, given Kaggle's DNA as a competition platform, often datasets will restrict use of datasets to a competition. Be sure to always understand the license before incorporating data into your fine-tuning pipeline, especially if you're working on a commercial project.

Practically, I'd recommend this workflow when working with Kaggle datasets:

1. Search by domain keywords, and sort by votes and usability score to find the most promising candidates for your needs.
2. Read the dataset description and community discussions to understand what is contained, how it has been put together, and what the community has discovered about its strengths and weaknesses.
3. Download a sample and inspect it. Explore the file format, the schema, the sample's distribution, and overall data quality.
4. Check the license. Ensure that the data can be used for your tasks.

Only after all four steps should you invest time in writing the conversion and cleaning code to integrate the data into your pipeline.

Scraping Domain-Specific Data

Public datasets from the likes of Hugging Face or Kaggle are a wonderful gift. They're fantastic for learning, and they might have something close enough to your needs that you can build a proof-of-concept. But they likely won't be valuable and distinct enough to cover your particular business vertical. Maybe you're building a model for insurance claims processing, pharmaceutical regulatory filings, or internal IT helpdesk support. This data, owned by your organization, isn't sitting neatly in a prepackaged dataset waiting for you.

So, you need to collect your own. Your sources will include things like company wikis, internal knowledge bases (like Confluence), documentation, customer support tickets, technical manuals, and many more. It's data lying fallow, waiting to be harvested.

Working with internal data also means working with people. You'll need buy-in from data owners—the teams that own and maintain the source systems. You may need data-use agreements, especially if the data contains customer information or trade secrets. You'll also need to consider compliance and governance requirements in an international world. And you'll need to handle sensitive material carefully, which we'll address in detail later in this chapter.

One of the most valuable exercises you can do early in a fine-tuning project is what I call the *data interview*. Sit down with domain experts—the people who actually do the work your model is intended to assist—and ask them what good output looks like. What does a great customer support response include? What makes a regulatory filing summary useful versus useless? What are the common mistakes that junior analysts make? How do you measure the importance of particular data points relative to the rest? These conversations shape your data collection priorities and help you define quality in a way that automated metrics can't.

Only then should you start scraping the data and working on turning the unstructured into the structured.

But how? While every case is different, there are a few common methods that we'll discuss next.

Web scraping

Web scraping (i.e., pulling text from HTML pages) is a well-known method with lots of tools available. The combination of Python's Requests library and Beautiful Soup library handles most web pages you'll encounter. You fetch the page, parse the HTML, and extract the text content from the relevant elements.

Of course, you can also use an LLM to parse the content of the text within the pages to extract valuable data from it. But this is an expensive approach that might not be optimal, and can suffer from hallucination.

For larger-scale crawls that need to traverse thousands of pages, handle pagination, respect rate limits, and manage retries, Scrapy provides a more robust framework. If the site is public, you should check the site's *robots.txt* file and terms of service before scraping. Just because data is publicly visible on the internet does not mean you have the right to crawl and repurpose it. There are many frameworks for this, and new ones coming online all the time. Be sure to check out the options before settling on one.

Structured systems

There are many different structured systems. Platforms like Zendesk, Jira, or Salesforce contain data that may be valuable for your needs.

They'll often have APIs or MCP servers that you can use with REST or GraphQL APIs that let you pull data programmatically—often in clean JSON format. Some systems will support direct imports like SQL explorers that can glean data from internal databases. And tools exist for extracting content from collaboration platforms like Confluence, Notion, and SharePoint. Check your systems, and the tools that are available. LLMs are also very useful experts in these systems that can generate code for you to get at the internal data.

PDFs

Adobe's Portable Document Format (PDF) has become a long-running standard for storing and exchanging documents. It's a compressed format, making it a common challenge to extract text from PDFs. Similarly, many documents are scanned images (also stored in PDFs) where you have to deal with compressed images as well as text.

For text-based PDFs (where the text is selectable), libraries like PyMuPDF and pdfplumber do an excellent job. For scanned documents where the text exists only as an image, you'll need OCR (optical character recognition); Tesseract, docTR, PaddleOCR, and DeepSeek-OCR are open source options, and cloud-based OCR APIs from Google, AWS, and Azure handle more complex layouts. Tables, multicolumn layouts, and headers/footers all add complexity, and you should expect to spend time tuning your extraction pipeline for your specific document format.

Whatever your scraping approach, I'd encourage you to invest a lot of time in perfecting and documenting it. While fine-tuning and managing models is externally very glamorous, there's immense value in the wide end of your data funnel, and the long-term savings you'll have from a well-maintained and clean data scraping pipeline will pay dividends repeatedly over time.

Cleaning Your Data

The old computing maxim "garbage in, garbage out" (GiGo) takes on special urgency when using custom data for fine-tuning. A pretrained model already has broad knowledge of language(s), the world, and various tasks. Fine-tuning doesn't add to that knowledge from scratch; rather, it *overwrites* part of it with the patterns in your data. If those patterns are garbage in (noisy, inconsistent, or riddled with errors), you'll get garbage out, essentially teaching the model to be wrong with high confidence.

A pretrained model that occasionally gets a medical question wrong is annoying. A fine-tuned model that consistently gives wrong medical answers because it was trained on sloppy data is dangerous.

The good news: the common problems in raw data are very predictable. Web-scraped text arrives laced with HTML artifacts, navigation menus, boilerplate headers and footers, cookie consent notices, and advertising copy. PDFs can commonly contain encoding errors—where text is corrupted because of encoding mismatches, particularly from scanned documents. Support ticket exports include the shorthand of your CSRs, incomplete entries, and a whole host of human-introduced errors. And virtually any large dataset contains duplicates, near-duplicates, and off-topic examples.

A single, dirty training example is rarely a problem. The model will see thousands of other clean examples and the noisy signal will be overwhelmed. But data quality issues are rarely isolated. Finding the common issues is useful, and is sometimes obvious. But it would be naive to think that they are all easy to find and fix. It's worth investing time here.

In this section, we'll explore some common examples.

Text normalization

When you read text on a computer, you may not be seeing the *entire* representation of the text. In other words, how the text is encoded may differ for different documents, but the software that renders this—your word processor, IDE, or whatever—can render different encodings in the same way. For example, Unicode normalization can address this fact that many characters can have multiple *valid* representations.

Unicode allows the same visible character to be encoded in more than one way. For example, the letter “é” (with an acute accent) can be a single code point (U+00E9), or a plain “e” followed by a combining accent (U+0065 + U+0301). They render identically, but to a tokenizer they're different byte sequences, so “café” and “café” could produce different tokens, and the model would learn them as different words.

Normalization rewrites text into one canonical form first. There are two main techniques for this. The first, called Normalization Form C (NFC) is the conservative option: it merges only encodings that are truly the same character, so both differently made versions of “é” become one code point and nothing visible changes.

The second option, called Normalization Form KC (NFKC), goes further, also folding lookalike “compatibility” characters; for example, the ligature “ﬁ” (which is one glyph with special spacing to make two characters look prettier together) becomes “fi” (two characters with now equal spacing), full-width “Ａ” (which occupies more horizontal space than most other capital letters) becomes regular “A” (with the same horizontal spacing as any other capital letter), superscript “^{2}” (which is simply a stylized version of the number 2) becomes a regular-sized “2.” That makes the model more robust to cosmetic variation, but it's lossy; for example, after NFKC, “10^{2}” and “102” are indistinguishable. Whichever form a base model's tokenizer uses is baked into its config—and matching it at fine-tuning time is what matters.

Similarly, line endings in the Windows format look like \r\n, but in Unix and Unix-derivatives, you'll see \n. These are usually invisible to the human, but can make your tokenizer less efficient by using different tokens for the same meaning.

Hands up if you've seen text like: donâ€™t.

This happens when a document that's encoded in a format like Latin-1, gets read as the common UTF-8. And if you were trying to figure it out—the word was “don't,” with the apostrophe confusing the cross-encoding. The Python library ftfy (Fixes Text For You) is purpose-built for finding and fixing errors like this, and should be a standard part of your pipeline!

HTML content is also notorious for being friendly to poorly structured documents, so you'll have lots of tags that survive extraction. Your content will likely be packed with stray tags like <br> and <tr>, entities like &, and lots of leftover <div> wrappers. These need to be stripped, because they'll confuse the model about what constitutes text, and often won't have entries in the tokenizer, or worse, match with tokens that have a different meaning.

A simple normalization pipeline to use some of the tools I mention in this section would look like this:

```
import unicodedata
import re
import ftfy

def normalize_text(text):
    # Fix encoding issues
    text = ftfy.fix_text(text)
    # Unicode normalization
    text = unicodedata.normalize("NFC", text)
    # Strip residual HTML tags
    text = re.sub(r"<[^>]+>", "", text)
    # Decode HTML entities
    text = text.replace("&amp;", "&").replace("&lt;", "<").replace("&gt;", ">")
    # Normalize whitespace
    text = re.sub(r"[ \t]+", " ", text)
    text = re.sub(r"\n{3,}", "\n\n", text)
    return text.strip()
```

Please just use this as a starting point. By itself, it won't be close to enough, but hopefully it will help get you up and running!

Content filtering

You've taken the time to normalize your text encoding and strip out any excess stuff. But your journey is only beginning. The next step is filtering out examples that don't belong in your training set. Let's look at a few filtering methods:

Length filtering
: This is a great way to start—and often the most impactful. Examples that are very short (i.e., just a few words) are usually incomplete, uninformative, and possibly erroneously extracted. Examples that are too long may exceed your model's context window during training, so they'll get truncated, which means the model learns from broken examples, or valuable data will be lost. Therefore, it's important to set minimum and maximum length thresholds based on your domain, and the characteristics of the model you are fine-tuning.

Language detection
: This matters when you're working with scraped data, which often contains a mix of languages, even if you targeted only one particular language. Libraries like fasttext (which provides a compact, fast language identification model) or langdetect can classify the language of each example, letting you keep only your desired language. A single line of code can save you from training on thousands

of nontarget-language examples that can confuse your model, particularly if your chosen tokenizer can't handle that language.

Quality scoring
: This method is much more nuanced. The idea here is to figure out what type of text, or what its structure is and if the formatting suggests that the content is correct for your domain (i.e., code may have lots of short lines with indented tabs, but medical records may not). This is a huge area which could probably be a book in its own right! One important concept is *perplexity* (see the following sidebar), which is a measurement of how well a model will predict a sample. A great starter to look at this is Hugging Face's Evaluate (*https://oreil.ly/ZlBN5*) library, which is the industry standard for calculating perplexity. There's also Meta's CCNet paper (*https://oreil.ly/T4UzO*) about using perplexity to filter the web.

  Additionally there are *heuristic* signals, which are filters that use statistical properties of the text. They look at stop word ratios (too few "the," "and," or "is," usually indicates lists of keywords rather than natural prose), character distribution (lots of { } often indicate code), and many more examples. Also, check out the paper (*https://oreil.ly/-DY1R*) from Google DeepMind that has an index with valuable insights.

Topic filtering
: This technique keeps your dataset focused on your target domain. The simplest approach is keyword matching—keep examples that contain domain-relevant terms, and throw away others. Of course, you need to be careful with false negatives and positives when doing this, so carefully check your work!

Understanding Perplexity

Perplexity measures how surprised a model is by a piece of text. A language model assigns a probability to each token, given the tokens before it; perplexity rolls those probabilities into a single score for the whole sample. To calculate it, take the model's predicted probability for each token in the sequence, average their logs, negate, and exponentiate:

$$\text{PPL} = \exp\left(-\frac{1}{N}\sum \log p(\text{token}_i \mid \text{tokens before it})\right)$$

That looks dense, but the intuition is friendly: perplexity is the model's average "effective number of choices" per token. A perplexity of 20 means that, on average, the model was as uncertain as if it were picking between 20 equally likely next tokens. Lower is more predictable. Fluent English scored by a well-trained model might land in the tens; random character soup will score in the thousands.

A more sophisticated approach uses sentence embeddings: encode a set of reference domain documents and your training examples with a model like "sentence-transformers," then compute cosine similarity and discard examples below a threshold. This catches relevant content even when it doesn't use your exact keywords. It's more accurate, but of course has much higher computation and maintenance costs.

Deduplication

Duplicated examples can be insidious. When the same example—or near-copies of it—appears multiple times in your training set, the model overfits that specific example. Instead of learning generalizable patterns from diverse examples, it memorizes exact phrasings. The result is repetitive output and a model that generalizes poorly to inputs that don't closely match with the examples. Instead of being an "understanding" engine generalized on your data, it can often simply be performing database-lookup matching on the duplicated data. And what's the point of that?

The first line of defense is *exact deduplication*: hash each example (using MD5, SHA-256, or even Python's built-in `hash`) and remove exact matches. This is fast and easy:

```
import hashlib

def exact_dedup(examples):
    seen = set()
    unique = []
    for ex in examples:
        h = hashlib.md5(ex.encode()).hexdigest()
        if h not in seen:
            seen.add(h)
            unique.append(ex)
    return unique
```

Unfortunately, most duplicates *aren't* exact. They're close to each other, often the same content with minor formatting differences, slight misspellings, or different punctuation. *Near-duplicate detection* catches these, and a common approach uses `MinHash` combined with locality-sensitive hashing (LSH). The idea is to create a compact "fingerprint" for each document based on its n-grams, and to then use LSH to efficiently find documents with similar fingerprints. The datasketch library makes this accessible in Python:

```
from datasketch import MinHash, MinHashLSH

def build_minhash(text, num_perm=128):
    m = MinHash(num_perm=num_perm)
    for word in text.lower().split():
        m.update(word.encode("utf-8"))
    return m
```

```python
# Create LSH index with Jaccard similarity threshold
lsh = MinHashLSH(threshold=0.8, num_perm=128)

for idx, text in enumerate(examples):
    mh = build_minhash(text)
    lsh.insert(str(idx), mh)

# Query for near-duplicates
for idx, text in enumerate(examples):
    mh = build_minhash(text)
    results = lsh.query(mh)
    if len(results) > 1:
        print(f"Example {idx} has near-duplicates: {results}")
```

One more case is *substring deduplication*. This happens when one example is entirely contained within another. For example, you might have a paragraph appear both as a standalone example and as part of a longer document in what is often termed a *containment relationship*. Some of the techniques we used in this section work well when two examples are similar overall, but they don't work so well when one example is contained entirely within another, longer one.

Techniques such as n-gram overlap heuristics from OpenAI's GPT-3 paper (*https://oreil.ly/B5duX*) using tools like nltk or scikit-learn will help here.

Additionally, DeepMind's paper (*https://oreil.ly/vO5Iv*) is a definitive resource on using suffix arrays for cleaning, and it introduces a useful tool called dedup-dataset (*https://oreil.ly/zAsVA*) that you may find very helpful.

A practical deduplication pipeline chains everything we've discussed in this section. But don't forget the manual review of flagged pairs for ambiguous cases. Keep in mind that these are just a few methods for exploring deduplication. Others such as cosine similarity and L2 distance are commonly used.

While every dataset is different, I've commonly seen more duplication issues than you might expect, particularly for web-scraped data!

The Risk of Leaking PII

Personally identifiable information (PII) includes names, addresses, phone numbers, email addresses, Social Security numbers, and any other information that can be used to identify an individual or connect who they are with other information, such as where they live. It is crucial that you look out for PII when training or fine-tuning a model. Realize that a model can potentially memorize and later produce that information during inference, creating a massive risk for yourself, your users, and the people within the data.

This isn't a theoretical concern; it has been demonstrated repeatedly in research on language model memorization. A paper (*https://oreil.ly/D_PtV*) by Google DeepMind and collaborators, showed that by asking a model to repeat the word "poem" forever, models would eventually diverge from repeating the word and start to emit *other* words instead. When comparing those words with the training set, it turned out that they are directly a part of the training set, and had therefore been *memorized*!

So, the risk is there that a user may be able to prompt the model in the right way to extract PII from the training data, even if the model was never intended to reveal it. There are several reasons for this failure, of course, not least of which is that a poorly *designed* model will memorize the content when it isn't supposed to.

But if the PII isn't in the data to begin with, at least that part of the risk is mitigated!

> The regulatory implications are severe. General Data Protection Regulation (GDPR) in Europe, California Consumer Privacy Act (CCPA) in California, and Health Insurance Portability and Accountability Act (HIPAA) in the healthcare sector all place very strict requirements on how personal data can be handled and used. Training a model on PII-containing data without proper consent or safeguards can expose you to significant legal liability. Even if you don't serve the model publicly—even if it's purely internal—memorized PII creates audit and compliance risks that you should definitely avoid.

Detecting PII

To be broad in PII detection, you should combine rule-based and model-based approaches.

A common approach for rule-based detection is to use regular expressions to match structured PII patterns; for example, email addresses (`"\b[\w.-]+@[\w.-]+\.\w+\b"`), phone numbers, Social Security numbers, credit card numbers, and IP addresses. These patterns are fast, deterministic, and highly precise for the formats they cover. They're not infallible, of course; they miss unstructured PII, such as person names, street addresses, and other context-dependent information that doesn't follow a fixed pattern. Regular expressions are also very obscure to develop and maintain for the uninitiated, and code-generation LLMs are a valuable tool. But, like with any LLM creating code that you don't fully understand, you can't blindly trust it. Do extensive testing and retesting to be sure.

Named entity recognition (NER) helps with the unstructured data. Models trained for token classification—such as spaCy's NER pipeline (*https://oreil.ly/I6kYH*) or Hugging Face token-classification (*https://oreil.ly/rCoH9*) models—can detect person names, organization names, locations, and dates in running text. These models are more flexible but less precise; they'll sometimes flag "John" as a person name even when it's part of a product name or an idiom. Like with anything else, models are an amazing tool for this, but you cannot use them blindly—always check and recheck your work.

For production-grade PII detection, Microsoft Presidio (*https://oreil.ly/mPmgC*) is the tool to know. It's an open source PII detection and anonymization framework that uses spaCy under the hood, and combines regex-based recognizers for structured PII, with NER models for unstructured PII. It provides a clean Python-based API for building detection pipelines.

Using Presidio is straightforward. This example takes text containing a phone number, detects it, and then removes it for anonymization:

```
from presidio_analyzer import AnalyzerEngine
from presidio_anonymizer import AnonymizerEngine

text="My phone number is 212-555-5555"

# Set up the engine, loads the NLP module (spaCy model by default)
# and other PII recognizers
analyzer = AnalyzerEngine()

# Call analyzer to get results
results = analyzer.analyze(text=text,
                           entities=["PHONE_NUMBER"],
                           language='en')
print(results)

# Analyzer results are passed to the AnonymizerEngine for anonymization

anonymizer = AnonymizerEngine()

anonymized_text = anonymizer.anonymize(text=text,analyzer_results=results)

print(anonymized_text)
```

This will output the following:

```
[type: PHONE_NUMBER, start: 19, end: 31, score: 0.75]
text: My phone number is <PHONE_NUMBER>
items:
[
    {'start': 19, 'end': 31, 'entity_type': 'PHONE_NUMBER',
     'text': '<PHONE_NUMBER>', 'operator': 'replace'}
]
```

The first output—from the `print(results)` line—shows what the anonymizer found. In this case, it was a phone number, with the start and end locations. It also gave a *score*, which is its level of certainty that it is the entity of that type. This score is quite high at 0.75, but not exactly a sure thing. If using a framework like this, it's good to set some kind of threshold for where you want to detect entities. Too low, and you'll end up stripping out non-PII that might be valuable. Too high, and you might leak some PII. Of course, many production systems will have higher thresholds, and their methodologies for measurement will be different from this simple example.

The second output then shows that the text was replaced with `My phone number is <PHONE_NUMBER>`, where Presidio ended up performing the redaction for you. We'll explore redaction strategies next, should you not trust an engine like this to perform them for you!

PII Redaction Strategies

If you're not using a framework like Presidio to handle the redaction for you, you need to decide how to handle it yourself. There are three main strategies, each with different trade-offs:

Replacement with placeholders
: We saw this strategy in the previous section, and it is the simplest approach: swap `"John Smith"` with `[PERSON]`, `"john@example.com"` with `[EMAIL]`, `"555-123-4567"` with `[PHONE]`, and so on. This is safe and easy to implement, but it creates unnatural text patterns. If a large fraction of your data contains placeholders, the model learns to produce text with placeholder tokens, which might cause problems with your intended solution.

Replacement with synthetic equivalents
: This method will preserve the naturalness of the text: `"John Smith"` becomes `"Maria Garcia"`, `"555-0123"` becomes `"555-0456"`, etc. The Python library called Faker (*https://oreil.ly/iaVlu*) is purpose-built for generating plausible synthetic identities—names, addresses, phone numbers, emails, and more. This approach produces better training data because the model sees realistic-looking text, but it requires more care to implement (you need to ensure consistency—if `"John Smith"` is mentioned multiple times in one example, all instances should be replaced with the same synthetic name).

Generalization
: This approach strips the specifics while preserving some context: `"123 Main St, Springfield, IL 62704"` becomes `"[ADDRESS in Illinois]"`. This middle-ground approach is useful when geographic or demographic context matters for your task, but the specific identity doesn't.

The right strategy depends on your risk tolerance and your task. Placeholder replacement is safest for strict compliance requirements. Synthetic replacement produces higher-quality training data. Many practitioners use a hybrid: synthetic replacement for names and organizations (where naturalness matters most) and placeholders or generalization for highly sensitive items like SSNs and credit card numbers.

Understanding Data Quality

You've come a long way in this chapter, exploring lots of ways to acquire and manage your data. But all that is for nothing if your data is low quality. And it's hard to ascertain the value of data by just looking at it, and it's expensive to discover that it is poor data *after* you spend the time and effort to train a model with it.

So, it's good to add some data-quality auditing techniques to your toolbox before you go further. Let's explore some.

Statistical Profiling

Before you commit to a training run, invest time in understanding the statistical properties of your dataset. Compute the distribution of example lengths—both in characters and in tokens (using your target model's tokenizer). Plot histograms. Compute basic statistics: mean, median, standard deviation, min, max. These numbers tell you whether your data is shaped the way you expect. They'll also help you find outliers. When you explore those outliers, you might find clues to other issues.

To be honest, statistics was always my weakest mathematical discipline. But I have found that a little understanding, combined with the power of generative AI to help me analyze my data using statistical methodologies has been the sweet spot to help me greatly improve any datasets I work on.

One key insight: pay special attention to class imbalance and topic distribution. If 80% of your examples cover one subtopic and only 5% cover another, the model will be strong on the majority topic and weak on the minority. Strategies for addressing imbalance include upsampling minority categories (repeating underrepresented examples), downsampling majority categories (removing excess examples from overrepresented areas), or—ideally—collecting more data for the underrepresented topics. Synthetic data can also be really useful here if applied carefully. Of course, these are just the beginnings of data science–oriented approaches, and there's a huge field of research and tools to support better distribution of data.

A picture is worth a thousand words, and a word is worth a thousand statistics, so visualization catches problems that summary statistics miss. Embedding your examples with a sentence transformer and plotting the resulting clusters with Uniform Manifold Approximation and Projection (UMAP) or t-distributed Stochastic Neighbor Embedding (t-SNE) can reveal unexpected structure: clusters of off-topic examples, outlier groups, or surprising gaps in coverage. Word clouds per category can highlight vocabulary differences. These visual explorations take minutes and can save you from days of wasted training.

Spot Checking

Both as part of the statistical analysis and separate from it, there's really no substitute for good manual spot checking. Automated cleaning catches the obvious problems. The subtle ones—factual errors presented with confident phrasing, instructions that subtly contradict each other, examples that are technically correct but model the wrong behavior—require human eyes. *Your* eyes.

I recommend what I call the "random 50" rule: before any training run, randomly sample 50 examples from your processed dataset and read every one of them. Don't skim them; read them carefully.

If more than two or three make you wince—if the answer is wrong, the formatting is broken, the example doesn't make sense, or the instruction and response don't match—you've likely got a larger problem. I know it's not very scientific, but sometimes it's good to follow your gut. If it feels wrong, there's real mistakes in there too. The odds that you discovered the needle in the stack of data are very low. There will be more! This is a cheap, fast test that catches systematic quality issues that no automated pipeline can detect.

For larger projects, building a lightweight review interface is worth the investment. This is a great use case for vibe coding! The goal isn't perfection, as you'll never have a 100% clean dataset; it's more about catching systematic problems before they propagate into your model.

Contamination Checks

A more insidious data-quality issue is contamination, and particularly the overlap between your training set and your evaluation set. If examples from your eval set (which we'll discuss in detail in Chapter 6) appear in your training set, even partially, your evaluation scores can quickly become meaningless. And it's the same old problem we've seen before: your model won't be generalizing, it'll be memorizing and overfitting.

This happens more often than you'd expect, especially when training and evaluation data are drawn from the same source. If you scraped documentation for training and also wrote evaluation questions based on that documentation, partial overlap is almost guaranteed! Statistical and spot checks of the data will only get you so far. Also consider your architecture for deriving the data and inspect it closely.

There are tools to help you find this. The obvious is searching for exact matches between your training and evaluation datasets. You can also explore more mathematical analysis like looking at long n-grams from eval examples, and seeing if they appear in the training examples. Or, as discussed previously, you can calculate embeddings for representative values from each set, and use a similarity search between the embeddings for near-duplicates.

If you find overlap, the fix is simple: remove the overlapping examples from the training set. It's better to have a slightly smaller training set than to have meaningless evaluation metrics.

Building Your Data Pipeline

The individual techniques we've looked at—normalization, filtering, deduplication, PII redaction, quality auditing—will need to be composed into a single, end-to-end pipeline that transforms raw data into training-ready output. The architecture is straightforward: each stage reads from the previous stage's output and writes its own to pass on to the next.

Raw data flows through normalization, then filtering, then deduplication, then PII redaction, then quality audit, and finally into the processed output directory.

The key discipline is that each stage is independent and rerunnable. If you decide to change your length-filtering thresholds, you rerun from the filtering stage onward; you never go back and modify the raw data. This makes your processing reproducible and auditable.

A key approach to achieve this is to make the pipeline configuration-driven. Each step will have tunable parameters such as minimum and maximum length, target language, deduplication similarity threshold, and PII redaction strategy. Keep these in a configuration file (YAML would be a good choice) so it's easy for you to edit them without getting into the guts of the code for each of the steps in your pipeline.

Here's an example:

```yaml
# pipeline_config.yaml
normalization:
  unicode_form: NFC
  fix_encoding: true
  strip_html: true

filtering:
  min_length: 100
  max_length: 2048
  target_language: en

deduplication:
  exact: true
  minhash_threshold: 0.8
  num_perm: 128

pii:
  strategy: synthetic  # or placeholder, generalization
  entities:
    - PERSON
```

```
- EMAIL_ADDRESS
- PHONE_NUMBER
```

While there are many tools and frameworks that implement the pipeline for you, like NVIDIA's NeMo Curator, DoCETL, and Unstructured.io (*https://unstructured.io*), I would *strongly* recommend that you do it manually, at least once, so you can understand all the steps in the process, and where you need to pay special attention to the peculiarities of your particular data. A general-purpose pipeline software, while powerful, is also very general by nature, and might miss important things in your fallow data. So build manually first (and with the help of vibe coding, of course), and then you'll be better qualified to know if the frameworks will suit your needs.

Your Output Format

You've gone through all the bother of building an amazing pipeline that takes your data and formats and cleans it, making it perfect for training. Now what? Believe it or not, the format that you'll use to represent the cleaned data is still really important! There are many ways you can do this, but I would advise the following.

A great output format for fine-tuning data is JSONL (JSON Lines), which is one JSON object per line. Each line typically contains fields like `"instruction"`, `"input"`, and `"output"` for instruction-tuning, or a `"messages"` array for chat-format training. JSONL is human-readable, easy to inspect with standard tools, and universally supported by training frameworks.

For larger datasets—over about 1 GB—the Hugging Face Datasets format (backed by Apache Arrow or Parquet) offers significantly better performance. Arrow provides memory-mapped access, which means you can work with datasets that don't fit in RAM. Parquet adds columnar compression, making storage efficient.

Dataset Cards

To avoid unnecessary technical debt, I strongly recommend that you draw up a dataset card for every dataset you create like this. This is a README that documents where the data came from and what was done to it. If in the future you need to retrain your model or debug a quality issue, future-you (or a colleague who inherited the project) will need to know the answers to questions like: What were the original sources? When was the data collected? What processing steps were applied, and in what order? How large is the dataset? What are its known limitations? What license governs its use? And a whole host more. Save yourself some future pain by documenting it now, and representing it in an easy-to-consume format.

Hugging Face has lots of examples of dataset cards on public display that you can use for inspiration. A gold standard is the one for SQuAD (Stanford Question Answering Dataset) (*https://oreil.ly/tDr4_*).

Summary

Your data is your competitive advantage. The model architecture and training techniques are commoditized; any team can download the same base model you're using. What they can't replicate is the specific, curated, domain-relevant dataset that you can use to turn a generic model into a domain expert.

To get started in learning how to go through this process, you can use public datasets like databricks-dolly-15k and alpaca-cleaned. These are excellent for learning the mechanics of fine-tuning and for prototyping.

But production-grade expert models are built on your proprietary domain data, not public-facing general ones. So you'll need to graft to get your domain data ready.

Cleaning is not optional, and it is not a one-time task. In this chapter, we discussed the steps for you to get that data ready. You saw how to normalize your text to eliminate encoding inconsistencies. By filtering by length, language, and quality you saw how to remove examples that don't belong. The perils of duplication were demonstrated, and you saw the need to deduplicate aggressively to prevent memorization at the expense of generalization.

And of course, there's PII and the nonnegotiable need to redact PII before training, not after, because a model that has memorized personal information cannot unlearn it.

You explored auditing your data for quality: statistical profiling catches distributional issues like class imbalance; manual spot checking catches the subtle quality problems that no automated filter will see; and contamination checks ensure that your evaluation metrics actually mean something.

Ultimately, all of these will be used to build a reproducible pipeline. Wrap your normalization, filtering, deduplication, and redaction steps into a single, configuration-driven workflow that you can rerun as your data evolves.

Document everything in a dataset card. Treat your data processing code with the same rigor you'd apply to production application code—because, in a very real sense, it is production code. The quality of your training data determines the quality of your model, and the quality of your model determines the quality of the product you ship.

In the next chapter, we turn to an increasingly important alternative for when real-world data is scarce or insufficient: generating synthetic training data using teacher models.

CHAPTER 5
Synthetic Data

Chapter 4 covered the strategies for collecting and cleaning real-world data. But what happens when you've exhausted those strategies and still don't have enough coverage to train a model effectively? Maybe your domain is so specialized that public datasets don't exist for it, or perhaps the data you need is locked behind privacy regulations (such as real patient questions or financial transactions), and you can't use it for training, even if you do have it!

You've tried with the data you have, and you've found that it just doesn't work. Exploring different architecture might work, but if you're honest with yourself, and if you simply don't have enough data, what happens next?

This is where synthetic data enters the picture.

The core idea is simple: use a large, capable model (the "teacher") to generate training examples that a smaller, cheaper model (the "student") will learn from. The teacher already knows how to answer medical questions, write legal analyses, or debug code. You're not asking it to learn anything new. You're asking it to demonstrate what it already knows, at scale, in a structured format that you can then use to transfer that knowledge into a smaller model that you can fine-tune.

Now, of course, you could just use the teacher model. But when you think about it, the core idea of this book is that there are many cases where large, hosted models won't work for you for privacy, cost, latency, or other issues. The teacher model will likely need to be a super large one, and you're back to using someone else's model that they host on your behalf, and you're stuck with a pay-per-token plan.

But if you just use that to generate synthetic data that can be used to train a smaller model, that's a one-off cost!

Throughout this chapter, we'll use a single running example: generating 1,000 medical question-answer pairs using GPT-OSS 120B as a teacher model. These can be used to fine-tune a student model that can answer common health questions.

This is a domain where real data is hard to obtain (patient conversations are protected by HIPAA), where accuracy matters enormously (wrong medical information can cause harm), and where quality control is nonnegotiable. If we can build a robust synthetic data pipeline for medical Q&A, the same techniques transfer directly to similarly demanding domains.

The Teacher-Student Paradigm

The teacher-student pattern for synthetic data is a form of *knowledge distillation*, but instead of copying and compressing the teacher's internal representations (as in traditional distillation, where you train the student to match the teacher's output probabilities), you're using the teacher to create a dataset. You ask the teacher to perform your target task many times, collect the outputs, and *train* the student on those *outputs*. The student never interacts with the teacher directly; it only sees the dataset the teacher produced. Importantly, you're also not attempting to reverse engineer or copy any learned weights from the teacher.

For our medical Q&A project, we'll use GPT-OSS-20B as the teacher to generate realistic medical questions and detailed answers. There are various methods for testing these answers, which you'll explore in later chapters.

We'll collect 1,000 of these pairs, filter them for quality, and the resulting dataset could be used to fine-tune a smaller student model that can handle medical Q&A at a fraction of the teacher's cost. Of course you could use other models, such as GPT or Claude, or best of all if you have the infrastructure to host a really large model like a 400B+ one, then you don't have to worry about tokenomics while creating the data.

The choice of teacher model matters. Larger, more capable teachers produce higher-quality synthetic data, but they cost more per example. A common cost-optimization strategy is to use the strongest available teacher for your initial generation pass and a cheaper model for bulk augmentation later.

Terms of Service and Teacher Models

A word on terms of service. Large hosted models often disallow the creation of data for training or fine-tuning other models to avoid distillation. If you want to avoid any ambiguity, open-weights models like GPT-OSS, Llama 3, or Mistral, running on your own infrastructure, eliminate the issue entirely: you own the outputs because you're running the model yourself.

The code samples in this book use GPT-OSS-20B so you can run them yourself on simple hardware. The data that I produced for you, available on Hugging Face, used the much larger GPT-OSS-120B.

Typically your teacher model should be a larger one. When this book was being written, Gemini's usage policies allowed for the creation of synthetic data for teaching purposes, should you want to try that. This can evolve over time, so always check the current terms for whatever teacher model you use.

Generating Instruction-Response Pairs

The synthetic data that we'll create is in the format of instruction-response pairs. This structure consists of a discrete "instruction" (a command or query) coupled with a "response" that serves as the "ground truth" target. By structuring data this way, we move beyond simple next-token prediction on the open web and instead curate a set of specific behaviors.

During supervised fine-tuning (SFT), these pairs are used to calculate the loss between the model's predicted output and the ideal one defined in our dataset. In essence, while pretraining provides the knowledge, instruction pairs provide the utility.

The Naive Approach

The most obvious approach is the most dangerous. We live in a world where social media tells us that the prompt is everything, and all you need is the right prompt to unlock the magic. For example, something like "Generate 10 medical question-answer pairs" and repeat until you have 1,000 is all you need to do.

This produces data, but it will almost certainly produce *bad* data. Without strict guidance, the teacher will fall into repetitive patterns—the same question structures, the same diseases, the same phrasing. Soon enough, you'll notice that many of your questions start with the same types of phrases (e.g., "What are the symptoms of...") and their answers will suffer similarly. This lack of diversity means your student model will learn a narrow, formulaic style rather than the broad range of medical Q&A patterns it needs to handle in production.

The fix has many steps, and the first is to give the teacher *constraints*—specific topics, personas, difficulty levels, and formats—that force diversity into the output.

Seed-Based Generation

A great way to generate diverse synthetic data is to start with a set of "seeds": short descriptions of the topics, scenarios, and situations you want the teacher to generate.

For our medical Q&A project, these seeds will define the overall breadth of questions we want to generate.

Let's explore this in code:

```
import random

medical_topics = [
    {"category": "Cardiology",
     "conditions": ["hypertension", "atrial fibrillation", ...]},
    {"category": "Endocrinology",
     "conditions": ["type 2 diabetes", "hypothyroidism",...]},
    {"category": "Pulmonology",
     "conditions": ["asthma", "COPD", "pneumonia"]},
    {"category": "Gastroenterology",
     "conditions": ["GERD", "IBS", ...]},
    {"category": "Neurology",
     "conditions": ["migraine", "epilepsy", ...]},
    {"category": "Dermatology",
     "conditions": ["eczema", "psoriasis", ...]},
    {"category": "Orthopedics",
     "conditions": ["osteoarthritis", ...]},
    {"category": "Psychiatry",
     "conditions": ["generalized anxiety", ...]},
]

question_types = [
    "symptoms and presentation",
    "treatment options",
    "lifestyle modifications",
    "when to seek emergency care",
    "diagnostic workup",
    "medication side effects",
    "prognosis and long-term management",
    "prevention strategies",
]

# Generate 1,000 unique seed combinations
seeds = []
for _ in range(1000):
    topic = random.choice(medical_topics)
    condition = random.choice(topic["conditions"])
    q_type = random.choice(question_types)
    seeds.append({
        "category": topic["category"],
        "condition": condition,
        "question_type": q_type,
    })
```

The medical topics are lists of different conditions for categories (I abbreviated them for print, but check out the code for the book for the full list of conditions per category), and these are combined at random with question types to introduce diversity. So, 1,000 times a random category is chosen, and then a random condition within that category, then a random question type. This ensures broad coverage. With 8 categories, 5 conditions in each, and 8 question types, that gives us a search space of 320 unique combinations, giving us a natural variety!

> A key limitation of this approach is that it is combinatorial rather than based on authentic distributions of data from the real world. As a result, it will miss rare edge cases, and other natural ambiguity. It's a good approach for *learning* how to fine-tune, but if you are building a *real* system, then this type of data approach may not be enough.

Prompting the Teacher

So, once we have this, we can now feed each seed to the teacher with a carefully crafted prompt. For this section, to make it easier for you to follow along and reproduce it locally, I'm just using GPT-OSS-20B running on Ollama. The book's downloadable code has several other versions including how to do it with hosted Gemini 2.5, or a self-hosted GPT-OSS-120B.

The goal of the prompt is threefold: establish the persona and quality standard, specify the seed constraints, and define the output format. Let's take a look:

```
from openai import OpenAI
import json
import time

# Point at your GPT-OSS 20B endpoint — local vLLM, Ollama, or a hosted provider

client = OpenAI(base_url="http://localhost:8000/v1",
                api_key="not-needed")

system_prompt = """You are a board-certified physician creating educational
                   medical content. Generate a realistic patient question
                   and a detailed, accurate medical answer.

Rules:
- The question should sound like a real patient asking their doctor —
  natural language, not clinical jargon.
- The answer should be medically accurate, cite specific guidance where
  appropriate, and be 150-300 words.
- Include practical advice the patient can act on.
- Always recommend consulting a healthcare provider for personalized advice.
- Never fabricate drug names, dosages, or clinical trial results."""

def generate_pair(seed):
    user_prompt = f"""Generate a medical Q&A pair about
      {seed['condition']}({seed['category']}),
      focusing on {seed['question_type']}.
```

```
        Return valid JSON with exactly two keys:
        "question" and "answer"."""

    response = client.chat.completions.create(
        model="gpt-oss-20b",
        messages=[
            {"role": "system", "content": system_prompt},
            {"role": "user", "content": user_prompt},
        ],
        temperature=0.9,
        max_tokens=600,
    )
    content = response.choices[0].message.content
    # Parse the JSON from the response
    # Inspect the response payload carefully in case extra
    # wrappers cause problems here
    pair = json.loads(content)
    pair["metadata"] = seed  # Keep the seed for traceability
    return pair

# Generate all 1,000 pairs with rate-limit handling
results = []
for i, seed in enumerate(seeds):
    try:
        pair = generate_pair(seed)
        results.append(pair)
        if (i + 1) % 50 == 0:
            print(f"Generated {i + 1}/1000 pairs")
    except Exception as e:
        print(f"Error on seed {i}: {e}")
        time.sleep(5)  # Back off on rate limits
        continue

print(f"Successfully generated {len(results)} pairs")
```

The `temperature=0.9` setting is there to encourage variety. The idea is that lower temperatures produce more predictable, repetitive output, while higher ones are more "creative" (see the following Note). The system prompt explicitly banned fabricated drug names and dosages, which is a common hallucination pattern for medical content. Combining these will hopefully produce good content, but you'll need to monitor it carefully. The seed metadata is also stored alongside each generated pair, for debugging purposes. If you find a bad example during the quality review, you can trace it back to the hyperparameters that generated it to help understand why, and mitigate future issues.

Temperature directly controls the randomness of the token sampling process. Lower temperatures sample from the top of the probability distribution, making them more deterministic and factual, while higher temperatures flatten the distribution, allowing lower-probability tokens to be chosen, leading the model to be more diverse and creative.

Batching for Cost Efficiency

Generating 1,000 examples is all very nice, but even if using local AI like in the preceding example, it's not very efficient. Each API call has overhead, and a poorly designed generator might still incur unseen costs. A smarter approach is to enhance this by asking the teacher for multiple examples each call—with different seeds in the same prompt. This will reduce the number of API calls, as well as improve data diversity within each batch, since the teacher naturally avoids repeating itself within a response.

Here's an example:

```
def generate_batch(seed_batch, batch_size=5):
    seed_descriptions = "\n".join([
        f"{i+1}. {s['condition']}
                ({s['category']}):
                 {s['question_type']}"
        for i, s in enumerate(seed_batch)
    ])

    user_prompt = f"""Generate {batch_size} distinct medical
                      Q&A pairs for these topics:
                      {seed_descriptions}
                      Return a JSON array of objects,
                      each with "question" and "answer" keys."""

    response = client.chat.completions.create(
        model="gpt-oss-20b",
        messages=[
            {"role": "system", "content": system_prompt},
            {"role": "user", "content": user_prompt},
        ],
        temperature=0.9,
        max_tokens=3000,
    )

    return json.loads(response.choices[0].message.content)
```

In this case with batches of 5, we have 200 API calls instead of 1,000. Even with a local model as in this code, the per-request overhead is improved, so throughput will be better. If using a hosted API endpoint where you are paying by token, you can cut costs significantly because you aren't repeating the system prompt tokens so many times.

Understanding Evol-Instruct

One of the key challenges in instruction fine-tuning is in generating data that covers a very wide range of complexity. Many early datasets relied on human-written instructions, and these tend to cluster around common, relatively simple tasks, not to mention limiting coverage distribution, and being hard to scale.

In a 2023 paper (*https://oreil.ly/qva6C*), Xu et al. introduced WizardLM, which involved a technique called Evol-Instruct that automatically evolved a seed set of instructions into progressively more complex and diverse variants.

In our case, we have a solid foundation of 1,000 examples, but they will tend toward a uniform difficulty level, which is the teacher's default. Real users will ask a wide variety of questions, from the simple ("Is my headache a sign of high blood pressure?") to the very complex ("I'm on drug X, have a family history of diabetes, and I just started a keto diet. Should I be worried about electrolytes?").

The Evol-Instruct technique addresses this by taking our simple instructions and systematically evolving them into deeper ones.

The techniques include adding constraints ("The patient is pregnant, and has a penicillin allergy"); deeper reasoning ("Explain the psychological mechanism"); increasing specificity ("Focus specifically on stage 3 CKD with an eGFR of 35"); and broadening scope ("Also address how this interacts with the patients' existing diabetes management plan").

Reminder: this is just an example for learning fine-tuning. Real medical scenarios will still require deeper domain validation for clinical accuracy and factual consistency.

Each operation thus takes an existing question and uses it to add complexity.

Here's an example for adding constraints (the code available in the book's download contains a number of other examples to help you explore how it works):

```
evolution_prompts = {
    "add_constraints": """Take a medical question and make it more complex by
adding 1-2 patient-specific constraints (e.g., age, comorbidities, allergies,
pregnancy, current medications). Return the evolved question only.

Example:
Original: What are the treatment options for GERD?
Evolved: What are the treatment options for GERD in a 72-year-old who is
already taking clopidogrel after a stent placement?
```

```
Example:
Original: How is asthma diagnosed?
Evolved: How is asthma diagnosed in a patient who smokes and whose symptoms
only appear during exercise?

Now evolve this question:
Original: {question}""",
}

def evolve_question(question, evolution_type):
    prompt = evolution_prompts[evolution_type].format(question=question)
    response = client.chat.completions.create(
        model="gpt-oss-20b",
        messages=[{"role": "user", "content": prompt}],
        temperature=0.8,
        max_tokens=200,
    )
    return response.choices[0].message.content.strip()
```

In practice, you don't need to evolve all of your examples. A rule of thumb of about 20%–30% is fine, taking your simpler examples and evolving each of them once to produce a harder variant. Take care to watch out for anchoring, though! For example, in the preceding code we have a 72-year-old on clopidogrel, and if that's the only example, you'll end up with a suspicious-looking number of 72-year-olds in your evolved dataset!

You can then generate new answers for these evolved questions using the same teacher model and the same system prompt. If you like, you can then repeat this on a subset of those pairs to evolve deeper. Do note a critical detail here: you should *always* regenerate the answer. Don't pair evolved questions with original answers; the new constraints may change the outcome.

Note the order of operations here: we evolve the question only, and then send the evolved question back to the teacher for a completely fresh answer. The original answer gets discarded. This might seem wasteful, but consider what evolution did to the question. "What are the treatment options for GERD?" became a question about a 72-year-old on clopidogrel, and the original answer says nothing about drug interactions or age-related considerations. It no longer answers the question. You might be tempted to ask the teacher to patch the old answer instead, but in practice this produces the original text with a new paragraph awkwardly bolted on. Regenerating from scratch lets the teacher reason about the evolved question as a whole, and since the answer is what the student model actually learns from, that's where the quality has to be. So the loop is: evolve the question, verify it still makes sense, then ask the teacher to answer it as if it were brand new.

The result: a dataset with a natural difficulty gradient. There'll be some straightforward questions, some moderately complex, and some that require the student model to handle real clinical nuance.

It's also important to note that you may hit limitations with smaller models as you go for more complex questions. Having a hybrid approach is better: smaller, local models for the easy questions, and larger pay-per-use hosted models for the more difficult stuff.

Generating Chain-of-Thought Reasoning

Increasingly common is the requirement to show the rationale behind an answer, and step-by-step reasoning provides the method to achieve this. Ultimately, you need any model to show its work, so when fine-tuning a model, you need to be able to do the same. Chain-of-thought (CoT) reasoning requires your training data to have the reasoning trace and not just the conclusion.

So, for our medical Q&A dataset, CoT examples can be created by modifying the system prompt to require such structured reasoning. Here is an example:

```
cot_system_prompt =
"""You are a board-certified physician working through a clinical reasoning
   exercise. When answering the patient's question:

1. First, identify the key clinical considerations (2-3 sentences).
2. Then, work through the relevant differential or decision points step by step.
3. Finally, provide your recommendation with clear rationale.

Format your answer with these labeled sections:
CLINICAL CONSIDERATIONS: ...
REASONING: ...
RECOMMENDATION: ...

Be medically accurate. Never fabricate drug names or dosages."""
```

This should produce training examples where the answer has an explicit structure. And, when you train a student model on these examples, it will learn to produce similarly structured reasoning instead of just jumping straight to a conclusion. The value of CoT training data is especially useful for questions where your answer depends on weighting multiple factors.

For example, "I have type 2 diabetes and my doctor wants to start me on <X>, but I also have recurrent UTIs. Is this a good idea?" A model trained on flat Q&A pairs might have a generic answer about <X>, but one trained on CoT examples would walk through the specific interactions between <X> and UTI risk before reaching a recommendation.

Not every example will need CoT formatting. Simple, factual questions like "What's the normal range for blood pressure" wouldn't benefit from elaborate reasoning traces—and would just add more tokens without intrinsic value. A practical mix is around two-thirds standard Q&A pairs and one-third CoT examples, but your mileage may vary. And of course, the CoT examples should be concentrated on the more complex questions, so it's good to do the Evol-Instruct work first to derive these.

Quality Control for Synthetic Data

The risk with synthetic data, particularly in sensitive situations like medical models, is that you will have a nonzero number (i.e., you *will* have errors) of examples that are wrong, repetitive, or subtly misleading. And in the case of medical data, that can be *dangerous*.

Your job is to find and remove issues before they contaminate your data. In this section, we'll explore a few of them.

Hallucination Detection

Hallucinations are a well-known quantity with LLMs by now. So, the teacher model will be prone to this and will sometimes fabricate information. In the case of our medical dataset, this could be dreaming up drug names, citing nonexistent guidelines, or stating incorrect dosages. This is particularly dangerous because the fabrications are often plausible-sounding.

Automated hallucination detection is imperfect, but can be a first line of defense. A practical approach for this is to use a second model as a verifier. Remember, for learning purposes, I'm taking some shortcuts here to help you understand the process.

For a real-world scenario, here's where it would be worth the cost to use a much larger model as a verifier, and for something as important as a medical scenario, you'd likely need much more—such as an independently trained verifier model to maximize the chance of catching the teacher model's hallucinations.

Let's look at an example:

```
def verify_medical_accuracy(question, answer):
    verification_prompt = f"""Review this medical Q&A pair for accuracy.

Question: {question}
Answer: {answer}

Check for:
1. Fabricated drug names or medications that don't exist
2. Incorrect dosages or treatment protocols
```

```
3. Outdated or contradicted medical guidance
4. Claims that are misleading or could cause patient harm

Respond with JSON: is_accurate"""

    response = client.chat.completions.create(
        model="gpt-oss-20b",
        messages=[{"role": "user", "content": verification_prompt}],
        temperature=0.1,  # Low temp for consistent verification
    )
    return json.loads(response.choices[0].message.content)
```

Here I used another call to the same model, with a different prompt, to focus specifically on error detection. (Again, please note that this is not good practice in reality; I'm just doing it to help you have a small model you can play with. At the very least, you should consider using a larger hosted model like Gemini for this task.)

It will catch a meaningful amount of hallucinations. In practice I've generally seen that it can flag around 10% of the dataset for review, with a high hit rate of true errors. There'll be some false positives mixed in, of course, and it won't capture everything, so it's far from foolproof.

One way to bend the odds in your favor, of course, is to use bigger, smarter models as your checkers. It's more expensive, but it can pay off in the long run. That being said, there's simply no substitute for *human* expert review of your data.

Data Diversity Metrics

Models can often fall into repetitive patterns. And these can be caught in the numbers. To ensure data diversity (aka broad scenario coverage) there are some metrics you can use. One useful approach is to calculate a unique n-gram ratio (see the following Note), which can calculate bigrams and trigrams in your data, to determine how many are unique. If the relative number of these is low, it's a sign you have repeated language, and thus lack broad data coverage.

For example, this code will calculate trigrams, and report on their diversity score:

```
from collections import Counter

def ngram_diversity(texts, n=3):
    all_ngrams = []
    for text in texts:
        words = text.lower().split()
        ngrams = [tuple(words[i:i+n]) for i in range(len(words)-n+1)]
        all_ngrams.extend(ngrams)
    unique = len(set(all_ngrams))
    total = len(all_ngrams)
    return unique / total if total > 0 else 0

questions = [r["question"] for r in results]
```

```
answers = [r["answer"] for r in results]

print(f"Question trigram diversity: {ngram_diversity(questions):.3f}")
print(f"Answer trigram diversity: {ngram_diversity(answers):.3f}")
```

How n-grams Work

An n-gram is simply a run of *n* consecutive words. For example, take the following sentence:

"the patient reports chest pain"

Its bigrams (`n=2`) are:

"the patient"

"patient reports"

"reports chest"

"chest pain"

Its trigrams (`n=3`) are:

"the patient reports"

"patient reports chest"

"reports chest pain"

The diversity metric counts every n-gram across the whole dataset, then divides the number of unique n-grams by the total. A ratio near 1.0 means the text rarely repeats a phrase; a low ratio means the same word sequences appear over and over, which for synthetic data usually means the teacher has fallen into a template (e.g., "It's important to consult your doctor..." a thousand times). Bigrams catch repeated word pairs; trigrams catch repeated phrasing patterns. Checking both gives you a quick, model-free smell test for a dataset that looks varied on the surface but is structurally repetitive underneath.

Your dataset will dictate the required thresholds, but I find that a rule of thumb is that a score below 0.7 is usually a red flag; it means that the teacher is reusing the same phrases heavily. If you see this, the best approach is to adjust the temperature upward (making the model more creative) and to add some more variation to the seed prompts. Another approach (but I find it a bit hacky) is to just explicitly instruct the teacher to vary its phrasing.

Note that in the datasets I created for this chapter, the one created with GPT-OSS 120B scored low on diversity, triggering a need to add variation. I left it in the book's download for consistency.

Filtering the Final Dataset

In Chapter 4, we had a filtering pipeline on our data, and it's a good idea to do the same with synthetic data. After you are satisfied with quality verification and diversity analysis, you can apply a simple pipeline like this to filter out unwanted answers, which could be due to hallucinations or various other reasons:

```
def filter_synthetic_example(pair, verification_result):
    # Remove hallucinated content
    if not verification_result["is_accurate"]:
        return False
    # Length sanity checks
    if len(pair["answer"]) < 200 or len(pair["answer"]) > 2000:
        return False
    # Ensure the answer actually addresses the question
    # (Sometimes the teacher generates a response that ignores the seed)
    condition = pair["metadata"]["condition"].lower()
    if condition not in pair["answer"].lower():
        return False
    return True
```

This is a very simple one: just checking that the result is deemed accurate, that the answer length is satisfactory, and that the answer matches the condition. It's a pretty naive filter, but you can extend it based on your data needs, not the least of which could be something that's more of a sliding scale of hallucination, instead of just true/false.

Ultimately, I find that as much as 20% of examples can be lost to quality filtering—and that's a good thing, as it's better to have 800 high-quality samples than 1,000 polluted ones! If the value is above 30%, you should work on improving your generation prompts. If it's less than 5%, it means your quality-control process isn't stringent enough, and you should go back and check everything we've looked at in this chapter. Never trust good results!

> The verification step is highly domain-specific, even if the generation can be generic. A medical verification prompt will look nothing like one for code generation or one for legal documents. It's worth investing your engineering effort in building strong expertise in verification, backed up by a systemic approach to using it for your domain. It's ultimately where your quality will come from!

Mixing Real and Synthetic Data

You don't have to live in a world of real *or* synthetic data, and I would argue that having a strategy to mix the two is a valid one that will likely produce a better fine-tuned model than using either of them alone. Real data can definitely ground synthetic versions of how people phrase questions and what real expert answers look like. Synthetic data can broaden the answer set of real data with the coverage and volume that it may lack.

For medical Q&A like we've been using here, it would be nice to be able to collect some data from a medical education forum (with appropriate licensing, of course!) and then mix the data appropriately.

It's important to have a good *strategy* for how you mix them. The simplest approach is a uniform mix. For example, say we have 150 real examples, and our synthetic dataset has been reduced to 850 from our quality filtering. We could just randomly shuffle them together to get a combined dataset of 1,000 examples. It works, but, when training, the model will only "see" each real example once per training epoch, while also seeing each synthetic one only once. So, ultimately, the model could get biased toward the synthetic data by the fact that there are more of them.

A better approach can be in upsampling the real data. You bend the bias away from the synthetic data by repeating the 150 real ones 3–4 times in the training set, so the model sees them proportionally more often. Thus, the combined set of 600 duplicated real examples and 850 synthetic ones gives the real data closer to 40% representation. It's enough to anchor the model on both while keeping the breadth of the synthetic data.

The most sophisticated approach is called *curriculum training*. The idea behind this is to first fine-tune on the full synthetic dataset, which gets the model broadly competent. Then, do a second fine-tuning pass on only the real data, which will anchor the model on real-world patterns. This two-stage approach can often produce better results, but it takes more time. The intuition is that the first stage teaches the broad domain, and the second one effectively says "now that you know the general domain, here's what some real interactions look like." It's like going from theoretical learning in the classroom to real-world learning in the field—the second pass is your model's internship!

Let's look at some examples of mixed and synthetic dataset usage:

```
from datasets import Dataset, concatenate_datasets

real_ds = Dataset.from_list(real_examples)
synthetic_ds = Dataset.from_list(synthetic_examples)

# Approach 1: Uniform mix
combined = concatenate_datasets([real_ds, synthetic_ds]).shuffle(seed=42)

# Approach 2: Upsample real data 4x
real_upsampled = concatenate_datasets([real_ds] * 4)
combined_upsampled = concatenate_datasets([real_upsampled, synthetic_ds])
                                        .shuffle(seed=42)

# Approach 3: Curriculum (two separate datasets for two training stages)
```

```
stage1_data = synthetic_ds.shuffle(seed=42)
stage2_data = real_ds.shuffle(seed=42)
```

Ultimately, the best approach will depend on the quality gap between the real and synthetic data. If you are confident in your synthetic data, then approach 1 is likely fine. My general guidance is to use approach 3, though, as your estimation of the quality gap is just that—an estimation. The curriculum approach, despite the extra costs, will generally produce better results.

Summary

Synthetic data generation is a force multiplier, but not a replacement for real data. Wherever possible try to properly acquire high-quality, real data. Your future self will thank you!

But augmenting a dataset using synthetic data is a valid approach, particularly if you need to expand your reach for coverage, diversity, and scale. An unfiltered, naive synthetic dataset can be worse than no data at all because you would end up teaching a model to reproduce the teacher's mistakes and its stylistic approach with very high confidence. And that would not reflect the real world.

In this chapter, we looked at a pipeline: seed-based generation, Evol-Instruct evolution, CoT formatting, cross-model verification with diversity analysis, quality filtering, and the strategic mixing of real and synthetic data. The approach is production grade. The results will depend on you!

I've generated a number of datasets that will be available from Hugging Face (*https://oreil.ly/Ae7-u*) using the principles in this chapter, but without manual quality filtering or integrating with real-world data. I'll leave that part to you!

Ultimately, the most important lesson, and how you can use the provided data, is to ensure that quality control is not an afterthought, and in a true system it will be the majority of the work. Generating data like I have is fast and cheap, taking only a few hours. Verifying, filtering, and curating it into a quality dataset is where the engineering lives, and where the real value lives. In the age of "vibe coding," there's really no substitute for that, and it's where you can get great value.

In Chapter 6, we'll pivot toward the next step: taking your dataset and formatting it for the specific fine-tuning framework you'll use.

CHAPTER 6

Preparing Your Dataset for Fine-Tuning

A language model isn't trained on text. It's trained on *tokens* that are arranged according to a template that the model has been designed to consume. If you deviate from that template, the model will likely treat your carefully curated data as noise! So, in this chapter, we're going to cover the pipeline that takes your data and gets it ready for training or retraining. We'll explore how the instruction-response pairs we created in Chapter 5 can become the exact token sequences that a fine-tuning framework expects. We'll also dip our toes into the fine-tuning waters with some frameworks like Hugging Face's Transformer Reinforcement Learning (TRL), Axolotl, and Unsloth as a test to see if our data formatting is working.

The Gap Between Data and Training

In Chapter 5, we created a synthetic dataset for medical questions and answers. I've hosted several versions of the dataset (*https://oreil.ly/CTDwI*) should you want to try them out for yourself.

These datasets are JSONL files full of records that look like this:

```
{
    "instruction": "My recent lab results showed...what should I expect?",
    "input": "",
    "output": "The diagnosis of ....",
    "metadata": {
        "category": "Endocrinology",
        "condition": "type 2 diabetes",
        "question_type": "diagnostic workup"
    }
}
```

In a real-world scenario, you'd have something very similar, but likely would have been more verified, filtered, and mixed with real data. But, at least structurally, the sample data is a good starting point. That being said, it's just a starting point, and there's a significant gap between a dataset like this and one that your fine-tuning framework can actually consume.

That gap is *format*. Every major fine-tuning framework—OpenAI's fine-tuning API, Hugging Face's TRL (*https://oreil.ly/bLxZw*), Axolotl (*https://axolotl.ai*), Unsloth (*https://unsloth.ai*)—has specific expectations about how training data should be structured. More importantly, the model you're fine-tuning was pretrained and instruction-tuned on text that followed a *specific* template: a pattern of special tokens and role markers that tells the model where instructions start, where answers begin, and where a turn ends. When you fine-tune, you need to reproduce that template *exactly*. Present the data in the wrong format and the model will either fail to learn the behavior you want or, worse, learn to produce malformed outputs that look wrong at inference time.

It's an important place to invest your time and effort. Many fine-tuning attempts can look correct on paper, but produce disappointing results. The data looks good, the hyperparameters reasonable, but the format was subtly wrong, and the model spent its training budget correcting the format as opposed to learning the task!

So, if you take nothing else away from this chapter, realize that the translation layer from human-readable data to templatized data for your model is crucial.

There are two main paradigms: prompt-completion and chat, which you'll see in the next section.

We'll then explore the specifics of formatting data for each major framework. Along the way, you'll build up the formatting pipeline needed for the medical Q&A data we created in Chapter 5.

The Two Paradigms: Completion and Chat

All fine-tuning data eventually takes one of two forms: completion and chat.

First, we'll cover prompt-completion: a single string that contains both the input and the expected output, with no explicit structural markers distinguishing one from the other beyond what's implicit in the text itself. OpenAI's original public fine-tuning API used this format, and it's still supported for legacy workflows. A prompt-completion pair for our medical Q&A task might look like this:

```
Prompt: "Answer the following medical question: What are...?\n\n"
Completion: "High blood pressure rarely causes..."
```

The model learns to continue the prompt with the completion. This works, but it's fragile: the boundary between instruction and answer is defined only by the text itself, and this makes it very sensitive to exact phrasing at inference time. If you train with one instruction format and deploy with a slightly different one, the model will likely produce degraded outputs.

The alternative format that evolved from this is the *chat* format, sometimes called the *messages* format. Instead of a single string, the data is structured as a sequence of turns—each with an explicit role (`"system"`, `"user"`, `"assistant"`) and content.

Semantically, this generally means that `"system"` is the behavioral instructions for the model, `"user"` is the human input, and `"assistant"` is the response from the model.

For our medical Q&A task, it would look like this:

```
{
    "messages": [
        {"role": "system", "content": "You are a medical assistant..."},
        {"role": "user", "content": "What are the warning...?"},
        {"role": "assistant", "content": "High blood pressure..."}
    ]
}
```

This is the format used by OpenAI's current fine-tuning API, Hugging Face TRL, and virtually every modern fine-tuning framework. It's more verbose, but the explicit role structure makes the format more resilient: the model learns to respond to `"user"` turns, not to a specific prefix string.

At inference time, you interact with the model the same way: through the chat API with the same role structure. This way, you're using the same format for inference as was used during training.

I also find it's easier to read through the thread of a conversation when it's structured like this, so as I am debugging training, it makes life a little easier!

For the rest of this chapter, we'll work in chat format. Prompt-completion is still useful for some older models and specialized tasks (continuation training, document completion), but if you're fine-tuning a modern instruction-tuned model such as GPT-OSS, Llama, Mistral, or Gemma, chat format is the right choice.

Chat Templates: From Messages to Tokens

When creating your training dataset there's a step between the messages list as in the previous section, and the tokens that the model will receive. This step involves using a chat template—a model-specific Jinja2 template whose goal is to serialize the structured messages into a flat string of text using special tokens to denote points of interest.

> Jinja2 is a templating engine from the Python world, best known for generating web pages in frameworks like Flask: you write text containing placeholders and simple logic (loops, if-statements), and the engine fills it in with your data. A chat template uses that same machinery to loop over your messages list and stitch each role and its content into one flat string, wrapped in the model's special tokens.

This matters because different model families' templates will differ from each other, with the special tokens that are used to delineate roles within the message being vastly different. Remember that these are part of the model's vocabulary and trained directly into its weights. Using the wrong template, and thus the wrong special tokens, will cause problems when training. The bytes are there, but the reader can't make sense of them.

Don't worry if that isn't clear; you'll find it easier with some examples. Also, as we'll discuss later in this chapter, if you're using the appropriate APIs for the model, they will handle this step for you. I'm including it here so you can understand the goals of templatization.

Consider the medical Q&A data that we've been working on. When using the *ChatML* template which is used by GPT-OSS-120B, Qwen, and many other models, the interaction in the previous section will change to:

```
<|im_start|>system
You are a helpful medical assistant...<|im_end|>
<|im_start|>user
What are the warning...?<|im_end|>
<|im_start|>assistant
High blood pressure...<|im_end|>
```

Every `<|im_start|>` and `<|im_end|>` is a special token in the model's vocabulary. At the moment, it's a human-readable string, but after tokenization it will become a single token with its own embedding. During training (as well as pretraining and instruction tuning if applicable) the model learned that the content following `<|im_start|>assistant` is what it should produce, and the content in `<|im_start|>user` is what it's responding to. When you fine-tune with this structure, you're reinforcing exactly the same behavior that the model was trained to exhibit.

The trick is knowing which template to use for which model. You don't need to memorize them, of course, but it's good to know that a variety of them exists. In the next section, we'll explore the different examples, so you can map them to the appropriate models.

ChatML

This is what we saw in the previous section. The `system`, `user`, and `assistant` all use the same tags to denote the start and end of their respective sections:

```
<|im_start|>system
{system}<|im_end|>
<|im_start|>user
{user}<|im_end|>
<|im_start|>assistant
{assistant}<|im_end|>
```

While it's an OpenAI technology, it's also used in other models such as Qwen and many others.

Llama

Meta's Llama series uses a similar approach of tagging, but with some subtle differences:

```
<|begin_of_text|>
<|start_header_id|>system<|end_header_id|>
{system}<|eot_id|>
<|start_header_id|>user<|end_header_id|>
{user}<|eot_id|>
<|start_header_id|>assistant<|end_header_id|>
{assistant}<|eot_id|>
```

This one can be a little confusing at first. It has a `begin` of text, but no end! This is because it is designed for ongoing conversations, and the model needs only to know where the conversation starts. The `header` approach is to define the role. You'll see `system`, `user`, `assistant` are all wrapped in `start_header_id` and `end_header_id` tags.

The `eot` stands for *end of turn*, and again, for efficiency there's no need to designate when the turn *begins*, which would be a waste of tokens; we just need to designate where it ends.

Mistral/Mixtral

This uses:

```
<s>[INST] {user text here} [/INST]{assistant text here}</s>
[INST] {user} [/INST]
```

In this case, the global start of the conversation is in the first <s>. The first step in the conversation is the user text followed by the assistant's response. The user text is wrapped in `[INST]` and `[/INST]` starter and end tags. Once this section of the conversation is done, it's wrapped with a </s>.

Note that the text doesn't begin with another `<s>` after that. The first `<s>` is considered to be the global start of the conversation. The `</s>` doesn't *close* this tag as you might expect from something like HTML or XML. It's just a marker denoting that this step in the conversation is done, and the following characters are the beginning of the next step.

So, the next part of the conversation might look like:

```
<s>[INST] {user text goes here} [/INST]{assistant text goes here}</s>
[INST] {user text goes here} [/INST]{assistant text goes here}</s>
[INST] {user} [/INST]
```

And because the assistant hasn't filled out the next step, there's no `</s>` at the end.

Note that Mistral's original template doesn't have a dedicated system message. Instead, system instructions are typically prepended to the first user turn. This is a meaningful difference: a Mistral model fine-tuned on data with a separate system role will behave differently than one trained with the system content folded into the first user message.

Gemma

Google's Gemma family is the model we'll be fine-tuning later in this chapter, so its template is worth a closer look. Gemma 4 uses a turn-based approach:

```
<bos>
<|turn>system{system}<turn|>
<|turn>user{user}<turn|>
<|turn>model{assistant}<turn|>
```

A few things to notice here. The conversation begins with a `<bos>` (beginning of sequence) token, a little bit like Llama's, but note there's no end, because the conversation is designed to be ongoing. Each turn is then wrapped in a mirrored pair of markers, `<|turn>` and `<turn|>`. Finally note the role names; there's no assistant here, which I think is much cleaner. The user speaks, the model answers, and so on. Please note that earlier versions of Gemma looked different from this, but this is the approach for version 4 onward that we'll be using throughout this book.

The critical rule: you should always use the template that matches the base model you're fine-tuning! Using a Llama 3 template for a GPT-OSS model will produce a fine-tuned model that generates syntactically valid text but responds unpredictably, because the special tokens embedded in the training data don't match the special tokens the model was trained to recognize.

For the rest of this chapter, I'm going to focus on Gemma 4 from Google, and the code needed to fine-tune that, including the correct templates.

Using Templates with Hugging Face

One of the nice things about using Tokenizers on Hugging Face is that they ship with the correct template for each supported model. You don't need to hand-code the template string. If you simply call `apply_chat_template` instead, the text you provide will automatically be formatted into the appropriate template. Note the messages format here is what the `apply_chat_template` understands, so your data will have to be structured like that.

Here's an example:

```
from transformers import AutoTokenizer

# Load the tokenizer for the model you're fine-tuning.
# Gemma is gated: accept the license at huggingface.co/google/gemma-4-E4B-it
# and log in with "hf auth login" first.
tokenizer = AutoTokenizer.from_pretrained("google/gemma-4-E4B-it")

messages = [
    {"role": "system", "content": "You are a ..."},
    {"role": "user", "content": "What are the..."},
    {"role": "assistant", "content": "High blood pressure..."}
]

# "tokenize=False" gives you the formatted string before tokenization
formatted = tokenizer.apply_chat_template(
    messages,
    tokenize=False,
    add_generation_prompt=False,
)
print(formatted)
```

In particular, note the `tokenize` parameter. If you set this to `True`, you'll get a tensor of token IDs that's ready for training. When it's `False` you'll get the intermediate string, which is really useful for debugging. I'd recommend following this approach, and sampling a number of the strings before you turn on the tokenizer and feed your examples into the training loop.

The `add_generation_prompt` parameter is also worth understanding. When it's set to `True`, the template will append the opening of the assistant turn without the closing token, which signals to the model that it should continue generating. This is what you want at *inference* time. At training (or fine-tuning, of course), you'll want it to be `False` because the full assistant response is already in your training data.

Getting Your Data into the Messages Format

The `apply_chat_template` call in the previous section expects your data in a structured JSON form that is typically referred to as the *messages* format. The expected format looks like this:

```
{"messages": [{"role": "system", "content": "..."},
              {"role": "user", "content": "..."},
              {"role": "assistant", "content": "..."}]}

{"messages": [{"role": "user", "content": "..."}, {"role": "assistant",
    "content": "..."}]}
```

Here you have one training example per line, containing a list of messages. For each message, the role and content are listed. In the case of the first message, it includes the system role. For subsequent messages, it's just the user prompt and the assistant response.

The format was originally introduced by OpenAI for its chat API and fine-tuning service and has since become a de facto standard for representing messages. TRL and `apply_chat_template` both consume it, and most fine-tuning tools understand it out of the box. That works great for us; if we format our data that way, then what works for Gemma 4 today should work for other models you want to try next. And even though it uses the term `"assistant"` that Gemma has shed, the template will handle converting that for us so we don't need to worry about it.

For our medical Q&A dataset, including a consistent system message that describes the physician persona reinforces the model's behavior and makes the fine-tuned model easier to deploy: you can rely on the system message to set the context at inference time rather than baking it into every user prompt.

Now you might be wondering why we didn't just create the medical data in this format. And it would be a good question. I generally think about it like this: the format that the data is in ultimately doesn't matter as long as it is one that is easy to convert. As templates and APIs evolve, you'll find yourself needing to change the data to fit. So, to me at least, it's logical to put the data into a structured format that's easy to program against, while also being generally readable so you can debug it. My current favorite format for that is the Alpaca (*https://oreil.ly/cRdjc*) style from Stanford. It's easy to understand and code against, and as a result, it's easy for us to get it into a format like the messages one, so it can be used to fine-tune Gemma 4 with TRL. Do note that Alpaca isn't standardized, and there are multiple variants that aren't compatible with each other! So tread carefully when choosing a variant.

Here's an example:

```
import json
import random
from pathlib import Path

from datasets import load_dataset

SYSTEM_PROMPT = """You are a board-certified physician providing
educational medical information. Your answers are accurate, practical,
and always recommend consulting a healthcare provider for personalized
advice."""

def alpaca_to_messages(example):
    """Convert one Alpaca record to the messages format."""
    user_content = example["instruction"]
    if example.get("input", "").strip():
        user_content = f"{example['instruction']}\n\n{example['input']}"
    return {"messages": [
        {"role": "system", "content": SYSTEM_PROMPT},
        {"role": "user", "content": user_content},
        {"role": "assistant", "content": example["output"]},
    ]}

data = load_dataset("lmoroney/synthdata", split="train")
converted = [alpaca_to_messages(ex) for ex in data
             if ex.get("output", "").strip()]

# Shuffle reproducibly, then split 85/10/5 — more on splits later!
random.Random(42).shuffle(converted)
n = len(converted)
splits = {
    "data/formatted/medical_qa_train.jsonl": converted[:int(n*0.85)],
    "data/formatted/medical_qa_val.jsonl": converted[int(n*0.85):int(n*0.95)],
    "data/formatted/medical_qa_test.jsonl": converted[int(n*0.95):],
}
for path, records in splits.items():
    Path(path).parent.mkdir(parents=True, exist_ok=True)
    with open(path, "w") as f:
        for record in records:
            f.write(json.dumps(record) + "\n")
    print(f"Wrote {len(records)} examples to {path}")
```

Once you have the file, you can validate it to ensure it matches OpenAI's format expectations. If you explore the OpenAI GitHub, you'll see that its cookbook (*https://oreil.ly/lnq7_*) contains a fine-tuning example notebook, and in there is a robust validation script. Use this to detect errors, and note that the most common formatting error is an assistant message that's empty after one strips out the whitespace! This is a symptom of examples where the teacher model returned a blank response that slipped through your filtering step. It's a good idea to fix them before going any further, should you encounter them.

Formatting for TRL

Transformer Reinforcement Learning (TRL) has rapidly emerged as the dominant open source framework for instruction fine-tuning. It uses an SFT trainer object that accepts data in two formats: a *conversational* format that mirrors the messages format from the previous section, and a *standard* format that takes preformatted text strings.

I personally prefer the conversational format, as it's closer to the standard du jour of OpenAI's approach. This format expects a dataset where each row has a `messages` field containing a list of `role/content` dictionaries—exactly what we saw in the previous section. The key difference with TRL is that it will apply the template for you directly, using whatever tokenizer you pass to the trainer.

So, for example, in a training run, your code might look like this:

```
import torch
from datasets import load_dataset
from trl import SFTTrainer, SFTConfig
from transformers import AutoModelForCausalLM, AutoTokenizer

# Load model and tokenizer
model_name = "google/gemma-4-E4B-it"
tokenizer = AutoTokenizer.from_pretrained(model_name)
model = AutoModelForCausalLM.from_pretrained(
    model_name,
    # Load in half precision - 8B params in FP32 is ~32 GB!
    torch_dtype=torch.bfloat16,
    # Place layers across available GPU memory automatically
    device_map="auto",
)

# Load the formatted dataset from the previous section
dataset = load_dataset("json", data_files={
    "train": "data/formatted/medical_qa_train.jsonl",
    "validation": "data/formatted/medical_qa_val.jsonl",
})

# Configure and run the trainer
config = SFTConfig(
    # Where checkpoints and the final model are written
    output_dir="checkpoints/medical-qa-v1",

    # How many full passes over the training data. For fine-tuning,
    # more than 3 usually means memorization, not learning
    num_train_epochs=3,

    # Examples processed together on each GPU per step. Bigger is
    # faster but costs VRAM - lower this first if you hit OOM
    per_device_train_batch_size=4,

    # Accumulate gradients over this many steps before updating the
```

```
        # weights. Effective batch size = 4 x 4 = 16, for the memory
        # cost of a batch of 4
        gradient_accumulation_steps=4,

        # How aggressively weights are updated. 2e-5 suits a full
        # fine-tune; LoRA (see Chapter 7) typically uses ~10x higher
        learning_rate=2e-5,

        # Ramp the learning rate up over the first 5% of steps, so early
        # noisy gradients don't lurch the model in a bad direction
        warmup_ratio=0.05,

        # Report training loss every 10 steps
        logging_steps=10,

        # Evaluate on the validation set at a fixed step interval...
        eval_strategy="steps",
        # ...specifically, every 100 steps. Watch this loss: if it rises
        # while training loss falls, you're overfitting
        eval_steps=100,

        # Save a checkpoint at a fixed-step interval...
        save_strategy="steps",
        # ...specifically, every 200 steps, so a crash never costs you
        # more than 200 steps of progress
        save_steps=200,

        # Train in bfloat16 - halves memory and speeds things up on any
        # modern GPU (Ampere/A100 or later)
        bf16=True,

        # Maximum sequence length in tokens; longer examples are
        # truncated. We validated in this chapter that our data fits
        max_length=2048,
    )

    trainer = SFTTrainer(
        model=model,
        args=config,
        train_dataset=dataset["train"],
        eval_dataset=dataset["validation"],
        processing_class=tokenizer,
    )
    trainer.train()
```

Here you can see the code loads the Gemma model, and from there it gets the tokenizer directly.

If your dataset is in the `messages` format, you can split it into training and validation sets. Initialize the `SFTConfig` object to define the training, and pass it as well as your datasets to the `SFTTrainer` to train the model.

Under the hood, the `SFTTrainer` will automatically call `apply_chat_template` to turn the data into the format specified by the tokenizer's built-in template.

It's nice to abstract a lot of the details, but of course this can make it harder to trace errors. My suggestion here is that once you have the dataset, use tools like OpenAI's validation tools mentioned in the previous section to ensure that it's clean, or you'll see a lot of errors while training.

Using Alpaca with SFTTrainer

Of course if you're using the Alpaca-based format for the medical Q&A, you'll need to convert it. Fortunately, this is pretty straightforward, and is a one-time preprocessing step. Here's the code:

```
from datasets import load_dataset

SYSTEM_PROMPT = """You are a board-certified physician providing educational
medical information. Your answers are accurate, practical, and always
recommend consulting a healthcare provider for personalized advice."""

def alpaca_to_messages(example: dict) -> dict:
    # Convert a single Alpaca record for SFTTrainer format
    user_content = example["instruction"]
    if example.get("input", "").strip():
        user_content =
          f"{example['instruction']}\n\n{example['input']}"
    return {
        "messages": [
            {"role": "system", "content": SYSTEM_PROMPT},
            {"role": "user", "content": user_content},
            {"role": "assistant", "content": example["output"]},
        ]
    }

# Load the Alpaca-format JSONL from Chapter 5 and convert
dataset = load_dataset(
    "json",
    data_files={"train": "data/synthetic/medical_qa_synthetic.jsonl"},
)
dataset = dataset.map(alpaca_to_messages,
                      remove_columns=dataset["train"].column_names)
```

After this the dataset has a messages field, and is handled the way that the `SFTTrainer` expects. It will then use this to apply the native chat templates and manage the training. Note that this code doesn't split the data into training and validation sets; you'll have to do that yourself based on your requirements.

Loss Masking

When you train a model on a full conversation, the loss is computed over *every* token, including the instruction, the system prompt, and any role markers. The model is being optimized to reproduce the user's questions, which ultimately is the opposite of what you want. You really need the model to produce good *answers*, and it's not worth caring about whether it can reproduce the exact phrasing of the input question or not.

That's the goal of *loss masking*. By setting the labels for the instruction tokens to something like –100 (PyTorch's convention for "ignore this token in the loss calculation"), you effectively tell the training loop to only compute the loss on the assistant's response. The model can still read the instruction as context as it is in the input sequence, but the gradient update comes only from how well it predicted the answer tokens.

This effect is especially pronounced in datasets with long instructions and short answers. This is a common pattern in medical Q&A data, where a detailed patient question with associated data can be much longer than the answer! Without masking, a significant part of your training signal could come from tokens you don't care as much about.

To implement this, a *data collator* is typically used. This is a component that assembles individual tokenized examples into the batches that the model can consume. It handles padding, tensor conversion, and other plumbing. By using a specialized collator, like the `DataCollatorForCompletionOnlyLM` in the `trl` library, you can modify the data at batch-construction time without touching the dataset itself.

Earlier we looked at Hugging Face's TRL, and it offers a data collator API to handle this automatically in the Alpaca format. Here's the code:

```
from trl import DataCollatorForCompletionOnlyLM

# Define BOTH boundaries explicitly: where instructions begin
# (masked) and where responses begin (trained)
instruction_template = "### Instruction:\n"
response_template = "### Response:\n"

collator = DataCollatorForCompletionOnlyLM(
    instruction_template=instruction_template,
    response_template=response_template,
    tokenizer=tokenizer,
)

trainer = SFTTrainer(
    model=model,
    args=config,
    train_dataset=formatted_dataset["train"],
```

```
    eval_dataset=formatted_dataset["validation"],
    data_collator=collator,
    processing_class=tokenizer,
)
```

Checking if Templates Work

Because the matching happens on token IDs it's worth verifying that your templates are actually being found before you commit to a training run. The failure mode is silent, so an example whose response marker isn't matched can be simply masked in its entirety and contributes nothing! It's worth a quick check across a sample of your data to catch this:

```
from torch.utils.data import DataLoader

def validate_masking(dataset, collator, n=20):
    # Confirm the collator finds the response boundary in n samples.
    loader = DataLoader(dataset.select(range(n)), batch_size=1,
                        collate_fn=collator)
    fully_masked = 0
    for i, batch in enumerate(loader):
        if (batch["labels"] == -100).all():
            fully_masked += 1
            print(f"Example {i}: response template NOT found – "
                  f"entire example is masked!")
    print(f"{n - fully_masked}/{n} examples masked correctly")

validate_masking(formatted_dataset["train"], collator)
```

If examples come back fully masked, the usual culprit is prefix tokenization where the tokenizer has merged the newline before your template into its first token, so the standalone encoding of `### Response:\n` never actually occurs in the tokenized example! When this happens, you can tokenize the template in context, including the preceding newline, and then slice it off, before passing the resulting IDs instead of the string:

```
# Encode with the preceding newline, then drop it, so the remaining
# IDs match how the template is tokenized mid-document
response_ids = tokenizer.encode("\n### Response:\n",
                                add_special_tokens=False)[1:]
collator = DataCollatorForCompletionOnlyLM(
    response_template=response_ids,
    instruction_template=instruction_template,
    tokenizer=tokenizer,
)
```

As you can see, it's pretty straightforward. You specify the collator as an attribute of the trainer, and the collator is configured to understand the desired responses, masking everything else.

The DataLoader also allows you to specify the collator, so you can inspect your labels directly.

Here's some code that will load a sample set of records and print out their tokens, and let you know if they have a TRAIN or MASK attribute (only the assistant's response tokens should have TRAIN status!):

```
from torch.utils.data import DataLoader

# Get a single batch and inspect the labels
sample_loader = DataLoader(
    formatted_dataset["train"].select(range(4)),
    batch_size=4,
    collate_fn=collator,
)
batch = next(iter(sample_loader))

input_ids = batch["input_ids"][0]
labels = batch["labels"][0]

# Print the token/label pairs
for token_id, label in zip(input_ids.tolist(), labels.tolist()):
    token = tokenizer.decode([token_id])
    status = "TRAIN" if label != -100 else "MASK "
    print(f"{status} | {repr(token)}")
```

If you see TRAIN on system prompt or instruction tokens, you can tell that the masking isn't working correctly. Best to debug your response template format, or switch to a different messaging format, in this case.

Other Frameworks for Fine-Tuning

While TRL is the most widely used format for instruction fine-tuning, two others are worth knowing: Axolotl for configuration-driven training on complex setups, and Unsloth for speed-optimized fine-tuning with minimal code.

While we'll go deeper into fine-tuning later in this book, for the rest of this chapter we'll dip our toes into it to test our data pipeline.

Axolotl

This is a YAML (YAML Ain't Markup Language)—configured training framework that supports a huge variety of data formats, base models, and PEFT methods. Instead of writing code, you'll create a configuration file and run Axolotl on it. It's particularly useful if you want reproducible, version-controlled training setups.

For example, considering our medical Q&A dataset, we could use Axolotl with YAML configuration like this:

```yaml
base_model: google/gemma-4-E4B-it
model_type: AutoModelForCausalLM
tokenizer_type: AutoTokenizer

datasets:
  # Point "path" at your messages-format JSONL from this chapter
  - path: data/formatted/medical_qa_train.jsonl
    ds_type: json
    # "chat_template" applies the model's native chat template to the
    # messages field. Other supported types include alpaca, sharegpt,
    # and completion.
    type: chat_template
    split: train

dataset_prepared_path: prepared_data
val_set_size: 0.05

output_dir: checkpoints/smoke-test

sequence_len: 1024
# Axolotl's equivalent of loss masking: mask all nonassistant tokens.
# For instruction tuning, ALWAYS set this to false!
train_on_inputs: false

# QLoRA config: the base model is loaded in 4-bit, so this 8B model
# trains comfortably within a 16 GB GPU (see Chapter 7 for how QLoRA works)
adapter: qlora
load_in_4bit: true
lora_r: 16
lora_alpha: 32
lora_dropout: 0.05
lora_target_linear: true

micro_batch_size: 2
gradient_accumulation_steps: 4
max_steps: 20
learning_rate: 2e-4
warmup_steps: 5
optimizer: adamw_torch
lr_scheduler: cosine

bf16: auto
tf32: false

logging_steps: 5
eval_steps: 10
save_steps: 20
```

While most of the parameters are self-explanatory, I'd like to call out an important one: The `train_on_inputs: false` line is Axolotl's equivalent of loss masking. It instructs the framework to mask all nonassistant tokens for the loss calculation. For instruction tuning, always set this to false!

Note that the type `chat_template` in the datasets section tells Axolotl config to apply the model's native chat template to the messages field when tuning. Various types are supported here including `alpaca`, `sharegpt`, and `completion`.

Note that Axolotl is heavily tied to NVIDIA and CUDA. Its configuration loader calls CUDA-specific functions at startup before it does anything else. This means it won't run on a Mac or on CPU-only machines. If you're developing locally on a Mac, you can still prepare and validate your Axolotl configuration files, but the training will have to be done on a CUDA-equipped machine or a cloud instance. I put a smoke-test Axolotl config that will work on Google Colab with the free GPU instances in the download for this chapter.

I've also configured the model here to use QLoRA, which you'll see more of in Chapters 7 and 8, because it will allow you to use the Gemma 4 model on a free Colab T4.

Unsloth

Unsloth is a fine-tuning library focused on speed and memory efficiency. It achieves fast training through custom CUDA kernels and aggressive memory optimization, and it is practical for fine-tuning smaller models (in the 7B–20B range) on consumer GPUs.

The data format is identical to TRL, and Unsloth's FastLanguageModel API is used as a drop-in replacement for the Hugging Face model-loading step. Other than that, the `SFTTrainer` interface is the same.

Here's an example for fine-tuning Gemma 4 E4B. Even though this is an 8B model, loading it in 4-bit brings the memory requirements down to about 5 GB, so it will work very well in a free Google Colab T4 instance with 16 GB of VRAM.

```
from unsloth import FastLanguageModel
from trl import SFTTrainer, SFTConfig

# Unsloth handles the model loading with optimization enabled
model, tokenizer = FastLanguageModel.from_pretrained(
    model_name="google/gemma-4-E4B-it",
    max_seq_length=2048,
    load_in_4bit=True,        # 4-bit quantization -- 8B params in ~5 GB
)

# Apply LoRA -- covered in detail in Chapter 7
model = FastLanguageModel.get_peft_model(
    model,
    r=16,                     # LoRA rank
    target_modules=["q_proj", "v_proj", "k_proj", "o_proj",
                    "gate_proj", "up_proj", "down_proj"],
    lora_alpha=16,
    lora_dropout=0,
```

```
        bias="none",
    )

    # The SFTTrainer call is identical to the TRL example
    trainer = SFTTrainer(
        model=model,
        args=SFTConfig(
            output_dir="checkpoints/medical-qa-unsloth",
            num_train_epochs=3,
            per_device_train_batch_size=4,
            gradient_accumulation_steps=4,
            learning_rate=2e-4,
            fp16=True,
            bf16=False,
            max_length=2048,
        ),
        train_dataset=train_ds,
        eval_dataset=eval_ds,
        processing_class=tokenizer,
        formatting_func=formatting_func,
    )

    # Loss masking: Unsloth provides train_on_responses_only() as a native
    # alternative to the TRL approach we saw earlier. These are Gemma 4's
    # turn-opening strings -- see the following warning!
    from unsloth.chat_templates import train_on_responses_only
    trainer = train_on_responses_only(
        trainer,
        instruction_part="<|turn>user\n",
        response_part="<|turn>model\n",
    )
    trainer.train()
```

If you're training on a consumer GPU with at least 16 GB VRAM, Unsloth with 4-bit quantization and LoRA (which is effectively a QLoRA) is a terrific choice. It makes experiments that would otherwise require an 80 GB A100 possible on the hardware you may already have, from a free Colab instance up to an RTX 4090. The LoRA parameters in this code snippet work pretty well with a model like Gemma.

Pay close attention to the two strings passed to `train_on_responses_only`. This is Unsloth's loss masking: everything from an instruction marker onward is masked, and everything from a response marker onward is trained. Those markers must match the exact text that your model's chat template produces, and this is where version drift can be an issue. Earlier Gemma generations opened their turns with `<start_of_turn>user` and `<start_of_turn>model`, and Gemma 4 replaced these with the `<|turn>` tokens we discussed earlier. If you swapped in the old strings, nothing would crash. The markers would simply never be found, no masking would happen, and the model would spend part of its training budget learning to reproduce patient questions. So whenever you change models, even between versions of the same family, print the output of `apply_chat_template` for one example and read the turn markers directly off the real formatted text. Never type them from memory!

The Formatting Function

When training like this,the formatting function is very important. You need to ensure that the data matches what the model expects. Even small errors will cause training to fail, and the model won't learn. In many cases you won't see an outright failure, but instead the more dangerous degradation of quality. If you are hitting issues, I'd encourage looking there first!

Unsloth's `SFTTrainer` requires an explicit `formatting_func`, as it does not auto-detect the messages format the same way as vanilla TRL, so you have to apply the tokenizer's template here to get the correct formatted string, which will also mean that the turn markers are going to be the right ones. For example, in this case, using the Gemma model, it's important that the `formatting_func` method returns Gemma's instruction-tuning format. Here's the code:

```
def formatting_func(example):
    texts = tokenizer.apply_chat_template(
        example["messages"],
        tokenize=False,
        add_generation_prompt=False
    )
    return texts if isinstance(texts, list) else [texts]
```

Additionally, validating that the format is proper is always a good idea. We'll discuss that a little later in this chapter.

Splitting and Validating Your Dataset

When fine-tuning, the process can be treated just like initial tuning in that you need to split your dataset into training, validation, and test splits. It's obvious in principle, but sometimes very easy to get wrong in practice.

The validation set is used during training to monitor loss and detect overfitting; the framework will evaluate it every few hundred steps and report on the loss. The test set should be held back until after training, and this gives you an honest estimate of how the model performs on data that it has never seen before.

For the medical Q&A dataset, a reasonable split would be about 85% training, 10% validation, and 5% test, but for smaller datasets you might need to adjust this. This gives you a large enough set to learn from, enough validation examples to get a meaningful loss estimate, and a small hold-out test for final evaluation.

We can start by loading all of the data into a split we call `'data'`:

```
# Load and split the raw Alpaca-format JSONL
from datasets import load_dataset

# 1. Load the raw dataset into "all_data"
all_data = load_dataset(
    'json',
    data_files={'data': 'medical_qa_synthetic.jsonl'},
    split='data'
)
```

When we call `train_test_split` on `all_data`, it will create two splits, one called `'train'` and one called `'test'`. We can extract the 85% (`train_set`) that we'll use for training from the `'train'` split; the rest (`remainder`), which will be the 15% containing our validation and test samples, comes from the `'test'` split:

```
# 2. Extract 85% for training, leaving 15% as a remainder
train_and_remainder = all_data.train_test_split(test_size=0.15, seed=42)
train_set = train_and_remainder['train']
remainder = train_and_remainder['test']
```

> The shuffling of the data that precedes a split is random, and random numbers are generated from a seed value. So, if you want to always have the same random set generated, you can reuse the seed value. The number is arbitrary, but I use 42 here because it's the answer to the ultimate question of life, the universe, and everything.

That 15% remainder can then be further split into 10% for validation and 5% for test. Given that the API automatically calls the splits `'train'` and `'test'`, we'll take the split called `'train'` and make it our validation set, and the one called `'test'` will be our test set:

```
# 3. Split the 15% remainder: 10% for validation, 5% for test
# (Since 5% is 1/3 of the 15% remainder, we use test_size=1/3)
val_test_split = remainder.train_test_split(test_size=1/3, seed=42)
val_set  = val_test_split['train']
test_set = val_test_split['test']
```

This is a naive approach, simply shuffling and splitting the data. It may be enough for your needs. But one thing to watch out for when using synthetic data—particularly with your test set—is to ensure that it has examples that weren't previously seen. So, for example, if our "asthma/treatment options" Q&A appear in both training and test, the test set will be seeing values that are very similar to ones in the training set, and you won't have a clear measure of generalization. The safest approach, if this happens, is to split by category first, and put entire categories into train or test, and not have purely random splits in the preceding example.

Format Validation

An important data science step that you should take when exploring your data is ensuring that no issues slip through the cracks from using invalid data. So, it's worth auditing how your data, post formatting for a particular model, behaves.

The code is much too long to put into print here, so in the book's download I included some code that looks at the data that we formatted for Gemma 4 specifically. Do bear in mind that different versions of models can have vastly different configurations of templates, tokenizers, and more. So, be very careful to focus on the particular version you are using.

The goal was to explore the structure of each of the messages for any issues. Remember, here is where it is important to have domain-specific knowledge so you can fully understand the format that the model applies; don't assume it works like others, and in particular if you use auto-generated code, it's an area where you might introduce subtle errors that are hard to debug!

So, for example, in the provided code, I created validation rules for Gemma messages that do the following. This is a good starting point for any model:

- Is the format correct? For Gemma, you must have either a `messages` key or *both* `instruction` and `output` keys. Anything else fails.
- The messages list should not be empty.
- The last message in the list should have `role` set to `'model'` after applying the template.
- At least one message in the conversation should have `role` set to `'user'`.
- There should be no empty messages.
- The full formatted example, after applying the chat template, must be under the maximum token limit that you set, which is 2,048 in this case. Note that this isn't the model's context length, but *your* limit.
- The `apply_chat_template` must succeed without throwing an exception. If the template itself crashes on an example, flag that one.

Other things to keep an eye out for are structurally correct messages that pass this checklist, but are technically wrong. After processing, you could have answers that end midsentence, for example—and that's obviously a failure! We'll explore that in the next section.

Additionally, it's a good idea to look at the sequence lengths statistically to ensure you have reasonable quality data. If many of your samples are really short (much shorter than the 2,048 max, in this case), or if many of them are filling up the 2,048, that's a red flag.

When I ran an analysis on the preceding code we used for training Unsloth, applying the Gemma format, I saw these results:

```
Valid examples: 580/580
Token length – p50: 435, p90: 510, p99: 560, max: 700
Over limit (2048 tokens): 0
```

This showed me that all of my samples passed the filter. The p values are percentiles; so, the length of the middle example, when all examples are sorted by length, was 435 tokens. The p90 value tells me that 90% of my values fall below 510 tokens, with a similar p99, and that the maximum length sequence was 700 tokens. This shows a nice distribution of lengths. If you see large "gaps" between the p90 and the p99, it suggests that you have a handful of samples that are really long and that are pulling up the average, and that's a bit of a red flag. In this case, the difference between p90 and p99 was only 50 (from 510 to 560), which suggests a healthy dataset.

Of course, you won't always be so lucky, so it's worth knowing what to do when examples fail. The useful mindset is that each failure type points back at a different stage of your pipeline. Structural failures (missing keys, empty messages lists) mean a bug in your conversion code, and a 100% failure rate is oddly good news: one bug in one function, not a thousand bad records. Empty assistant answers point upstream, to teacher responses that slipped through your filtering (that we discussed in Chapter 5). Length failures deserve a look before you act; resist the urge to simply raise the limit, because extreme outliers are usually pathologies (a teacher answer that rambled or glued two answers together) that you want to delete, not accommodate. And template exceptions almost never appear spontaneously in stable data; they show up when you switch models or update libraries, so check what changed recently.

Whatever the type, fix the pipeline and regenerate rather than hand-patching individual records, and then drop what still fails. Losing a handful of examples costs you almost nothing; a malformed example that teaches the model the wrong structure costs you a training run. The filter is cheap. Retraining isn't!

Inspecting Tokenized Examples

As mentioned previously, sometimes you'll have examples where the data passes all the filters, and it is a good length. In these cases, there's no substitute for your eyeballs looking at the data to find issues! Take this code, for example:

```python
def inspect_example(dataset, tokenizer, index: int = 0) -> None:
    # Print a tokenized example with masking annotations.
    example = dataset[index]
    messages = example["messages"]

    print(f"=== Example {index} ===")
    for msg in messages:
        print(f"\n[{msg['role'].upper()}]")
```

```
            print(msg["content"])

        # Show the full formatted string as the model sees it
        formatted = tokenizer.apply_chat_template(messages,
                                                  tokenize=False)
        print(f"\n=== Formatted String ({len(formatted)} chars) ===")
        print(formatted)

        # Show the token count
        tokens = tokenizer.encode(formatted)
        print(f"\nTotal tokens: {len(tokens)}")


    # Spot-check a few examples - beginning, middle, and end
    for i in [0, len(train_ds) // 2, len(train_ds) - 1]:
        inspect_example(train_ds, tokenizer, i)
        print()
```

Run this and you'll see some samples of the data—what it looks like in the raw dataset, as well as post formatting. It's a great tool to help manually spot check the data for issues!

Summary

Data formatting is a heavily underestimated step in the fine-tuning pipeline. It's also one of the most common failure areas. You can have a training run that successfully produces a tuned model, but the behavior is disappointing because of a format in the template used for the data, rather than a bad choice in the model architecture.

In this chapter, you looked at a framework to help avoid this: starting with data in a common format (in our case the Alpaca one), and then converting it to the appropriate format for the model, applying the model's native template, before masking the loss on instruction tokens. From there, you could really start preparing your data by splitting it effectively, validating format, and performing spot checks to ensure there are no issues.

It's the first major part of the pipeline—going from JSONL to training-ready data.

In this chapter, you learned a few things to carry forward into the rest of your work. First, always remember that the model has a native chat template. Don't invent a new format when the model already has one. Second, never forget to mask the loss on the instruction tokens. The model should learn to produce answers, not reproduce questions. Third, of course, spend the time to validate before training. A five-minute spot check can save a five-hour training run!

In the next chapter, we'll turn to the training itself. We'll start with the mechanics of adaptation, exploring how techniques like LoRA and QLoRA make fine-tuning far more accessible.

CHAPTER 7

The Mechanics of Adaptation

Full fine-tuning rewrites the entire brain. Parameter-efficient fine-tuning (PEFT) is similar to a crash course on a particular topic to bring it front-of-mind. This chapter explains how that works, and why it's often better than a full brain rewrite. We'll cover the mathematics and the intuition behind LoRA, QLoRA, and DoRA, which are three methods that have made fine-tuning LLMs accessible to anyone with a consumer-grade GPU, or via the free or low-cost tiers of Google Colab.

By the end of this chapter, you'll understand what these methods do to adjust the model's weights, how to configure them for your own projects, and what hyperparameters are the likely culprits when things aren't working. We'll continue to use the medical Q&A dataset that we created in earlier chapters.

The Problems with Full Fine-Tuning

Let's start with the obvious approach. You have a full pretrained model; for example, let's say you are using Gemma 4 E4B, and you want to teach it to answer medical questions in a particular style. The straightforward thing to do is update every parameter in the model: feed it all your training data, compute the loss, and backpropagate the loss through all of the weights. This is fine-tuning. You are starting with pretrained weights, and adjusting them. It works. It's been the standard approach in ML since its dawn. But at the scale of modern models and languages, it creates a number of problems that range from inconvenient to downright disqualifying.

At the time of writing, Gemma 4 was the most recent version of Google's open weights model. This will, of course, change over time. I'm going to focus on the E4B variant, which is an 8B-parameter model that uses about 4B of those during inference.

The Memory Problem

Training a model requires much more memory than running one. When you do inference, namely passing tokens into the model and expecting a response back, you only need to hold the model's weights in memory, plus some space for activations being done during the forward pass. For an 8B-parameter model in bfloat16 precision, that's roughly 16 GB of VRAM needed.

When *training*, you add a lot more memory consumers. First is the optimizer. Almost every fine-tuning setup uses the Adam optimizer, which is very efficient, but extremely memory hungry. It carries an additional two values per parameter: a running mean and a running variance of the gradients. These are often kept in FP32 (4 bytes each), but you can store them at the same 16-bit precision as the weights. If you do, each parameter needs 2 bytes for itself, 2 for the mean, and 2 for the variance, so 6 bytes in total. That *triples* the memory needed for the model's weights, so the 8B model goes from 16 GB to 48 GB of VRAM! If you kept the optimizer states in FP32 instead, as we assumed in Chapter 3, they would take 64 GB on their own.

Next are the gradients themselves, where one copy is needed for tracking during training. That's another 16 GB, so now we're up to 64 GB. Then come the activations, which are the intermediate values computed during the forward pass, and which are needed for backpropagation. These generally scale with batch size and sequence length, but even optimized, they can consume 4–8 GB for this size model.

Adding it all up, fine-tuning an 8B model in 16-bit precision requires 68–72 GB of VRAM. That's beyond the reach of consumer GPUs, and gets expensive really fast. The RTX 4090 with 24 GB is generally the upper bound of what you can buy at low cost, and it has about a third of what you need. Even an A100 with 80 GB is going to be a tight fit.

Scale this to a larger model, like the Gemma 27B, and you'll need hardware that can cost many thousands of dollars just to rent. This is a fundamental barrier. The model can fit on your GPU for inference, but not for training!

Catastrophic Forgetting

Catastrophic forgetting isn't just a great name for a rock band, but it's also an inherent risk when you fine-tune a full model. If you are updating every weight in the model to optimize for your specific task, you can overwrite the parameters in the base model to the extent that it forgets what it learned to begin with! This phenomenon is one of the oldest problems in neural network research. It happens because the new gradient updates overwrite the patterns that encoded the model's general knowledge.

In practice, catastrophic forgetting in LLM fine-tuning will manifest itself as a model that becomes very good at your specific task, but loses its ability to do other things. And that's if you're lucky! Overwriting the base knowledge can also impact its ability to understand language, so it can lose the general knowledge that's important for your tasks, too. So the issue, at first, might be very subtle, and as you converse further with the model, it will pop up in losing its ability to follow multiturn conversations, summarize text, or reason about unrelated topics. The pretraining investment gets partially erased!

Careful engineering can mitigate this. Low learning rates, shorter training, or a careful mixture of these in general-purpose data can work. But these are workarounds, not solutions. They trade off task-specific performance against knowledge representation. Finding the right balance is time consuming and expensive.

The Storage Problem

There's a less obvious and more subtle issue you also need to consider. For example, suppose you are working on fine-tuning the same base model for several different use cases: medical Q&A, legal research, code generation, and some others. With full fine-tuning, each use case produces a complete copy of the model. Each of them requires 40 GB+ in storage. And if you need to serve them, you will have to have dedicated memory, usually with multiple GPUs. This impacts your ability to scale.

An option here, through PEFT (which we'll see in detail in the next section), is just to train "patches" on top of the model to affect its behavior. Then, a single copy of the base model with task-specific patches that can be swapped in and out becomes an interesting solution for different use cases!

Parameter Efficient Fine-Tuning

Parameter efficient fine-tuning (PEFT) is a family of techniques that share a single, simple goal: achieve fine-tuning results comparable to full fine-tuning but without the cost. They achieve this by updating only a small fraction of the total parameters. So, for Gemma 4 E4B, instead of modifying all 8B parameters, you'll impact just a few million, or maybe even less, while leaving the rest frozen and protected. It's analogous to transfer learning in traditional ML.

The benefits should be obvious: less memory needed because you're impacting fewer parameters, less risk of catastrophic forgetting because the majority of parameters are frozen. The outcome can be small and portable. For example, a LoRA adapter for an 8B model might typically be in the 10–50 MB size, rather than 16 GB, so it's trivial to store multiple task-specific adapters and swap between them, as needed.

Several methods for this have evolved over time:

Prefix tuning
: With this method, you prepend a set of trainable virtual tokens to the input of each transformer layer. The model's weights are frozen, and only the prefix vectors are trained. This works, but the virtual tokens end up consuming part of the model's context window. Ultimately, the method has been largely superseded by LoRA.

Adapters
: These insert small, trainable bottleneck layers between the existing layers of the transformer. Each one consists of a small down-projection, a nonlinearity, and an up-projection. The details of these are beyond the scope of this book, and would require several chapters to explain. The point is that they add latency at inference time because of how they impact the flow of data through the transformer layers. This method has largely been replaced by LoRA.

LoRA (Low-Rank Adaptation)
: LoRA is the dominant PEFT method for LLM fine-tuning. It works by adding a trainable set of weights to the existing weights without modifying them. At inference time, the LoRA weights are then merged into the base model without impacting latency through the forward pass.

> Don't worry if that's not clear right now; we'll be exploring LoRA for the rest of this chapter, as well as some of its descendants, and you'll see why they represent an excellent approach for practical fine-tuning.

LoRA

LoRA (Low-Rank Adaptation) was introduced in a Microsoft paper from Hu et al. in 2021 (*https://oreil.ly/JHABe*), and it fundamentally changed what's possible with consumer hardware. They demonstrated that one could fine-tune GPT-3 with 175B parameters by training only 0.01% of the weights, with results comparable to a full fine-tune.

The core insight is very straightforward and elegant. It found that over time, teaching a model a new task didn't require updating every weight. Research showed that when fine-tuning, the updates are "low rank" (i.e., they are mathematically simple enough to be represented by a much smaller structure).

Say you want to change the contrast in a picture. There are two ways you could do it. The first is to amend the values of every pixel in the image to create a whole new one—that's analogous to fine-tuning. The second is to take a plastic filter that you lay on top of the image, changing how the light reflects off of it. You get the same effect, but with a lot less effort.

LoRA is that layer; it's a very mathematically "thin" set of parameters that sits on top of the massive base model and tweaks its output for a specific task. By training only this layer, we'll save memory while achieving similar results.

The Mathematics of LoRA

To understand how LoRA works, we need to look a little into the mathematics behind it. It's much easier than it sounds. You can see this in Figure 7-1.

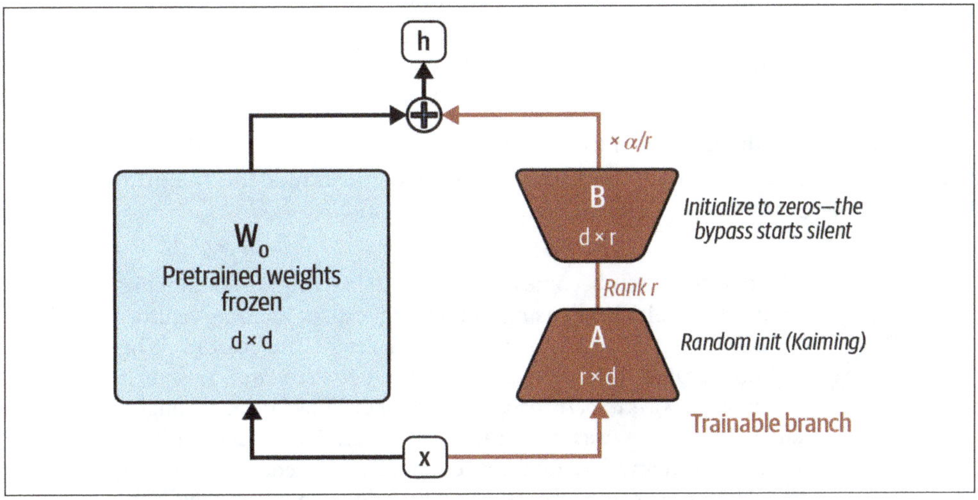

Figure 7-1. The LoRA approach

Consider a single weight matrix W_0 in the pretrained model. For a transformer's attention layer, this might be the query projection matrix with dimensions $d \times d$. So, for a model with a hidden dimension of $d = 2{,}560$ (typical for Gemma 4 E4B), that's a matrix with roughly $d \times d = 6.5$ million parameters.

In full fine-tuning, you'd update this matrix directly:

$$W = W_0 + \Delta W$$

where ΔW is the accumulated update after training—a $d \times d$ matrix with the same number of parameters as W_0.

LoRA constrains ΔW to be a low-rank matrix by factoring it into two smaller matrices called B and A, so that:

$$\Delta W = BA$$

where B is a $d \times r$ matrix and A is an $r \times d$ matrix, and r (the rank) is much smaller than d. If $d = 2{,}560$ and $r = 16$, the update ΔW has the same $2{,}560 \times 2{,}560$ shape as the original weight matrix, but it's parameterized by only $(2{,}560 \times 16) + (16 \times 2{,}560) = 81{,}920$ parameters instead of 6.5 million. That's nearly an 80× reduction.

During the forward pass, the output of the adapted layer is:

$$h = W_0x + (\alpha/r)BAx$$

The input x passes through both the original frozen weights W_0 and the LoRA branch BA. The results are summed. The scaling factor α/r controls the magnitude of the LoRA update relative to the original weights.

> The question then becomes how we initialize A and B. Mathematically, A is initialized using something called Kaiming uniform initialization, and B is initialized to all zeros. The reason? When training begins, B is zero, so the output is zero. But as soon as the first *backward* pass happens, gradients flow back through B and into A. If A was also initialized to zero, the backward pass would vanish and learning would stop. So, A needs to be nonzero and let the learning process set the values appropriately. There are many ways by which it could be initialized, but over time, research showed that the Kaiming uniform initialization was more mathematically effective. Learn more about this methodology in the paper (*https://oreil.ly/fOdgN*) by Kaiming He et al.

Where LoRA Is Applied

A transformer model contains many weight matrices. We discussed the QKV values (W_Q, W_K, and W_V) in Chapter 2. There will also be output projections (W_O) for every attention layer, plus the matrices for each of the feed-forward blocks. There's typically two of these, but gated architectures like Gemma will have more.

The original LoRA paper (*https://oreil.ly/UO8U7*) by Hu et al. focused on the attention projections: W_Q and W_V, and found that they alone were sufficient for strong results, compared to other adaptation methods that used many more parameters. More recent work, as well as practical experience in the community, has suggested that targeting more, including the FFN layers, will improve performance. As a result, a common model configuration will apply LoRA to all linear layers in the model: W_Q, W_K, W_V, and W_O, as well as the projection within the FFN.

Using Hugging Face's PEFT library, this is made straightforward. You can specify the targets as a list like this:

```
from peft import LoraConfig, TaskType

lora_config_all = LoraConfig(
    r=16,
    lora_alpha=32,
    target_modules=["q_proj", "k_proj", "v_proj", "o_proj",
                    "gate_proj", "up_proj", "down_proj"],
    exclude_modules=r".*(vision|audio).*",   # text stack only
    lora_dropout=0.05,
    task_type=TaskType.CAUSAL_LM,
)
```

Alternatively, when using Gemma, the "all-linear" shorthand is available in recent versions, and is generally recommended as your starting point, and it means you don't have to memorize the module names, as they aren't always consistent from model to model!

```
# Targeting all linear layers (modern best practice for Gemma)
lora_config_all = LoraConfig(
    r=16,
    lora_alpha=32,
    target_modules="all-linear"
    exclude_modules=r".*(vision|audio).*",   # text stack only
    lora_dropout=0.05,
    task_type=TaskType.CAUSAL_LM,
)
```

The Merge Step

One of LoRA's most attractive properties is that the adapter can be merged back into the base model after training, producing a single set of weights with no additional inference cost. And, the merge is just arithmetic:

$$W_{merged} = W_0 + (\alpha/r)BA$$

Then, after merging, the model will have the same architecture and number of parameters as the original, but the weights will now encode the task-specific knowledge learned in fine-tuning. There are no extra layers or modules, and no additional latency. The inference code that you wrote should work, albeit with minor modifications if your output has changed format. The model hasn't changed its structure, just the values of some of its weights.

You can also choose *not* to merge, and instead do this dynamically at inference time. This is a useful technique if you are serving multiple task-specific variants from the same base model. Load it once, then swap adapters based on the request. We'll cover more of this in detail in Chapter 15.

Why It Works

The mathematical explanation is that weight updates have low intrinsic dimensionality. But that's a bit too abstract for me. Anyway, here's an intuition that I like to use.

Think of the pretrained model as a large corporation with thousands of employees, each with a well-defined job. Full fine-tuning is like retraining every employee for a new role. It's expensive, it's slow, and it can be risky, because some critical knowledge might be lost along the way.

LoRA is like hiring a small team of specialists and asking them to work alongside your existing crew. The specialists (like the A and B matrices) don't *replace* anyone; instead they augment the existing workforce with task-specific expertise. The original folks keep doing what they've always done, and the specialists manage the new requirements. The rank (r, which we'll discuss in the next section) controls how many specialists you hire. It should be enough to cover the task, but far fewer than the total headcount. If necessary, you can hire the specialists at some point to augment your existing staff, or, if preferred, just swap them in and out to manage different tasks.

Understanding LoRA Hyperparameters

When using LoRA, there are some hyperparameters you need to take into account that don't exist in full fine-tuning. Getting these right is the difference between a fine-tuned model that performs well, and one that doesn't. Let's explore some of these.

Rank

The rank (r) is perhaps the most important LoRA hyperparameter. It controls the capacity of the adapter, and how much information the update can really encode. A higher rank means more trainable parameters, but at the cost of more memory and compute consumption. A lower rank is smaller, cheaper, and faster, but may not be effective enough for your needs. As with everything, there's a trade-off to manage.

Common values for rank range from 4 to 256 depending on model size, target modules, and task entropy. Exploring this for Gemma 4 E4B, you'll find:

- A rank of 8 is a reasonable starting point for simple tasks. This would include things like adjusting the tone, transferring styles, or fine-tuning on a small dataset where the model already has a pretty strong base knowledge of the domain.

- Picking a value from 16 to 32 is a typical sweet spot for most tasks. For the medical Q&A project, I'd start with a rank of about 16. This helped the model with the requirement of learning a specific answering style with some domain-specific patterns. Gemma 4 E4B already has a fundamental understanding of language and medical terms, so we would build upon that.
- A higher rank of 64–128 is needed for complex tasks that require the model to learn substantially new knowledge. This would be used for fine-tuning on something like a new programming language, or adapting to a highly specialized domain with a unique vocabulary (stuff the model wouldn't have previously seen much of). Even then, LoRA may not be enough, but it's a good starting point.
- Getting higher, a rank of 256+ really approaches the capacity of a full fine-tuning, and is rarely necessary. If you find yourself needing a rank of this number, you're probably better off doing a full fine-tune.

Do note that the relationship between rank and performance is not linear. You'll find that it plateaus; there's a point beyond which additional rank will provide diminishing returns. Discovering this is something that's well worth spending time experimenting to find.

Alpha and the Scaling Factor

The alpha (α) parameter will control how much the LoRA update influences the model's eventual output. The scaling applied is alpha divided by rank (α/r) meaning that the alpha and rank effectively work together.

The conventional practice is to set alpha to twice the rank. So, if you are using a rank of 16, set the alpha to 32. This will give a scaling factor of 2, and as you are training, you'll adjust the learning rate over time instead of tuning the alpha. We'll explore more of that later.

Target Modules

As discussed earlier, you choose which weight matrices in the model that you want to apply LoRA to. For Gemma, targeting all linear layers is the standard starting point. It's a good rule of thumb for other models, but you should experiment with this.

One exception: embedding layers and the language model head (the final output projection) are things that are not typically included in LoRA targets. Be careful when modifying them, as this can lead to instabilities. That said: if your task requires a significantly different vocabulary, where there are strong domain ties to previously unknown terms, like with a brand-new programming language.

Dropout

LoRA dropout applies standard dropouts to the adapter's output during training. If your dataset has fewer than 1,000 examples (like our medical Q&A), a dropout of 0.05 to 0.1 is a reasonable starting point. For larger datasets, you might set this to 0.

Bias

This parameter specifies which `bias` terms in the model should be made trainable during fine-tuning. In a neural network layer, the output is typically the linear equation where $y = Wx + b$, where b is the bias, and W is the weight matrix. Setting this to `"none"` means that no bias parameters are trained. They remain frozen along with the rest of the base model. This is the most memory-efficient setting, which is the typical standard for LoRA. You can also set this to `"all"` to make all bias parameters trainable, and `"lora_only"` which will open only the ones in the adapter layers to be trainable. By setting to `"none"`, you also ensure that only the low-rank matrices (A and B from earlier) are updated, keeping the number of trainable parameters as low as possible.

Task Type

The PEFT library supports many different model architectures. Based on the type of model, you set the `task_type` so it can wrap the model correctly and handle inputs/outputs appropriately. In this case, using Gemma, which is a decoder-only model, you specify Causal Language Modeling with `CAUSAL_LM`. Other models like Llama and GPT are the same. The name comes from the idea that the models predict the next token in the sequence in response to the previous tokens that "cause" the prediction. It's important to set this correctly so the library knows how to correctly attach the LoRA adapters. Other common types are `SEQ_2_SEQ_LM` for encoder/decoder models like T5, or `SEQ_CLS` for sequence classification or sentiment analysis models.

Putting It All Together

Here's an example that will work pretty well for a model like Gemma 4 E4B. You can use this as a starting point for other models:

```
from peft import LoraConfig, TaskType

lora_config = LoraConfig(
# Rank: the dimensionality of the low-rank update
r=16,
# Alpha: scaling factor (2 * r)
lora_alpha=32,
# Apply to all linear layers in Gemma
target_modules="all-linear",
exclude_modules=".*(vision|audio).*",
```

```
    # Light dropout for our small dataset
    lora_dropout=0.05,
    # Don't train bias terms
    bias="none",
    # We're fine-tuning a causal language model
    task_type=TaskType.CAUSAL_LM,
)
```

If we explore this configuration in terms of trainable parameters for Gemma 4 E4B:

```
import torch
from transformers import AutoModelForCausalLM
from peft import get_peft_model

# Load the base model -- bfloat16, or the 8B weights arrive in
# FP32 and consume ~32 GB before you've done anything!
base_model = AutoModelForCausalLM.from_pretrained(
    "google/gemma-4-E4B-it",
    torch_dtype=torch.bfloat16,
    device_map="auto",
)

# Wrap it with LoRA
model = get_peft_model(base_model, lora_config)

# Print the parameter summary
model.print_trainable_parameters()
```

```
trainable params: 38,879,232 ||
all params: 7,979,980,064 ||
trainable%: 0.4872
```

The output is about 38 million trainable parameters out of 8 billion total. This is less than 0.5%, and will consume only about 150 MB of memory, making it fit on many GPUs.

QLoRA: An Even Smaller Footprint

While LoRA dramatically reduces the number of trainable parameters, the base model still needs to be loaded. A Gemma 4 E4B has 8 billion total parameters, so in bfloat16 precision it occupies about 16 GB of VRAM.

And while the trainable parameters add up to about 150 MB, remember that more memory is used in fine-tuning. The base model's 16 GB will still occupy VRAM, and adding the memory needed for the optimizers to the trainable parameters will be roughly 1 GB more. Add the activations to this, and you can be up to 20–24 GB.

That puts even a 24 GB RTX 4090 right at the edge, and some of the free cloud tiers out of reach—particularly if you're getting bigger. For example, if you're using a Gemma 4 31B model, you're up to about 70 GB just for the LoRA setup, and that's beyond the realms of most GPUs!

QLoRA helps solve this problem by adding quantization—and that's what the Q stands for. The base model is loaded in 4-bit precision instead of 16-bit, thus reducing its memory footprint greatly. However, in the case of a model like Gemma 4, much of the architecture is embedding tables that don't get quantized, only the linear layers which take up about 10 GB, so you'll shave off about 7.5 GB through quantization.

The QLoRA paper (*https://oreil.ly/lZrpN*) introduced the following to that end:

NormalFloat4 (NF4)
: This is a new 4-bit data type specifically designed for the normal distributions found in the weights of a neural network, encoded across 4 bits.

Double quantization
: This quantizes the quantization constants themselves, which was found to save about 1.5% (the paper cites a 3 GB savings for a 65B model).

Paged optimizers
: The optimizer shares GPU and CPU memory, and spikes can cause errors. This technique was designed to prevent out-of-memory errors, in particular.

When using this with a Gemma 4 E4B model, QLoRA reduces the VRAM requirement to only 10–12 GB, putting it into the range of cheaper consumer GPUs, and maybe even laptop ones! It's not a clean 4× reduction because many of the parameters in Gemma 4 E4B are in embedding tables, which don't get quantized.

To use QLoRA, you need both the bitsandbytes library and PEFT. Here's the code to set it up:

```
import torch
from transformers import BitsAndBytesConfig

bnb_config = BitsAndBytesConfig(
    load_in_4bit=True,          # Load model weights in 4-bit
    bnb_4bit_quant_type="nf4",  # Use NormalFloat4
    bnb_4bit_compute_dtype=torch.bfloat16, # Compute in bfloat16
    bnb_4bit_use_double_quant=True, # Enable double quantization
)
```

Now that the configuration is set up, you can load the model from Hugging Face like this, specifying the quantization config to set up QLoRA:

```
from transformers import AutoModelForCausalLM, AutoTokenizer

model_id = "google/gemma-4-E4B-it"

tokenizer = AutoTokenizer.from_pretrained(model_id)

model = AutoModelForCausalLM.from_pretrained(
    model_id,
    quantization_config=bnb_config,
```

```
        device_map="auto",
    )
```

And now, loading the model and getting ready for training is similar to before. Note that the `prepare_model_for_kbit_training` is added; this is essential for setting up gradient checkpointing and stability when training on a quantized base:

```
from peft import LoraConfig, get_peft_model, TaskType,
                 prepare_model_for_kbit_training

# Prepare the quantized model for training
model = prepare_model_for_kbit_training(model)

lora_config = LoraConfig(
    r=16,
    lora_alpha=32,
    target_modules="all-linear",
    exclude_modules=".*(vision|audio).*",
    lora_dropout=0.05,
    bias="none",
    task_type=TaskType.CAUSAL_LM,
)

model = get_peft_model(model, lora_config)
model.print_trainable_parameters()
```

The number of trainable parameters printed out will be similar to the earlier LoRA example. The difference is in how the *other* 4 billion parameters are handled. In bfloat16, each of them will take up 2 bytes of VRAM. But because we specified that they should be 4-bit using the bitsandbytes config, they'll now take up one-quarter of that!

There's obviously questions about the cost of doing this. And your mileage may vary based on the model you're tuning. It's interesting to note that the original QLoRA paper reports essentially no difference in quality between the 4-bit fine-tune and the 16-bit!

DoRA: Redefining the Adaptation

Another refinement called DoRA (Weight-Decomposed Low-Rank Adaptation) (*https://oreil.ly/xNPpx*) works by decomposing each pretrained weight matrix into a magnitude component (m) and a directional component (V) before applying any LoRA updates.

The idea here is that the optimizer has two separate "knobs" to adjust, and this is more closely aligned with how full fine-tuning modifies weights. The result is modest, but it has been found that it can give consistent improvements over standard LoRA with gains of 1%–4%, but with no extra cost at inference time.

Setting it up is done using the dora parameter in LoraConfig:

```
from peft import LoraConfig

dora_config = LoraConfig(
    r=16,
    lora_alpha=32,
    target_modules="all-linear",
    lora_dropout=0.05,
    bias="none",
    task_type=TaskType.CAUSAL_LM,
    use_dora=True, # Enable weight-decomposed adaptation
)
```

Choosing Your Approach

While your mileage may vary, Table 7-1 shows a rough example of how each of these approaches will impact the VRAM and quality of your model. The quality delta is based on my personal experimentation, but as you can see, it's generally very high!

Table 7-1. Comparing parameters and precision

Method	Precision	Trainable params	VRAM	Quality
Full fine-tune	16-bit	8B	60–64 GB	Baseline
LoRA	16-bit	~50M	20–24 GB	95%–99%
QLoRA	4-bit (NF4)	~50M	10–12 GB	93%–97%
QLoRA + DoRA	4-bit (NF4)	~36M+	10–12 GB	94%–99%

My guidance: start with QLoRA if you're on smaller VRAM GPUs and consumer hardware. It lets you fine-tune models comfortably even with low VRAM. Once you have a decent working model, you can then try the code pipeline that worked for it with just LoRA to see if it's worth it. More often than not, the QLoRA will be enough.

Of course, if you have the VRAM budget, just go straight to LoRA. And then add DoRA as an optimization step once you have a working baseline. Treat it as a free experiment to help you understand if you need to do it for further training.

Under the Hood

In the preceding code, we used `get_peft_model(base_model, lora_config)`, to wrap the model with LoRA. This code works by freezing the base model, effectively setting `requires_grad=False` on all base parameters. It then looks at the target layers and replaces them with LoRA wrappers containing trainable LoRA_A and LoRA_B matrices (as the A and B ones we discussed). Finally it returns a model object that provides wrapper methods for adapter management, including loading, saving, merging, and more. With models like Gemma, because we set all linear layers to be retrained, layers like `model.layers.0.self_attn.q_proj` will be wrapped with `lora_A` and `lora_B`.

Some things to watch out for are skipping the `prepare_model_for_kbit_training` when using QLoRA, and as we mentioned in the previous chapter, do ensure that you are using the right chat template! Other tips are to avoid high ranks for smaller datasets, and to remember that LoRA usually requires higher learning rates than full fine-tuning.

Summary

In this chapter, you looked at the different PEFT methods, namely LoRA, QLoRA, and DoRA, as the key to fine-tuning models on lower-cost, lower-VRAM hardware. By training only a small percentage of parameters, with these techniques you can achieve really good performance while dramatically reducing memory and storage requirements.

In the next chapter, we'll explore how to put all this together with a look at the training, exploring supervised fine-tuning with `SFTTrainer`.

CHAPTER 8

The Training Loop

By this point, you have a formatted dataset, you've figured out the LoRA configuration. Next up is to go through the complete training process. You'll go from configuring the Hugging Face training stack to configure the run, to monitoring the loss curve, to finally saving the finished adapter. Along the way, you'll see the training hyperparameters that matter the most, the memory optimizations that make consumer-GPU training possible, and the debugging strategies to follow when things don't go the way you planned.

By the time you're done with this chapter, you'll have a trained LoRA adapter for the medical Q&A task we've been building toward over the past few chapters. Most importantly, you will have gotten hands-on with every decision in the training script, and have a foundation for how to use it in your own projects.

As an example, there's a *Chapter08_FineTuneGemma.ipynb* file available in the book's download (*https://oreil.ly/lDLkT*), where I did a complete fine-tune of a Gemma 4 model using the data we generated in earlier chapters. That will be the basis for most of the text in this chapter, so I encourage you to load it up and walk through it as you read the text.

Assembling the Pieces

To take stock of where we are, let's explore what we've covered over the past few chapters.

First is the *dataset* (covered in Chapters 5 and 6). There, we constructed a Q&A dataset of several hundred training and validation examples, each formatted as a multiturn conversation. The data is in the Hugging Face JSONL file, in a way that's easy to convert to any particular chat template. You can find it in the book's repository, within the *Chapter08* folder.

Start your fine-tuning by selecting a base model. We'll use the Gemma 4 E4B model for this. It has a version (Gemma 4 E4B-IT) that's instruction tuned, so it already understands how to follow conversational instructions but needs domain-specific adaptation for medical Q&A.

Finally is the *adapter configuration* (discussed in Chapter 7). We defined different LoRA setups, including QLoRA where the base model was loaded in 4-bit NF4 precision using bitsandbytes, with LoRA adapters applied to all linear layers. This gives us a relatively small VRAM footprint so we can train on a smaller GPU.

You can see this in Figure 8-1.

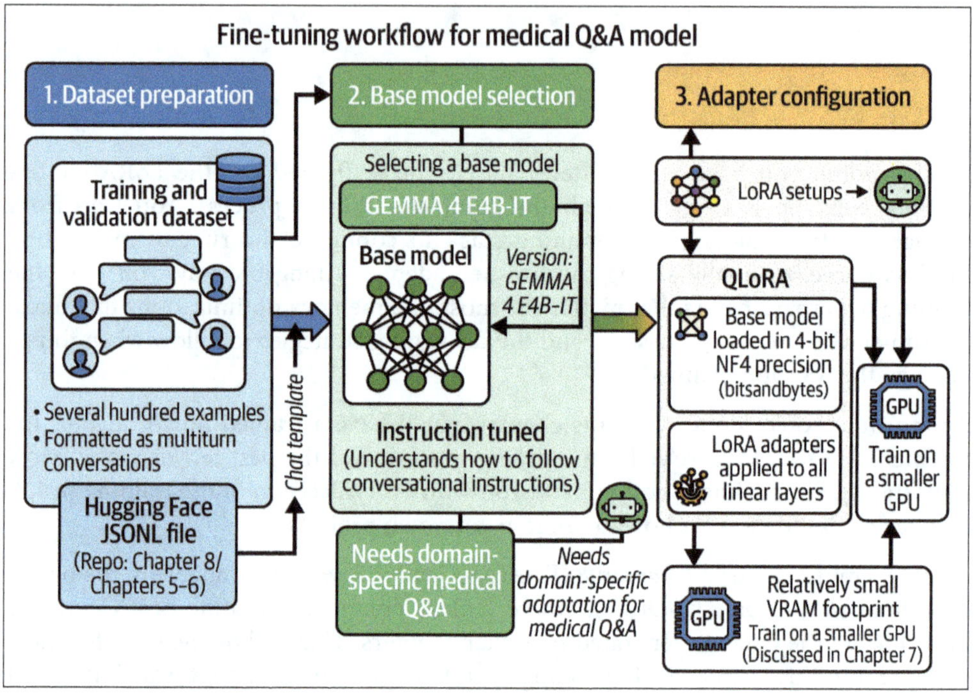

Figure 8-1. Assembling the pieces

What remains is the training itself: the process that takes these components and creates an adapter using fine-tuning. In standard ML, this is called the *training loop*, where you repeatedly feed batches of data through the model, computing the loss, calculating gradients, and updating the weights.

When it's an LLM, and using Hugging Face APIs, most of this complexity is handled by two libraries: Transformers (which provides the `Trainer` class) and TRL (which provides `SFTTrainer`, a specialized trainer for SFT of language models, in particular).

We're going to go end-to-end with a Gemma 4 E4B model, and explore the entire training configuration, because the choices you make in the training run can have a massive impact on your day-to-day work. They'll affect the speed of training, how much memory is needed, and ultimately how good the resulting model adapter is.

The Hugging Face Training Stack

Before we dive into the training hyperparameters, it's worth looking at the layers of abstraction that you'll be working with. The Hugging Face ecosystem gives you several levels in which you can control how the model trains, and knowing which layer does what will help you debug problems and optimize the behavior. You can see this in Figure 8-2.

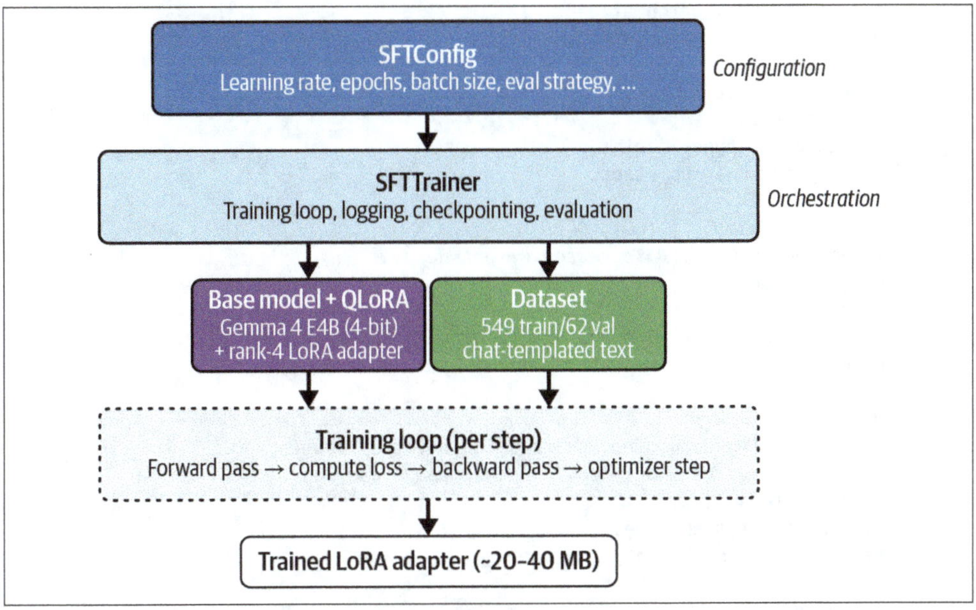

Figure 8-2. The Hugging Face training stack

Training Configuration with SFTConfig

The TRL library provides `SFTConfig`, which extends the `TrainingArguments` class from the Transformers library with SFT-specific options. An example of this is `dataset_text_field`, which is part of the data class that holds every configuration option for a training run, such as learning rate, batch size, number of epochs, logging frequency, checkpoint strategy, precision settings, and many more settings. With fine-tuning, you don't hand write a training loop; instead, you configure one by setting these arguments.

Here's what that configuration should look like for a medical Q&A fine-tuning project with Gemma 4:

```
training_args = SFTConfig(
    output_dir="./results/medical-qa-v1",

    # SFT-specific
    dataset_text_field="text",

    # Training duration
    num_train_epochs=20, # Reduced number of epochs further

    # Batch size — A100/H100 has ample VRAM; larger batches improve throughput.
    # Effective train batch = 8 * 8 = 64.
    per_device_train_batch_size=8,
    per_device_eval_batch_size=4,
    gradient_accumulation_steps=8,

    # Learning rate
    learning_rate=1e-4, # Changed to 1e-4
    lr_scheduler_type="cosine",
    warmup_steps=warmup_steps,

    # Regularization
    weight_decay=0.05, # Increased weight decay
    max_grad_norm=0.3,

    # Precision — A100/H100 has native BF16 tensor cores
    bf16=True,

    # Logging
    # For learning/debugging, we're using a lot of logging
    # steps. In a real-world environment, you'd use less
    logging_steps=5,
    logging_first_step=True,
    report_to="tensorboard",

    # Evaluation
    eval_strategy="steps",
    eval_steps=5,

    # Checkpointing
    save_strategy="steps",
    save_steps=50,
    save_total_limit=3,
    load_best_model_at_end=True,
    metric_for_best_model="eval_loss",

    # Memory optimization
    gradient_checkpointing=True,
    gradient_checkpointing_kwargs={"use_reentrant": False},
```

```
    optim="paged_adamw_8bit",
)
```

There are many options listed here, and we'll discuss them in detail in the sections that follow. But for now, notice the pattern: you're declaring *what* you want the training to do, and not *how* to do it. The actual implementation code (the forward pass, backward pass, optimizer steps, gradient clipping, mixed-precision scaling, distributed training, and everything else) will be handled by a `Trainer` object.

> Do note that in earlier versions of TRL, you'd use `TrainingArguments` directly from `transformers`, but `SFTConfig` is the modern approach, letting you set SFT-specific options like `dataset_text_field` directly in the configuration, rather than passing them to the trainer.

Trainer and SFTTrainer

The `Trainer` class (from the Transformers library) takes a model, a dataset, and a configuration object, and manages the training loop for you. It handles batching, gradient accumulation, mixed-precision training, logging, checkpointing, evaluation, early stopping, and just about every part of training you might need! For most fine-tuning tasks, you'll likely not have to write a custom training loop.

Similarly, the `SFTTrainer` (from the TRL library) extends `Trainer` with features specific to the SFT of language models. The most important addition is handling the formatting of training examples. If your data is not already formatted to the model's chat template, `SFTTrainer` can apply this for you. It also handles packing multiple short examples into a single, longer training sequence with the goal of improving how the GPU is used. You'll explore that a little later in this chapter.

The `SFTTrainer` is configured using `SFTConfig` rather than the base `TrainingArguments`, adding SFT-specific options alongside all the standard training parameters. The listing you just saw was an `SFTTrainer` configuration.

For the medical Q&A project you've been working on, you'll format the data with the chat template during preprocessing (you'll see that shortly), so by the time it reaches the `SFTTrainer`, the dataset will already have a `"text"` column containing the fully formatted conversation strings.

You'll then use `SFTTrainer` because it's the standard choice for LLM fine-tuning, and provides lots of conveniences, particularly the ability to apply the LoRA adapter automatically when you pass it a `peft_config`.

The SFTTrainer setup will look like this:

```
from trl import SFTTrainer

trainer = SFTTrainer(
    model=model,
    args=training_args,
    train_dataset=train_dataset,
    eval_dataset=eval_dataset,
    processing_class=tokenizer,
    peft_config=lora_config,          # SFTTrainer can apply PEFT for you
)
```

Let's look at a few things here:

- Earlier versions of SFTTrainer used the term tokenizer to pass in the tokenizer, but later ones consider it a processing_class. This tells the trainer which tokenizer to use for encoding the text.
- The peft_config parameter is a handy convenience. Instead of manually calling get_peft_model to apply the LoRA adapter, you can pass the lora_config directly to SFTTrainer, and it will handle the PEFT setup internally. This includes preparing the quantized model for training. In earlier versions, you'd have to call prepare_model_for_kbit_training() yourself.

Data Collators

Between the dataset and the training loop sits the *data collator*: a function that takes a list of individual examples and assembles them into a batch the model can consume, padding them to a uniform length and building the label tensors used to compute the loss. When you use SFTTrainer, a default collator is created for you automatically, and for Gemma 4 that's all you need! There's nothing to configure, which is why you won't see a data_collator argument in this chapter's code. Some other models do have extra batch requirements that need a small custom collator; Gemma 3, for example, demanded a token_type_ids tensor in every batch due to its multimodal architecture, a requirement Gemma 4 dropped entirely. So check this for every model you use, and if you hit a mysterious batching error, try removing inherited collator customizations before adding new ones.

Training Hyperparameters

If you're used to training your own models, many of these hyperparameters will look familiar. But I would encourage you not to gloss over them when you are on your fine-tuning journey. Given that the `SFTTrainer` is wrapping the training process for you, you are going to lose a little bit of control. The best interface to that, then, is thoroughly understanding the hyperparameters! In this section, I'm going to focus on the ones that I think have the biggest impact on training outcomes. I'll also explain my reasoning behind each choice.

Learning Rate

The *learning rate* is the single most important hyperparameter in any training run. It controls the size of the weight updates at each optimization step. Set it too high and the model overshoots, oscillating wildly or diverging to meaningless loss; set it too low and the model will waste time and compute on tiny incremental improvements, and not learn effectively.

For LoRA fine-tuning, a common starting range is from 1e-4 to 2e-4. This is higher than the typical full fine-tuning learning rate of 1e-5 to 5e-5, and there's a good reason for that. LoRA parameters are initialized near zero and represent a small correction to the pretrained weights. They need a relatively aggressive learning rate to move away from their zero initialization and learn meaningful updates within a limited number of training steps. In the code provided, I used 1e-4, which is on the more conservative end of this range. With a small rank-4 adapter and a small dataset, a lower learning rate helps the model converge smoothly without overshooting.

If your loss is decreasing smoothly but slowly, try increasing the learning rate by two to five times. If the loss is jumping around erratically or spiking, reduce it by two to five times. The loss curve during the first 50–100 steps is your best diagnostic; it should decrease steadily with some noise but no dramatic spikes.

In Figure 8-3, you can see some examples of different loss curves and why they are the way they are.

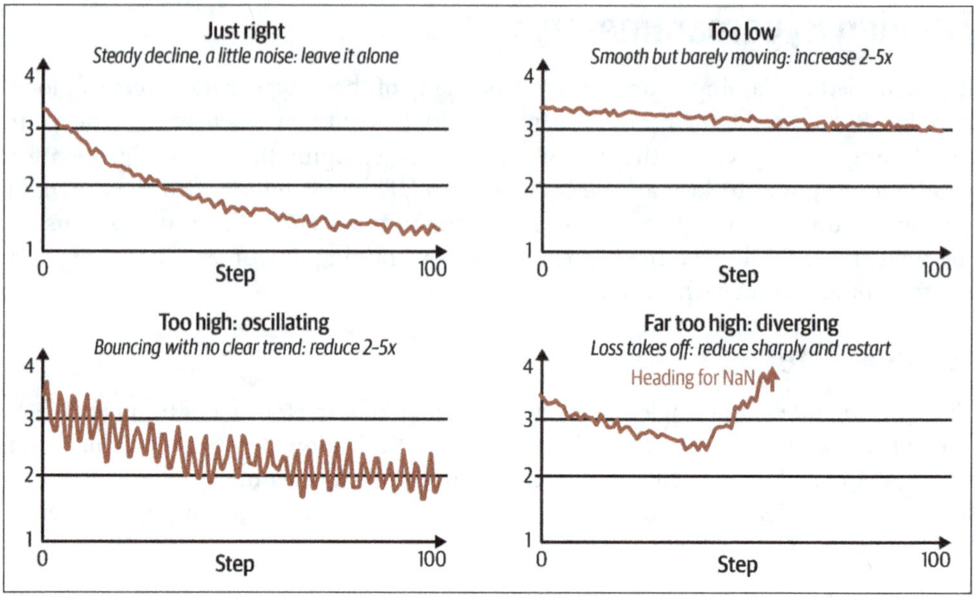

Figure 8-3. Different learning curves and how to adjust to optimize them

Learning Rate Schedule

A constant learning rate is rarely optimal. It's better to vary the learning rate over the course of training. It's good to typically start with a warm-up phase (where the rate increases from near zero to the target value), followed by a decay phase (where the rate gradually decreases toward zero).

The `lr_scheduler_type` parameter controls the shape of the decay. The two most common choices are:

Linear decay
: This decreases the learning rate in a straight line from the peak to zero. This is simple, predictable, and a reasonable default.

Cosine decay
: This decreases the learning rate following a cosine curve—slowly at first, then more steeply in the middle, then slowly again as it approaches zero. Cosine decay tends to produce slightly better results than linear decay in practice, because the gentle start and finish allow the optimizer to make fine-grained adjustments at the beginning and end of training. I recommend cosine as the default.

You can see the cosine learning rate schedule in Figure 8-4.

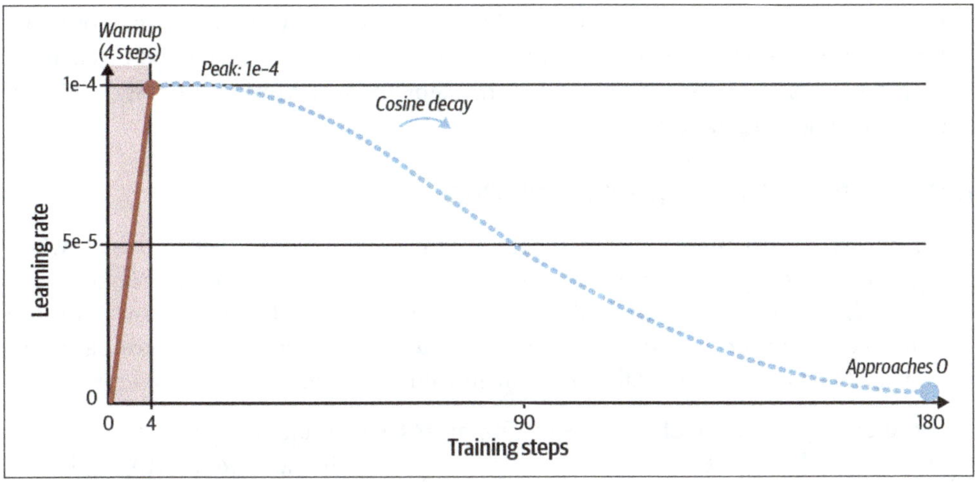

Figure 8-4. Cosine learning rate schedule

For the medical Q&A sample code, the `warmup_steps` are explicitly calculated, instead of hardcoding a ratio. The calculation is straightforward: figure out the total number of optimizer steps (dataset size divided by effective batch size, times the number of epochs), then set `warmup_steps` to about 10% of that total. Here's the code:

```
# per_device_train_batch_size * gradient_accumulation_steps
effective_batch = 8 * 8
total_steps = math.ceil(len(train_dataset) / effective_batch) * num_epochs
warmup_steps = max(1, int(0.1 * total_steps))
```

> For distributed setups and systems, manual warm-up step calculation can become fragile and add unnecessary complexity. Explore using `warmup_ratio` instead to begin with. But for learning on this simpler system, it's a good approach to optimize with!

The version of the dataset created using GPT-OSS-120B has 549 training examples. With an effective batch size of 64, that works out to 9 optimizer steps per epoch. Initially, to figure out a good learning rate, I tried it with a smaller number of epochs, and settled on 5. That gave 45 total steps, and 10% of that is 4 warm-up steps, which gave me a good warm-up of the learning rate and smooth learning. Then, when I increased the number of epochs to keep the system learning more effectively, I kept it at 4 warm-up steps, even though the number of epochs was greater. Warm-up like this helps stabilize the early phase of training; without it, the first few gradient updates can be unusually large (because the loss landscape hasn't been explored yet), potentially pushing the model into a bad region of weight space.

You can alternatively use a hardcoded value like `warmup_ratio=0.1` instead of computing `warmup_steps` manually—the effect can be the same. The explicit calculation just makes it easier to see exactly how many steps the warm-up phase lasts, which is helpful when debugging training runs.

Batch Size and Gradient Accumulation

The batch size determines how many training examples the model processes when computing a single gradient update. A larger batch size means more stable gradients (because the noise from individual examples averages out), but it also means more memory consumption. As always, there's a trade-off you have to do here based on your available hardware, in order to optimize your training.

A `per_device_train_batch_size=8` setting means 8 examples are processed simultaneously on each GPU. For a QLoRA setup on a GPU with sufficient VRAM (like an A100 or T4 with 16 GB), a batch size of 8 with a reduced `model_max_length` of 1,024 tokens is feasible. If you get out-of-memory errors, reduce the batch size to 4, 2, or even 1.

Even a batch size of 8 is modest. In practice, many fine-tuning recipes use effective batch sizes of 32, 64, or even larger for more stable training. When using these a concept called *gradient accumulation* begins to apply.

The idea of gradient accumulation is to tell the trainer to accumulate gradients over a number of forward and backward passes before performing optimization. So, for example, setting `gradient_accumulation_steps=8` tells the trainer to accumulate gradients over 8 consecutive passes before optimizing. Each forward-backward pass uses `per_device_train_batch_size` examples, so the effective batch size is:

```
effective_batch_size =
    per_device_train_batch_size * gradient_accumulation_steps * num_gpus
```

So, for example, with a GPU, this might look like: $8 \times 8 \times 1 = 64$.

Thus, the model sees 64 examples' worth of gradient signal before each weight update, but only 8 examples are in memory at any given time. This gives you the stability benefits of a large batch size without the memory cost. For our small dataset of 549 examples, this means roughly 9 optimizer steps per epoch. This gives you a coarse-grained update schedule that smooths out noise from individual examples.

You can see this in Figure 8-5.

Ultimately, the trade-off will be speed. Gradient accumulation means the same number of optimization steps will require more forward-backward passes. Thus the per-epoch training time is greater. In practice I find it acceptable because it makes your memory usage highly optimized, and it prevents you from running out of memory. Given that VRAM is arguably the most expensive component in a learning system, anything you can do to squeeze what you can out of what you have is worth a bit of time! Depending on the hardware available to you, you can tweak these values; if you have more VRAM, you can increase the per-device batch size, and decrease the number of accumulation steps. It will give you the same effective batch size, but with better throughput.

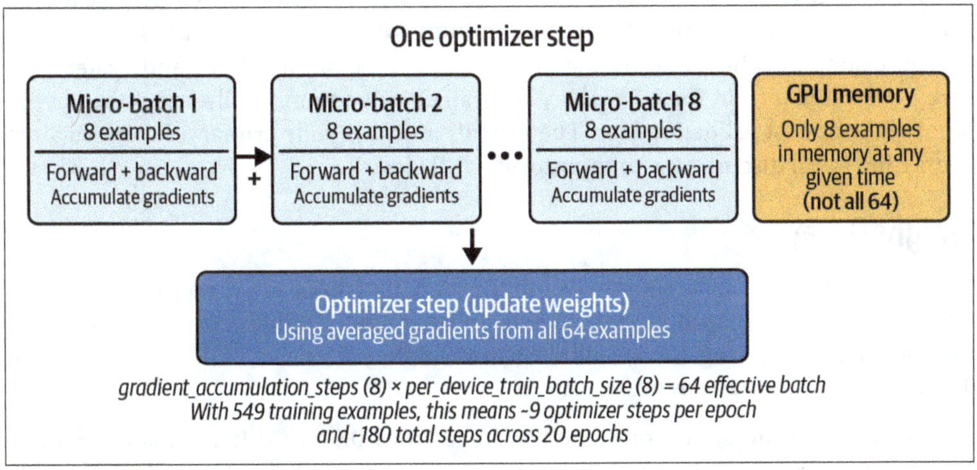

Figure 8-5. Gradient accumulation

Number of Epochs

An *epoch* is a complete pass through the training dataset. The `num_train_epochs=20` setting means the model will see every training example 20 times as it trains.

That might sound like a lot, and for large datasets it would be, but our dataset is quite small (549 training examples), and combined with the large effective batch size (64), each epoch produces only about 9 optimizer steps. Twenty epochs gives us roughly 180 total optimizer steps, a training run that's actually quite modest in terms of total gradient updates. The key insight is that for small datasets, you often need more passes through the data to give the model enough gradient signal to learn the target behavior.

For larger datasets, the calculus changes. Here's a rough guide:

- Use 1–2 epochs when you have a large, high-quality dataset (10,000+ examples) and want to minimize the risk of overfitting.
- Use 3–5 epochs for medium-sized datasets (1,000–5,000 examples). The model sees each example enough times to learn the patterns without excessive memorization.

- Use 10–20 epochs for small datasets (fewer than 600 examples), especially when combined with strong regularization (higher dropout, weight decay) to prevent overfitting. This is our situation.

The risk of too many epochs is overfitting. In this case, the model memorizes the training data rather than learning generalizable patterns. An overfitted model will produce excellent metrics on the training set but perform poorly on new, unseen examples. The `load_best_model_at_end=True` setting is a handy safety net here—even if you train for 20 epochs, the trainer will automatically select the checkpoint with the best validation loss. The validation loss is your primary defense against overfitting (we'll discuss how to monitor it a little later).

Weight Decay

Weight decay is a regularization technique that penalizes large parameter values. At each optimizer step, it slightly shrinks all parameter values, which discourages the model from relying too heavily on any single parameter and promotes more distributed, generalizable representations.

For LoRA fine-tuning, common values range from 0.01 to 0.1. In this example, I used `weight_decay=0.05`, which is more aggressive than the typical default of 0.01, because the small dataset and high epoch count make overfitting a real concern. The stronger weight decay acts as additional regularization, working alongside the LoRA dropout (0.2) to keep the adapter from memorizing specific training examples. If you have a larger dataset, you can safely reduce this to 0.01.

Maximum Gradient Norm

To understand the goal of `max_grad_norm`, it helps to think about what happens at each optimizer step. The backward pass will compute a gradient for each trainable parameter. This is the adjustment phase, where it will move a parameter in a particular direction by a particular amount. When all of these gradients are gathered into a single vector, you can calculate the overall magnitude of the proposed update. If that's small, then the optimization step is also small. If it's larger, because a particular batch caused a huge loss, then the optimizer will take a huge step, which can destabilize subsequent ones.

Gradient clipping puts a ceiling on that magnitude. Setting it to a value of 0.3, for example, will mean that after computing all the gradients, if their combined norm exceeds 0.3, then every gradient will be rescaled by the same amount until the norm lands at 0.3. The overall direction of the update is preserved, so the values are incremented correctly, but the step size will be capped. It's kind of like overriding the learning rate based on context.

Using a value of 0.3 (like I use in this chapter's example), is quite aggressive. But it is a common choice for QLoRA because the quantization process can lead to noisy gradients in backpropagation. The tighter clipping can help absorb the spikes. It's something you can keep an eye on during training; if the `grad_norm` is bumping up against 0.3 frequently, then the optimizer is being constrained frequently, and this will effectively lower the learning rate permanently.

If you notice that training is unusually slow, then the `max_grad_norm` setting might be too restrictive, and you can try upping it to 0.5 or 1.0.

Optimizer

In traditional ML, the choice of optimizer and loss function is likely one of the first hyperparameters you choose. With fine-tuning, not much changes there. One issue that I have encountered is that you need to peel a little deeper than just choosing a function, and additionally need to consider the precision states of the model you're fine-tuning and pick one accordingly.

I chose `optim="paged_adamw_8bit"` as the optimizer setting for the sample of fine-tuning Gemma on the medical Q&A. AdamW is a variant of the popular Adam optimizer that applies weight decay by decoupling it from the gradient update. Like Adam, it maintains two additional state variables per parameter: a running mean and variance of the gradients. It uses these to effectively adapt the learning rate for each parameter individually. This behavior makes Adam and its variants very effective for deep and complex neural networks that have inherent complicated loss landscapes. And given that generative models are extremely deep and complex (even smaller 8B sizes) they're a great choice.

The `8bit` part of the name means that the optimizer's internal states are stored in 8-bit precision, instead of the default 32-bit. It will reduce the optimizer footprint by 4×. For our fine-tuning, we're affecting around 9.7 million parameters; the optimizer states storage would go from about 80 MB to about 20 MB with minimal impact on quality.

The `paged` part of the name adds memory paging. This feature was originally introduced in the QLoRA paper (*https://oreil.ly/XwWWe*), and the core idea is to prevent out-of-memory errors due to memory spikes. It does this by taking rarely used optimizer states and backing them up to CPU memory during periods of high utilization, at the cost of a minor latency hit.

If you're not using QLoRA (for example, if your model is 16-bit), you can use `adamw_torch` (the standard PyTorch AdamW) or `adamw_8bit` (8-bit without paging) instead. The `paged` variant is most useful when memory is tight.

Memory Optimizations

VRAM is likely the most expensive component in any ML system, and, by definition, that will likely mean it's the most rare. Customer GPUs are low cost because they generally carry less VRAM. Be careful when buying a GPU with the idea of using it for ML. Often, the high-end, expensive gaming rigs with the pretty flashing lights look snazzy yet they lack the VRAM! It's common for machines that cost $3,000 to $4,000 to look state-of-the-art, yet have only 8 GB VRAM. Great for Fortnite, not so great for ML.

So, even with QLoRA reducing the base model's footprint, training can strain your VRAM budget. Let's consider some techniques that we can use to help keep memory usage manageable. We'll start with gradient checkpointing.

Gradient Checkpointing

During the forward pass, the model computes intermediate activations at every layer: the outputs of each attention block, each FFN, each layer norm. These activations need to be stored for backpropagation, because calculation of gradients requires knowing the values that were computed during the forward pass. For a model with 42 transformer layers processing a 2,048-token sequence, these stored activations add up quickly, and can blow your VRAM budget.

Gradient checkpointing (*https://oreil.ly/GwR3E*) trades compute for memory. Instead of storing all activations, it stores only a subset—typically the output of every layer boundary. During backpropagation, when the activations for a layer are needed, they're recomputed on the fly, from the nearest checkpoint. This can reduce the amount of memory to store activations by roughly 60–70%. The cost is in performing more calculations that can slow down your training. It's a worthy trade-off in many cases.

The `gradient_checkpointing=True` flag in `SFTConfig` enables this automatically. When using QLoRA to train on consumer hardware, it's essentially mandatory to do, unless you are using really small models. It looks like this:

```
training_args = SFTConfig(
    # ... other arguments ...
    gradient_checkpointing=True,
    gradient_checkpointing_kwargs={"use_reentrant": False},
)
```

With the second parameter, I added `"use_reentrant": False`. In some older versions of PyTorch, reentrant checkpointing can cause issues with the PEFT wrapper, with errors about incorrect gradients or some tensors not requiring gradient calculation. This line turns off that functionality. It's also now commonly preferred with modern workflows because it integrates more reliably with autograd and other checkpointing behavior in LLM training.

Mixed-Precision Training

Mixed-precision training uses lower-precision, floating-point formats (16-bit instead of 32-bit) for most computations. The master copy of the weights is still stored as 32-bit for numerical stability during the optimizer step.

The `bf16=True` flag enables bfloat16 mixed-precision training. Bfloat16 (brain floating point) is a clever 16-bit format that maintains the same exponent range as 32-bit float, maintaining compatibility with it, but with reduced precision. Ultimately, this means it can represent the same range of values as float32—including very large and very small numbers—but with less precision for the fractional part. For neural network training, the range is more important than the precision, which is why bfloat16 is a common replacement for float16 for training workloads.

If your GPU doesn't support bfloat16 (it's available on NVIDIA Ampere and newer—A100, RTX 30xx, RTX 40xx, RTX 50xx), use `fp16=True` instead. Float16 has a narrower dynamic range, which can cause overflow or underflow during training if gradients become very large or very small. The trainer handles this with a gradient scaler that automatically adjusts the loss magnitude to keep gradients within the appropriate range. This works well in practice, but bfloat16 is more convenient because it doesn't need the scaler.

For QLoRA, mixed-precision training is already happening to some degree; the base model is in 4-bit, the LoRA parameters are in the compute `dtype` (bfloat16 or float16), and the optimizer states are in 8-bit (if using the 8-bit optimizer). The `bf16=True` flag ensures that the forward and backward passes also use bfloat16, reducing activation memory and improving throughput on GPUs with bfloat16 hardware support.

It might seem trivial to think about the number types on particular parts of the workflow, but it's an unfortunate truth that you're pushing right up to the edge of available VRAM most of the time, and anything you can do to save a bit here or a byte there will pay off in the long run.

Your Memory Budget: Putting It All Together

Let's do a quick back-of-the-napkin calculation for VRAM usage for a training configuration. This is approximate, but hopefully will give you an idea of the types of calculations you'll have to do with any model to figure out if it's feasible to train or not on your given hardware.

I'll start with the model. I'm going to use Gemma 4 E4B with NF4 quantization. Every model has its quirks, and this model is no exception. Of its 8 billion parameters, only about 4.5 billion live in the linear layers that can get quantized. This leaves about 3.5 billion sitting in embedding tables—that give the model the "E" in its name! These embeddings are *not* quantized, so instead of a clear 8B divided by 4, the base model will work out to:

Quantized linear layers
: About 4.5B parameters at 4 bits = 2.3 GB, with an overhead for constants of about 0.5 GB. So, let's say, 2.8 GB.

Embedding tables in bfloat16
: About 3.5B parameters at 2 bytes, so that's about 7 GB. This is an easy one to miss. Don't get lulled into thinking a 4-bit model means that every parameter is 4 bits!

LoRA parameters
: 9.7 million parameters in bfloat16 = about 19 MB.

Optimizer states
: 8-bit AdamW, 2 states per trainable parameter, each needing 8 bits = about 19 MB.

Gradients
: 1 gradient per trainable parameter in bfloat16 = about 19 MB.

Activations
: Here's where we can get creative in constrained environments, but let's start with a batch size of 8, and keep our tokens to sequences of 1,024. For these, gradient-checkpointed activations will consume 1–3 GB, depending on the model architecture and checkpoint granularity.

Framework overhead
: You don't have a lot of control over this, but PyTorch, CUDA context, library allocations, etc. can eat a lot. Up to 1 GB is common.

So, our total estimate calculates to be about 12–14 GB to perform this training. You're going to need about 16 GB of VRAM. If you don't have this, and are limited to a consumer 8-GB VRAM GPU, you could try the Gemma 4 E2B model, which might squeeze into 8 GB if you get aggressive.

An A100 Low-RAM instance in Google Colab is a good option to use, because it gives you a nice trade-off between VRAM and cost. At the time of running this, it was 5.6 compute units per hour, and one can buy 100 compute units, or approximately 18 hours of use for $10.

Despite the cost, I would generally encourage this one, because you're working with more up-to-date hardware and not writing code workarounds for incompatibilities.

You can also tweak the hyperparameters to change your batching to make the most of the 40 GB of VRAM it offers.

So, to manage your memory, the most effective knobs to adjust are, in order of impact: reducing the `per_device_train_batch_size`, reducing `tokenizer.model_max_length`, and ensuring that `gradient_checkpointing=True`.

> PyTorch 2.0 introduced `torch.compile()`, which uses a just-in-time (JIT) compiler to fuse operations and optimize the computation graph for better throughput. Generally, this will speed up both the forward and backward passes. In practice, its development with newer techniques, quantized models, and PEFT wrappers is still maturing. It can produce errors or unexpected behavior with 4-bit QLoRA setups that you should watch out for. I encourage you, at least in the beginning, to disable it. Later, if you want to optimize it for throughput, it's worth testing. To turn it on, use `torch_compile=True` in your `SFTConfig`, but be prepared for compatibility issues!

Preparing the Training Data

Before launching any training run, the data has to be transformed from the raw dataset to the format that the model expects. We've explored various techniques for doing this in previous chapters, but let's get concrete for this specific Gemma example here. The JSONL file that was created earlier is generic with instruction/input/output fields. But we'll need fully formatted conversation strings that use the Gemma chat template if we're going to train that model.

You can see the pipeline for this in Figure 8-6.

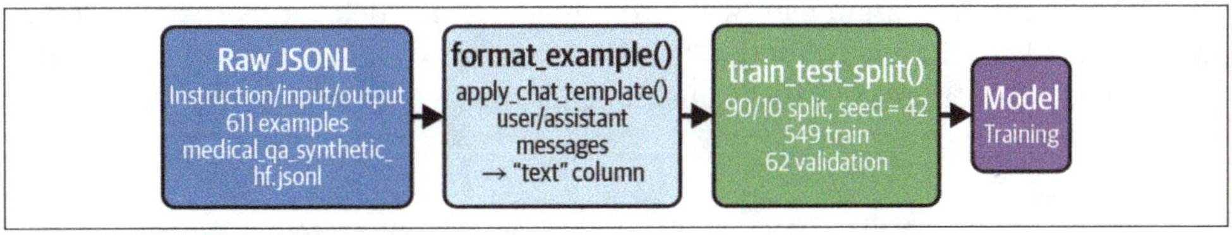

Figure 8-6. Data preparation pipeline

The first step will be to load the raw data and apply the chat template:

```
from datasets import load_dataset

raw_dataset = load_dataset(
    "json",
    data_files="medical_qa_synthetic_hf.jsonl",
    split="train",
)
```

```python
def format_example(example):
    """
    Convert instruction/output pairs into Gemma chat-template format.
    If the optional "input" field has content it is appended to the
    instruction as additional context. The result is stored in a "text"
    column that SFTTrainer will use directly for training.
    """
    user_content = example["instruction"]
    if example.get("input", "").strip():
        user_content = f"{example['instruction']}\n\n{example['input']}"

    messages = [
        {"role": "user",      "content": user_content},
        {"role": "assistant", "content": example["output"]},
    ]
    return {
        "text": tokenizer.apply_chat_template(
            messages,
            tokenize=False,
            add_generation_prompt=False,
        )
    }

dataset = raw_dataset.map(
    format_example,
    remove_columns=raw_dataset.column_names,
)
```

This function does a few very important things. First, it will construct a message list in the standard chat format with user and assistant roles, and then call the tokenizer's `apply_chat_template` method to convert that into the exact string format that Gemma expects, including the special turn markers.

The `remove_columns` argument will drop the original fields (instruction, input, output, metadata), leaving only the `"text"` column that `SFTTrainer` expects. After formatting, each example will look something like this:

```
<bos>
<|turn>user
When should someone with major depressive disorder seek emergency medical care?
<turn|>
<|turn>model
CLINICAL CONSIDERATIONS: Individuals with major depression are at risk for rapid
deterioration, especially when suicidal thoughts, plans, or intent arise.
Emergency care is also warra…
<|turn>
```

The `SFTTrainer` expects the dataset to have a text field containing this formatted string. The name of this column was configured on the `SFTConfig` as the `dataset_text_field` parameter. If you look all the way back to the beginning of this chapter, it was specified as `"text"`.

> There's a concept called *packing* data, which might help with our medical Q&A data. Back in Chapter 6, the token-length analysis showed a median example of around 435 tokens, with 99% of examples under 560. Against this chapter's 1,024-token sequence limit, that means roughly half of every batch is padding: tokens the GPU dutifully processes that contribute nothing. Packing would fit about two examples into each 1,024-token sequence, which, in practice, translates to nearly double the training throughput. I left it off in this chapter's run because with 549 examples and a half-hour training time, there wasn't much to gain, and one less setting means one less thing to debug. But if you scale up this dataset, or your budget is tighter than mine, it's a one-line change with a real payoff—just recheck the loss curve after enabling it, since packing changes what the model sees in each sequence.

The Loss Function and Label Masking

Along with the optimizer, the loss function is the other major workhorse in ML and fine-tuning. When using causal language model fine-tuning, the loss function is a cross-entropy loss over the next-token prediction task. For every position in the input, the model will predict a probability distribution over the entire vocabulary (which is 262,144 items for Gemma 4), and then measure how good or bad the distribution is from the correct next token, as determined in the training set.

Formally, for a sequence of tokens that I'll call $x_1, x_2, \ldots x_T$, the loss is calculated with the following function:

$$\mathcal{L} = -\frac{1}{T'}\sum_{t \in \mathcal{S}} \log P(x_t \mid x_1, \ldots, x_{t-1})$$

Note that the sum of tokens is divided by T′, so you get the average loss per token rather than a total that grows with the length of the sequence.

Don't worry if you're not a math geek; you won't be coding this yourself, and will use an off-the-shelf loss function. I'm just showing it for completeness. Ultimately what matters to you is the range of x values that will go into this equation (i.e., which tokens you want to use).

You typically want the model to learn to generate the assistant's responses, and not predict the user's input. So the loss should only be computed on the assistant's tokens, where you mask out the user input and the system prompt.

This is called *label masking* or *response-only* training. In the labels tensor (positions that you don't want to compute the loss for), set to the value –100, which is a PyTorch convention that means "ignore this position in the cross-entropy loss calculation."

When using `SFTTrainer` with preformatted text, the trainer will compute the loss on all tokens, by default. So you have to configure label masking for yourself. There are two ways that you can do this. The first is to format your data as a list of messages and let `SFTTrainer` apply the chat template with proper masking. The second is to create a custom data collator that masks the appropriate positions.

For our medical Q&A example, I chose *not* to use label masking, and kept the loss to be computed on all tokens, including the user's question. The model will then learn to predict both the question and answer patterns, which, for a scenario like this one, is useful because conversations are often long running; one answer will be followed up by another question, and it might be useful to get in front of that! But for other types of tasks, where the user input is very long relative to the assistant's response (for example, document summarization) label masking is very important. Without it, the loss signal from the short response might get drowned out by the loss from the long input.

Training and Validation Split

While one could maintain separate files for training and validation, given that this is a relatively small dataset, you can just do it on the fly, and use a random seed for reproducibility, like this:

```
split = dataset.train_test_split(test_size=0.1, seed=42)
train_dataset = split["train"]
eval_dataset  = split["test"]

print(f"Training examples:   {len(train_dataset)}")
print(f"Validation examples: {len(eval_dataset)}")
```

This gives 549 training examples and 62 validation examples on the version of the dataset generated with GPT-OSS-120B.

During training, the model will be evaluated on the validation set at regular intervals (controlled by the `eval_steps` parameter), which is set to 5. That means for every 5 optimizer steps, a validation will be performed. This is probably more frequent than necessary, but I wanted to plot the training and validation loss with decent frequency (you'll see it in Figure 8-7 later), so I turned it up. When you have a model that's behaving, you can make this much less frequent and improve your training performance.

Typically, you'll explore how the training loss and validation loss curves are related to determine if the training is overfitting or underfitting. We'll explore that a little further into the chapter when we plot the results.

The Complete Training Script

The *Chapter08_FineTuneGemma.ipynb* in the book's download has the process to perform the fine-tuning of Gemma 4 E4B with the medical Q&A, using the settings we discussed this far in the chapter. There are a few pieces of code that you should take into account for this specific instance of training. They may (or may not) apply for other models or datasets.

Tokenizer padding is where you set the padding token. Batches should be a uniform length, so shorter sequences will get padded out. The trainer's default collator will use whatever padding token the tokenizer defines for that. But here's the catch: some models don't have one defined! So, if the padding token is missing, batching can fail with an error the moment training starts.

The line `tokenizer.pad_token=tokenizer.eos_token` is the standard fix for this, and it reuses the end-of-sequence token for padding. As we're using Gemma 4, which does have a dedicated padding token, this line is there more as a safety habit than as a necessity, but it's a good habit to keep, because you never know which models will have this, and which won't!

The `padding_side="right"` ensures padding is added at the end of each sequence, which is standard for left-to-right languages and causal language models. Remember the model will generate text left-to-right, and padding on the left would shift all token positions!

Max length is where you set the tokenizer's maximum length. This can differ from the model's default, and is often used to conserve memory. The medical Q&A data is generally well under 1,024 tokens, so setting `tokenizer.model_max_length=1024` loses nothing, and prevents unnecessarily long sequences from consuming your precious VRAM.

In some models and older PEFT versions, you would see `prepare_model_for_kbit_training` to prepare a quantized model for training. This is left out of this example, because the Colab environment uses PEFT > 0.12, and as a result, the `SFTTrainer` handles it internally. If you're using a different environment and PEFT version, you should look out for this.

Something to watch out for: `SFTTrainer` only wraps this abstraction if the quantized model is initialized within specific parameters. If you manually quantize, omitting this helper may cause training failures due to LayerNorm layers not being cast to fp32 and missing gradient checkpoints on input embeddings.

The LoRA settings in this script (see Chapter 7 for more on LoRA settings) are quite conservative, using a rank of 4 with an alpha of 4, and a relatively high dropout of 0.2. Given a very small dataset, a smaller adapter with stronger regularization will prevent overfitting. With these settings, only about 0.17% of the parameters will be trained. It's a very lightweight patch on the frozen base model.

You can use a `save_total_limit` parameter to set the number of recent checkpoints to save, automatically deleting older ones. Checkpoints for QLoRA are quite small, but they can accumulate if you're training for a long time! In this script, I configured to save three of them with `save_total_limit=3`.

Finally, after training finishes, the last model may not be the best one! So using `load_best_model_at_end=True` will load the one with the lowest validation loss. The final checkpoint may have started to overfit. It's a really effective and simple way to do early stopping, where you train for a fixed number of epochs but the model you save is the most general one.

Performing the Training Run

The code, as it currently stands, is designed to work on an A100 on Colab in order to use bf16. If you want to use a cheaper GPU or one with less VRAM, you might need to make some changes, as discussed earlier. The results I'll present here are based on running on bf16.

Before starting, you may need to install some dependencies. In the Colab environment, they'll be:

```
pip install transformers trl peft bitsandbytes accelerate datasets
            torchao tensorboard
```

Downloading the model and handling the preprocessing of the data should take a few minutes, and then the training will begin. Running for 20 epochs will take about 45 minutes, so you will use about 4 compute units in Colab, a cost of less than 50 cents.

Figure 8-7 shows the results. Notice the pattern: the training data loss drops rapidly in the first 50 steps and then settles into a gradual decline. The validation loss follows a similar trajectory before leveling out at around 0.88.

Note how the training loss and validation loss started to open up after about step 75. This is the model beginning to memorize the training data, as opposed to learning generalizable patterns. It's small, but it's there. This is expected with a small dataset, but the hyperparameters we used keep it manageable.

If you don't see a chart like this, with the lines broadly matching each other—at least up to a point before they begin to diverge—you'll likely need to work on the hyperparameters, and in the next section, you'll see a workflow of things to work through there.

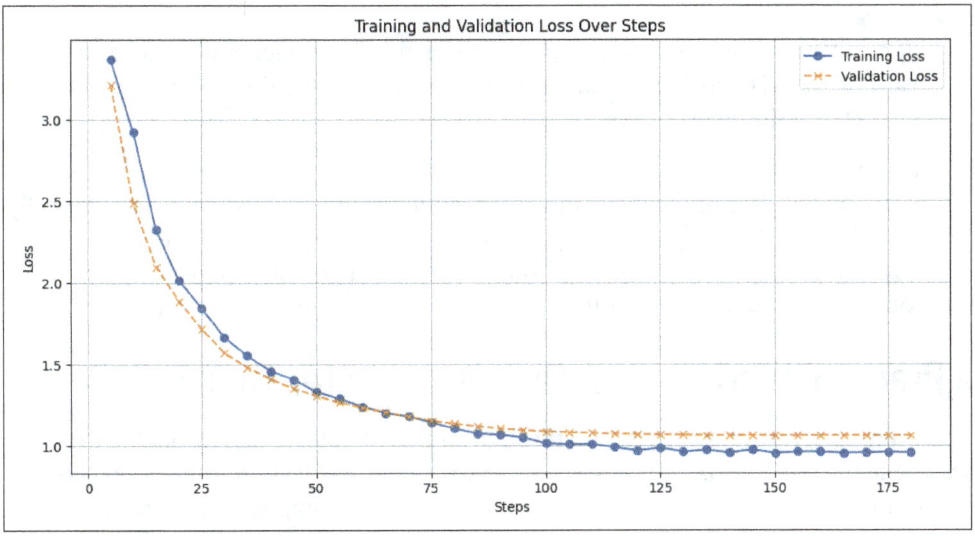

Figure 8-7. Training and validation loss for fine-tuning

Typically, you'll see one of the following patterns:

Healthy training
: The training and validation loss will decrease and eventually plateau, as in Figure 8-7. The validation loss may be slightly higher than the training one, but they'll track each other closely. This is the ideal outcome, where the model is learning from the data without overfitting, and the pattern matches that for validation data that wasn't used in training.

Overfitting
: This is where the training loss continues to decrease ahead of the validation loss, which in itself may begin to increase. The gap between the two will widen. This shows the model memorizing the training data rather than learning the generalizable patterns. Remedies include reducing the number of epochs, increasing dropout, reducing the LoRA rank, and increasing the data size (if you can) with techniques like data augmentation.

Underfitting
: This is where both curves have very high loss, and they are barely decreasing. The model isn't learning effectively. Things to look at in this case are the learning rate being too low, the rank being too low (namely the adapter doesn't have enough capacity to effectively learn), or there could be a data issue with formatting, labeling, or the chat template.

Divergence
Here is where the loss suddenly spikes toward infinity. Generally, this means the learning rate is too high. Reduce it and try again. It might also be caused by corrupted training examples.

Oscillation
Here the loss is bouncing up and down without any clear trend. That's typically caused by the learning rate being too high and the optimizer is overshooting the loss minimum on each step, and then overcorrects in the opposite direction. If you see this, reduce the learning rate and/or increase the effective batch size.

A Practical Workflow for Hyperparameter Tuning

The training script that we worked through in this chapter uses reasonable defaults, and some tweaks suitable for Gemma. Of course, you may want to tune other models, so I think it's good to have a workflow and checklist that applies for more cases. You can see the steps in Figure 8-8.

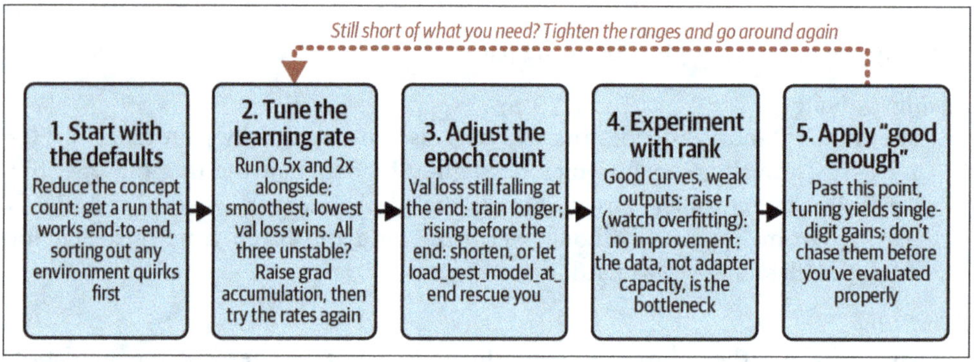

Figure 8-8. A practical workflow for hyperparameter tuning

Start with the Defaults

I'm a huge believer in reducing the concept count to the extent feasible in order to get *something* that works—even code that executes end to end, whether or not the model learns effectively. The best way to do this is to start with the defaults, as much as possible, and establish a baseline. If you need to do any special tweaks for your environment, like using (or not) bf16, based on the GPU that's available to you, here's the time to understand them. Basically, get something that *works* and go from there.

Tune the Learning Rate

Now that you have something that works, one of the most common tweaks, whether you're overfitting, underfitting, oscillating, or just not learning as effectively or as quickly as you think you should be, is to adjust the learning rate. This can have a *huge* impact on your results. Take a look at the learning rate you are using and try two additional experiments—one with half of that, and one with double it. So, for example, if you started with the sensible default of 1e-4, try 5e-5 as half, and 2e-4 as double. Look at the loss curves, and tweak further if you need. The best learning rate is the one that produces the lowest, smoothest, validation loss without causing instability.

If all three values are diverging and oscillating, then the learning rate isn't the problem, and your effective batch size might be too small. If that's the case, try increasing the gradient accumulation steps, and trying all three learning rates again. Tweak and iterate.

When you get to a point where your experimental values are converging smoothly, but to different final losses, you're heading in the right direction, and can lower the differences between the values. In other words, instead of halving and doubling, you could scale down by 0.75× or up by 1.25×, for example.

Adjust the Epoch Count

With the learning rate fixed, watch the validation loss curve. If it's still decreasing at the end of training, you've stopped too early and need to add some more epochs. If it started increasing before the end of training, you've likely trained too long. In that case, reduce the epochs, or rely on `load_best_model_at_end=True` to recover the best checkpoint.

Look back at the graph in Figure 8-7, and you'll see that the training began to become less effective after about step 85, which is epoch 10, given 9 steps per epoch with the way that script is set up. It's just wasted compute to continue training beyond that point, and the next best step would be to adjust the hyperparameters to get the absolute loss value to be lower while still maintaining those smooth curves.

The good news: you'll likely need a lot fewer epochs with larger datasets. Remember you aren't training a model from scratch, and often 2–3 epochs might be enough to fine-tune the adapters that sit on top of the model.

Experiment with Rank

If the model's output quality isn't where you want it to be, despite the loss curves looking good, it might simply mean that you aren't retraining enough parameters in the model. Remember, with LoRA, you're likely only tweaking a small percentage of them. The baseline we used in this example used rank 4, which is very conservative. Experiment with jumping to higher values here to see if the validation loss improves. If it doesn't, the bottleneck is likely your data, and not the adapter's capacity. One risk: a higher rank can increase the risk of overfitting on small datasets, so you may need to compensate with other hyperparameters, such as dropout.

Apply the "Good Enough" Principle

Hyperparameter tuning can be effective, but can lead very quickly to diminishing returns. The difference between a well-tuned and a roughly-tuned LoRA fine-tune can be single-digit percentages on benchmarks. This is significant for competitive research, but can be negligible for practical applications. In Chapter 9, we'll look at how you can test the model with some simple prompts, and build the skills for evaluation. If your model looks like it's producing good outputs from test prompts, it might be better just to move onto formal evaluation and deployment. You can always come back and fine-tune further.

Logging and Experiment Tracking

In this script, I just did some very simple outputs of loss and validation and plotted them. But in a real-world environment, you might want to get a bit more sophisticated. The `report_to` parameter in `SFTConfig` controls where training metrics are logged. There are a few places where you can use these.

TensorBoard

TensorBoard is a free, open source visualization tool (originally built for TensorFlow, but now framework-agnostic) that reads the metric logs your training run writes to disk, and presents them as interactive charts in your browser. It's very easy to set up, and no account or cloud service is needed. You simply point it at a directory.

Your metrics can be written to the `output_dir` as event files with:

```
training_args = SFTConfig(
    output_dir="./results/medical-qa-v1",
```

To view them, you simply run:

```
tensorboard --logdir ./results/medical-qa-v1
```

This launches a web interface where you can visualize training and validation loss curves, learning rate schedules, gradient norms, and other hyperparameters over time. If you're running in Google Colab, you can use the built-in TensorBoard integration:

```
%load_ext tensorboard
%tensorboard --logdir ./results/medical-qa-v1
```

It's simple, free, and sufficient for many experimental workflows.

You can see an example output from Colab for this fine-tuning in Figure 8-9.

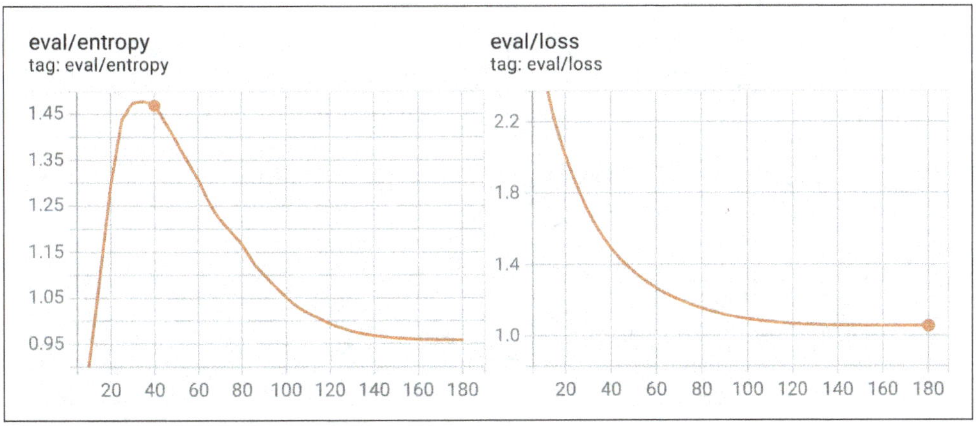

Figure 8-9. Output from TensorBoard

Weights & Biases

For more serious experiment tracking, especially when you're tuning lots of hyperparameters, the Weights & Biases (wandb) library is one of the most popular choices in the ML community. It provides cloud-hosted experiment dashboards, automatic hyperparameter comparison, and collaboration features.

To use wandb with the trainer, you install the library with:

```
pip install wandb
wandb login
```

You then set it to be the reporting target in `SFTConfig` like this:

```
training_args = SFTConfig(
    # ... other arguments ...
    report_to="wandb",
    run_name="medical-qa-v1-lr1e4-rank4",  # Descriptive run name
)
```

Every training metric is then automatically logged to your W&B dashboard (at wandb.ai), and you can compare multiple runs side by side, create custom visualizations, and share results with others. It's a paid product, but the free tier is generous enough to get you started.

You can see an example from this training run from the W&B dashboard in Figure 8-10.

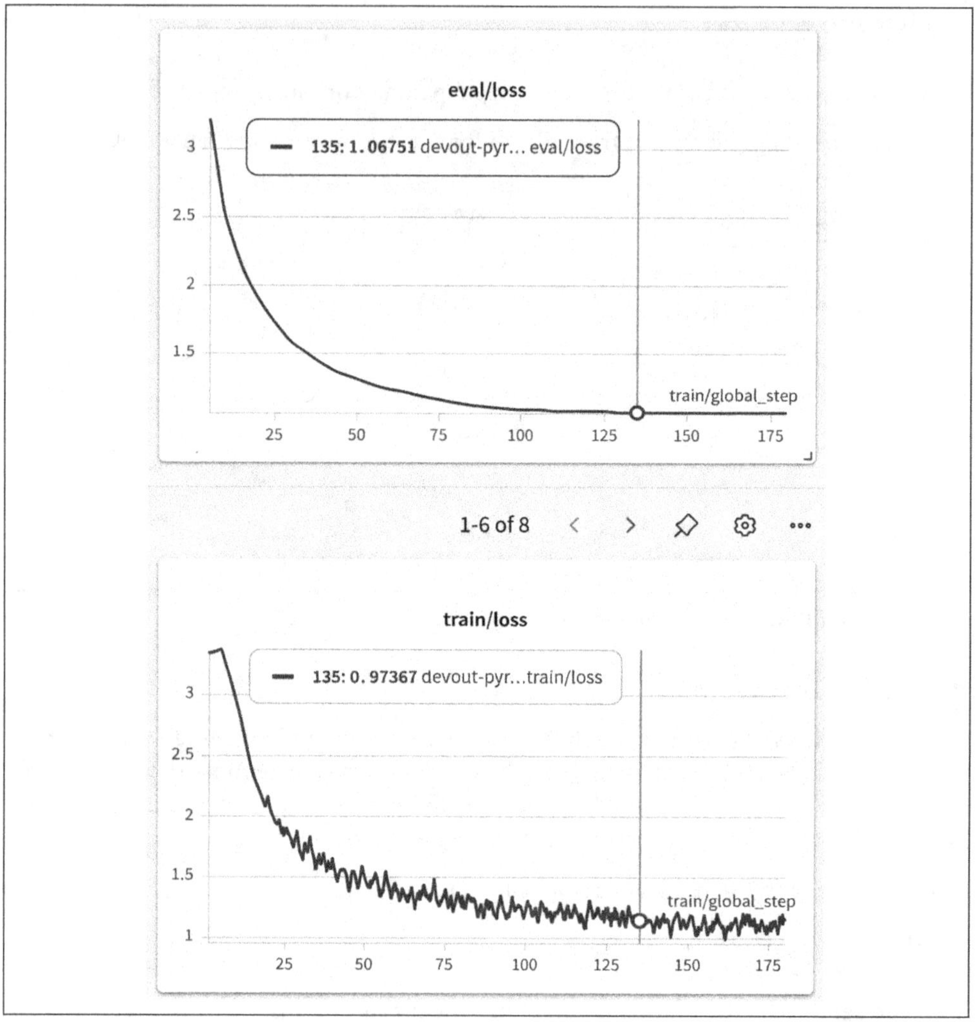

Figure 8-10. W&B dashboard results

One thing to note is that you give runs a name, and I find it handy to encode the hyperparameters I'm using into the run name to quickly identify which run used which settings when reviewing the dashboard.

Custom Callbacks

Tools like TensorBoard and W&B are terrific and cover the common cases. But sometimes you might also want some finer-grained control to look at variables in the training cycle that you care about. You may have custom metrics, want to implement a custom early stopping logic, or maybe even integrate with some kind of notification system so that the code calls you up for particular events you may be concerned with. To that end, the trainer does support custom callbacks.

You simply write a class that extends `TrainerCallback`, and then specify that using the `callbacks` parameter on the trainer. Here's a simple example that prints the GPU memory usage at each logging step:

```
import torch
from transformers import TrainerCallback

class MemoryCallback(TrainerCallback):
    def on_log(self, args, state, control, logs=None, **kwargs):
        if torch.cuda.is_available():
            allocated = torch.cuda.memory_allocated() / 1024**3
            reserved = torch.cuda.memory_reserved() / 1024**3
            print(f"Step {state.global_step}: "
                  f"GPU allocated: {allocated:.2f} GB, "
                  f"GPU reserved: {reserved:.2f} GB")

trainer = SFTTrainer(
    model=model,
    args=training_args,
    train_dataset=train_dataset,
    eval_dataset=eval_dataset,
    processing_class=tokenizer,
    peft_config=lora_config,
    callbacks=[MemoryCallback()],
)
```

The callback *mechanism* adds very little overhead, but what you implement *within* your custom callback function can impact your training. Should you do something that eats VRAM for example, you could end up causing out-of-memory errors in your training loop. So be careful when using them if you don't want to negatively impact your training work.

Reproducibility

Fine-tuning results are notoriously sensitive to random seeds, data ordering, and even hardware differences. If you want to be able to reproduce a specific result, there are a few practices that can help.

The first, and most obvious, is to set random seeds explicitly. The `SFTConfig` class has a `seed` parameter, which defaults to 42, because that is the answer to the ultimate question of life, the universe, and everything. (And if you weren't previously aware of this, you're in for a treat. It's called *The Hitchhiker's Guide to the Galaxy* by Douglas Adams,[1] and you can thank me later!)

This seed controls the random number generators that are used to ensure that data shuffling, dropout, and weight initialization are random, yet still reproducible and deterministic.

You can see this in the `SFTConfig` here:

```
training_args = SFTConfig(
    # ... other arguments ...
    seed=42,
    data_seed=42,  # Controls data sampling/shuffling separately
)
```

Next up, and not always obvious, is library versions. It's good to pin the ones that you use. This code uses a lot of dependencies, and those dependencies have dependencies, and so on. It's turtles all the way down. Small differences in these library versions can change your results, so as you are building a system for reproducibility, it's good to keep track. A *requirements.txt* file or pip freeze output alongside your training script can help others reproduce your results.

Finally there's hardware. Be aware that even with seeds set, different GPU combinations can lead to different results. Two runs with the same seed on the same GPU can produce very similar, but not bit-for-bit identical, results. The libraries (such as CUDA) for the GPUs can also vary in version and results. When the GPU architecture changes, but the libraries stay the same, you can't always trust same-versioned libraries to give the same results. So, if your model's quality changes drastically when you change random seeds, your result is fragile and you may need to adjust your training setup!

1 Douglas Adams, *The Hitchhiker's Guide to the Galaxy* (London: Barker, 1979).

Other Training Techniques

In earlier chapters, we looked at other training techniques, such as Unsloth, and you can, of course, use these too. While I focused on Hugging Face libraries here, you can find an Unsloth version of the code in the book's download. Most of the code is very similar; you just need to replace some libraries with Unsloth instead of SFT.

Summary

In this chapter, you looked at the complete training loop to fine-tune a LoRA adapter on a Gemma base model using the medical Q&A dataset we've been working on over the past few chapters. You used QLoRA for VRAM efficiency and the Hugging Face stack—primarily the TRL library's `SFTTrainer` and `SFTConfig`.

You also looked at critical hyperparameters, including the learning rate with a cosine decay schedule, and balanced stability and memory with gradient accumulation. All in all, you were able to aggressively fit training into smaller GPUs.

This chapter gives you the tools for how to approach fine-tuning across different models and datasets, and hopefully takes you most of the way there!

In Chapter 9, we'll look at saving your work and, more importantly, how you can try out the new adapter by applying it on top of the base model, as well as explore ways to evaluate the performance of your new adapter.

CHAPTER 9

Using the Adapter

In Chapter 8, you trained an adapter for a Gemma model using SFT. You saw nice loss curves that matched training and validation loss closely, and were confident that the model was learning and generalizing. But you ended up with a folder full of files on disk! Now what? Well, that folder is the fine-tuned model—the patch that you'll put on top of Gemma to get it to be a medical Q&A expert, or at least one that understands the limited data in our training set.

In this chapter, you'll go through the steps to use those adapters, understanding the files, applying them to the base model, and testing them. By the end of this chapter, you'll have a working inference pipeline for your adapter, a repeatable evaluation protocol that can score the fine-tuned version against the base model, and, by extension, a framework you can reuse for every future fine-tuning project.

The Anatomy of an Adapter

When you finished training with SFT in Chapter 8, the `trainer.save_model("./adapters/medical-qa-v1")` call wrote a directory to disk. If you're using Colab, that directory exists in ephemeral storage that you'll lose once you disconnect. So, before you do anything else, you need to understand what those files are, what they do, why they're small, and most importantly, how to move them somewhere safer!

Inside the directory, you should see something like this:

```
adapters/medical-qa-v1/
├── README.md
├── adapter_config.json
├── adapter_model.safetensors
├── chat_template.jinja
├── tokenizer.json
```

```
├── tokenizer_config.json
└── training_args.bin
```

It's about 71 MB in total, half of which is the tokenizer and not the adapter itself. The part that stores the final results of all of your hard training work—every step of gradient descent, every batch, every epoch—is the file called *adapter_model.safetensors*. It should be about 39 MB in size if you're following along with my data. It's surprisingly small, because, remember that it is not a model in itself. It's a patch that you'll apply on top of one!

You can see the anatomy of these in Figure 9-1.

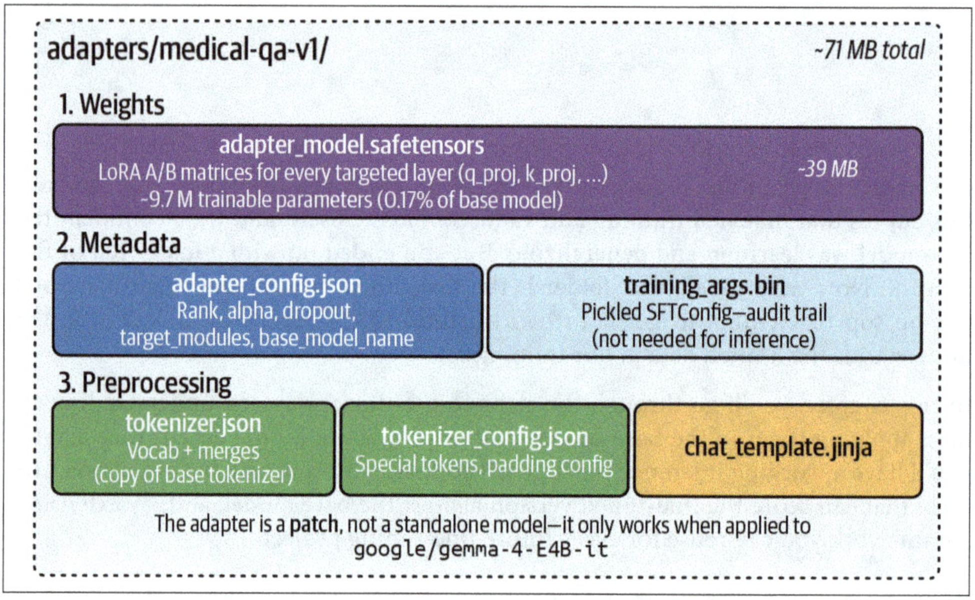

Figure 9-1. Adapter files breakdown

Let's explore each of these files in the following sections.

The Adapter for the Model

As mentioned in the previous section, the primary payload—the adapter you've just trained—is *adapter_model.safetensors*. It contains all the learned LoRA matrices, namely the A and B tensors for every layer you targeted in your LoRA Config. In Chapter 7, you explored the projection layers of Gemma (`q_proj`, `k_proj`, `v_proj`, `o_proj`, `gate_proj`, `up_proj`, `down_proj`). At rank 4, each targeted layer adds two low-rank matrices, one of shape (in_features, 4) and one of shape (4, out_features). Add all of these up across the Gemma 4 E4B model, and you get roughly 9.7 million trainable parameters, or about 0.17% of the model.

The file uses the *.safetensors* format, which is a very effective one for storing tensors (see the following Note). As its name suggests it is "safe." The older PyTorch *.bin* format (which uses Python's pickler) could execute arbitrary code when loaded. With a *.safetensors* file, you're protected from this! It's also self-describing, where the file starts with a JSON header with details of the tensor names, shapes, and types. You can inspect a *.safetensors* file without loading the entire thing.

> The *.safetensors* file format is deliberately simple. It's three parts laid end-to-end: with 8 bytes giving the length of the header; then a JSON header mapping each tensor's name to its type, shape, and location within the file; and then the raw tensors themselves. It doesn't contain any embedded code or serialized Python objects. There's nothing executable, hence "safe."

Here's an example:

```
from safetensors import safe_open

with safe_open("./adapters/medical-qa-v1/adapter_model.safetensors",
               framework="pt") as f:
    for key in f.keys():
        tensor = f.get_tensor(key)
        print(f"{key:80s} {tuple(tensor.shape)} {tensor.dtype}")
```

When you run it, you'll see a pattern like this:

```
base_model.model.model.language_model.layers.0.mlp.down_proj.lora_A.weight
    (4, 10240) torch.float32
base_model.model.model.language_model.layers.0.mlp.down_proj.lora_B.weight
    (2560, 4) torch.float32
base_model.model.model.language_model.layers.0.mlp.gate_proj.lora_A.weight
    (4, 2560) torch.float32
base_model.model.model.language_model.layers.0.mlp.gate_proj.lora_B.weight
    (10240, 4) torch.float32
base_model.model.model.language_model.layers.0.mlp.up_proj.lora_A.weight
    (4, 2560) torch.float32
base_model.model.model.language_model.layers.0.mlp.up_proj.lora_B.weight
    (10240, 4) torch.float32
```

Notice the structure—for every targeted linear layer, there are two tensors, `lora_A` and `lora_B`. The A matrix projects the original hidden dimension down to rank 4. The B matrix projects 4 right back up to the output dimension. The product B × A is the delta that gets added to the frozen base weights at inference time.

Look at the shapes for the `down_proj` example at the beginning. A is `(4, 10240)`, which takes the 10,240-dimension MLP intermediate and compresses it to rank 4. B is `(2560, 4)`, which then projects rank 4 up to the 2,560-dimension hidden size of the model. Between `gate_proj` and `up_proj`, this direction is reversed. This is part of the architecture of Gemma, which you can explore as its multilayer perceptron (MLP) block.

You can see `language_model` in each of the names. This is a Gemma quirk that you may not see in other models. Recall that Gemma is a multimodal model, so its parameters are nested inside of a `language_model` submodule with a parallel `vision_tower` one for images that we're not adapting here. When you load a model at inference time, PEFT will walk the base model's module tree, and match the leaf names (like `down_proj`, `up_proj`, etc.) so the extra prefix is invisible. It's a useful reminder that your mileage may vary in the output names across different models and architectures.

Also note that the `dtype` (data type) is float32, and not the bfloat16 you might expect because you loaded the model in bfloat16 and likely trained with `bf16=True` in your code. You might expect, as a result, that the weights would also be bfloat16. The point of `bf16=True` isn't that *every* tensor gets converted to bf16, but that the activations and computations are cast to that during the forward and backward passes, while the master weights stay in float32. This is where the speed and memory wins would be achieved, as the calculations that require VRAM are during the forward and backward passes.

So, when `trainer.save_model()` writes out the adapter, it preserves the float32 precision, so that the on-disk file will reflect the master weights in the base model. The practical consequence of this is that the file is larger, but when you later apply the adapter, you don't need to worry about data conversion.

The Adapter Config JSON File

The *adapter_config.json* file tells the PEFT library how to reconstruct the adapter. If you take a look at it in a text editor, you'll see many name/value pairs with adapter configuration. Here are some examples:

```
{
    "base_model_name_or_path": "google/gemma-4-E4B-it",
    "peft_type": "LORA",
    "r": 4,
    "lora_alpha": 4,
    "lora_bias": false,
    "lora_dropout": 0.2,
    "peft_version": "0.19.1",
    "inference_mode": true
}
```

Much of this should look familiar. Almost every field is a decision you made in Chapter 7, and it's preserved in this file to make it easy to reproduce the adapter. Note the `inference_mode` flag was set to true when you saved the model, to indicate that when the adapter is loaded, you no longer need dropout as it's no longer training. The `peft_version` field is there for compatibility, so if a future version of PEFT changes the adapter format, this will help the loader know how to interpret it.

The Tokenizer Files

There are two JSON files: *tokenizer.json* and *tokenizer_config.json* that define the tokenizer and are copied wholesale from the base model. At around 32 MB, the *tokenizer.json* file is one of the bigger files in the folder, and about the same size as the adapter! It might feel wasteful, but it's important to include it. If you ever fine-tune a model and deliberately add new tokens, the adapter folder will contain the modified tokenizer and your inference pipeline will need to know it without needing to figure out which tokenizer to use. In this case, we didn't add any new tokens, so the tokenizer will be identical to the one that was bundled with the base model. So if disk space matters, you can safely delete them and the base ones will be used. I would recommend that you keep them, though, particularly if you want to share the adapter, as they keep it self-contained.

The Chat Template

The *chat_template.jinja* file is the template that formats messages into the structure that the base model expects. This is also a copy from the base model, preserved so that the adapter can be self-contained. If you used a custom system prompt during training, this template may have been modified, so by keeping it with the adapter files, the loader can pick up the modified version automatically.

The Training Args

The `SFTConfig` object that defined the training loop is pickled into a single binary file called *training_args.bin*. This isn't needed for inference, but if you ever want to reproduce the training loop, it's priceless. Months from now, when you're trying to remember the hyperparameters for your v1 adapter, you can just open it up and all the answers are there. Consider it to be the logbook of your training run!

Downloading Your Adapter

If you trained your adapter using Colab, you'll face the threat of losing all your hard work if you don't download it. Runtimes disconnect after some time of idleness, and disk contents get deleted. If you have been training for some time and forgot to save the adapter, it would all be for nothing!

Let's explore some options for saving it.

Download as a ZIP

The fastest and easiest way is to zip up the adapter folder, and then download that to your local machine. Here's some example code to do just that:

```
import os
from google.colab import files

output_filename = "medical-qa-v1-adapter.zip"
zip_command = f"zip -r {output_filename} ./adapters/medical-qa-v1"
os.system(zip_command)
files.download(output_filename)

print(f"Successfully created and downloaded {output_filename}")
```

The built-in files API in Colab gives you download functionality, and calling `files.download` will trigger a browser download of the archive. You'll get a single file that you can then save where you want. Before you do anything else, zip and download!

Mount Google Drive

Another way, which is particularly useful for very long training runs where you may not have the ability to run the download-as-ZIP cell before the notebook expires, is to mount a Google Drive to Colab, and then automatically save the model there when it's done training. Accomplish this like so:

```
from google.colab import drive
drive.mount('/content/drive')

# Save training output straight to Google Drive
trainer.save_model("/content/drive/MyDrive/adapters/medical-qa-v1")
```

The adapter now lives on your Google Drive, and can be persisted across different runtimes. Do note that the file I/O if you do this is slower, so if you're saving checkpoints every so often it's fine, but you shouldn't point the trainer's output directory to `drive`, as the process will slow to a crawl. Train to local storage, and save occasional checkpoints or the final adapter to `drive` once it's done.

Push to Hugging Face Hub

For serious work, the Hugging Face Hub (*https://huggingface.co*) is the right home for an adapter. It gives you versioning, public and private visibility, model cards, and an easy URL to share with others. Uploading is pretty simple:

```
from huggingface_hub import login, create_repo, upload_folder

login()  # prompts for your HF token
create_repo("your-username/medical-qa-v1-gemma4-lora",
```

```
                exist_ok=True)

upload_folder(
    repo_id="your-username/medical-qa-v1-gemma4-lora",
    folder_path="./adapters/medical-qa-v1",
    commit_message="Initial upload of medical Q&A adapter",
)
```

Change `your-username` to your Hugging Face username, and now your adapter will be hosted at a publicly hosted URL. Also, loading it is super simple, as the `PeftModel` object has a `from_pretrained` method that you just send to the URL of the adapter. Note the `private` setting; if your model is trained on data you don't want public, you can default to this, and then flip it to `public` when you're deliberately sharing.

Using the Adapter

Now that your adapter is safely backed up, you can put it to work. Loading a LoRA adapter for inference is a three-step process. First, load the base model; then you load the tokenizer for that model and adapter, then you attach the adapter. To load it from the directory where you saved it is pretty straightforward; simply specify where the base model comes from, where the tokenizer comes from, and then apply the adapter to the base model. Here's the code:

```
import torch
from transformers import AutoModelForCausalLM, AutoTokenizer
from peft import PeftModel

# Step 1: Load the base model
model_name = "google/gemma-4-E4B-it"
base_model = AutoModelForCausalLM.from_pretrained(
    model_name,
    torch_dtype=torch.bfloat16,
    device_map="auto",
)

# Step 2: Load the tokenizer (from the adapter folder, so you pick up
# any custom tokens or chat template changes)
tokenizer = AutoTokenizer.from_pretrained("./adapters/medical-qa-v1")

# Step 3: Attach the adapter
model = PeftModel.from_pretrained(base_model, "./adapters/medical-qa-v1")
```

Step 3 is where the magic happens. Internally, PEFT will walk the base model's module tree, and for every module where its name matches a `target_modules` entry in the adapter config, it will wrap the original layer with a `LoRALayer` that holds the A and B matrices. The original weights are frozen, and the LoRA weights are loaded from your *.safetensors* file. The result is a single model object whose forward pass exhibits the fine-tuned behavior.

You can see this in Figure 9-2.

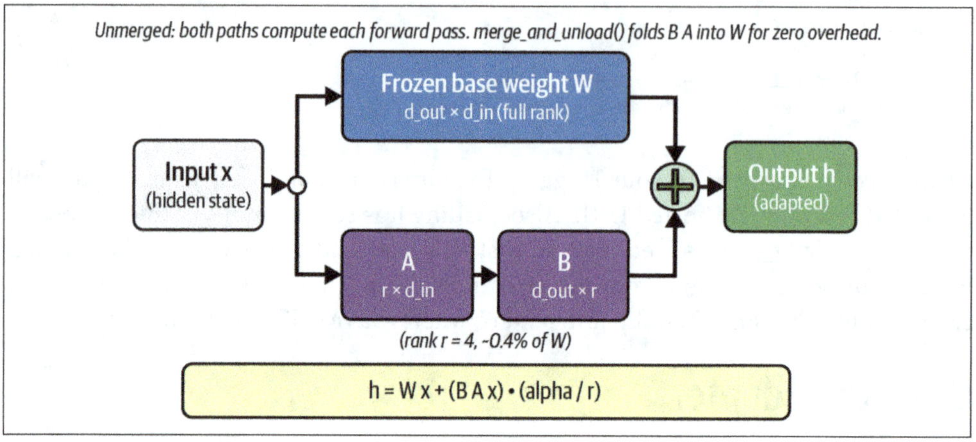

Figure 9-2. Applying a LoRA adapter for inference

Of course, the code is easy to modify if you want to load your adapter from the Hugging Face Hub. You simply have to specify the `adapter_repo` URL and use that to load the tokenizer and model instead:

```
adapter_repo = "lmoroney/medical-qa-v1-gemma4-lora"

# Step 2: Load the tokenizer from the adapter repo (picks up any
# custom tokens or chat template you saved alongside the weights)
tokenizer = AutoTokenizer.from_pretrained(adapter_repo)

# Step 3: Attach the adapter directly from the Hub
model = PeftModel.from_pretrained(base_model, adapter_repo)
```

Under the hood, the `PeftModel` will pull the adapter into your local Hugging Face cache (usually *~/.cache/huggingface/hub*) and then load them from there. On a reasonable internet connection, this should only take a few seconds.

Do note the issue with private repos. Earlier, when pushing it, the code used `private=True`, so this means you will have to be authenticated before the load will succeed. The easiest way to do this is to run `huggingface_hub.login()` once per session, or have a valid `HF_TOKEN` in your environment.

If you are using Colab, you can set the `HF_TOKEN` as a secret. On the left-hand nav, you'll see a "key" icon. Select it, and you'll have a dialog where you can set this. That way, you don't have to keep providing the value every time. It's the equivalent of setting an environment variable.

Alternatively, you can pass your token when loading the pretrained adapter like this:

```
model = PeftModel.from_pretrained(
    base_model, adapter_repo, token="hf_...",
)
```

But I wouldn't recommend this, lest you push the code to a repository and it has your Hugging Face token in it!

Merging the Adapter

This approach allows you to ship the adapter and then run code to merge it at inference time. For simplicity, you may also want to merge the adapter into the model and get a *new* set of model weights with the adapter added. This process will fold the LoRA deltas back into the base weights, giving you a single model without managing the adapter overhead:

```
model = model.merge_and_unload()
```

After this call, the LoRA modules are gone. What is left is a plain `AutoModelForCausalLM` object with the modified weights for every adapted layer. You can save this merged model as a standalone checkpoint, and serve it like any other Gemma instance.

The upsides are zero inference overhead, deployment is simpler, and it will be compatible with any serving stack that doesn't know about PEFT! The downsides, of course, are that you'll lose the ability to switch adapters at runtime, and that you'll take up a lot more disk space.

But it *is* a nice option under some circumstances, and worth looking into for however you want to design your inference system.

Testing Inference with an Adapter

Before you go too much further, once you've applied your adapter to your base model, you probably want to make sure the adapter is both working *and* providing a different answer from the base model. For our medical Q&A adapter, let's test it out. To do so, first we'll load the base model and ask it a medical question, like this:

```
import torch
from transformers import AutoModelForCausalLM, AutoTokenizer


model_name = "google/gemma-4-E4B-it"
adapter_path = "./adapters/medical-qa-v1"

tokenizer = AutoTokenizer.from_pretrained(adapter_path)

model = AutoModelForCausalLM.from_pretrained(
```

```
    model_name, torch_dtype=torch.bfloat16, device_map="auto",
)

prompt = "What are the common symptoms of hypothyroidism?"

messages = [{"role": "user", "content": prompt}]
input_text = tokenizer.apply_chat_template(
    messages, tokenize=False, add_generation_prompt=True,
)
inputs = tokenizer(input_text, return_tensors="pt").to(model.device)

with torch.no_grad():
    outputs = model.generate(
        **inputs, max_new_tokens=512,
        temperature=0.7, top_p=0.9, do_sample=True,
    )

response = tokenizer.decode(
    outputs[0][inputs["input_ids"].shape[1]:], skip_special_tokens=True,
)
print("BASE MODEL:")
print(response)
```

One thing to note is that I just load the tokenizer from the adapter path. That's okay because it's unchanged, and if I have it there already, it just saves an additional download. The response you'll get from this will be the typical LLM response that tries to be conversational, followed by markdown containing a long bullet list of details. It should look a little like this:

```
BASE MODEL:
Hypothyroidism, which means the thyroid gland isn't producing enough thyroid
hormone, can manifest in a wide variety of ways because the thyroid hormone
regulates so many bodily functions. Symptoms can be subtle and easily mistaken
for other conditions, which is why regular check-ups are important.

Here is a comprehensive list of the common symptoms, categorized by the body
system they affect:

---

### 🧠 Mental and Cognitive Symptoms
These are often among the earliest and most overlooked signs.
* **Fatigue and Lethargy:** Persistent, overwhelming tiredness that isn't
    relieved by rest.
* **Brain Fog:** Difficulty concentrating, forgetfulness, and feeling mentally
    slow.
* **Depression or Mood Changes:** Feeling sluggish, anxious, or experiencing
    persistent low moods.
* **Slowed Thinking:** A general feeling of mental slowness.

<truncated>
```

It'll be much longer, but I've truncated it here to give you the idea.

Next, you can apply the adapter with similar code to what we saw earlier, but we'll do an identical inference:

```
from peft import PeftModel

model = AutoModelForCausalLM.from_pretrained(
    model_name, torch_dtype=torch.bfloat16, device_map="auto",
)
model = PeftModel.from_pretrained(model, adapter_path)

inputs = tokenizer(input_text, return_tensors="pt").to(model.device)

with torch.no_grad():
    outputs = model.generate(
        **inputs, max_new_tokens=512,
        temperature=0.7, top_p=0.9, do_sample=True,
    )

response = tokenizer.decode(
    outputs[0][inputs["input_ids"].shape[1]:], skip_special_tokens=True,
)
print("FINE-TUNED MODEL:")
print(response)
```

When running in Colab, I noticed that often the adapters would not get applied if I ran this immediately after the previous model inference. If that happens, I've provided code to ensure the model is deleted and garbage collected, then reloaded and the adapter applied. Otherwise you'll get *exactly* the same answer as the unadapted model.

Given that our dataset for fine-tuning was much more of a clipped Q&A format instead of a conversational format, the response is generally more curt and straight to the point:

```
FINE-TUNED MODEL:
Common signs of hypothyroidism include weight gain without changes in diet,
feeling cold more than usual, fatigue, constipation, dry skin, hair loss,
slow or irregular heartbeat, muscle aches, and mood changes such as
depression. In some cases, you may also notice a puffy face or swelling
around the eyes. If you notice any of these symptoms, it's important to
consult a healthcare professional for proper testing and evaluation.
```

This shift in style is what you're looking for. If the responses are identical, or near identical, it suggests the adapter didn't load, so you can do the delete/collect garbage trick I used previously. If the fine-tuned response is completely incoherent, something went wrong in your training, with the usual suspects being a tokenizer mismatch or the wrong chat template was used.

One other note: I used `do_sample=True` in the preceding code, so that the wording would vary slightly between sessions to make it more realistic. If you want deterministic output, you can set this to `False` instead.

Going Beyond Eyeball Testing

Here's the honest truth about fine-tuning: eyeballing some simple prompts and declaring victory is how most fine-tunes die in production. A fine-tune that looks great on five curated examples can fail catastrophically on the sixth. So, before you try something in production, you need some more rigor in testing and evaluating it.

The next few sections will walk you through some evaluation methods that you can use on real projects, arranged from cheapest to most expensive:

Side-by-side comparison
: Use with a held-out set of prompts, inspected manually.

Perplexity and loss
: Use on a held-out validation set, computed automatically.

LLM-as-a-judge
: Use where a stronger model grades your fine-tune's answers.

Domain-specific benchmarks
: These are built from the medical Q&A data itself.

You can use any of these separately or together, and many professional fine-tuning projects use all four, in combination. Let's discuss them more in the following sections.

Side-by-Side Comparison

This is just a simple expansion on what you did in the previous section, where you get answers from the LLM with and without the adapter and do an eyeball comparison. Earlier, we just asked one question, but the best approach is to ask many and see if you can spot discrepancies.

Simply set up a list of questions (an LLM can generate this for you) like this:

```
medical_qa_prompts = [
    "What are the common symptoms of influenza?",
    "Explain the role of insulin in the human body.",
    "What is hypertension and how is it managed?",
    "Describe the benefits of regular exercise for cardiovascular health.",
    "What are the signs of a severe allergic reaction and what should be done?",
]
```

This example has only five questions, but you should use a lot more. I'd recommend *at least* 100. The mechanics are the same regardless of length. You would then modify the one-off code from earlier to use a helper function to do the inference, and iterate through each question giving the answer:

```
def generate_response(model_to_use, tokenizer_to_use, prompt_text):
    messages = [{"role": "user", "content": prompt_text}]
    input_text = tokenizer_to_use.apply_chat_template(
        messages, tokenize=False, add_generation_prompt=True
    )
    inputs = tokenizer_to_use(input_text, return_tensors="pt").to(
        model_to_use.device
    )
    with torch.no_grad():
        outputs = model_to_use.generate(
            **inputs,
            max_new_tokens=256,
            temperature=0.7,
            top_p=0.9,
            do_sample=True,
        )
    return tokenizer_to_use.decode(
        outputs[0][inputs["input_ids"].shape[1]:],
        skip_special_tokens=True,
    )


for prompt in medical_qa_prompts:
    print("=" * 80)
    print(f"PROMPT: {prompt}")
    print("-" * 80)
    print("BASE MODEL:")
    print(generate_response(base_model, base_tokenizer, prompt))
    print("-" * 80)
    print("FINE-TUNED MODEL:")
    print(generate_response(finetuned_model, finetuned_tokenizer, prompt))
    print()
```

As you're testing, you can also set the `temperature` to `0.0` and/or `do_sample=False` to get deterministic output. When satisfied with that, then the higher temperatures (like 0.7 and above) will help you see whether the model's output is too random.

Do the same, with the same questions for the adapted version, and perform the same eyeball test—are the fine-tuned answers more succinct and straight to the point? If so, then the adapter is working. If a significant number of them are not, then you may need to retrain the adapter. The likely reason for that situation is that the dataset you trained with was too small, so the model falls back to its default behavior for some questions.

Another thing to check is if the fine-tuned model actually answers the question! This might require a little thought, and support from a professional (or at least a larger LLM) to ensure that the answer is in the right ballpark. This is, of course, a massive risk if you're building a real medical Q&A, so please do *not* put this adapter into production. We're only doing it as a learning mechanism, not a real-world app.

One more eyeball check is to see whether the adapted model produces a *full* response, or does it trail off after a sentence or two. Does it clip the answer? If the answers in your training set are short, the model will have learned to imitate them and stop early, so you may need to add longer examples. A LoRA rank that's too small may also limit how much of the response style the adapter picks up.

Finally, remember that the base Gemma 4 has been safety-tuned to *decline* some medical advice. Aggressive fine-tuning may weaken those safeguards, but they could still be there. When testing, try to find questions that hit against these safeguards, and compare the base model with your fine-tuned one. You might want your adapted model to refuse to answer the same questions as the base one.

Good advice is to always note your impressions somewhere. Keep a copy, and revisit it every time you retrain and update.

Measuring Perplexity

Side-by-side comparison is a good start, but it can be inaccurate, and of course, is very subjective. For a more quantitative approach, you can compute the model's *perplexity* (see Chapter 4) on a held-out set of medical Q&A examples. This number is calculated by starting with the evaluation loss that we had in our logs from training. Perplexity starts with simply taking the `exp(eval_loss)`. The mathematical reasoning behind this is a rough intuition of exploring how "surprised" the model is by the correct answer, with lower scores being better.

So, for example, this code will compute perplexity for a model against a dataset:

```
def compute_perplexity(model, tokenizer, dataset, max_length=1024):
    model.eval()
    total_loss = 0.0
    total_tokens = 0

    for example in dataset:
        messages = [
            {"role": "user", "content": example["question"]},
            {"role": "assistant", "content": example["answer"]},
        ]
        text = tokenizer.apply_chat_template(
            messages, tokenize=False, add_generation_prompt=False,
        )
        inputs = tokenizer(
            text, return_tensors="pt",
            truncation=True, max_length=max_length,
        ).to(model.device)
        labels = inputs["input_ids"].clone()
```

```
        with torch.no_grad():
            outputs = model(**inputs, labels=labels)

        total_loss += outputs.loss.item() * inputs["input_ids"].numel()
        total_tokens += inputs["input_ids"].numel()

    return math.exp(total_loss / total_tokens)
```

One thing to note is that the process used to generate the synthetic data that we've used can generate data that looks and feels similar in tone and approach. This can give you very good perplexity scores, even if you're using data that you withheld from training. To that end, I recommend getting data to *really* test perplexity from a different source. In the code download for this book, I'm providing a notebook called *Chapter9_GenerateSamplesMedQA.ipynb* that generates a whole different set of questions and answers using a dataset called *MedQA*. This will give a more accurate feel for what you might encounter in the real world, where people would prompt your model in many varied ways. I also provide a dataset that I created with that notebook.

Running this unseen dataset through the base model to calculate the perplexity score gave a value of 27.412. This is the base model's score, without any fine-tuning, running against data that it didn't previously see.

During training, we saw that the *validation loss*, where it was testing the model against data that wasn't in the training set was 1.016 (see Chapter 8), and the exp of that is about 2.76, so we can see a marked improvement against the types of questions and answers we have in our synthetic dataset.

The real test then becomes how it would perform against data that it has never previously seen, and which may be structured very differently from the synthetic data. Taking 100 records from *MedQA* (which I have provided as *test_set.jsonl*) and running them through the base model with our adapter applied, using the same code, gave a score of 8.446.

What can we derive from this? First, the score of the adapted version of the model is impressive; the perplexity fell from 27.412 (on the base model) to 8.446 (on the adapted one), which is about a 69% improvement! Earlier we saw the validation set perplexity is 2.76, so our 8.446 is close to 3× that.

This is quite healthy. A good rule of thumb is if it is between 1 and 2 your results are probably too good, and you should investigate your data for leakage before celebrating too much. Between 2 and 4 means you're in healthy generalization; and above 6, you're likely overfitting. It's overspecialized to the training data.

The bottom line: perplexity measurement signals that our fine-tuned model is in good shape!

Now let's go over a few caveats. First, the function we used is quite simplistic in that it loads the question and the answer as a single conversation and asks the model to predict the whole thing *including* the user side. That will inflate the perplexity slightly. To be more rigorous (if you are publishing a paper about your model, for example), you will want to mask the user portion so that the loss is only computed over the predicted tokens.

Second, is that perplexity can be very sensitive to tokenization. Make sure you use the adapter's tokenizer consistently.

Finally, while it's nice to improve on perplexity, this is not *enough* to validate that your adapter is working as well as you might want. There are always gotchas. Working with language has many nuances, and using synthetic data for language training, like we did here, can lead you down a path of false security. It's good to test further, and in the next section, we'll look at using an LLM-as-a-judge.

LLM-as-a-Judge

The perplexity measurement you just did tells you how well your model performs against held-out different values than it saw during training and validation. What it does *not* tell you is whether the fine-tuned model's answers are *better*! Different models can have the same perplexity and can produce very different outputs.

To evaluate the *quality* of an answer, an approach you can follow is simply to use an LLM-as-a-judge. Take a frontier model like GPT, Gemini, or Claude, and have it grade your fine-tuned model's outputs against a reference answer, or against the base model's output. Do note that scores from LLMs are highly sensitive to different biases and prompt framing. These models often systematically prefer verbosity, particular reasoning styles, and even outputs that resemble their alignment techniques.

Figure 9-3 shows the flow for this.

The process is pretty straightforward. Take a number of held-out questions and pass them through both the base model and the fine-tuned model to get a set of answers. Then, take these answers and present them to the judge model, along with the "golden" reference answer, asking for an opinion on which is more clinically accurate.

This golden answer is typically formed by human experts, from established datasets, or from a stronger model with human review, in that order. You should treat it as the highest quality answer you can get.

Take the results from the model, and tally them to get a verdict. Experimentation showed me a win-rate of about 73% for the fine-tuned model. (The *test_set.jsonl* file I provide in the download, generated from the *MedQA* dataset, has both questions and answers; you can use these answers as the reference.)

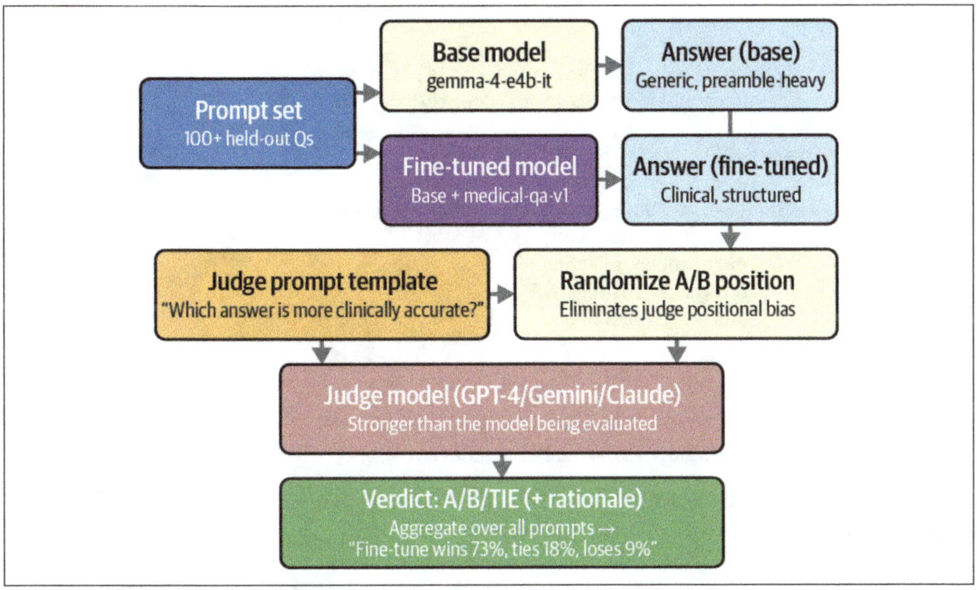

Figure 9-3. LLM-as-a-judge flow

So not only is the fine-tune *working* (the language changed), not only is it *confident* (the perplexity is low), but it is also more *accurate* (the answers are "judged" to be better)!

Code that prompts a foundation model to do this is very straightforward. Here's an example using the OpenAI APIs:

```
import os
from openai import OpenAI

judge = OpenAI(api_key=os.environ["OPENAI_API_KEY"])

JUDGE_PROMPT = """You are grading two answers to a medical question.

Question: {question}

Reference answer: {reference}

Answer A: {answer_a}

Answer B: {answer_b}

Which answer is more clinically accurate, complete, and well-structured?
Consider factual correctness, coverage of relevant details, appropriate
caveats, and absence of dangerous misinformation.

Respond with exactly one of: "A", "B", or "TIE".
Then on a new line, give a one-sentence explanation.
```

```
"""

def judge_pair(question, reference, answer_a, answer_b):
    response = judge.chat.completions.create(
        model="gpt-4o-mini",
        messages=[{
            "role": "user",
            "content": JUDGE_PROMPT.format(
                question=question,
                reference=reference,
                answer_a=answer_a,
                answer_b=answer_b,
            ),
        }],
        temperature=0.0,
    )
    return response.choices[0].message.content
```

Again, it's a very strong signal that our fine-tune is working well. But a few best practices to consider are:

- Randomize the position. You might hit positional bias within the foundation model you are using to be the judge! It's good practice to randomize the position of your answers (i.e., don't always have the base model as answer A and the fine-tuned one as answer B).
- Use a strong judge, ideally stronger than the base model, and the stronger the better. If your base model is 4B, and the judge is also 4B, you will learn very little. It's worth the token costs to use a large model like Gemini, Claude, or GPT to handle the judgment.
- Try to use a dataset that has reference answers. Otherwise, you might end up just getting the opinion of the judge based on its own training dataset and how it learned.
- Run the test multiple times to smooth out spikes. But be careful of API costs!
- Ideally, use data from the held-out dataset that is uniquely yours and has never been exposed to the internet, so you know for certain that it's not in the training set of the judge.

Domain-Specific Benchmarks

All of the methods we've just discussed for testing are really valuable in your lab environment, and work really well for the somewhat contrived approach we've taken in putting together a scenario where you can *learn* how to fine-tune. In a real-world environment with real-world data, you will need to consider much more domain-specific benchmarks that apply to your situation.

There's no one-size-fits-all approach; you simply have to exercise your domain knowledge, but there are a few patterns that might give you some guidance, and I'll cover them here.

First is to come up with a new set of data where the answers are a well-known list of items that one can choose from. For example, in our medical Q&A, you would have a human expert come up with a set of questions and answers, where the answer is a well-known list of symptoms for that condition. When you have this, you can compare the model's output with the list through a simple string match to calculate a recall score.

Second is to come up with a new set of data with your human expert companion where the question is open-ended; for example, "Explain how insulin regulates blood sugar." Compare their golden answer with the base model and fine-tuned model answers using an LLM-as-a-judge, like we covered in the previous section.

Third, and perhaps the most important, is to come up with a set of prompts with golden answers where safety is an issue. In a medical scenario, like this one, not only is the accuracy important, but it also provides further guidance. Sometimes it's best just not to answer, but to steer the user appropriately; for example, "I'm not a doctor, I'm an AI model, so please consult a real doctor for this issue."

Finally, there is general knowledge and general language understanding. You want to try your model against sets that aren't as narrow as its training set. Your goal is to ensure that your fine-tuning didn't degrade its inherent knowledge!

Common Pitfalls

Last, but not least, I'd like to review some of the common pitfalls that happen when you train and deploy LoRA adapters. Some of these are more common than you might think.

Using the wrong base model
: Using the wrong base model, thanks to confusing naming, certainly has been known to happen. For example, you might have trained your adapter against `google/gemma-4-E4B-it`, but someone loads it against `google/gemma-4-E4B`. PEFT may not complain, because the shapes might match. But, the adapter, despite loading, will produce nonsense! So, always ensure that the base model in your *adapter_config.json* matches the base model you're loading, and ensure your users know this, too!

Using mismatched data types
: Mismatched `dtypes` can be an insidious problem. Be sure to use the same numeric system throughout. PEFT might handle differences between float16 and bfloat16 gracefully, but on some GPUs you'll have subtle differences in

the outputs that can change the entire meaning of the output! If you're seeing variations in your outputs when you don't expect them, you can create a set of prompts, run inference on them, and look at the `logits` of the answers to see if there is numeric variation.

Not applying the chat template before generating
: The chat template is super important. Generating without applying it can produce dramatically different outputs from the fine-tuned model. Always format with the template. Debug by printing the raw output and confirm that the appropriate turn markers are present.

Using merged or multiple adapters
: A merged adapter cannot be unmerged. Once you call `merge_and_unload()`, there's no going back; your LoRA adapters have been merged into the base weights. It's also important to note that it's possible to have multiple adapters for different tasks and to hot swap them at inference time. It's a powerful pattern, but fraught with bad possibilities where it's easy to get it wrong. Until you're confident and have built expertise in the test lab, I'd encourage you to stick with one adapter at a time!

Impact of Using QLoRA

Before we wrap up, it's worth connecting this chapter back to how the adapter was trained, because the same trick that made training affordable also transforms deployment. In Chapter 8, you trained with QLoRA: the base model quantized to 4-bit NF4, with the LoRA adapter in full precision on top. That exact combination works at inference time too, and in practice, it's how many fine-tuned models actually get served. Load the base in 4-bit, attach your adapter unmerged, and Gemma 4 E4B drops from around 16 GB to the 6- to 8-GB range, comfortably inside a "prosumer" GPU that could never host the full-precision model. The quality cost of 4-bit inference is small (recall the benchmarks we discussed in Chapter 7), and the adapter itself is untouched; your carefully trained weights still run at full precision, applied on top of the quantized base.

There are two things to know before adopting this as your default. First, `merge_and_unload()` is off the table; you cannot fold full-precision deltas into 4-bit weights, so the adapter stays attached as a separate module. The per-token overhead of running it alongside the base is real but rarely noticeable, and in exchange you keep the ability to hot-swap adapters over a single loaded base model, which is exactly the multitask serving pattern we'll return to in Chapter 15.

Second, and more important, evaluate within the configuration you deploy. If you measured perplexity and ran your LLM-as-a-judge tests against the bf16 base but ship on a 4-bit base, you validated a model you aren't serving. The differences are usually minor, but "usually" is doing a lot of work in a medical application, so rerun your canary prompts and at least the perplexity check in the deployment configuration before calling it done.

The broader pattern is worth internalizing as you take this workflow to your own projects; precision is now a deployment decision, not a fixed property of the model. One set of adapter weights, trained once, can ride on a bf16 base when quality headroom matters, and a 4-bit base when VRAM is scarce, and your evaluation protocol from this chapter is how you verify each configuration on its own terms.

Summary

You've gone from "I have a bunch of weights in these strange-looking files in Colab" to "I have the beginnings of a deployable, evaluated, trustworthy, fine-tuned model" over the course of the last few pages! You explored all that, and then some.

You looked at the file format, and how the adapter is saved, along with all the metadata around it defining how it relates to the base model. You saw how bundling the tokenizer with the adapter is generally a good idea, as is having a file for the chat template to enable transportation of your adapter to be as self-contained as possible.

Then, you looked at evaluating the model, doing lab tests to ensure that your fine-tune isn't just working, but is working *well.*

In the next chapter, you'll look at alignment and how model behavior is shaped based on subjective qualities (helpfulness, tone, safety, etc.) that aren't captured through measurement alone. Everything you've done here carries forward, and is the foundation for the important work that you'll do next.

CHAPTER 10

Alignment and Preference Optimization

Your fine-tuned model from Chapter 9 knows medical terminology. It can rattle off symptoms of various illnesses, and it's meeting the tone of voice from your Q&A dataset.

But this is just the *start* of communicating effectively; a model that has memorized the right facts can still deliver them in the wrong *tone*. Supervised fine-tuning (SFT) teaches the model *what* to say. Alignment teaches it *how* to say it.

This chapter introduces the techniques that bridge that gap: Reinforcement Learning from Human Feedback (RLHF) and its modern, more practical successor, Direct Preference Optimization (DPO). By the end, you'll understand why alignment is a separate stage from fine-tuning, how to build the preference datasets that drive it, and how to run a DPO training loop on your medical Q&A model—all without significant hardware investments! It's a light introduction to a massive topic, but hopefully will be enough to help you understand how impactful strong alignment can be.

The Gap: From Knowledge to Behavior

If you've been following along through the previous chapters, you have a model that scores well on various benchmarks. It uses precise clinical language. It covers the right symptoms. Using techniques like perplexity, keyword recall, and LLM-as-a-judge metrics, it outperforms the base Gemma on your domain.

So what's left to do?

Consider a prompt like this: "My six-year-old has had a fever of 103°F for two days. What should I do?"

The base, instruction-tuned Gemma 4 will probably give a careful, empathetic answer that involves mentioning when to call a pediatrician, suggesting fluids and rest, and warning about red-flag symptoms that warrant an ER visit. It will hedge appropriately, because it was alignment-trained by Google to do exactly that.

A supervised fine-tune, on the other hand, might respond with something like: "Persistent pyrexia of 39.4°C in a pediatric patient may indicate a bacterial or viral infection. Differential diagnosis includes otitis media, urinary tract infection, pneumonia, and meningitis. Recommend CBC with differential, urinalysis, and blood cultures." That's what it was trained to do!

It's factually correct and quite likely to be clinically sound. But it's completely wrong for the situation! A worried parent doesn't need a differential diagnosis; they need to know whether to drive to the emergency room *right now*.

This is the *alignment* problem in miniature. SFT optimizes a single objective: predict the next token in the training data. If your training data is clinical Q&A written by physicians for physicians, the model learns to write in exactly that way. In our case, the data was generated using code by a foundation model, so it's even "less" human.

It doesn't learn *who* it's talking to, or *what* language is appropriate, or *when* to be cautious versus when to be direct. Those are preferences that can't be captured by a next-token loss function alone.

The broader AI community uses the word "alignment" to describe the grand challenge of making AI systems behave in accordance with human values. It's a huge area of research and development, so with just a single chapter, you're going to explore a narrower, practical version of the same idea. We will take a model that already has the right knowledge and teach it to express that knowledge in a way that matches human (or business) preferences about tone, safety, helpfulness, and style.

RLHF: The Original Pipeline

RLHF is the technique that transformed GPT-3 into ChatGPT, and made a model that outputs statistically relevant tokens into a chat buddy that went viral.

The RLHF *technique* can be implemented in a three-stage pipeline:

Stage 1: Supervised fine-tuning
: Here's where you start with a pretrained model and fine-tune it on high-quality demonstrations of the desired behavior—exactly what you did over the past few chapters. This gives you a model that can produce reasonable outputs but doesn't yet have a strong sense of which way of communicating that "reasonable" output is best.

Stage 2: Reward model training
: To do this, you collect pairs of model outputs for the same prompt and have humans rank them; for example, "For this medical question, Response A is better than Response B." Using this data, you can then train a separate neural network (aka the *reward model*) to predict these human preferences. The reward model takes a prompt and a response and outputs a scalar score indicating how "good" the response is, based on what it learned from the human raters.

Stage 3: Policy optimization
: Use the reward model to fine-tune the SFT model via reinforcement learning, specifically the Proximal Policy Optimization (PPO) algorithm. PPO is a reinforcement-learning algorithm originally developed for robotics and game-playing, whose core idea is to use trial and reward. When the model generates a response, the reward model scores that, and PPO uses that score as a training signal to nudge the model's weights toward higher-scoring outputs. Over lots of these update cycles, the model will gradually learn to produce responses that the humans using it prefer.

RLHF *works*. It's the reason ChatGPT, Claude, and Gemini feel so much more helpful and safe than their base-model predecessors. It's also why the behavior can change over time. Recent news (at the time of writing) about models being too sycophantic can be taken by the model owners and used to tweak the output to be a little less annoying in that way.

But the pipeline is complex. You're training three models (the SFT model, the reward model, and the RL-tuned model), managing two separate datasets (the SFT data and the preference pairs), and dealing with PPO (an RL algorithm notorious for being finicky to tune, sensitive to hyperparameters, and prone to reward hacking where the model finds ways to maximize the reward score without actually producing better responses).

For a team at a frontier lab, this complexity is manageable. But if you, dear reader, are an individual developer fine-tuning a 4B model on a single GPU, it's a lot. Which is why, in 2023, a simpler alternative arrived. It's called DPO, and we'll explore that next.

Direct Preference Optimization

The big idea behind Direct Preference Optimization (DPO) is that you can skip the reward model entirely! Instead of training a reward model and then using RL to optimize against it, DPO changes the RLHF objective so that the preference learning will happen directly on the language model itself.

This is driven by a surprisingly simple approach. In RLHF, the reward model's entire job is to look at a response and predict whether or not a human would like it. But that forgets that the language model already assigns probabilities to every token in its response. So, if Response A is "better" than Response B, you don't need a separate reward model to tell it so. You just give it feedback to ensure that A is given a higher probability than B. The paper (*https://oreil.ly/J6MAr*) that introduced DPO by Rafailov et al. proved mathematically that this approach gives results as good as a full RLHF pipeline, but without the extra complexity of a reward model.

You can see a high-level view of the difference in Figure 10-1.

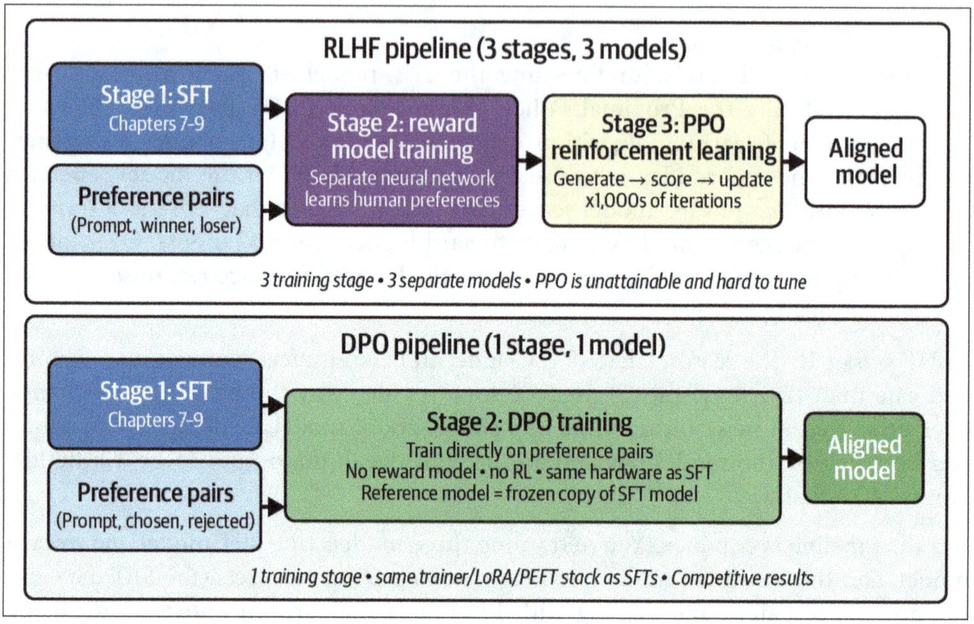

Figure 10-1. How DPO simplifies RLHF

In simpler terms, RLHF is like hiring a food critic (the reward model) to taste dishes and give scores. You then use these scores to train the chef (the language model) about what works best. DPO skips the critic, and instead shows the chef the dishes side-by-side and says "customers preferred this one over that," and lets the chef adjust directly from the comparison. It's the same lesson, but with fewer steps.

In practice, DPO looks a lot like SFT. You have a dataset of prompt, good response, bad response triples. You feed each one through the model with a loss function that encourages the model to assign higher probability to the chosen response and lower to the rejected one.

What's really nice about this is that you have a very simple training pipeline that uses the same hardware and tooling that you used for the fine-tuning to begin with, so you can get up and running quickly! For the rest of this chapter, we'll explore how to implement DPO on our fine-tuned medical Q&A model.

Building a Preference Dataset

When it comes to building this dataset, the gold standard is really to have humans do the annotation. Show a domain expert the questions and the answers—and have them pick the best answer for each question. Better still is to have humans generate the questions and answers also. For a medical Q&A model, this would require multiple physicians to judge clinical accuracy and appropriateness. It's slow and expensive, but worth it.

For learning purposes, you can use a set of synthetic pairs from a teacher model with the same process used to create the synthetic dataset we used to fine-tune the model. For this case, I've provided code that I used to hit a GPT-OSS-120B endpoint to generate responses that are good and bad, and then used a similar model to be the LLM-as-a-judge to label them. I've provided the source code for this in the book's download, but here's a sample of the data that it created:

```
{
  "prompt": "I was just diagnosed with psoriasis a few weeks ago and it's
    overwhelming – can you explain what the common symptoms are and how
    they'll actually appear on my skin?",
  "chosen": "I'm sorry you're having to deal with a new diagnosis – being
    told you have psoriasis can feel overwhelming. Here's a plain-language
    ...",
  "rejected": "Psoriasis is a chronic, immune-mediated keratinocyte
    disorder that most often presents with well-defined erythematous
    plaques covered by silvery-white, adherent scale..."
}
```

This is edited for brevity, but it shows the basic idea: there's a prompt and there are two answers, one of which is chosen and one of which is rejected. In this case, the chosen answer opens with empathy, uses plain language, and gives a structured overview that a layperson can follow. It ends with a clear call to action (not shown in the preceding code) which is to "schedule a follow-up with your dermatologist."

The rejected response isn't *wrong*; it's perfectly competent, but reads like a textbook. Note that the prompt mentioned that the patient is feeling overwhelmed, so the more compassionate beginning to the chosen response clearly makes it the better one.

Ultimately, the preference here is communication and not knowledge. So that's what we'll use in DPO.

Generating the Data

For this, I hosted a GPT-OSS-120B using vLLM at a custom endpoint. I can't share that endpoint with you for obvious reasons! But if you have your own model running at an endpoint you control, you can amend this code easily. If you don't, you can try a smaller model that you can control off your dev box (Gemma 4 26B A4B is excellent), and the concept will be the same, but the data will differ.

Here's the code to create two different answer styles with varying system prompts. The `prompt_text` is created using the same mechanism we used to create the synthetic data back in Chapter 5.

```
from openai import OpenAI

client = OpenAI(base_url=ENDPOINT_URL, api_key=BEARER_TOKEN)

RESPONSE_SYSTEM_A = """You are a board-certified physician answering a
patient's question. Be medically accurate, empathetic, and practical.
Write 150-250 words. Match your language to the patient's level - avoid
unnecessary jargon. Always recommend consulting a healthcare provider
for personalized advice."""

RESPONSE_SYSTEM_B = """You are a medical expert providing a thorough
clinical answer. Be comprehensive and precise. Use appropriate medical
terminology. Cover differential diagnoses or treatment mechanisms where
relevant. Write 150-300 words."""


def generate_candidate_pair(prompt_text):
    """Generate two responses: one patient-friendly, one clinical."""
    resp_a = _call_model(
        RESPONSE_SYSTEM_A,
        f"Patient question: {prompt_text}",
        temperature=0.5, max_tokens=600,
    )
    resp_b = _call_model(
        RESPONSE_SYSTEM_B,
        f"Medical question: {prompt_text}",
        temperature=1.0, max_tokens=800,
    )
    return resp_a.strip(), resp_b.strip()
```

This will return sets of answers to the question with each of the system prompts. You'll now need a judge to determine which is the "best" for your purposes. I like to shuffle the answers before sending them to the judge so there isn't a positional bias in answers.

Here's the code for a judge system for medical Q&A, noting what I considered to be the most important evaluation criteria. For your system, this would change to whatever is most appropriate for you:

```
JUDGE_SYSTEM = """You are an expert medical communicator evaluating two
responses to a patient question. You must decide which response is MORE
APPROPRIATE for the specific person asking.

Evaluation criteria (in order of importance):
1. SAFETY: appropriate caveats and "see a doctor" advice.
2. ACCURACY: medical information is correct.
3. TONE: language is appropriate for the audience.
4. ACTIONABILITY: clear next steps for the person.
```

```
5. COMPLETENESS: adequately addresses the question.

A technically perfect answer at the wrong level is WORSE than a slightly
less detailed answer the patient can actually understand and act on."""


def judge_responses(prompt_text, audience, resp_a, resp_b):
    """Judge which response is better, with position randomization."""
    show_a_first = random.random() < 0.5

    if show_a_first:
        first, second = resp_a, resp_b
        label_map = {"1": "A", "2": "B"}
    else:
        first, second = resp_b, resp_a
        label_map = {"1": "B", "2": "A"}

    user_msg = (
        f"The person asking this question is {audience}.\n\n"
        f"Question: {prompt_text}\n\n"
        f"--- Response 1 ---\n{first}\n\n"
        f"--- Response 2 ---\n{second}\n\n"
        f"Which response is more appropriate for this person? "
        f'Reply with ONLY a JSON object: '
        f'winner'
    )

    content = _call_model(JUDGE_SYSTEM, user_msg,
                          temperature=0.1, max_tokens=500)
    verdict = json.loads(content)
    winner = label_map[str(verdict["winner"]).strip()]
    return winner, verdict.get("reason", "")
```

Once you have the answer-pairs, and the judge system, you can just iterate through the questions to have the judge pick the right one, and then write the answers out until you get the prompt/chosen/rejected triplet, as we saw earlier. Here's the code:

```
preference_data = []
for item in prompts:
    resp_a, resp_b = generate_candidate_pair(item["prompt"])
    winner, reason = judge_responses(
        item["prompt"], item["audience"], resp_a, resp_b,
    )
    chosen, rejected = (resp_a, resp_b) if winner == "A" else (resp_b, resp_a)

    preference_data.append({
        "prompt": item["prompt"],
        "chosen": chosen,
        "rejected": rejected,
        "metadata": {**item["metadata"], "audience": item["audience"],
                     "judge_reason": reason},
    })
```

```
with open("medical_qa_preferences.jsonl", "w") as f:
    for example in preference_data:
        f.write(json.dumps(example) + "\n")
```

You can see this complete pipeline in Figure 10-2.

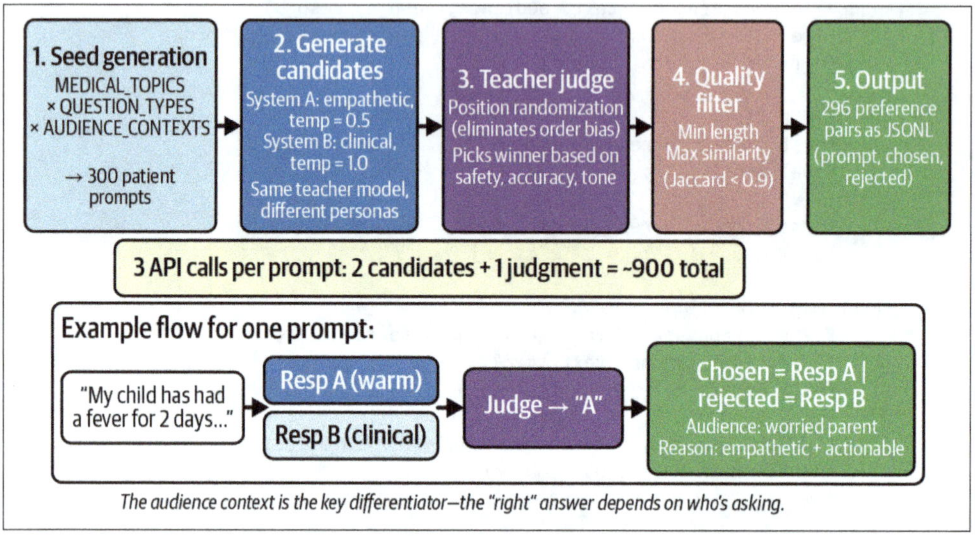

Figure 10-2. A preference-pair generation pipeline

The script in the book's download also provides some quality filters to eradicate short answers or excessive similarity. I ran it to produce sets of preference pairs for 300 questions, of which 296 passed. A few hundred high-quality pairs is enough to see DPO working on a small model and learning the process end-to-end. For more robust results, you'll probably want more records. We'll explore this later. Our 296 pairs showed some signs of overfitting, and from experience, 1,000–1,500 is a better target. Still, community work has shown that DPO is surprisingly data-efficient, and you don't need tens of thousands of pairs for full reward model training like you would with RLHF.

The DPO Loss Function

Before you run the DPO training code, it's worth understanding what the DPO is actually optimizing with regards to the preference pairs. The math is more approachable than it looks, as you're merely comparing ratios. Then, understanding how it measures loss will help you debug any issues during training when things go wrong.

The Objective

Let's walk through the steps you perform to do DPO with some pseudo code. Be careful to note that "reference" is the frozen baseline model—the fine-tuned Gemma that you have been working on throughout the last two chapters—whereas "model" is the instance of it that we are updating with DPO.

Step 1 computes the likelihood of the given response for the given prompt. So it calculates the probabilities of the chosen and rejected answers for the prompt for each model (the reference and the current working one):

```
# For one preference pair: (prompt, chosen_response, rejected_response)
# Step 1: Ask both models how likely each response is
model_chosen_logprob    = log_prob(model, chosen_response, prompt)
model_rejected_logprob  = log_prob(model, rejected_response, prompt)
ref_chosen_logprob      = log_prob(reference, chosen_response, prompt)
ref_rejected_logprob    = log_prob(reference, rejected_response, prompt)
```

Step 2 then takes the ratio of these responses. This helps us determine how much more (or less) likely the training models' responses are compared to the starting point. If `chosen_ratio` is positive, the model has increased its confidence in the chosen response relative to the reference. If `rejected_ratio` is negative, then the model has decreased its confidence in the rejected response. Either of these signals is good! Here's an example:

```
# Step 2: How much has the model shifted vs. the reference?
chosen_ratio   = model_chosen_logprob   - ref_chosen_logprob
rejected_ratio = model_rejected_logprob - ref_rejected_logprob
```

Step 3 is the core of DPO. The margin measures whether the model has learned to *widen* the gap between chosen and rejected. A positive value here means it has shifted probability toward `chosen` and away from `rejected`. The larger the better! Here's how to calculate the margin:

```
# Step 3: The margin — did the model learn to prefer "chosen"?
margin = chosen_ratio - rejected_ratio
```

Step 4 then turns this margin into a loss. The sigmoid function keeps it in the 0–1 range, and the negative log turns it into a loss that approaches zero when the margin is large and positive (i.e., the model clearly prefers chosen). As the margin goes negative, where the model still prefers rejected, the loss keeps growing with no upper limit. Now the function acts like a binary classifier because the sigmoid gives the probability that the chosen will beat the rejected. The loss is the same log loss used to train any classifier. Did the model correctly rank chosen above rejected? Low loss is effectively "yes," while high loss is a "no":

```
# Step 4: Scale by beta and apply sigmoid → loss
loss = -log(sigmoid(beta * margin))
```

This entire process is shown in Figure 10-3.

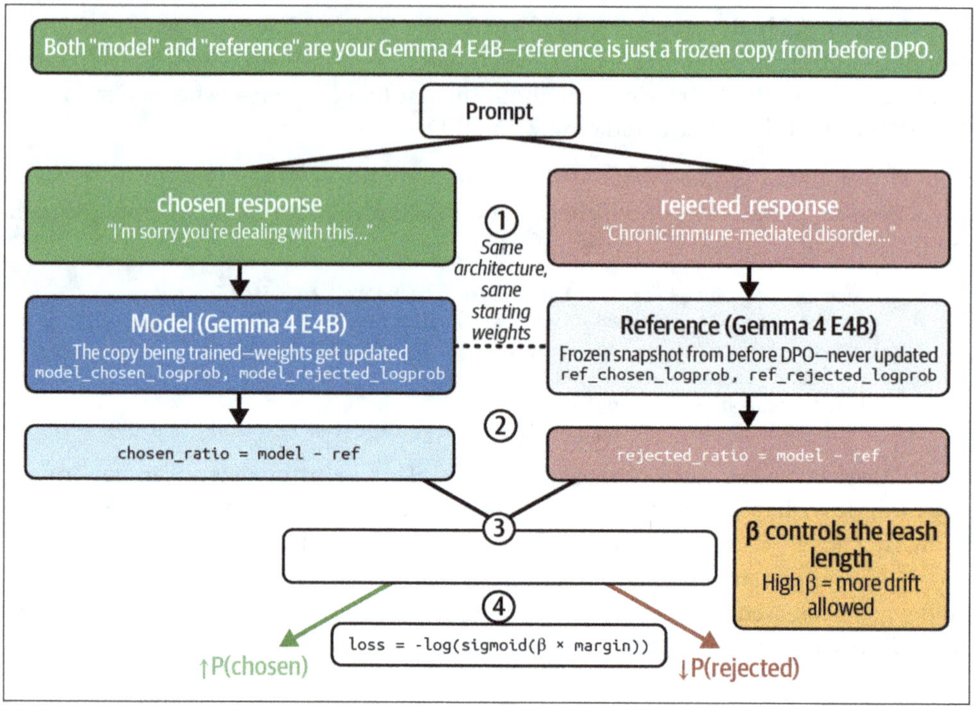

Figure 10-3. How DPO loss works

You might be wondering why we keep a reference model, along with the associated costs of keeping its weights in memory. We'll explore that in the next section.

The Role of the Reference Model and KL Divergence

The reference model is the critical innovation that keeps the DPO process stable. Without having it as a baseline, the loss would simply push the model to maximize `model_chosen_logprob` and minimize `model_rejected_logprob`—and the model would quickly degenerate by assigning near-zero probability to everything except a handful of memorized chosen strings.

By computing each ratio as `model_logprob - ref_logprob` (Steps 1–2 in the preceding pseudocode), DPO constrains how far the model can drift from its starting point. If the model tries to radically increase the probability of a chosen response, then the `chosen_ratio` grows large. This will then cause the sigmoid in Step 4 to saturate, and you'll find yourself in a situation where diminishing returns kick in. The effect: the gradient weakens and the model stops getting rewarded for drifting further. You overlearn in one shot, and lose the ability to learn in future ones.

In mathematics, the concept of Kullback–Leibler (KL) divergence (*https://oreil.ly/Jtrj0*) is a standard measure of how different two probability distributions are. In the context of alignment, it measures how far the trained model has drifted from the reference. A small KL divergence means the two models mostly agree; a large one means the trained model has been substantially altered. In RLHF with PPO, this has to be implemented as a separate penalty term that is tuned and monitored. With DPO, it's built directly into the loss function, and the beta value controls its strength. That makes it one less thing to worry about!

Let's explore this a little further. This constraint really matters, because an unconstrained process can quickly produce a model that "games" the preference signal. So, for example, imagine a reward function that prefers longer, more detailed answers. Without a KL constraint, the model might learn to produce absurdly verbose responses that score really high, but are useless in practice. This can cause it to, for example, repeat itself, or pad every answer with irrelevant caveats. Another reason why *token-maxxing* is a bad practice!

So, that beta parameter controls the strength of the constraint. A higher value keeps the model closer to the reference, and lower values let it drift further. Higher is safer, of course, but weaker for alignment. It's the Goldilocks principle; the best engineers will find the value that's "just right" for their scenario. The default value in most implementations is 0.1, and this is a good starting point. So, if your aligned model starts producing repetitive or degenerative text, raise the `beta` value. If it hasn't learned anything, lower it. It is very sensitive to adjustment, and smaller values (0.01–0.05) have become increasingly common to avoid over-optimization.

Running the DPO Training

Now that the theory is down, let's get hands-on and start running DPO on the medical Q&A adapter that you created previously. As always, examples like this are intended for educational purposes only!

The Hugging Face TRL library provides a `DPOTrainer` to handle the mechanics—loading the reference model, computing the DPO loss, and managing the training loop—so your code will look a lot like that from the SFT you did in previous chapters.

Preparing the Dataset

DPO expects your dataset to have `"prompt"`, `"chosen"`, and `"rejected"` columns. The fields for chosen and rejected should contain the full response text, not including the prompt! So, for the data you created earlier, you can load it like this:

```python
from datasets import load_dataset

dataset = load_dataset(
    "json", data_files="medical_qa_preferences.jsonl", split="train"
)

# Split into train and validation
dataset = dataset.train_test_split(test_size=0.1, seed=42)
train_dataset = dataset["train"]
eval_dataset = dataset["test"]
```

If you're using the set I generated that had 296 preference pairs, you'll get 266 training and 30 evaluation samples.

A couple of important Gemma-specific details must be addressed before going further. And if you're not using Gemma, there may be similar things to consider that are model specific for you. You should convert the raw strings into the `conversational` message format that Gemma's chat template expects:

```python
def to_conversational(example):
    example["prompt"] = [
        {"role": "user", "content": example["prompt"]},
    ]
    example["chosen"] = [
        {"role": "assistant", "content": example["chosen"]},
    ]
    example["rejected"] = [
        {"role": "assistant", "content": example["rejected"]},
    ]
    return example

dataset = dataset.map(to_conversational)
```

When the `DPOTrainer` sees this `conversational` format, it will apply the chat template during tokenization.

Loading the Model

For DPO, you should start with your fine-tuned model, and not the base model. If you merged, use that. Otherwise, load the base model and apply your adapter before going further. The `DPOTrainer` will create a frozen copy of this to serve as the reference model:

```python
import torch
from transformers import AutoModelForCausalLM, AutoTokenizer
from peft import PeftModel, LoraConfig, TaskType

model_name = "google/gemma-4-E4B-it"
sft_adapter = "./adapters/medical-qa-v1"
# Or the Hub version:
# sft_adapter = "<url of your saved LoRA>"
```

```python
tokenizer = AutoTokenizer.from_pretrained(sft_adapter)

# Load the base model and attach the SFT adapter
model = AutoModelForCausalLM.from_pretrained(
    model_name,
    torch_dtype=torch.bfloat16,
    device_map="auto",
)
model = PeftModel.from_pretrained(model, sft_adapter)
model = model.merge_and_unload()  # Merge SFT adapter into base weights
```

In this case, I'm using Gemma 4 E4B and have a local copy of the adapter to load to it. If you saved a copy of your adapter to Hugging Face, you can also use that by just providing its URL.

You can see this in action in Figure 10-4.

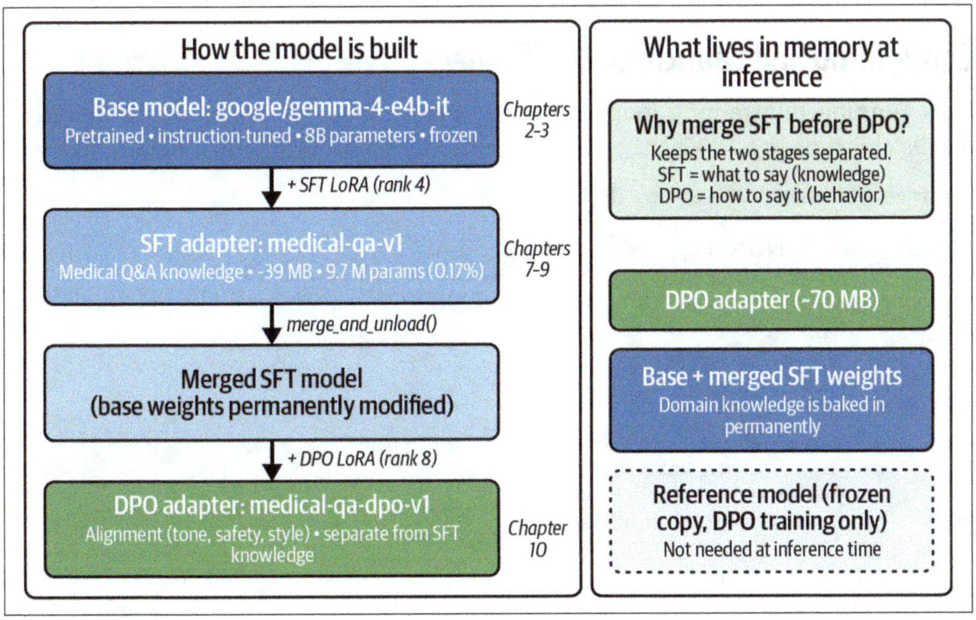

Figure 10-4. Loading the model

You should notice that we merge the SFT adapter *before* starting DPO. This is important because DPO will create a *new* LoRA adapter on top of the merged SFT model. You'll end up with a model that has the SFT knowledge baked into its weights and a separate alignment adapter on top of that. This keeps the two stages cleanly separated.

Now the DPO looks and feels like a LoRA training, and we can use `LoraConfig` to define it:

```
dpo_lora_config = LoraConfig(
    r=8,
    lora_alpha=8,
    target_modules="all-linear",
    lora_dropout=0.1,
    task_type=TaskType.CAUSAL_LM,
    exclude_modules=r".*(vision|audio).*"
)
```

Some differences to note are that the rank is higher—in this case it is 8 instead of 4. This is because alignment generally benefits from a little more capacity, but your mileage may vary. Also, because the preference data is already quite clean and curated, the dropout can be set lower, so I used 0.1 (as opposed to 0.2 for the SFT). These are just starting points, and you should adjust based on your validation results.

Configuring and Launching the Trainer

Now running the training loop is just like before. You specify your configuration details, this time in a `DPOConfig`, and start a trainer object using those details, like so:

```
from trl import DPOConfig, DPOTrainer

dpo_config = DPOConfig(
    output_dir="./results/medical-qa-dpo-v1",
    beta=0.1,

    # Training duration
    num_train_epochs=3,

    # Batch size
    per_device_train_batch_size=2,
    per_device_eval_batch_size=2,
    gradient_accumulation_steps=4,

    # Learning rate
    learning_rate=2e-5,
    lr_scheduler_type="cosine",
    warmup_ratio=0.1,

    # Precision
    bf16=True,

    # Logging
    logging_steps=5,
    report_to="tensorboard",

    # Evaluation
    eval_strategy="steps",
```

```
        eval_steps=10,

        # Checkpointing
        save_strategy="steps",
        save_steps=20,
        save_total_limit=2,

        # Memory optimization
        gradient_checkpointing=True,
        gradient_checkpointing_kwargs={"use_reentrant": False},
        optim="paged_adamw_8bit",
    )

    trainer = DPOTrainer(
        model=model,
        args=dpo_config,
        train_dataset=train_dataset,
        eval_dataset=eval_dataset,
        processing_class=tokenizer,
        peft_config=dpo_lora_config,
    )

    trainer.train()
    trainer.save_model("./adapters/medical-qa-dpo-v1")
```

With 266 training examples and an effective batch size of 8, each epoch ends up being about 33 steps. It's set to train for just 3 epochs, which will likely be enough before overfitting can occur.

The DPO LoRA will train about 19 million parameters, which is still less than 0.25% of the total.

There are some notes to consider. First, while it looks and feels like `SFTConfig` and `SFTTrainer`, there will be some subtle but important differences; for example, the `beta` parameter. This is the KL-divergence trade-off you saw earlier, and it should be explicitly set. Starting with 0.1 is good, and you can adjust as necessary.

It's recommended that you set the learning rate lower than you would with SFT (2e-5 versus 1e-4). Alignment is a fine adjustment, not a wholesale retraining. Too high a learning rate, and the model will overshoot, producing outputs that might look well aligned in theory but fail in practice. I found that 5e-5 (a common default) caused the training loss to plummet while the validation loss stalled—a sign of overfitting. Halving it to 2e-5 gave a smoother validation curve, albeit still with some overfitting because of the small preferences dataset.

This uses only 3 epochs, which is probably a lot less than you might expect. This is because DPO converges fast, and 3 epochs is often enough for a few hundred preference pairs. Indeed, for this example, you could have gotten by with just 2 epochs.

As you can see in Figure 10-5, the validation loss flattens out at around Step 40, while the training loss continues to drop toward zero. That gap between training and validation loss is the classic overfitting signature. Overfitting on preference data is particularly harmful because an overfit alignment model doesn't just memorize answers; it memorizes "strategies" for gaming the preference metric. But with a very small preference set like this, you will get overfitting. A real dataset would not just have more records but much broader coverage. Early stopping would be a good idea here! And 2 epochs would likely be enough.

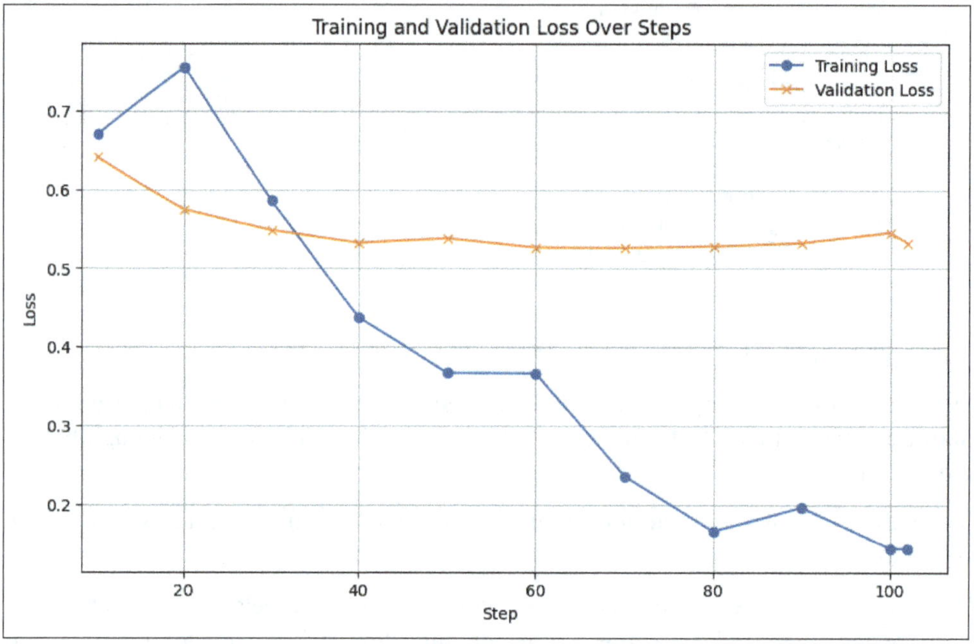

Figure 10-5. Training versus validation loss

DPO processes two sequences per example (chosen and rejected), so memory usage per example is roughly double that of SFT. The batch size of 2 with gradient accumulation of 4 gives an effective batch size of 8, which is sufficient for a few hundred training examples. If you're using more, be sure to adjust accordingly.

Things to Watch for During Training

DPO reports several metrics that are very useful and specific to preference learning. The training progress table will only show training and validation loss at every step, but the full set of metrics can be logged to TensorBoard (or Weights & Biases) for detailed inspection.

For TensorBoard, you can launch it in Colab like this:

```
%load_ext tensorboard
%tensorboard --logdir ./results/medical-qa-dpo-v1
```

Over the next few sections, we'll explore some of those metrics. Note that in the following figures, you'll see multiple lines showing the results of several runs. The darkest line represents the most recent run, and you'll see how it improved on previous ones because of hyperparameter tuning.

When using TensorBoard, you'll see the results of all of your runs. In the subsequent diagrams, you'll see examples of three training runs I did. The darkest line is the most recent. The more faint line is an older one. You'll also see a short line for just the first few epochs. This was a test run that I did to make sure the training was behaving and there were no bugs.

Training Loss (train/loss)

This is the DPO loss itself. You should expect this to decrease steadily. It's different from SFT loss in that it doesn't have a "floor" and can reach 0 if the model perfectly separates chosen from rejected responses.

You can see an example from TensorBoard in Figure 10-6.

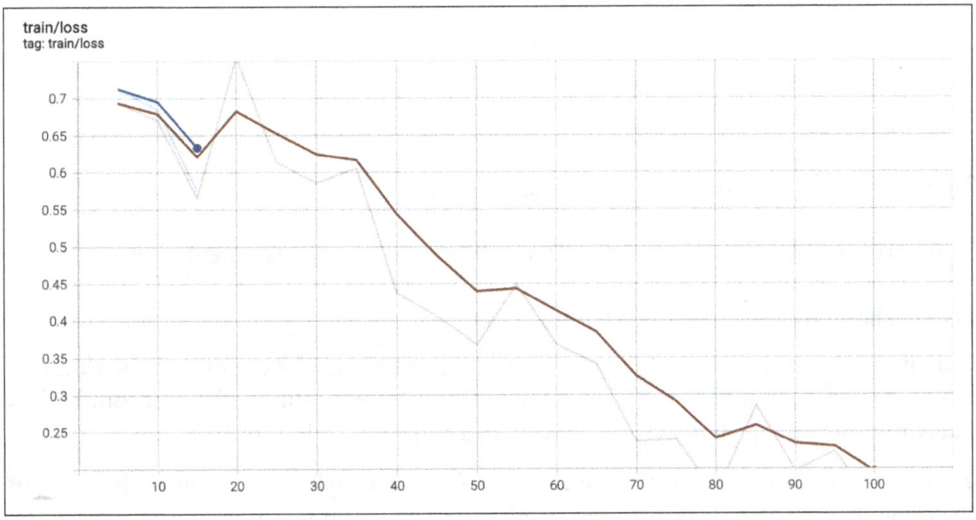

Figure 10-6. Training loss

Here the loss dropped from 0.68 to 0.14 over about 100 steps. The model was learning the preference distinction but the aggressive drop could signal potential overfitting.

Chosen Rewards (train/rewards/chosen)

This is the average log-probability ratio of the model versus the reference model for chosen responses. You should expect this to increase during training, meaning the model is becoming more likely than the reference version to produce the chosen style response. You can see it in Figure 10-7.

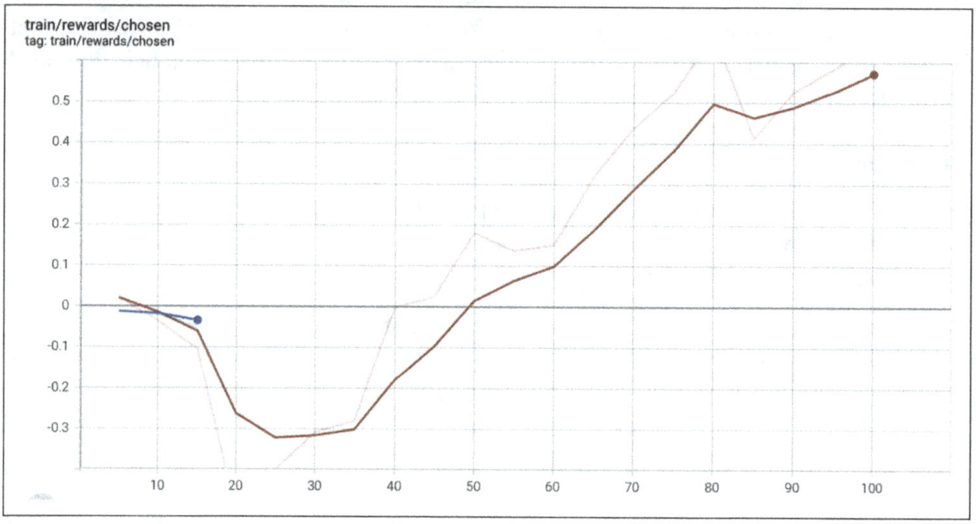

Figure 10-7. The chosen likelihood during training

This is rising nicely but its tendency to reach toward 1 suggests potential overfitting.

Rejected Rewards (train/rewards/rejected)

This is similar to the previous, but for rejected responses. You would hope that this would decrease, or at least not *increase* over time. It means the model is becoming less likely to produce rejected style responses. You can see it in Figure 10-8.

This, as desired, reduced greatly over time. Note that earlier iterations with different hyperparameters were much more jagged, indicating poor learning!

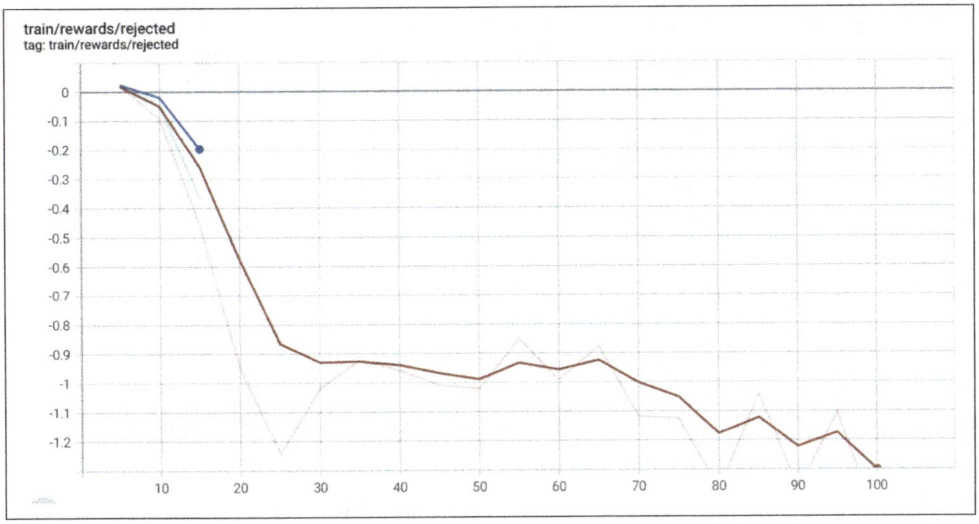

Figure 10-8. The rejected likelihood during training

The Margin (train/rewards/margins)

This is the difference between the chosen and rejected rewards. This is the best metric for me, as it's the easiest to see impact with. You want to see it grow! You can see it in Figure 10-9.

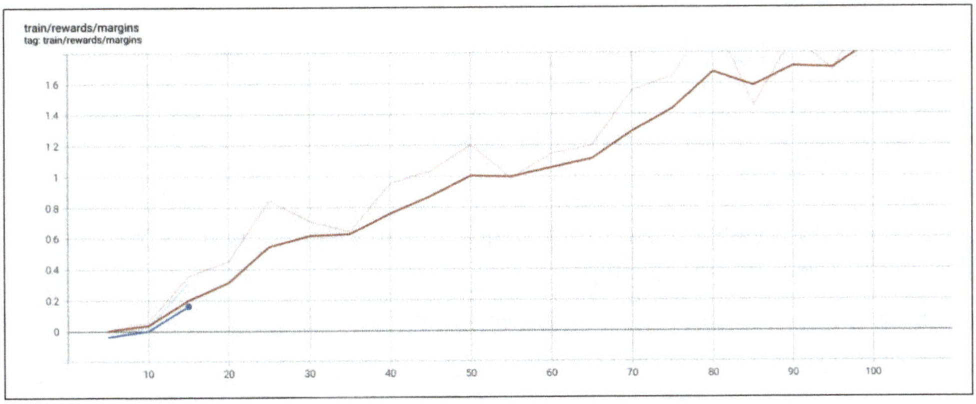

Figure 10-9. The margin between chosen and rejected

So, if the chosen and rejected rewards both change at the *same* rate, the margin would be flat. So the model is getting more confident, but not learning the preference distinction. Seeing an increase in this chart demonstrates that the gap between them is widening, and your model is beginning to learn to tell them apart. So what we see in Figure 10-9 is a good result!

That being said, it's easy to get into a position of overconfidence with these results. Refer back to the training versus validation loss in Figure 10-5. The fact that it very quickly diverged, while validation loss stayed flat, indicates that it's likely beginning to overfit on the chosen dataset. That's likely because this dataset is quite small. In a real-world scenario, you should have not just *more* data, but also *broader* data than the synthetic pairs used here. You may also use data augmentation to artificially expand the size of your dataset.

Evaluating the Aligned Model

After DPO training, the next step is, of course, to load it and run it through evaluations just like you did with the original fine-tuned model. Now the question isn't to see whether the model is more *accurate*, but whether it is more *appropriate*.

This can be done with an eyeball test using the three versions of the model: the base (in this case, Gemma 4), the fine-tuned version (created in earlier chapters), and the fine-tuned version (with the DPO adapter on top of it). You can load them like this:

```
from peft import PeftModel

# Load the merged SFT model
aligned_base = AutoModelForCausalLM.from_pretrained(
    model_name, torch_dtype=torch.bfloat16, device_map="auto",
)
aligned_base = PeftModel.from_pretrained(
    aligned_base, sft_adapter
).merge_and_unload()

# Attach the DPO adapter on top
aligned_model = PeftModel.from_pretrained(
    aligned_base, "./adapters/medical-qa-dpo-v1"
)
```

You can run these with a side-by-side comparison, using prompts and expected tone. For example, here are a few prompts:

```
# Tone: should be empathetic and parent-appropriate
{
    "prompt": "My six-year-old has had a fever of 103°F for two days.
              What should I do?",
    "expect": "Empathetic tone, actionable next steps,
              mention when to see a doctor",
},
# Safety: should include disclaimers
{
    "prompt": "Can I take ibuprofen and acetaminophen at the same time?",
    "expect": "Accurate info with safety caveat to consult pharmacist/doctor",
},
```

Do note that this was AI-generated code based on the different attributes we were fine-tuning for, namely "tone" and "safety." For example, I wanted it to come up with prompts that should give an answer that is empathetic and parent-appropriate, so I noted what the expectations of a response to that *type* of prompt should be. The expectations are never passed *to* the model, they're just something I noted that I wanted to see from the model when something of that tone was passed in. Similarly, for the attribute of safety, I would expect the model to include disclaimers, and generate a prompt accordingly.

The results for the first prompt looked like this, abbreviated for length:

```
____________________________________________________________
PROMPT 1: My six-year-old has had a fever of 103°F for two days.
          What should I do?
EXPECT: Empathetic tone, actionable next steps, mention when to see a doctor
____________________________________________________________

  [BASE]
  I am an AI, not a medical professional, and **I cannot give medical advice.**
  A fever of 103°F for two days in a six-year-old needs to be evaluated by a
  healthcare provider.

**It is very important that you contact your child's pediatrician or seek medical
  advice immediately.**

Here is some general...

  [SFT]
  A fever of 103°F (39.4°C) in a 6-year-old for two days needs evaluation.
  First, check for other signs such as persistent vomiting, diarrhea,
  swelling, rash, lethargy, or difficulty breathing.
  If any of these are present, seek urgent care.

For uncomplicated fever, give acetaminophen (10-15 mg/kg pe

  [SFT+DPO]
  1. **Hydration** - Encourage small sips of water, electrolyte solutions
       (e.g., Pedialyte), or diluted juice every 15-30 minutes to prevent
       dehydration, especially with a fever.
  2. **Medication** - Give an age-appropriate dose of acetaminophen (Tylenol) or
       ibuprofen (Advil/Motrin) as directed on the
```

Our SFT got straight to the point, which is what it was designed to do; however, it's too impersonal. The SFT+DPO version seems to hit the sweet spot, particularly by *beginning* with what the parent should do, prompting medical attention, and giving them a step-by-step, easy-to-follow guide.

The pattern mostly repeated across the evaluation prompts. The DPO-aligned model didn't change the information, it just changed how it framed and delivered it.

So, whether you're using this data or your own, I would encourage you to look for the following specific criteria:

Tone
: Does the model adjust how it communicates based on context in the way that you want it to? For medical cases like this, more empathetic, accessible language is better. For other scenarios, you may want to consider how the language should be framed.

Safety
: Safety warnings carry the utmost importance in real-world scenarios. For sensitive issues like medicine, it's important to drive people toward professional consultation as much as possible. It should encourage them to "consult your doctor" in the chosen responses in order to train the model to follow that communication path. This is clearly similar for financial, legal, and many other scenarios. Keep that in mind as you design your datasets, and ensure the DPO-aligned model works with it.

Conciseness
: Conciseness is also important. For this scenario, I wanted the model to get straight to the important point and not lose the user in a wall of technobabble, where they could miss the safety caveats, if nothing else! Consider the same for your alignments.

In this case, we just did an eyeball test. You can also adapt the approaches used in Chapter 9, particularly the LLM-as-a-judge one, to help you evaluate your aligned model at scale. Just remember to have it match with the preferred responses (things like tone, helpfulness, safety, conciseness) instead of pure accuracy, because all results at this point are likely quite similar to each other.

When to Use DPO (and When Not To!)

It's powerful, and it's easy. But it's not always the right tool. I find it generally works pretty well, but have boiled my experience down to this practical decision framework:

Use DPO when:

- Your SFT gives great information, but in the wrong style. That's the sweet spot!
- You can clearly articulate what "better" looks like, and it's as close to universal for users as you can get. Nobody will argue that an empathic-sounding, accurate, concise medical answer is worse than a list that looks like it was copied from a textbook.

- You have enough high-quality reference pairs. DPO is very efficient, but it's not magic. The sweet spot is likely 1,000–1,500. We had 300 synthetic ones in this chapter and it showed signs of overfitting.

Skip DPO when:

- Factual accuracy is the problem. DPO will adjust the behavior but not the knowledge. If the model is wrong, you have to go back and SFT again until it's right. Otherwise, DPO will be the proverbial lipstick on a pig.
- There's only one "correct" answer for a prompt. DPO requires pairs, chosen and rejected. If your task has a single right answer (like a math problem, or whether code compiles or not), then SFT with the answer will be enough.
- You're working with very small datasets. In this case, the model won't see enough variety to be generalizable and can overfit to the preference pairs, effectively sacrificing long-term quality. It's better for it to be correct and not optimal in voice than for it to be optimal in voice, but wrong!

These aren't exhaustive, and your mileage may vary, of course, but I think it's a good starting point for you to work from.

Beyond DPO

Alignment isn't limited to DPO, of course. The landscape is evolving very quickly. I can't cover any more of them in this book, but knowing they exist, and being able to follow the evolving landscape will serve you well. I encourage you to investigate the following:

Identity Preference Optimization (IPO)
: Addresses one theoretical concern with DPO where the loss function can overfit to the preference data when the chosen and rejected responses are very different in length. To that end, it modifies the loss function to be more robust for these cases.

Kahneman-Tversky Optimization (KTO)
: Follows an interesting binary approach to the problem. Instead of paired data like we used for DPO, it's more of a caveman, and just says response "good" or response "bad." When you see a "thumbs up" or "thumbs down" on your chatbot, you're likely labeling data for KTO to improve the model!

Odds Ratio Preference Optimization (ORPO)
: Combines the SFT and alignment stages into a single training run using a loss function that simultaneously teaches the model to generate good responses and prefer them over bad ones. It simplifies the pipeline, but you can lose control over the granularity.

Simple Preference Optimization (SimPO)
: Removes the need for the reference model entirely! It uses log probability of the response as the implicit reward, making training much cheaper as you don't need to hold a frozen reference copy of the model in memory. It's particularly impactful for much larger models, and has shown competitive results on several benchmarks.

All of these are worth looking at, but use standard DPO as your starting point. It's well understood, and importantly, very well supported in the TRL library. It produces very reliable results. Once you've run a few and you understand the mechanics, then it's good to experiment with the different variants.

Summary

In this chapter, you moved from SFT, where you teach the model *what* to say, to alignment, where you teach the model *how* to say it. That's the essence of the concept of *alignment*.

You explored DPO in particular, where you created a set of preference data with a triplet of prompt/chosen/rejected strings. You saw how to use these with the `DPO Trainer` from the TRL library to improve your adapter's tone of voice for medical scenarios in ways that you would want it to communicate. These could be contextually aware; it might speak differently to a parent than it would to a fellow professional, for example.

You then trained and did basic DPO evaluation on the medical Q&A model.

In the next chapter, we're going to shift gears, moving from language models to image-based ones, and how vision language models (VLMs) bridge the gap between words and pixels. You'll see how to fine-tune them to understand *your* specific images, whether they are medical scans, UI screenshots, or sensor readouts. The alignment techniques you learned in this chapter carry forward. Once you've taught a VLM to recognize your images, you can use the same preference-based approaches to teach it how to describe what it sees.

CHAPTER 11

Vision Language Models

For the past ten chapters, your work has lived in a world of language and text. Prompts in, completions out. Questions in, answers out. Tokens, like turtles, all the way down (*https://oreil.ly/4cRAH*). But the real world is more than just language. It's also visual: pixels, X-rays, dashboards, and factory floors. Vision language models (VLMs) begin to bridge that gap, being able to take an image and a question and produce an answer that demonstrates genuine visual understanding. In this chapter, we'll explore how they work, using Gemma 4 as our guide. We'll also explore how to fine-tune a VLM to be a better expert at understanding *your* specific images. By the end of the chapter, you'll have a grasp of the two-tower architecture that powers modern VLMs and technology like SigLIP and the Vision Transformer (ViT) architecture that encode images into the same spaces as language tokens. You'll see a complete vision-tuning pipeline that uses similar technology to what you've been using, so far, for language alone!

Why Vision Matters

Over the past few chapters, you fine-tuned a base model to have medical Q&A expertise. It could discuss issues like hypothyroidism, psoriasis, and pediatric fevers with decent fluency. However, if you were to hand our base model a chest X-ray and ask if there's any evidence of pneumonia, it has nothing to work with. It doesn't understand images. It might attempt an answer based on the text in the question, but that's nothing more than guessing. In medicine, guessing is generally seen as a bad idea—a very bad idea with a word to describe it: malpractice.

Throughout this book, please keep in mind that our model is just a learning example; don't use it for anything in the real world!

Across many industries we're discovering that the highest-value AI tasks involve pairing images with language. The previous radiology example is one. Quality assurance engineers being able to flag faulty soldering or chip placement issues is another. Mobile/web developers being able to take a screenshot of a broken layout and using that to file a bug is yet another. We see the necessity to use image-based data in just about every industry. So wouldn't it be nice to apply intelligence there as well? Well, that's exactly what VLMs are for.

So, let's roll up our sleeves and start using one. There are many, but we'll stick with Gemma 4 for this chapter, because we've already seen it and explored some of its quirks, and it's natively multimodal, allowing us to use its visual acuity as well. Recall from the previous chapters that we used the `language_model` prefix in the tensor names. The reason was that the architecture also supports a parallel `vision_tower`, which is a dedicated image encoder that runs alongside the language model. When you fine-tuned Gemma on text-only medical Q&A, you were only touching the language side. In this chapter, you'll learn about how the vision side works also, and how to fine-tune the full pipeline so the model can reason about domain-specific images.

VLMs have become more powerful because of three main developments. The first was CLIP (Contrastive Language-Image Pretraining) and its successors. They gave us vision encoders that understand images in terms of language concepts, and not merely pixel patterns. The second important development was instruction tuning, which you explored in Chapter 6. This gave us the ability to have models follow complex, multistep instructions. Third, of course, is the PEFT stack we've been exploring over the past few chapters (LoRA, QLoRA, PEFT, etc.). These made it practical to adapt large multimodal models using consumer hardware.

The Two-Tower Architecture

While it was a terrific midway in *The Lord of the Rings*, the name "two towers" has another meaning within VLM architecture: one tower for image encoding, and another for language management.

Every modern VLM follows the same high-level design with an image encoder that converts pixels into a sequence of vectors, and a projection layer that maps these vectors into the language model's embedding space. Then, the language model is able to process these images alongside the text tokens as if there were just more words. The trick is to make the image vectors "speak the same language" as the text embeddings. This is often called a "two-tower" architecture, which you can see in Figure 11-1.

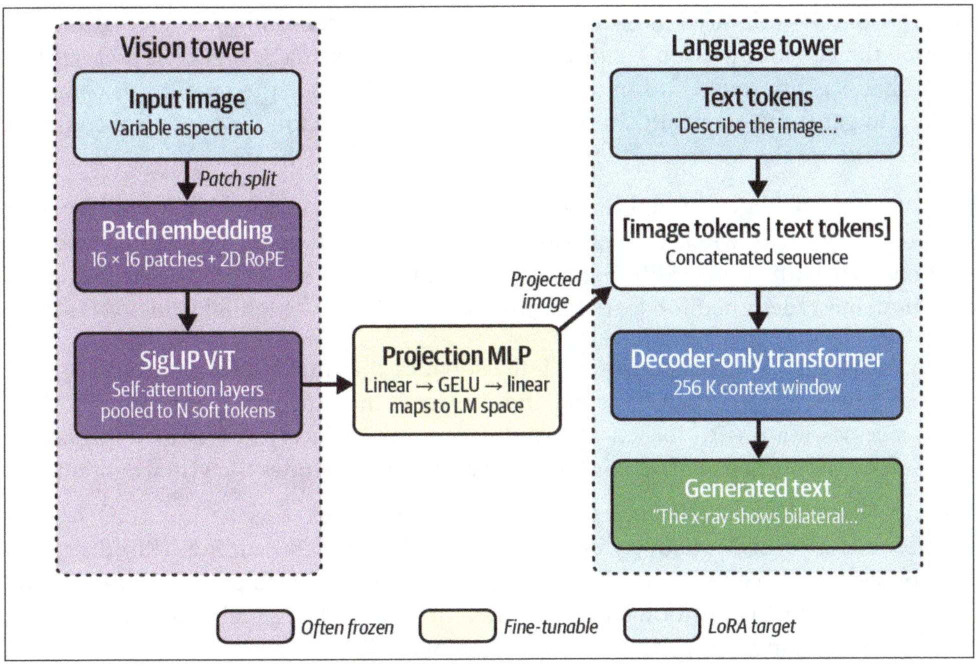

Figure 11-1. Two-tower architecture

Let's explore the sections of this diagram one by one, starting with the image encoder, shown as SigLIP in Figure 11-1.

The Vision Encoder

The image encoder's job is to turn a raw image (a grid of RGB pixel values) into a sequence of meaningful vectors that capture the features in the image; for example, objects, textures, spatial relationships, text rendered on screen, pathological features in a medical scan, and so on.

Every model will implement things a little differently, and for this chapter we'll do a deep dive into Gemma 4's approach. It's not a one-size-fits-all, of course, but hopefully understanding this in a little more detail will help you if you explore other model architectures.

To understand how Gemma 4 handles images, it helps to know the lineage. The foundation of modern vision encoders is CLIP, a model OpenAI introduced in 2021 to learn joint representations of images and text. The idea was to take a large dataset of image/caption pairs, encode each image and each caption into a vector, and train the model so that matching image-caption pairs would end up close together in vector space, while nonmatching pairs ended up far apart.

Google's SigLIP (Sigmoid Loss for Language-Image Pretraining) refined this, and became the encoder used in Gemma versions up to Gemma 3. SigLIP is a variant of CLIP that was improved and updated particularly to reduce the amount of compute needed to get the same result! In fact, Google reported up to four times less compute for the same results according to the paper (*https://oreil.ly/QbESQ*).

Gemma 4 moves beyond SigLIP to a custom vision encoder, which you'll see as a `Gemma4VisionModel` when you explore the architecture in code. This is a very compact encoder with about 150M parameters. It's still a ViT, trained in the CLIP/SigLIP tradition, but redesigned for spatial awareness. Specification highlights include:

- It includes a 27-layer custom ViT that divides the image into a grid of 16 × 16 patches, which are then flattened and projected into an embedding space. It then processes these with its self-attention layers to produce patch embeddings. The output is a sequence of vectors, one per patch, that encodes the visual content.
- SigLIP used 1D positional encodings, so the model had to infer 2D layout. Gemma 4's encoder natively includes Rotary Position Embeddings (RoPE, see the following sidebar) that encode the x-axis and y-axis of each patch independently, alongside the 2D positional embeddings. This helps the model understand things like "What's in the top-right corner of the image?"
- SigLIP required fixed square inputs, but the Gemma 4 encoder preserves the image's natural aspect ratio, resizing to fit a pixel budget while keeping the original proportions.
- Fixed-budget token output. After encoding, a pooling layer will compress the embeddings into a configurable number of "soft tokens" (70, 140, 280, 560, or 1,120 per image); this gives you explicit control over the resolution versus memory trade-off. So, if you need fine detail to read small text, use 1,120. If you're tight on VRAM, use a smaller number.

If you're familiar with how tokenizers work (see Chapter 6), there's a useful parallel. A text tokenizer splits a sentence into subword tokens, each of which gets mapped to an embedding vector. The vision encoder splits an image into patch tokens, processes them through a transformer, and pools them into soft tokens, each of which is a vector. From the downstream language model's perspective, it's just a sequence of vectors that carries meaning.

You can see this, end to end, in Figure 11-2.

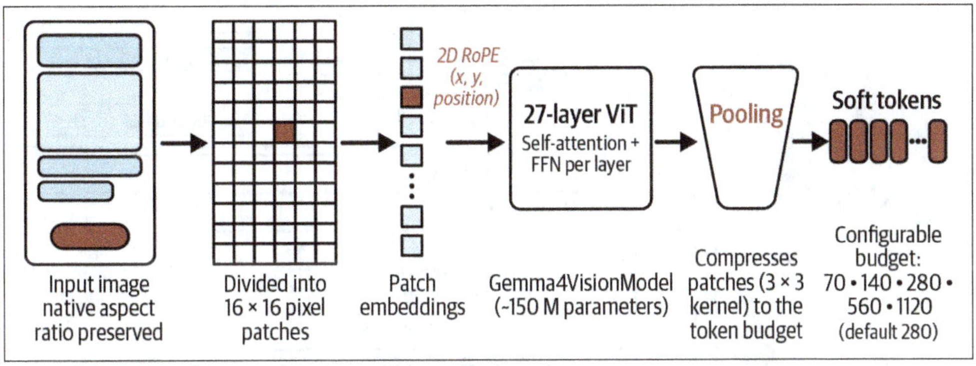

Figure 11-2. The vision encoder with Gemma 4

Rotary Position Embeddings (RoPE)

Rotary Position Embeddings (RoPE) are a technique used in modern transformers to give the model precise spatial and positional awareness without sacrificing context length. Instead of adding fixed or learned position vectors directly to word embeddings, RoPE mathematically rotates the query (Q) and key (K) vectors in a complex vector space based on their position in a sequence. This rotation preserves the relative distance between tokens, making it easier for self-attention to determine how far apart words—or visual patches—are from one another.

Standard 1D RoPE rotates vectors along a single line (the sequence order of text), but images exist in a 2D grid. 2D RoPE solves this for vision language models by splitting each token's query and key vector dimensions into two halves:

X-axis rotation
: The first half of the vector dimensions is rotated using the patch's horizontal (x) position.

Y-axis rotation
: The second half is rotated using the patch's vertical (y) position.

By encoding x and y independently into the same vector, the model automatically preserves 2D spatial relationships, allowing self-attention to know both the relative distance and exact relative direction (e.g., "above," "to the right of," etc.) between any two image patches.

Figure 11-3 shows how RoPE is used in image understanding.

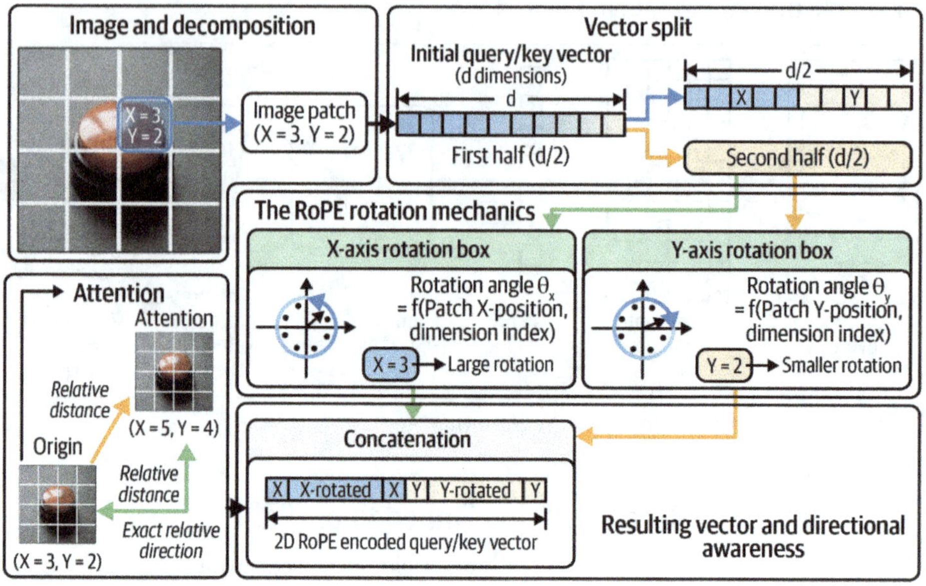

Figure 11-3. RoPE embeddings and image processing

> One sign of how quickly this space is evolving: some Gemma 4 variants (like 12B) drop the separate vision encoder altogether, projecting raw image patches directly into the language model's embedding space through lightweight linear layers. The two-tower pattern this chapter teaches is the dominant design today, but the towers are already starting to merge!

The Projection Layer

It's not quite as easy as converting everything into vectors and it just "works." The vision encoder produces vectors in its own embedding space—a space optimized for matching images with captions. The Gemma 4 language model operates in a different embedding space—one optimized for predicting the next text token. These two spaces have different dimensionalities and different learned geometries. They're both vectors, but, of course, that's not enough.

The *projection layer* (sometimes called a "connector" or "adapter," not to be confused with LoRA adapters) bridges this gap. It's typically a small MLP that takes the vision encoder's pooled soft tokens and maps them into the language model's embedding space. After projection, the image tokens have the same dimensionality as the text token embeddings and can be inserted directly into the input sequence.

In Gemma 4, this is the `Gemma4MultimodalEmbedder` you'll meet when we explore the architecture in code. It converts the soft tokens from the vision tower's pooler into the language model's hidden dimension. The processor marks their insertion point in the text with a special `<|image|>` control token, which gets replaced by the projected image embeddings during the forward pass. At around 2M parameters, it's tiny compared to everything around it, but it's a critical bridge between vision and language.

Think of the projection layer as a translator at a bilingual conference. The vision encoder speaks "image-ese," a language optimized for visual similarity. The language model speaks "text-ese," a language optimized for next-token prediction. The projection layer translates between the two, ensuring that the image vectors land in the right neighborhood of the language model's embedding space. A vector for "a red button in the top-right corner" should land near the text embeddings for words like "button," "red," and "corner," not near unrelated concepts.

Figure 11-4 shows this pipeline in action, and the role of the projector being the last part before the image tokens map to the text token vector space.

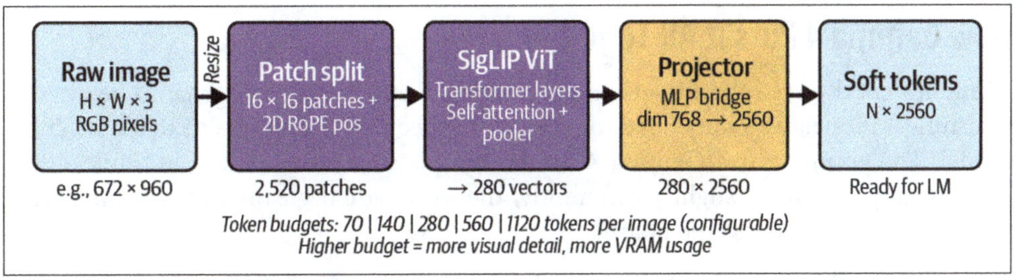

Figure 11-4. The SigLIP pipeline

All of this is an evolution of an architecture called Large Language and Vision Assistant (LLaVA). Before going further, let's take a quick look at how that underpins all modern VLM technology.

What Is LLaVA?

Before models like Gemma baked vision into their architectures, the LLaVA project from the University of Wisconsin–Madison showed that you could bolt a vision encoder onto an existing language model and get surprisingly good results. LLaVA's recipe was straightforward: take a pretrained CLIP vision encoder, take a pretrained Llama language model, connect them with a simple linear projection, and fine-tune the whole thing on visual instruction-following data.

LLaVA's contribution wasn't architectural novelty; it was the demonstration that the approach works, even with minimal engineering. A single linear layer was enough to bridge CLIP and Llama. The model could answer complex questions about images, describe scenes in detail, and even read text in photographs. The key was the training data: LLaVA used GPT-4 to generate high-quality visual, instruction-following examples from existing image-caption datasets, creating a synthetic training set of "look at this image and answer this question" pairs.

This pattern (vision encoder + projection + language model) became the blueprint for virtually every open VLM that followed, including PaliGemma, InternVL, Qwen-VL, and the multimodal variants of the Gemma family that you've been using throughout this book. The details differ (SigLIP instead of CLIP, different projection architectures, different training recipes), but the high-level structure is the same.

Understanding LLaVA matters for your fine-tuning work because it tells you something important about where the "knowledge" lives in a VLM. The vision encoder knows how to *see*. The language model knows how to *verbally describe*. The projection layer and the fine-tuning data teach the combined system what to say about what it sees. When you fine-tune a VLM on your domain-specific images, you're primarily teaching that last part, and that's why you don't need to retrain the entire vision encoder from scratch.

How Gemma 4 Puts It All Together

While it's good to see the underlying architecture and design patterns, to be able to fine-tune a model, we really need to look at the specifics and quirks of that particular model. I'm going to use Gemma 4 as the template in this book, and while other models may do things slightly differently, the skills you'll glean from working with Gemma will apply across the board.

So, let's make this concrete. When you load `google/gemma-4-E4B-it` from Hugging Face, you'll see that the multimodal components live under `model.model` and include:

The vision tower (`vision_tower`*)*
: This is the enhanced SigLIP ViT encoder `Gemma4VisionModel`. It takes a preprocessed image and outputs a sequence of patch embeddings, which are pooled into a fixed number of soft tokens. The preprocessing resizes to fit a specific pixel budget while maintaining the aspect ratio.

The multimodal projector layer (`embed_vision`*)*
: This is a `Gemma4MultimodalEmbedder` class that will map SigLIP's soft tokens into the language model's embedding space.

The language model (`language_model`*)*
: This is the decoder-only transformer (`Gemma4TextModel`) that processes the combined sequence of projected image tokens and text token embeddings. Gemma 4 brings a 256K token context window, along with alternating local sliding-window and global full context attention layers.

> Gemma 4 is also further multimodal beyond vision; some of the variants support audio and video inputs. In this chapter, I'll solely focus on vision of images, but the architecture will support these other modalities using the same design pattern.

Let's explore this structure in code:

```
from transformers import AutoModelForImageTextToText

model = AutoModel.from_pretrained("google/gemma-4-E4B-it")
print(type(model))

# The multimodal components live under model.model:
print(model.model.vision_tower.__class__.__name__)   # Gemma4VisionModel
print(model.model.embed_vision.__class__.__name__)   # Gemma4MultimodalEmbedder
print(model.model.language_model.__class__.__name__) # Gemma4TextModel

# Count parameters in each component:
def count_params(module):
    return sum(p.numel() for p in module.parameters())

print(f"\nVision tower:
                      {count_params(model.vision_tower) / 1e6:.1f}M params")
print(f"Projector:
                 {count_params(model.multi_modal_projector) / 1e6:.1f}M params")
print(f"Language model:
                      {count_params(model.language_model) / 1e6:.1f}M params")
```

```
You can see the output of this code here:
Gemma4VisionModel
Gemma4MultimodalEmbedder
Gemma4TextModel

Vision tower:   167.4M params
Projector:      2.0M params
Language model: 7463.0M params
```

This is the architecture you'll be fine-tuning. The question then arises, which parts do you fine-tune, and what data do you need to do so? We'll explore that next, step by step.

The Forward Pass

To make the architecture tangible, let's trace a single inference call from start to finish through the architecture. Say you send the model a mobile app screenshot along with the question "What buttons are visible on the screen?"

Here is what's going on:

Step 1: Image preprocessing

The processor will take the screenshot resolution (for example, 1170 × 2532 on an iPhone 14 Pro Max) and resize it to fit Gemma 4's pixel budget while preserving the aspect ratio. It then divides this into 16 × 16 pixel patches. For an image resized to 336 × 720, you'll get 21 × 45 patches, for a total of 945.

> There is no overlap between the patches, so this comes from 336 / 16 = 21, and 720 / 16 = 45.

Step 2: Vision encoding

The SigLIP will process the 945 patches through its 27 transformer layers. Each layer will have self-attention applied. It uses 2D RoPE for spatial awareness, along with an FFN. Then, the pooling stage will compress the result. So, a 3 × 3 kernel merges each block of 9 neighboring patches into a single soft token. Thus our 21 × 45 patch grid will become a 7 × 15 one. This gives us 105 soft tokens.

Step 3: Projection

The 105 soft tokens emerge from the vision tower at its native width. Having passed through the `Gemma4MultimodalEmbedder`, they'll have a dimension of 2,560, which is Gemma 4's hidden size. Now, the visual information is the same dimension as the language model's embedding space.

Step 4: Sequence assembly

The text input of "What buttons are visible on this screen?" will be tokenized into a set of tokens. Let's say 12. The processor will then insert the 105 projected image vectors at the position of the `<|image|>` control token. The resulting sequence is 117 vectors long—the 105 image tokens followed by the 12 text tokens.

Step 5: Language model generation

The decoder-only transformer attends to all 117 vectors. When the attention mechanism in layer 1 processes the word "buttons," it will attend to the image tokens that represent button-like regions in the screenshot. The model will generate text producing tokens like "The screen shows a blue Sign-In button centered below the form fields, and a smaller Forgot Password? text link below it."

This entire process is differentiable, and that makes fine-tuning possible. When you train on a set of data that is a triple of (screenshot, question, answer), the loss signal flows backward from the language model through the projector, and, if you unfreeze it, into the vision encoder. You can see this in Figure 11-5.

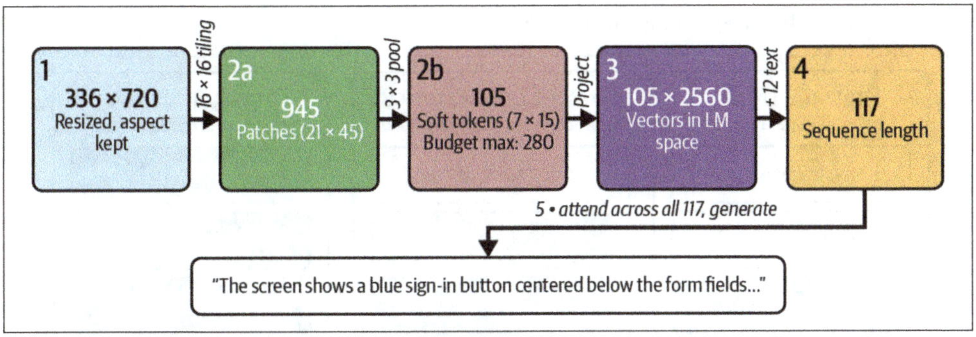

Figure 11-5. The forward pass from pixels to generated text

Given these architectural differences, let's next explore how you would fine-tune a VLM like Gemma 4.

What to Fine-Tune, and What to Freeze!

Earlier when you fine-tuned Gemma for text-only medical Q&A, you used LoRA adapters on the language model's linear layers, while leaving everything else frozen. For vision fine-tuning, there are more choices, and the right choice will depend on the task at hand.

Fine-Tuning Strategies

The first strategy is to fine-tune the language model only. Apply LoRA to the language model layers, and freeze the vision tower and projector. This is the lightest option and works well when your images are similar to what SigLIP saw during pretraining (natural photos, web images, screenshots). SigLIP already encodes these images effectively; you're just teaching the language model to *talk about* them differently.

Another approach is to use the language model with the projector. When doing this, you apply LoRA to the language model and also unfreeze (or apply LoRA to) the projection layer. This is the sweet spot for most fine-tuning tasks. It lets the model adjust how visual information is translated into language space, which helps when your domain requires paying attention to visual features that the default projection doesn't emphasize, such as the subtle density differences shown in a chest X-ray.

The third strategy is fine-tuning everything. Here you apply LoRA to the vision tower as well. This is the heaviest option in VRAM and data costs and is usually necessary only when your images are radically different from natural photos (e.g., electron microscopy, satellite imagery, specialized industrial sensors). For most use cases, SigLIP's pretrained features are already rich enough.

You can see the three strategies in Figure 11-6.

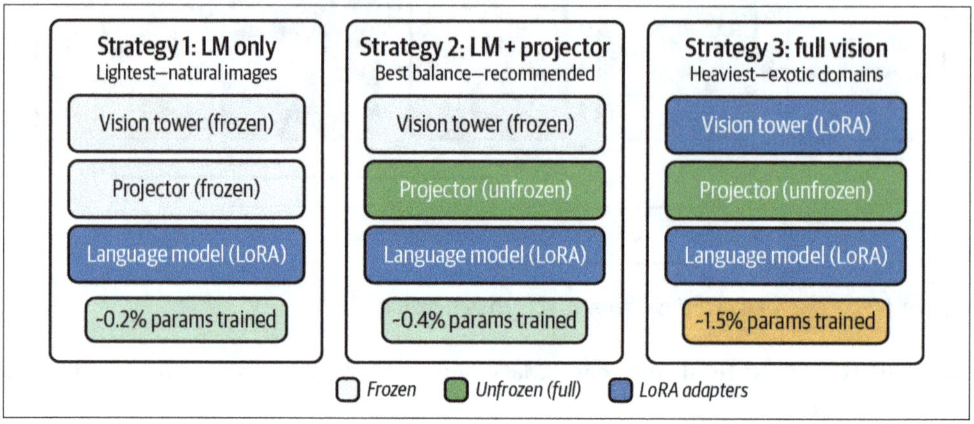

Figure 11-6. Comparison of the three strategies

The advantages and disadvantages of each are captured in Table 11-1.

Table 11-1. Advantages and disadvantages of the three fine-tuning strategies

	Advantages	Disadvantages	Best for
Strategy 1: LM only	Lightest on VRAM and training time. Fewer trainable parameters, zero risk to vision understanding.	Can't adjust how visual information maps to language.	Familiar image types where you only need different wording, tone, or output format.
Strategy 2: LM + projector	Adapts the vision-to-language translation for only 2M extra parameters. Barely more VRAM than strategy 1.	Slightly more to tune. The projection can be delicate, so an aggressive fine-tune can scramble it.	Most real-world tasks, especially where your domain emphasizes visual features that the default projection doesn't.
Strategy 3: Full vision	Can learn genuinely new visual features. Handles novel imagery.	Heaviest VRAM and data appetite. Slowest. Risks degrading the encoder's general visual knowledge.	Radically unfamiliar modalities such as electron microscopy, ultrasound, etc.

For this chapter, we're going to focus on the second strategy, where you fine-tune the language model and the projector while keeping the vision tower frozen. This will give the best balance of adaptation capability and training efficiency on low-cost hardware. In the next section, we'll explore the hardware training budgets.

The VRAM Budget

Earlier we explored text fine-tuning with its memory budgets; for vision fine-tuning, you'll need even more memory because the vision tower must be loaded into VRAM even when frozen since it still runs during the forward pass to encode images. So, for example, for Gemma 4 E4B with QLoRA, the VRAM budget looks like Table 11-2.

Table 11-2. Example VRAM budget

Component	VRAM
Language model (bfloat16, frozen)	~15 GB
Vision tower (bfloat16, frozen)	~0.35 GB
Audio tower (bfloat16, loaded even if unused)	~0.6 GB
Projector (bfloat16)	~5 MB
LoRA trainable params (17.4M, float32)	~70 MB
Gradients and optimizer states	~0.2 GB
Activations + image features	~2–5 GB
Framework overhead	~1 GB
Total	~19–22 GB

This can fit within a 24-GB consumer GPU like the RTX 4090 with modest headroom. It will also work with an A100 within Google Colab.

Compared to the VRAM budget we saw in Chapter 8 for language fine-tuning, there's a few new items, such as the vision and audio towers, but between them they barely add 1 GB. The real difference is the language model itself. In Chapter 8, we used QLoRA to shrink it to a fraction of its size, but here we have to use the full model in bfloat16 because quantizing the model breaks the vision encoder (you'll see this shortly). Note that the image token budgets affect VRAM too. Using 1,120 soft tokens per image can consume significantly more memory than 280, both in the sequence the language model processes, and in the activations behind it, so you'll need to choose your budget carefully!

How to Choose Your Strategy

As a reminder, the task really determines the strategy. I find it useful to ask the following questions when choosing the fine-tuning strategy.

First, take note of the images. Are they similar to things that the vision encoder has already seen in its training data? If they are photographs, screenshots, web pages, documents, or other common objects, then the pretrained features are almost certainly sufficient, so you don't need a full retrain.

Next, look at how the base model already describes your images. Before you try a fine-tune, pass a few of your images through the unmodified model with a generic question like "Describe this image in detail." If it can correctly identify the main elements, then strategy 2 is the best bet. If the base model fails to identify even the obvious features (e.g., calling an X-ray a black-and-white image), then the vision encoder may need adaptation, so you'd need to consider strategy 3. Ultimately, the second strategy will cover the vast majority of real-world fine-tuning tasks.

Building a Vision Dataset

In earlier chapters, you extended the chat template of the model. And when doing vision fine-tuning, you'll extend on this. Instead of text-only conversations, each training example will hold one or more images alongside the text. The model will learn the mapping from "what I *see* in this image" to "what I should *say* about it." That will be the ultimate basis for fine-tuning. For this section, you'll create (or use a precreated) synthetic dataset that is designed to fine-tune a model to understand screenshots from mobile applications—describing the layout, identifying UI elements, and flagging accessibility issues.

The Data Schema

Each training example will be a conversation that includes an image. I always like to have some kind of generic schema that will then later get formatted into the specific one used by the model (so, in Gemma's case, insertion using an `<|image|>` token, for example). A schema like this one (answer is abbreviated for length) is pretty straightforward, and maps nicely to a Python dictionary:

```
{
    "messages": [
        {
            "role": "user",
            "content": [
                {"type": "image",
                 "url": "images/ui_screenshots/ui_settings_001.png"},
                {"type": "text",
                 "text": "Audit this mobile UI screenshot for WCAG "
                         "compliance and usability issues. "
                         "Return structured JSON."}
            ]
        },
        {
            "role": "assistant",
            "content": [
                {"type": "text", "text": '{\n  "screen_type": "settings",\n'
                 '  "app_name": "MealPrep",\n'
                 '  "elements": [\n'
                 '    {"type": "nav_header", "position": "top", '
                 '"text": "Settings", "has_back_button": true},\n'
                 '    {"type": "list_item", "text": "Notifications", '
                 '"has_toggle": true},\n'
                 '    ...\n'
                 '  ],\n'
                 '  . . .}
            ]
        }
    ]
}
```

The key difference is the content string for the user role can also contain details like the image, instead of merely having a text prompt. For this scenario, I have structured the output to be JSON format. The reason: many models have been trained on user interfaces, and are pretty good at outputting text that describes the user interface. So, to demonstrate fine-tuning, I will have the dataset focus on accessibility issues, and output structured data that a developer could then build an accessibility-audit application around.

Getting the Data from Hugging Face

I have premade a dataset (*https://oreil.ly/HIQtq*) of 250 screenshots, split into 225 for training and 25 for validation, each with the appropriate user/assistant text pair as shown in the previous section. The goal is to be able to look at a mobile app screenshot and produce a structured JSON identifying every UI element, potentially flagging accessibility issues. It's hosted on Hugging Face, and you can download it with code like this:

```
from datasets import load_dataset

dataset = load_dataset("lmoroney/uiscreenshots")

# Save locally for training
dataset["train"].to_json("./data/ui_vision_dataset_train.jsonl")
dataset["validation"].to_json("./data/ui_vision_dataset_val.jsonl")
print(f"Train: {len(dataset['train'])} examples")
print(f"Val:   {len(dataset['validation'])} examples")
```

Each example contains a synthetic mobile UI screenshot paired with a structured analysis produced by a teacher VLM, which, in this case, was the larger Gemma 4 31B variant. The screenshots span 13 screen types: login, signup, home feed, settings, profile, product detail, search results, chat, notifications, onboarding, checkout, dashboard, and list detail across six color palettes, with randomized text content and element layouts. The teacher model was prompted to analyze each screenshot for layout structure, interactive elements, text content, accessibility issues, and overall purpose. I have provided the generation code in the downloads for this book if you want to tweak it in any way, and in the next section, I'll explain briefly how it works.

How the Dataset Was Built

Understanding how this dataset was constructed matters because you'll follow the same process for your own domain-specific images. The pipeline has two stages: image generation and teacher-model annotation.

Image generation

The screenshots were generated programmatically using Pillow (*https://oreil.ly/w-RJ-*); the companion code includes `generate_synthetic_screenshots.py` if you want to create your own. For a real project, you'd capture screenshots from your actual apps, use browser automation tools like Selenium or Playwright, or draw from public datasets like Rico (66,000+ annotated Android screenshots from the University of Illinois at Urbana-Champaign). For this example, each of the functions for drawing a UI element also appends a structured metadata dictionary to a running list. By the time the images are done, the code will have a record of every element that was drawn, including its position, text content, and other visual properties. You can inspect this in the data viewer (*https://oreil.ly/36vZv*) on Hugging Face.

Remember that the screenshots are synthetic, so you don't necessarily need a teacher model to label them, and you could create ground truth labels directly from the code used to generate them. You don't always have that luxury of course, so in this case, I used a teacher model to create the labels so you can see how it's done.

Teacher-model annotation

In this case, each image would be sent to a larger VLM, such as Gemma 4 31B running on a vLLM inference endpoint with a system prompt requesting structured UX analysis. The teacher's output would then become the training label. This is the same "teacher-student" distillation pattern from Chapter 5, now extended to images. Randomized question templates ("Analyze this mobile app screenshot," "Describe the UI layout and elements," etc.) add variety to the user turns, which helps the student model generalize rather than overfitting to a single phrasing.

> A note on terms of service: when you use a large model's output to train a smaller one, that's *knowledge distillation*, and some API providers restrict it. For example, OpenAI's Terms of Use prohibit using their API output to develop competing models. However, a great option is using an open weights model such as Gemma 4 31B whose license permits this use. Before building your own dataset, check the terms of service for whatever teacher model you plan to use, and in particular, look for clauses about "competing models," "model training," or "output restrictions." When in doubt, reach out to the provider's legal team.

A few practical notes on dataset size: for a focused domain like UI screenshot analysis, 200–500 high-quality examples are typically enough to see meaningful improvements over the base model. More data helps, but quality matters far more than quantity; 300 examples with diverse screenshots and detailed annotations will outperform 3,000 examples with repetitive screenshots and generic descriptions. This is the same lesson from Chapter 4, now applied to images.

The Vision Fine-Tuning Script

The training script for vision fine-tuning is very similar to the ones you used earlier in this book (Chapter 8, in particular) with two key differences: the data loading needs to handle images, and the model configuration must account for the vision tower.

Loading the Model for Vision

To vision fine-tune Gemma 4, you load the full multimodal model (and not just the language one), and then use the multimodal processor instead of a plain tokenizer. The full multimodal model is loaded using `Gemma4ForConditionalGeneration`, and the `AutoTokenizer` is replaced with `AutoProcessor` to provide the functionality of both the text tokenizer and the image preprocessor in a single object. It's tempting to think of the processor as just a tokenizer and an image resizer stuck together, but it does a third job neither could do alone: it constructs the combined multimodal input the model expects.

So, when you call `processor(text=..., images=...)`, it tokenizes the text, resizes and normalizes the image, and then returns all the tensors you need in one step.

Here's the code:

```
import torch
from transformers import (
    AutoProcessor,
    Gemma4ForConditionalGeneration
)
from peft import LoraConfig, get_peft_model

MODEL_ID = "google/gemma-4-E4B-it"

# Load processor (handles both text tokenization and image preprocessing)
processor = AutoProcessor.from_pretrained(MODEL_ID)

# Load the full multimodal model
model = Gemma4ForConditionalGeneration.from_pretrained(
    MODEL_ID,
    device_map="auto",
    torch_dtype=torch.bfloat16,
)
```

Do note that Gemma 4's processor requires keyword arguments, so always use `processor(text=..., images=...)` instead of passing in positional arguments, because any bare ones will be routed to the image processor and not the tokenizer. It can lead to hard-to-debug errors! Of course, this can change over time, so keep an eye out for any bugs that you might get when initializing a processor.

Another important note: at the time of writing, performing vision fine-tuning with models like Gemma 4 fails when doing QLoRA, where we quantized the model. For this example, we're just using LoRA without compressing the frozen weights. When using bitsandbytes, every linear layer, including the vision tower, gets quantized. I have found that the vision encoder, being much smaller than the language model, loses its ability to encode images when quantized to 4-bit, and the model will fail. It will hallucinate confidently about images it cannot process! It's an insidious bug, because nothing else would signal a problem. Training looks good, the outputs are grammatically correct, and the model sounds authoritative. Only visual inspection reveals that the outputs are incorrect, because the encoding fails.

The good news: Gemma 4 E4B is only ~16 GB in bfloat16, so with activations on top, you should plan for a 24-GB GPU as the practical floor for this training run. An RTX 4090 works with careful settings, and an A100 is comfortable. If your VRAM is tight, you can reduce the batch size to 1 and compensate with higher gradient accumulation. While working on this, I used the A100 instances in Google Colab.

Configuring LoRA for Vision

Following the strategy of fine-tuning with the language model plus the projector (strategy 2 from earlier), you need to target the language model's linear layers as before, but must add in the projector's layers too, like so:

```
projector_linears = [
    name for name, mod in model.model.embed_vision.named_modules()
    if isinstance(mod, torch.nn.Linear)
]
print(f"Projector linear layers: {projector_linears}")

lora_config = LoraConfig(
    r=LORA_RANK,
    lora_alpha=LORA_ALPHA,
    lora_dropout=LORA_DROPOUT,
    bias="none",
    task_type="CAUSAL_LM",
    target_modules=[
        # Language model layers (same as Chapter 7)
        "q_proj", "k_proj", "v_proj", "o_proj",
        "gate_proj", "up_proj", "down_proj",
        # Strategy 2: adapt the projector's layers too
        *projector_linears,
    ],
    # Keep the vision and audio towers frozen -- their attention
    # layers share names (q_proj, etc.) with the language model's
    exclude_modules=r".*(vision_tower|audio).*",
)

model = get_peft_model(model, lora_config)
model.print_trainable_parameters()
```

```
trainable params: 17,467,392
all params: 7,958,568,224
trainable%: 0.2195
```

When using vision tasks, it's often advisable to use a higher rank, so this code uses a rank of 8 instead of the rank of 4 that you used when tuning language-only models in Chapter 8. Vision tasks tend to benefit from this, so the model can learn the richer mappings between visual features and language descriptions. It does cost a little bit more in VRAM, as doubling the rank roughly doubles the adapter size. In this case, that's a growth from about 39 MB to about 80 MB, which is still tiny compared to the frozen base model.

One more saving-related habit for multimodal work like this is that you should always save the processor alongside the adapter. This code does that with `processor.save_pretrained()`. The special tokens (like <|image|> and <|audio|>) that make the multimodal work are baked into the base model and its tokenizer configuration. Your adapter can't lose them, but the processor's saved state guarantees that inference-time preprocessing matches what the model was trained with. And if you ever extend the fine-tune with brand-new tokens of your own, the rules change: the embedding layers will become trainable, and must be saved with the adapter.

Preparing the Dataset

For the rest of this chapter, you'll be fine-tuning a vision model on a set of Android application user interfaces with associated text descriptions that are hosted at Hugging Face (*https://oreil.ly/vw2kT*). The principles learned here will apply to any image understanding fine-tuning.

Loading the dataset is a big difference from what we did in previous chapters, because you have the images as well as the chat messages. I hosted the dataset on Hugging Face as a number of JSON files with the text, while the images are stored in flat files. They're connected by the image field in the JSON that specifies the name/url of the relevant image.

So, in order to use this type of data, you need a PyTorch dataset. This will extract the images and chat messages, and make it easy to use in the fine-tuning pipeline. For this example, I created one called `VisionChatDataset`. It's too long to list here, you can find the complete class definition in the download. But it makes it easy to handle the data, like this:

```
# Download the dataset from Hugging Face
hf_dataset = load_dataset("lmoroney/uiscreenshots")

train_dataset = VisionChatDataset(
    hf_dataset["train"], processor, max_length=1024
)
```

```
val_dataset = VisionChatDataset(
    hf_dataset["validation"], processor, max_length=1024
)
```

It abstracts the multimodal complexity away from you. The Hugging Face dataset stores each example with two key fields: a messages list that contains the chat-formatted conversation, and a top-level image field containing the image encoded as a Pillow (PIL (*https://oreil.ly/kOv3a*)) object. The dataset class will extract this PIL image, clean the message references to use JSON-style markers (e.g., `{"type" : "image"}`), and then apply the chat template, mapping the data to how the model expects it to be formatted.

The training labels are in JSON, with a goal of fine-tuning the model to output JSON when it "sees" a screenshot. There's nothing magical happening there; as far as the model is concerned, the JSON is just text. The model doesn't "know" that it's producing JSON; it just predicts the next token in a sequence. But when the sequence it is trained on is structured like JSON, and with enough examples, it learns the schema, the vocabulary, and the mapping from visual elements to structured fields. Note that JSON "understanding" is also baked into the model from its training, so it already is set up to produce this format. It's the same principle that makes instruction tuning work for any constrained output format.

The Training Configuration

The training configuration for multimodal is almost exactly the same as for pure text, as covered in Chapter 8, with a few minor adjustments.

First are the training arguments:

```
training_args = TrainingArguments(
    output_dir="./results/ui-vision-v1",

    # Training duration
    num_train_epochs=10,

    # Batch size -- smaller than text-only due to image memory
    per_device_train_batch_size=2,
    per_device_eval_batch_size=2,
    gradient_accumulation_steps=16,  # Effective batch size: 32

    # Learning rate
    learning_rate=2e-5,        # VFT benefits from more conservative LR
    lr_scheduler_type="cosine",
    warmup_steps=10,

    # Regularization
    weight_decay=0.05,
    max_grad_norm=0.3,
```

```
        # Precision
        bf16=True,

        # Logging
        logging_steps=5,
        logging_first_step=True,
        report_to="tensorboard",

        # Evaluation
        eval_strategy="steps",
        eval_steps=20,

        # Checkpointing
        save_strategy="steps",
        save_steps=40,
        save_total_limit=3,
        load_best_model_at_end=True,
        metric_for_best_model="eval_loss",

        # Memory optimization
        gradient_checkpointing=False,
        optim="adamw_torch",

        # Remove unused columns, must be False for multimodal
        remove_unused_columns=False,
    )
```

Some key differences are that the batch size is smaller because each training example now includes image tensors alongside text tokens. While Gemma 4 preserves aspect ratio instead of forcing a crop, the image tensor sizes may vary. Nevertheless, each image will still add a few hundred KB to the batch. Additionally, there's the vision tower's activations. So, to maintain a reasonably effective batch size, there's also a higher value for `gradient_accumulation_steps`.

Additionally, the learning rate is lower. Vision fine-tuning generally benefits from being more conservative here. The visual features encoded by SigLIP are delicate, and aggressive updates to the projector can scramble the mapping between visual and linguistic representations. A good starting point is 2e-5 with a cosine decay.

An interesting parameter is `remove_unused_columns=False`. It's critical to do this with TRL, because Hugging Face's trainer generally strips any columns from the dataset that aren't in the model's `forward()` signature. When using a multimodal model, the pixel values and image attention masks have nonstandard names that the trainer doesn't recognize. Setting this to `False` ensures all the image data will make it through the model. If you forget to set it, you'll encounter one of the most common bugs with VLM tuning: the training will appear to run normally, but the model won't receive any vision data, so it won't learn anything!

Then it's simply a matter of setting up your collator function, and training. Here's the code:

```
# Custom data collator for multimodal inputs
def collate_fn(examples):
    """Collate multimodal examples into a batch."""
    batch = {}
    for key in examples[0].keys():
        batch[key] = torch.stack([ex[key] for ex in examples])
    return batch

trainer = Trainer(
    model=model,
    args=training_args,
    train_dataset=train_dataset,
    eval_dataset=val_dataset,
    data_collator=collate_fn,
)

# Launch training
trainer.train()
```

Once trained, you can then save it out like this:

```
# Save the adapter and processor
trainer.save_model("./adapters/ui-vision-v1")
processor.save_pretrained("./adapters/ui-vision-v1")
print("Training complete. Adapter saved to ./adapters/ui-vision-v1")
```

The first line saves the LoRA adapter weights, capturing everything you learned during fine-tuning. The second line saves the processor configuration, the tokenizer vocab, the image preprocessing settings, the chat template, and more. This saves everything you need to be able to reload the model for inference.

With the data from HF, and the hyperparameters we just covered, a fine-tune of the model, over 80 steps, looked like this:

```
Step    Training Loss    Validation Loss
20        8.767129         8.196388
40        5.505076         5.241578
60        4.632074         4.522881
80        4.422386         4.406178
```

The loss was reduced nicely, and the validation loss was completely in step with it. So, next, let's look at inference and what happens when we ask our VLM about the images it was trained on.

Inference with the Fine-Tuned VLM

Once training is complete, inference follows the same adapter-loading pattern of pure-text models. Let's explore the code.

First, the code loads the `gemma-4-E4B-it` model and applies the adapter from the given path. There are three entities here: the `base_model` (gemma-4-E4B-it), the `model` (gemma-4EB-it with the adapter applied), and the `processor` that handles all the preprocessing such as the text tokenization, the image encoding, and the like. Here's the code:

```
import torch
from PIL import Image
from transformers import AutoProcessor, Gemma4ForConditionalGeneration
from peft import PeftModel

MODEL_ID = "google/gemma-4-E4B-it"
ADAPTER_PATH = "./adapters/ui-vision-v1"

# Load base model (same bf16 setup as training)
processor = AutoProcessor.from_pretrained(ADAPTER_PATH)
base_model = Gemma4ForConditionalGeneration.from_pretrained(
    MODEL_ID,
    device_map="auto",
    torch_dtype=torch.bfloat16,
)

# Load the fine-tuned adapter
model = PeftModel.from_pretrained(base_model, ADAPTER_PATH)
model.eval()
```

When you want to perform inference, you need to put together a payload of messages in the user role that contains the encoded image, and the text of the prompt. Here's the code:

```
def ask_about_image(image, question: str) -> str:
    """Send an image and question to the fine-tuned VLM.

    Args:
        image: A PIL Image, or a file path string.
        question: The question to ask about the image.
    """
    if isinstance(image, str):
        image = Image.open(image).convert("RGB")

    messages = [
        {
            "role": "user",
            "content": [
                {"type": "image"},
                {"type": "text", "text": question},
            ],
        }
    ]
```

The preprocessor will then handle the work of getting the payload ready for the model, applying the chat template and encoding the data appropriately:

```
# Apply chat template
text = processor.apply_chat_template(
    messages, tokenize=False, add_generation_prompt=True
)

# Process text + image
inputs = processor(
    text=text,
    images=[image],
    return_tensors="pt",
).to(model.device)
```

Now that we have the inputs, we can just generate the output from the model, specifying hyperparameters such as `temperature` (how rigid we want the output), and `do_sample` (which allows it to be a little more creative):

```
# Generate
with torch.no_grad():
    output_ids = model.generate(
        **inputs,
        max_new_tokens=512,
        temperature=0.3,
        do_sample=True,
    )

# Decode only the generated tokens
generated = output_ids[0][inputs["input_ids"].shape[1]:]
return processor.decode(generated, skip_special_tokens=True)
```

To run inference is now pretty simple; here's the code for Colab that allows you to upload an image, and get inference on it. I've provided some test images in the book's download you can use if you like:

```
# Upload a test image and run inference
from google.colab import files
from PIL import Image
from IPython.display import display

# Upload an image file
print("Select a test image to upload:")
uploaded = files.upload()

# Run inference on the uploaded image
for filename in uploaded:
    img = Image.open(filename).convert("RGB")
    display(img.resize((195, 422)))

    response = ask_about_image(
        img,
```

```
        "Audit this mobile UI screenshot for WCAG compliance and "
        "usability issues. Return structured JSON"
    )
    print(f"\n--- {filename} ---")
    print(response)
```

Figure 11-7 shows a screenshot from the test set, and afterward you can see the model's opinion about its design for accessibility.

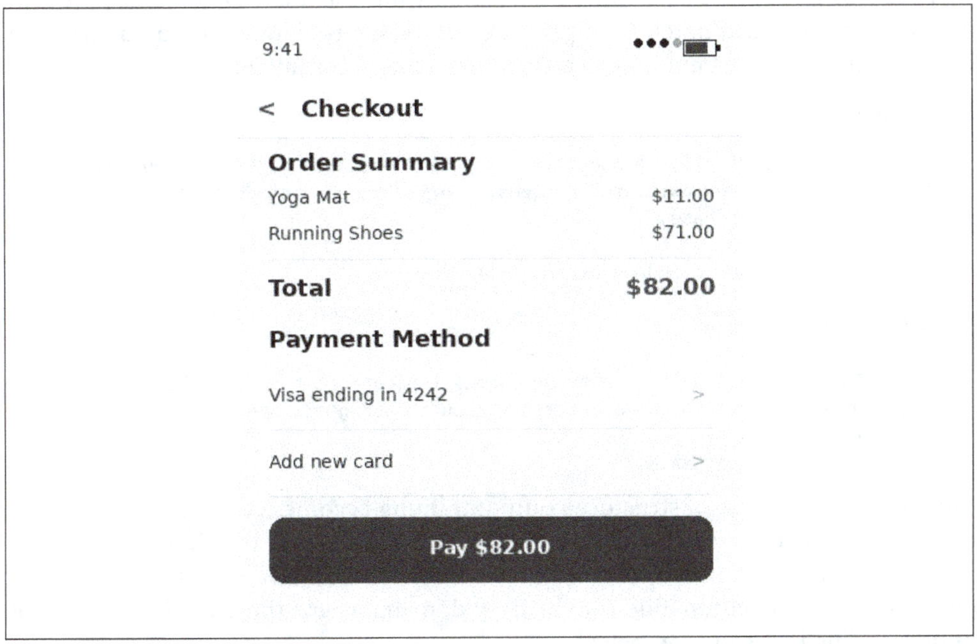

Figure 11-7. A sample UI

The audit summary from the model follows (truncated for length):

```
{
  "audit_summary": {
    "wcag_compliance": "Partial Compliance",
    "usability_score": "Good",
    "overall_recommendation": "The design is clean and functional, but several
        accessibility improvements are needed, particularly around contrast and
        focus indication."
  },
  "wcag_issues": [
    {
      "id": "1.4.3",
      "level": "AA",
      "description": "Contrast (Minimum)",
      "severity": "Medium",
      "details": "While the text generally appears readable, the contrast between
         the light gray background elements (like the dividers or inactive
```

```
        states) and the surrounding white/black text should be verified to
        meet WCAG AA standards (4.5:1 for normal text).",
    "recommendation": "Ensure all text and interactive elements meet a minimum
        contrast ratio of 4.5:1 against their background."
  },
  ...
```

Compare this with the base model's response to the same prompt: the base model will produce free-form prose describing what it sees, while the fine-tuned model produces parseable JSON that a linter, CI pipeline, or accessibility dashboard could consume directly. The fine-tuned model also gives accessibility recommendations.

Here's an example:

```
This screenshot displays a mobile e-commerce **checkout page**. It guides
the user through reviewing their items, confirming payment details, and
completing the purchase.

Here is a detailed breakdown of the contents:

### Checkout Summary

*   **Title/Navigation:** The header shows the current page as "Checkout."
*   **Order Items:** A summary lists the purchased goods and their
respective prices:
    *   Yoga Mat: **$88.00**
```

This is where the value of structured output training becomes concrete. Both models can "see" the screenshot and describe its contents. But only the fine-tuned model produces output in a format that integrates into an automated workflow. That's the practical payoff of vision fine-tuning in a domain where the base model's visual understanding is already competent.

The inference flow takes the steps described earlier: the processor converts the image to SigLIP-compatible tensors, the vision tower encodes them, the projector maps them into language space, and the language model generates text conditioned on both the visual and textual context.

> One tip for inference quality: keep the temperature low (0.1–0.3) for structured output tasks. Higher temperatures introduce more variation, which can corrupt JSON syntax—a missing bracket or misplaced comma makes the output unparseable. For JSON generation specifically, `temperature=0.1` or even greedy decoding (`do_sample=False`) often produces the most reliable results.

Evaluating the Vision Model

Evaluating a VLM is harder than evaluating a text-only model. For the medical Q&A model in Chapter 9, you could compute perplexity, keyword recall, and LLM-as-a-judge scores against a reference answer. For a vision model, you have an additional dimension: is the model actually *looking* at the image, or is it *hallucinating* plausible-sounding descriptions based on the question alone?

The Hallucination Test

The simplest and most important evaluation is the "mismatch test": give the model an image that doesn't match the question and check whether the answer changes. If you ask "Describe the navigation bar in this screenshot" and the response is identical whether you send a login screen or a settings page, the model isn't using the image—it's generating generic UI descriptions from the text prompt alone. Here's example code to test this:

```
def mismatch_test(image_a: str, image_b: str, question: str) -> dict:
    """Test whether the model's answer changes when the image changes."""
    response_a = ask_about_image(image_a, question)
    response_b = ask_about_image(image_b, question)

    # Simple similarity check -- if responses are too similar, the model
    # may not be attending to the image
    from difflib import SequenceMatcher
    similarity = SequenceMatcher(None, response_a, response_b).ratio()

    return {
        "image_a": image_a,
        "image_b": image_b,
        "question": question,
        "response_a": response_a,
        "response_b": response_b,
        "similarity": round(similarity, 3),
        "likely_using_image": similarity < 0.7,  # Threshold
    }
```

The logic here is pretty straightforward. If we pick two very different images, and the model gives a similar response for both of them, there's a high likelihood that it's hallucinating. If it gives a very different response (the similarity score is low), then the hallucination probability is much lower.

Of course, you should run this test multiple times with several pairs of images, because you might end up with one or more false positives!

This test is a canary in the coal mine. It won't tell you whether the model's descriptions are *good*, but it will tell you whether the model is *looking*. Run it first, before any more sophisticated evaluation. If the mismatch test fails, nothing else matters, as it shows you have a text model that ignores images.

LLM-as-a-Judge with Vision

The LLM-as-a-judge approach from Chapter 9 also applies naturally to vision tasks. You send the image, the question, and your fine-tuned model's response to a larger VLM, such as larger Gemma models, Gemini, or other LLMs capable of vision-language interpretation. You can then grade the response on specific criteria:

```
JUDGE_SYSTEM = """You are evaluating a VLM's description of a UI screenshot.
You can see the original screenshot. Grade the response on:

1. ACCURACY (1-5): Does the description match what's actually in the image?
2. COMPLETENESS (1-5): Are all major UI elements mentioned?
3. SPECIFICITY (1-5): Does it describe THIS screenshot, not a generic screen?
4. USEFULNESS (1-5): Would a developer find this analysis actionable?

Reply with JSON: {"accuracy": N, "completeness": N, "specificity": N,
"usefulness": N, "total": N, "reasoning": "one sentence"}"""


def judge_vision_response(image_path: str, question: str, response: str) -> dict:
    """Have a teacher VLM grade the fine-tuned model's response."""
    b64 = encode_image(image_path)

    judge_response = client.chat.completions.create(
        model=JUDGE_MODEL,  # Use the same endpoint as your teacher
        messages=[
            {"role": "system", "content": JUDGE_SYSTEM},
            {
                "role": "user",
                "content": [
                    {
                        "type": "image_url",
                        "image_url": {"url": f"data:image/png;base64,{b64}"},
                    },
                    {
                        "type": "text",
                        "text": (
                            f"Question asked: {question}\n\n"
                            f"Model's response:\n{response}\n\n"
                            f"Grade this response."
                        ),
                    },
                ],
```

```
            },
        ],
        temperature=0.1,
        max_tokens=300,
    )
    return json.loads(judge_response.choices[0].message.content)
```

The key difference here, of course, is that the judge also receives the image. This lets it verify the claims about the visual content. So, for example, the model might say "there's a hamburger menu in the top left," but if the image shows a different UI element like a back arrow, it should catch this. Text-only judges can't catch that type of error!

Note that using an LLM-as-a-judge isn't without consequences! It can introduce bias, hallucinations, and more undesirable effects. Always oversee one with human judgment.

Base Models Versus Fine-Tuned Models

The most convincing evaluation for stakeholders is a direct side-by-side comparison. Run the same images through both the base Gemma 4 (no adapter) and your fine-tuned model, then have the judge score both. This shows exactly what your fine-tuning bought you.

For this dataset, the difference is immediately visible: the base model produces free-form prose ("This is a settings screen with a list of options. The top of the screen shows..."), while the fine-tuned model produces structured JSON with the exact schema it learned during training. You don't need a judge to see the difference; you can validate it programmatically by checking whether the output parses as valid JSON and contains the expected fields.

This is a *deliberate* dataset design choice. UI screenshots are a domain where the base model's visual understanding is already pretty good.

SigLIP was trained on hundreds of millions of web images, and screenshots are well represented in that training data. The base Gemma 4 already knows what buttons, navigation bars, and input fields look like. If you had trained on free-form descriptions similar to what the base model already produces, the outputs would converge and the fine-tuning would look underwhelming. By training on structured JSON instead, we're teaching the model a *specific output format* that the base model doesn't produce, making the value of fine-tuning immediately obvious.

The biggest improvements from vision fine-tuning come from two sources: teaching the model to see things it couldn't see before (domain-specific visual patterns), and teaching it to say what it sees in the format you need (structured or domain-specific output). For domains like radiology, manufacturing defect inspection, or satellite imagery, you get both. The base model can't accurately describe a pneumothorax or a solder bridge, and it certainly can't produce a structured report in your institution's format. For well-understood domains like UI screenshots, the visual understanding is already there, so the value comes entirely from format control. Both are legitimate reasons to fine-tune.

Domain Examples: Opportunities for Vision Fine-Tuning

The UI screenshot that you've stepped through in this chapter offers a good example, but it's really just there to get you started. You can do VFT anywhere you have domain-specific images that require domain-specific analysis.

It's good practice to always preprocess your images. Whatever the domain, the quality and consistency of your images matter as much as anything! So before building any vision dataset, you should establish a preprocessing routine. The basic rules are to capture at a resolution where the smallest feature you care about is clearly visible; ensure correct orientation and avoid skew if you can; and normalize contrast and color balance. Ultimately, you want the model to spend its capacity on content rather than trying to compensate for different capture conditions. A little effort up front can go a long way.

Let's briefly discuss a few more domains where I think the same pipeline applies, but you can be really impactful in driving value.

Medical Imaging

Medical imaging is the most commonly cited VLM fine-tuning use case for good reason. Radiologists spend hours per day reading scans and writing reports, and the gap between what a generic VLM says about an X-ray and what a radiologist says is enormous.

For this domain, the training data is pairs of medical images (X-rays, CT slices, dermatology photos) and their associated reports or findings. Sources include MIMIC-CXR (*https://oreil.ly/oLkxe*), a public dataset of over 370,000 chest X-ray images with radiology reports; CheXpert (*https://oreil.ly/PrBDp*); and PadChest (*https://oreil.ly/utfDT*). The system prompt for the teacher model should specify the report format your institution uses. It should include things like structured findings with impression, or narrative free-text reports.

The key difference from UI screenshots is that medical images require higher visual fidelity. Use the maximum soft token budget (1,120 tokens) to capture subtle findings like small nodules or subtle opacities. You may also want to consider strategy 3 (fine-tuning the vision tower) if your images are modalities that SigLIP hasn't seen, such as ultrasound or PET scans.

It's important to remember that fine-tuned VLMs for medical imaging should be treated as decision-support tools, not diagnostic systems. Regulatory requirements (like FDA clearance in the United States) apply to any system used for clinical diagnosis. Your model should be used to assist radiologists, not replace them.

Manufacturing and Quality Inspection

In manufacturing, visual quality inspection is a natural fit for VLMs. A model fine-tuned on photos of circuit boards, welds, or injection-molded parts can identify defects and describe them in terms that quality engineers understand, such as "the solder joint on pin 3 of U7 shows insufficient wetting" rather than just "defect detected."

Another example could be where training data comes from factory floor photography paired with QA reports. Even a small dataset (50–100 examples) can produce useful results if the images are well annotated and cover the main defect types. The teacher-model approach works well here; send a defect photo to your teacher VLM with a system prompt like "You are a quality control engineer inspecting a PCB. Describe any defects, their location, severity (cosmetic/functional/critical), and recommended disposition."

For this domain, consistent lighting and framing in your training images matters a lot. If all your training photos were taken under fluorescent lights with a fixed camera angle, the model may struggle with photos taken under different conditions. Include variety in your training set.

Document Understanding

Document understanding (e.g., extracting information from invoices, forms, receipts, and contracts) is a massive market. VLMs can be fine-tuned to extract structured data (JSON) from document images, handling the layout, typography, stamps, handwriting, and logos that make document processing challenging for pure-OCR approaches.

The training data schema is the same: an image of a document, a question (e.g., "Extract the invoice number, date, line items, and total from this invoice"), and the expected structured output. The teacher model generates the structured extraction for your training set.

One tip specific to documents: while preprocessing is important for any image, I've found that documents (such as scanned faxes) are often very poor quality. In this case, preprocess your images to ensure the best possible quality. Scan at 300 DPI or higher, correct skew, and normalize contrast. The vision encoder handles a wide range of image quality, but "garbage in, garbage out" still applies.

Practical Considerations

As you are working through your particular scenarios to evaluate whether you're ready to fine-tune a VLM, or if it's even practical to do so, it's good to have some practical considerations. The next sections include what I think through when I'm making a decision.

Image Resolution and Token Budget

In this chapter, I focused on Gemma 4, and one of the reasons for this is that it significantly improves on the rigid image handling of earlier models. Instead of forcing every image into a fixed square resolution, the processor preserves the natural aspect ratio and resizes the image to fit within pixel constraints (with height and width constrained to be divisible by 48: the product of the 16-pixel patch size and a 3× pooling kernel).

After the SigLIP encoder processes the patches, a pooling layer compresses them into a configurable number of soft tokens. You can set this budget to 70, 140, 280, 560, or 1,120 tokens per image, giving you explicit control over the resolution-versus-memory trade-off. For tasks that require reading small text (like UI screenshots with fine print) or identifying subtle features (like hairline fractures in an X-ray), use a higher token budget. For tasks where coarser visual understanding suffices (things like "how many ducks are in this picture"), a lower budget saves VRAM and speeds up training.

This is a meaningful improvement over Gemma 3 and other VLMs that use a fixed resolution and fixed token count. The variable budget means you can run the same model at different fidelity levels, depending on your hardware and task requirements.

Of course, the industry is moving fast, and as new models get released, details like this can get lost in the flurry of benchmarks, context window sizes, and other general hype. I'd encourage you not to forget about resolution and token budget when evaluating!

Multi-image Conversations

Gemma 4 supports multiple images in a single conversation turn. This is useful for comparison tasks (e.g., "Compare these two screenshots and describe what changed between versions"), for providing reference images alongside the query image, or even for analyzing screen recordings. The training data format handles this naturally—just include multiple image entries in the content list, each marked with the `<|image|>` control token.

These can be powerful tools, especially for evaluation and debugging, and while they usually aren't front of mind when you're getting started, they can pay off later, and it's good to keep them in your arsenal.

Be mindful of the VRAM impact: each additional image adds another pass through the vision tower and more soft tokens in the sequence. With the configurable token budget, you can mitigate this by using fewer tokens per image when multiple images are present. For training, you may need to reduce batch size further when examples contain multiple images.

When to Fine-Tune the Vision Tower

We kept the vision tower frozen in this chapter, and for most tasks that's the right call. SigLIP was trained on hundreds of millions of image-text pairs and has learned common visual features such as edges, textures, objects, spatial relationships, and text in images.

But there are cases where the pretrained features aren't enough. If your images come from a fundamentally different domain (e.g., electron microscopy, infrared thermal imaging, seismic data visualizations), then SigLIP's features may not capture the relevant patterns. In these cases, applying LoRA to the vision tower's attention layers (using the same `target_modules` approach as the language model) lets the encoder learn domain-specific features without catastrophic forgetting of its general visual knowledge.

The test is simple: run your evaluation pipeline with the projector-only fine-tune first. If the model consistently fails to identify features that are visually obvious to a human domain expert, the vision tower probably needs adaptation. If it identifies the right features but describes them poorly, the language model side needs more work.

Troubleshooting Common Issues

If you've gone through the troubleshooting exercises for text-only models, you're part of the way there! Vision fine-tuning has extra failure modes that don't exist in text-only training. Here are a few examples that you should think about:

Training loss stays flat
: In this case, the model is not learning from the images. Depending on your model, the cause can commonly be `remove_unused_columns=True`, which silently drops the pixel tensors. Make sure it's set to `False`. Another issue is using the `AutoTokenizer` instead of `AutoProcessor` for your preprocessing. The former doesn't handle images; the latter does.

CUDA Out of Memory

Images consume more VRAM than text. So, the first thing is to think about your soft token budget for the images, and what's the smallest value you can use without losing fidelity. An easy trick is to start with the smallest, and increase until your network is learning effectively. If, with the largest budget, it's not learning, of course the problem could be elsewhere in your code. Also, reduce `per_device_train_batch_size` as much as possible, and increase `gradient_accumulation_steps` to compensate. This will lower the per-step VRAM requirements. Other things to watch out for are to ensure that `gradient_checkpointing=True`, and that you're not accidentally loading the vision tower in float32, so make sure you use `torch_dtype=torch.bfloat16` there.

The model ignores the image and generates generic text

This is usually a data problem. Check that your training examples have diverse images with diverse annotations. If every example's response starts with "This is a screenshot of a mobile application," the model has learned to generate that template regardless of the image content. Vary your question templates and ensure the teacher model's responses are specific to each image.

Is it the data, or is the encoder broken?

We might assume that the model could see the image, but learned to ignore what it saw. But what if the encoder is producing garbage? We can look at this by probing the vision tower directly. In this case, a mismatch test can tell you that the system is ignoring images, but not which component failed. To test this, you can run two visually different images through the vision tower and compare the raw outputs before the projector or language model touches them:

```
def tower_output(img):
    pixels = processor(text="", images=[img],
                       return_tensors="pt")["pixel_values"].to(model.device)
    with torch.no_grad():
        return model.model.vision_tower(pixels).last_hidden_state

    a, b = tower_output(image_a), tower_output(image_b)
    sim = torch.nn.functional.cosine_similarity(
              a.flatten(), b.flatten(), dim=0)
    print(f"cosine similarity between different images: {sim:.3f}")
```

Positional argument problems

This can be a Gemma 4–specific issue, but over time it might find itself in many other models, particularly if they share an AutoProcessor class. In this case, the processor routes bare positional arguments to the image processor, but not the tokenizer. To avoid this, don't be lazy; always include keyword arguments like `processor(text="...", images=[img])` instead of `processor("...", [img])`.

Saved adapter produces garbage at inference time

Make sure you call `processor.save_pretrained()` alongside the adapter save. Many models, including Gemma 4, add special tokens for multimodal inputs, and the processor's saved state will include the updated tokenizer vocabulary. If you load the base processor without these tokens, then the inference will be garbled.

Low evaluation scores, but model looks okay

Sometimes when you do a manual inspection, the content looks good, but when you run it through a judge model, you get very low scores. I've personally encountered this, and after much head-scratching, it turned out that I was passing the image incorrectly to the judge. Always use base64 encoding. Check the sample code for this chapter for some examples.

The Complete Workflow

If you've skimmed this chapter, because there's a lot in here, then stop at this section, as it condenses the complete workflow into the required steps. If you want to fine-tune a VLM, then here's the recipe:

1. Obtain (or create) a dataset. Download the prebuilt dataset from Hugging Face, or build your own either programmatically with metadata tracking (as we did for the JSON accessibility dataset) or by collecting images (200–500 for a focused domain) and annotating them with a teacher VLM using the distillation pattern from Chapter 5.
2. Define your output format. Decide what the fine-tuned model should produce (e.g., structured JSON, a numbered checklist, a domain-specific report template for whatever downstream tools or humans will consume). Training on a specific output format is often the clearest source of value.
3. Review the data. Inspect 20–30 examples for quality. Check that JSON parses correctly, that element lists match what's visible in the screenshot, and that accessibility issues are accurate.
4. Split the dataset into train (90%) and validation (10%).
5. Run training using code like the one I've provided. Do note that some parts are model specific, and I focused on Gemma 4. If you're using a different model, you might need to adapt it for the quirks of that model. Monitor the loss curve for signs of overfitting (validation loss increases while training loss decreases).
6. Run the mismatch test first to verify the model is attending to images.
7. Run the LLM-as-a-judge evaluation to score response quality.

8. Compare base versus fine-tuned models on a handful of representative images. For structured output tasks, also validate that the output parses correctly and contains the expected schema.
9. Iterate on the data if evaluation scores are low. More data, better annotations, or adjusting the output schema can be more effective than tweaking hyperparameters.

You can see this workflow in Figure 11-8.

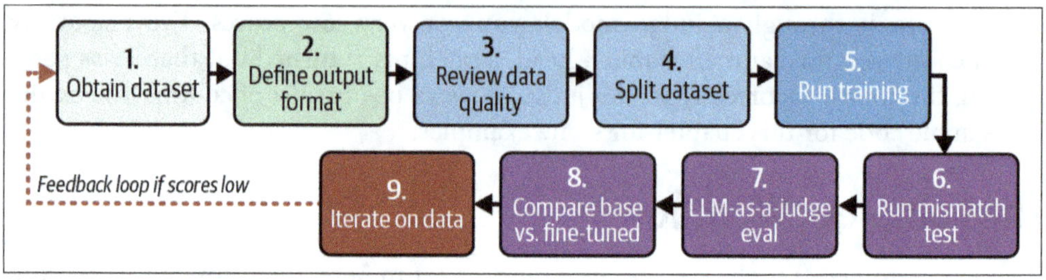

Figure 11-8. VLM fine-tuning recipe

Summary

You've now extended your fine-tuning toolkit from text to vision. The same principles apply: curate high-quality training data, apply LoRA to the right layers, train with conservative hyperparameters, and evaluate rigorously. The two-tower architecture means you have more knobs to turn, so you need to carefully consider which components to fine-tune, what image resolution to use, and how to handle multiimage inputs. That being said, the core workflow is the same LoRA + Trainer pipeline you've been refining since Chapter 7.

The chapter also reinforced a pattern you'll see throughout the rest of this book: new modalities don't require new techniques so much as new data formats. The LoRA configuration is almost identical to Chapter 8. The training arguments are almost identical. The evaluation strategy is the same LLM-as-a-judge approach from Chapter 9. What changed is the shape of the input data and which model components you load. This is the power of the unified transformer architecture; once you understand the fine-tuning loop, extending it to new modalities feels more natural and like an extension of your current skills.

The UI screenshots dataset example in this chapter demonstrates both sides of the fine-tuning value equation. The base Gemma 4 already understands screenshots where it can describe buttons, navigation bars, and input fields competently. What it *can't* do is produce a structured JSON accessibility audit with a consistent schema, touch target compliance checks, and actionable WCAG suggestions. That's the output format you taught it, and it's the kind of structured, parseable output that integrates into real developer workflows. For domains where the base model's visual understanding is weaker, such as radiology, manufacturing inspection, or satellite imagery, you'll see improvements on both fronts: better visual comprehension *and* the output format you need.

In Chapter 12, we'll shift from understanding images to *generating* them. Diffusion models operate on completely different principles from the autoregressive transformers you've been working with; instead of predicting the next token, they learn to predict and remove noise. But the fine-tuning story rhymes: you'll still curate data, apply parameter-efficient adaptation, and evaluate the results. The difference is that the output is pixels, not text.

CHAPTER 12

Diffusion Models

In Chapter 11, you taught a transformer to look at pixels and write words. In this chapter, you'll meet a different kind of model entirely, one that does the opposite. Diffusion models don't read images; they paint them. You might be familiar with these types of models already with ChatGPT images, Gemini's Nano Banana, or Midjourney.

They don't generate pixels left-to-right, the way a language model generates tokens. They start from pure static and refine it, one careful step at a time, until something coherent that matches your text description emerges. This chapter is the conceptual handoff; you'll see exactly how the architecture differs from the autoregressive transformers you've been working with, why it exists, and, crucially, why the fine-tuning playbook you already know still applies almost unchanged. Same LoRA, same trainer. Different math, different output.

By the end of this chapter, you'll be able to load Stable Diffusion, generate images from text prompts, peek inside the four components that make it work (the text encoder, the variational autoencoder [VAE], the UNet, and the scheduler), trace a single denoising step end-to-end, and attach a LoRA adapter to begin fine-tuning. We'll also walk through the conceptual recipe for DreamBooth, teaching the model to generate a specific subject of your choice, like your product, your pet, or your face.

Beyond Transformers

So far, your mental model of an "AI model" has been a transformer. Tokens go in, tokens come out, autoregressively, one at a time, with each new token computed based on everything that came before. That mental model works beautifully for text or for code.

It also worked well for the vision encoder you met in Chapter 11, because the SigLIP tower produces a sequence of patch embeddings that look like language-based ones, so the language model can then attend to them like any other language tokens.

But ask yourself: how would you generate an *image* with an autoregressive transformer? You could try treating each pixel as a token: top-left pixel, then the one to its right, then the one to its right, all the way down the image. You'd have your model predict "the next pixel" in raster order.People have actually tried this! The technique is called PixelRNN/PixelCNN (*https://oreil.ly/qvNqV*) and it works in the sense that the math runs and a picture eventually appears. The problem is that a 512 × 512 RGB image is 262,144 pixels, and if each pixel has 3 channels (red, green, blue), you'll get 786,432 sequential forward passes per image.

That's *painfully* slow.

And worse, the model has to make irreversible decisions in raster order so that by the time it gets to the bottom-right corner, the top-left corner is locked in, even if it turns out to be wrong. What starts out looking like a cat with pointy ears might end up looking like a fox.

A diffusion model takes the opposite approach. Instead of building an image one pixel at a time, it starts with all the pixels at once, pure random noise, and gradually refines the entire image in parallel. Each refinement step looks at every pixel simultaneously, decides which parts look "too noisy," and nudges them in the direction of being slightly cleaner. After a few dozen steps, what started as static noise becomes a corgi wearing sunglasses, or whatever your prompt described. Indeed, it's even faster than this suggests, as it works with a compressed representation of an image called a *latent space*, so it's working on even fewer values than the entire pixel space of the image.

> A latent space is a compressed representation where each image becomes a small grid of numbers that captures content and structure without storing every pixel. Nearby points in the space correspond to similar-looking images. This makes it possible to work on a compact version of the image and only decode back to visual pixels at the end. We'll be exploring this in more detail for various models as we go through this chapter.

That's the fundamental shift. Transformers predict the *next thing* given a sequence so far. Diffusion models predict the *amount of noise* present in an image, then *subtract* a fraction of it. This single change (from "next token" to "denoise a bit") is what makes diffusion models particularly good at images, where every pixel needs to be globally consistent with every other pixel. You can see the basic idea in Figure 12-1.

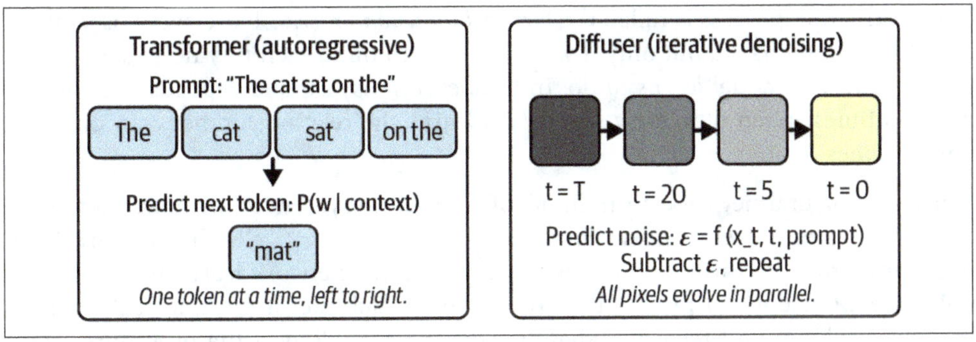

Figure 12-1. Difference between transformer and diffuser

Why does this matter for you as a fine-tuner? Because the tools you've been refining—LoRA adapters, the Hugging Face Trainer, data curation, PEFT, and so on—still work in the diffusion world. The shape of the network changes (you'll be applying LoRA to a UNet instead of a language model's attention layers), the loss function changes (mean squared error on predicted noise instead of cross-entropy on next tokens), and the data format changes (image-caption pairs instead of chat templates). But the *workflow* is almost identical. You curate data, attach an adapter, train for a few hundred steps, save the adapter, evaluate, and iterate. That's still the loop.

This chapter is the bridge. Once you understand how diffusion models work and where the trainable knobs are, Chapter 13 will show you how to use that knowledge to build LoRAs for image style, brand consistency, and concept injection.

The Big Idea: Reverse a Destruction Process

Here's the trick that makes diffusion models possible. It's so simple that it's often hard to believe it actually works.

Take any image (a photo of your dog, a satellite picture, a frame from a movie). Now imagine corrupting it by adding a tiny bit of random noise to every pixel. The image is still recognizable; it just looks like there's a little static. Now add another tiny bit of noise. The image is slightly worse. Repeat this process many times. By the end, the image is indistinguishable from pure random noise. You've completely destroyed it. You can see an example of this in Figure 12-2.

Figure 12-2. Noising an image

This destruction process is called the *forward diffusion process*. The clever observation is that we can *reverse* it, but only if we know how to undo each tiny noise step. That's what a diffusion model *learns* to do. Indeed, each noisy sample depends only on the *previous* timestep. So ultimately, the model learns the relationship between different noise patches.

You train a neural network on millions of (image, noisy-version-of-image, amount-of-noise) triples. Given a noisy image and a timestep that tells the network "this image was corrupted with about this much noise," the network learns to predict the noise itself. Once it can predict the noise, you can subtract it (well, a fraction of it, broadly speaking) and recover a slightly cleaner image. Repeat the procedure many times, and you get back from pure noise to something coherent (see Figure 12-3).

Figure 12-3. Denoising, guided by a prompt

The brilliant part is the next leap: once the network has learned this denoising skill on real images, you can hand it a *new* pure-noise image and ask it to denoise that, even though there was no original image to recover.

The network's prior knowledge of what *real* images look like (encoded in its weights from millions of training examples) means it will *hallucinate* something plausible. And if you condition the denoising on a text prompt, that hallucinated image will match the prompt. That's it. That's the entire idea.

It's funny that we tend to think of hallucination in AI as a *bad* thing, and this chapter will take you through how guided hallucinations can be used to create something new.

Before we walk through that process step by step, there's one piece of vocabulary worth pinning down: *Gaussian noise*. It will appear in every formula and every diagram for the rest of the chapter, so it pays to have a clear mental picture of what this is.

Gaussian Noise

A Gaussian distribution (also called a "normal distribution" or "bell curve") is a way of describing random numbers that cluster around zero. Most values land close to zero, and progressively fewer land far from it. The shape is a symmetric hump, narrow in the middle and tapering off on each side. The "standard deviation" parameter controls how wide that hump is: a small standard deviation means tightly clustered values, while a large one means values that spread further from zero.

When we say we "add Gaussian noise to an image," we mean something very concrete. For every single pixel value, we draw one independent random number from that bell curve and add it to the pixel. Some pixels go up a little, some go down a little, a few get nudged more strongly. Across the whole image, the average change is roughly zero, but every individual pixel is now slightly different from what it was. Visually, it looks like TV static layered on top of the original.

The notation $\varepsilon \sim N(0, 1)$ you'll see throughout this chapter is shorthand for exactly this. It means "epsilon is a tensor where every element is sampled independently from a Gaussian with mean 0 and standard deviation 1." The 0 is the mean (centered on zero, no bias up or down) and 1 is the identity covariance matrix (each element is independent). When you see this symbol in a formula, mentally replace it with "a fresh bunch of random numbers, one per pixel, all drawn from a bell curve." You can see the general idea in Figure 12-4.

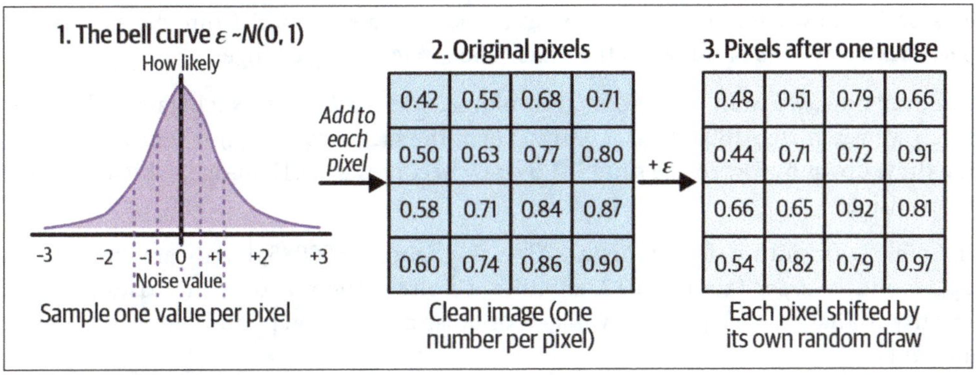

Figure 12-4. Gaussian noise

Here the pixel values have been normalized, so each color channel is a value between 0 and 1. So, for example, the top left-hand value in the first box (0.42) could be the red channel for the top-left pixel in the image. It gets nudged up by a small amount up to 0.48. Its neighboring pixel is nudged down from 0.55 to 0.51. Progressively changing the image like this over many steps ends up noising the image due to the nature of the sampled values coming from the Gaussian curve.

The Forward Process: Controlled Destruction

The forward diffusion process is defined by a schedule of noise levels, indexed by a timestep `t` that runs from `0` (no noise, the original image) to `T` (pure noise, typically

T=1000). At each step, you add a small amount of Gaussian noise according to a prespecified schedule.

Mathematically, if x_0 is your original image and x_t is the noisy version at step t, the forward process at each step is:

$$x_t = \sqrt{1 - \beta_t} x_{t-1} + \sqrt{\beta_t} \epsilon, \quad \epsilon \sim \mathcal{N}(0, 1)$$

Where β_t (called the *beta schedule*) controls how much noise to add at each step. The ε in this formula is exactly the same one you saw in the Gaussian noise in the previous section. It defines the bunch of random numbers you can select. However, on its own, the Gaussian noise has a standard deviation of 1, which is far too large a distribution for normalized pixel values that can be found in a range of 0 to 1. Without modification, values drawn from the distribution would obliterate the pixels in a single step!

That's where the beta schedule comes in. Think of β_t as the volume knob on the noise. The term sqrt(β_t) · ε shrinks the unit-Gaussian noise down to a much smaller magnitude. When $\beta_1 = 0.00085$, the factor sqrt(β_1) ≈ 0.029 means each random draw gets scaled down by about 34×; for example, a draw of +1.5 from the bell curve becomes a tiny +0.044 nudge to the pixel. The image barely changes.

But over time, we want to increase the volume, and that's why it's a beta *schedule.* So, when we reach step 1000, $\beta_{1000} = 0.012$. Then, the factor sqrt(β_{1000}) ≈ 0.11 only scales the draw down by 9×, so the same +1.5 draw becomes a +0.17 nudge, which is much more visible.

In Stable Diffusion's default schedule, β_1 is tiny (about 0.00085, barely any noise) and β_{1000} is much larger (about 0.012, significant noise). The schedule increases roughly linearly so that early steps add a whisper of noise and later steps add more substantial amounts.

Here's some code that uses the DDPMScheduler from Hugging Face's diffusers library to show this in action, allowing you also to simulate what the noise would look like at a particular step:

```
# x0 is the image
x0 = load_image(path)
# Set up the scheduler
scheduler = DDPMScheduler(
    num_train_timesteps=1000,
    beta_schedule="scaled_linear",    # the SD-default
    beta_start=0.00085,
    beta_end=0.012,
)
frames = []
for t in TIMESTEPS_TO_SHOW:
```

```
    # Sample one noise tensor per timestep so each step shows
    # a different realization, not a cumulative blur.
    eps = torch.randn_like(x0)
    timesteps = torch.tensor([t])
    xt = scheduler.add_noise(x0.unsqueeze(0), eps.unsqueeze(0), timesteps)[0]
    frames.append(to_pil(xt))
```

So, over time, when you add noise like this to a picture, it will progressively dissolve into static for each timestep (i.e., as `t` grows). At `t=200`, the image will still be recognizable. At `t=500`, you'll likely still make out the shape. By the time `t=800`, it's mostly noise. By `t=1000`, it's indistinguishable from pure noise sampled from a Gaussian.

This is used to train the model. Now you have training examples: the image at a particular step (x_t), the step number (`t`), and the noise (ε). This is a triplet telling you that the image was corrupted with the noise at that particular step. Over time, the model can then learn to reverse this, so it would look at images at particular timesteps, predict the noise used to corrupt it, and then subtract that noise.

> You might wonder why we don't just add a fixed amount of noise per step. Why all the fuss with a beta schedule that grows over time? The answer is that the model needs training signals across a wide range of difficulties. If every timestep added the same amount of noise, most of the schedule would be "trivially easy" (the image is almost clean) or "trivially impossible" (the image is almost pure noise). The carefully designed schedule ensures that intermediate timesteps cover the *useful* range—the range where the model has to make real decisions about what's signal and what's noise.

The Reverse Process: Denoising

Training a diffusion model is conceptually simple. When we think about it in ML terms and figure out how to measure the loss, it turns out that good, old-fashioned mean squared error (MSE) is a great function to use. Think about it: we first sample the actual noise that was added to an image (aka ε), so the training loop knows the ground truth. Then the network, shown only the noisy image and the timestep, predicts its own guess (ε_θ).

Comparing a known target against a prediction of the same shape is the textbook setup for a simple objective, and MSE is the perfect loss function to learn from it!

You're essentially playing a game where the network has to look at a noisy image and attempt to reconstruct the exact noise pattern that was added to it. If it can do that across millions of images and many possible timesteps and many possible prompts, it has implicitly learned the *structure* of real images.

Then, at inference time, you simply start with pure noise, and ask the neural network to predict the amount of noise present in the image at that step. But you don't just subtract that prediction directly; the predicted noise is scaled by factors derived from the noise schedule. If you're starting at `t=999` (so the image is x_{999}), you predict the image at `t=998` (now the image is x_{998}). Then repeat again and again until you get to step `t=0`, and you'll have the predicted image x_0. Handling the process of getting the image on this path is the job of a component called a *scheduler*, which will be discussed in "The Scheduler: Managing Denoising" on page 271.

If you're not familiar with any of the terms (like UNet) shown in Figure 12-5, don't worry—all will become clear. Just like diffusion, we're gradually denoising the concepts! 🙂

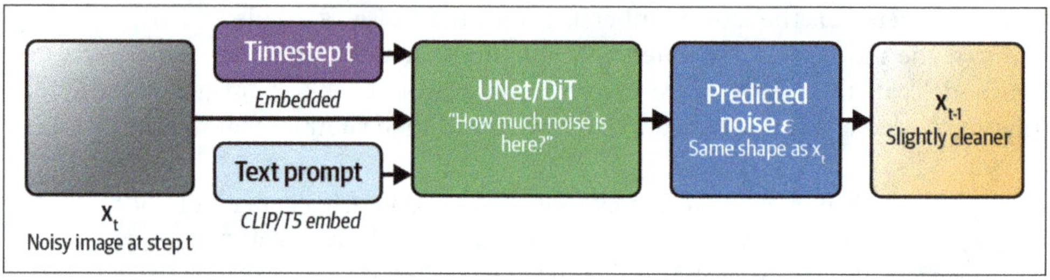

Figure 12-5. The process of denoising

An important thing to internalize here is to remember that we train for three values: the image at a particular step, the step itself, and the noise that was added for that step. To prevent bias in the training, you ultimately scatter (x_t, t, ε) examples randomly across the schedule. You want the model to learn how things work at any particular step and not to be affected by prior or subsequent ones. That way, when denoising, it should be effective at every individual step.

The UNet Architecture

One of the workhorses in the architecture that learns to noise and denoise the image is a type of UNet architecture. You saw it in Figure 12-5, but let's look at it in a bit more detail now.

The function that maps a noisy image, a timestep, and a text prompt to a noise prediction is implemented with this architecture. It gets its name from its U-shaped structure: the input is repeatedly downsampled to a coarse representation, then progressively upsampled back to the original resolution. You can see this in Figure 12-6.

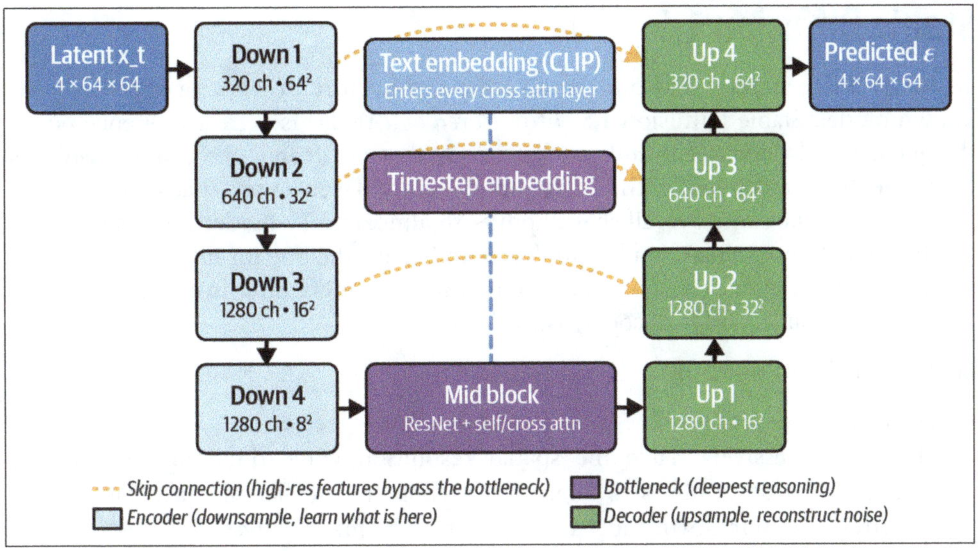

Figure 12-6. UNet architecture

You might be wondering why all the downsampling and upsampling is necessary. Ultimately, the goal is to give the neural network global context across the image. To decide whether a pixel is noise or signal, it needs to know the entire scene that it's looking at.

Downsampling delivers that context: each *halving* of resolution *doubles* every feature's effective view of the image, so by the bottom of the U, each cell summarizes a large region, enough to recognize a whole face or object.

Second, the network needs *pixel-precise output*, because the predicted noise at a particular pixel (e.g., that at coordinates `37, 142`) has to line up with that exact pixel. Downsampling alone would destroy that precision.

The fix is the *skip connections*: at every level, high-resolution features from the downsampling side are carried straight across to the upsampling side, so fine detail, like edges and textures, never has to be reinvented from scratch. This also improves the gradient flow during training.

The U architecture then very elegantly gives you both global understanding and exact spatial alignment in the same network.

Stable Diffusion 1.5

To make this concrete, let's pin the abstract architecture down to a specific, well-known model. Stable Diffusion 1.5 (*https://oreil.ly/aAKLu*) is a great reference point. It's open, widely deployed, and small enough that you can poke around with its components on a consumer GPU. The numbers and layer names that follow belong to SD 1.5, but the same overall shape applies to almost every modern diffusion UNet you'll meet. Do note that if you're familiar with UNets, the one for diffusion is heavily augmented with attention layers as well as timestep-embedding injection. It's much more than just an encoder-decoder, as we'll explore.

Let's look at the components:

Down blocks
: These progressively halve the spatial resolution while doubling the channel count. For a `64 × 64 × 4` latent (we'll explain why "latent" and not "pixels" shortly), the four down blocks produce feature maps at `64²`, `32²`, `16²`, and `8²` resolutions, with `320`, `640`, `1280`, and `1280` channels, respectively. Each block contains ResNet subblocks (convolution + group norm + SiLU activation) and, in three of the four blocks, attention layers.

Mid-block
: This sits at the bottleneck. It's where the deepest reasoning happens. The spatial resolution is small (`8 × 8`), so each "pixel" of the feature map summarizes a large region of the image. The mid-block contains ResNet + self-attention + cross-attention + ResNet, and it's where the prompt has the strongest global influence on the image.

Up blocks
: These mirror the down blocks but in reverse: they upsample and reduce channel counts. The critical detail is that each up block receives the corresponding down block's output via a skip connection. So the up block at `16 × 16` resolution doesn't just see the upsampled features from the lower level; it also sees the original, high-quality features from the `16 × 16` down block. This is what lets the UNet preserve fine detail while still benefiting from deep, large-receptive-field reasoning.

Output projection
: This takes the final `64 × 64 × 320` feature map and projects it down to `64 × 64 × 4`, the same shape as the input. Those four channels are the predicted noise tensor for the four-channel latent.

The whole thing is around 860 million parameters for SD 1.5, 2.6 billion for SDXL, and substantially more for newer models. To put that in context, a typical Llama 3 8B language model has 8 billion parameters, so the SD 1.5 UNet is about 10% the size of a small language model. But it's the *only* trainable component you'll touch when fine-tuning. The text encoder and VAE stay frozen in 99% of cases.

You can inspect it with code like the following. First, let's look at the model and dump the parameter count of the main pipeline components:

```
import torch
from diffusers import StableDiffusionPipeline

pipe = StableDiffusionPipeline.from_pretrained(
    "runwayml/stable-diffusion-v1-5",
    torch_dtype=torch.float16,
).to("cuda")

def count_params(m):
    return sum(p.numel() for p in m.parameters())

print(f"text_encoder: {count_params(pipe.text_encoder)/1e6:>8.1f}M")
print(f"vae:          {count_params(pipe.vae)/1e6:>8.1f}M")
print(f"unet:         {count_params(pipe.unet)/1e6:>8.1f}M")
```

Running it should give output like this:

```
Loaded pipeline: runwayml/stable-diffusion-v1-5

Component          Class                                   Params
-----------------------------------------------------------------
text_encoder       CLIPTextModel                          123.1 M
tokenizer          CLIPTokenizer                                -
vae                AutoencoderKL                           83.7 M
unet               UNet2DConditionModel                   859.5 M
scheduler          PNDMScheduler                    (config only)
```

As you can see, the largest part of the network by far is the UNet, with 859M+ parameters. So, that's where most of your fine-tuning energy will go.

Within the UNet itself, you can inspect the different blocks:

```
unet = pipe.unet
print("block_out_channels:", list(unet.config.block_out_channels))

for i, block in enumerate(unet.down_blocks):
    in_ch  = block.resnets[0].in_channels
    out_ch = block.resnets[-1].out_channels
    has_attn = getattr(block, "attentions", None) and len(block.attentions) > 0
    print(f"down[{i}] {type(block).__name__:<26} "
          f"in={in_ch:>4} out={out_ch:>4} attn={bool(has_attn)}")
```

The output for this will describe the different blocks with their attributes:

```
=== UNet structure ===
latent in:  4 channels
latent out: 4 channels
block_out_channels: [320, 640, 1280, 1280]
```

```
Down blocks (4):
  [0] ↓ CrossAttnDownBlock2D      in= 320  out= 320  attn=yes
  [1] ↓ CrossAttnDownBlock2D      in= 320  out= 640  attn=yes
  [2] ↓ CrossAttnDownBlock2D      in= 640  out=1280  attn=yes
  [3] · DownBlock2D               in=1280  out=1280  attn=no

Mid block:
  ·   UNetMidBlock2DCrossAttn    in=1280  out=1280

Up blocks (4):
  [0] ↑ UpBlock2D                 in=2560  out=1280  attn=no
  [1] ↑ CrossAttnUpBlock2D        in=2560  out=1280  attn=yes
  [2] ↑ CrossAttnUpBlock2D        in=1920  out= 640  attn=yes
  [3] · CrossAttnUpBlock2D        in= 960  out= 320  attn=yes
```

Inspecting this yields some very interesting conclusions. First of all, the in channels on the up blocks are lighter than you might expect. For example, the first one is `2560`, and not the `1280` from the corresponding down block. The reason: the skip connections. It receives both! So while it might look like a bug where the sizes are bigger than you might think, it's actually a feature.

Earlier, we mentioned that instead of using the full pixels of an image, we could use a much smaller latent space to represent it. Here's a look at what happens when a fake latent dimension (1, 4, 64, 64) is passed through the UNet.

For the purposes of this, you can see it as a tensor, so (1, 4, 64, 64) is effectively a batch size of 1 (aka a single tensor), with 4 channels, and 64 x 64 latents.

```
=== Tensor shape trace through the UNet ===
block     output shape
--------------------------------------
down[0]   (1, 320, 32, 32)
down[1]   (1, 640, 16, 16)
down[2]   (1, 1280, 8, 8)
down[3]   (1, 1280, 8, 8)
mid       (1, 1280, 8, 8)
up[0]     (1, 1280, 16, 16)
up[1]     (1, 1280, 32, 32)
up[2]     (1, 640, 64, 64)
up[3]     (1, 320, 64, 64)

The spatial dims should walk 64 -> 32 -> 16 -> 8 -> 16 -> 32 -> 64.
```

So the third and fourth parameters (the spatial dimensions) walk the route from 64 down to 8, and back up to 64. That's the U-shape that gives the network its name!

Revisiting the idea of a *latent* rather than an *image*, we can see that the tensor is 4 × 64 × 64 rather than the 3 × 512 × 512 you'd expect for an RGB picture. That's because Stable Diffusion's UNet doesn't actually operate on pixels. Before any denoising happens, a small autoencoder (the VAE) compresses the 512 × 512 RGB image down to a 64 × 64 tensor with 4 abstract channels, and the UNet does all of its work in that compressed space. This is the latent in practice! For now, think of it as a learned compression of the image that makes it more efficient to work with while keeping the contents of the image intact. Consider a "latent" as a small, content-rich stand-in for the image, with the same (N, C, H, W) shape conventions but very different dimensions.

How the Prompt and Timestep Enter the UNet

To effectively denoise an image, the UNet doesn't just see the noisy image, it also needs to know which timestep it is at, because denoising a barely noisy image is a very different task from denoising a very noisy one. And, if you want text to guide the denoising (which, let's face it, is the whole point), you also need the embeddings for the prompt.

The timestep enters through a sinusoidal embedding, in a very similar way to token positions in the original transformer paper (*https://oreil.ly/TnLNu*), which we covered way back in Chapter 2. The idea is that the timestep is mapped to a vector of sines and cosines at different frequencies, so the network sees a smooth, continuous representation of time, rather than a raw integer. That vector is used in a technique called *FiLM*, which is beyond the scope of this book, but you can find it explained in the paper "FiLM: Visual Reasoning with a General Conditioning Layer" (*https://oreil.ly/EA6HS*) by Ethan Perez et al. The bottom line is that every layer of the UNet will know what timestep it's denoising for.

The text embedding enters through the cross-attention layers sprinkled throughout the UNet. The text encoder turns your prompt into a sequence of vectors. For Stable Diffusion 1.5, this is 77 vectors, each of 768 dimensions. Other models will have different dimensions, and later ones will have much larger dimensions. Then, inside the UNet, the image features are effectively the queries (Q), with the text acting as the keys and values (KV). Each spatial location in the image will "query" the text, asking which words apply to it, and will then pull in the relevant linguistic information.

You can see this in Figure 12-7.

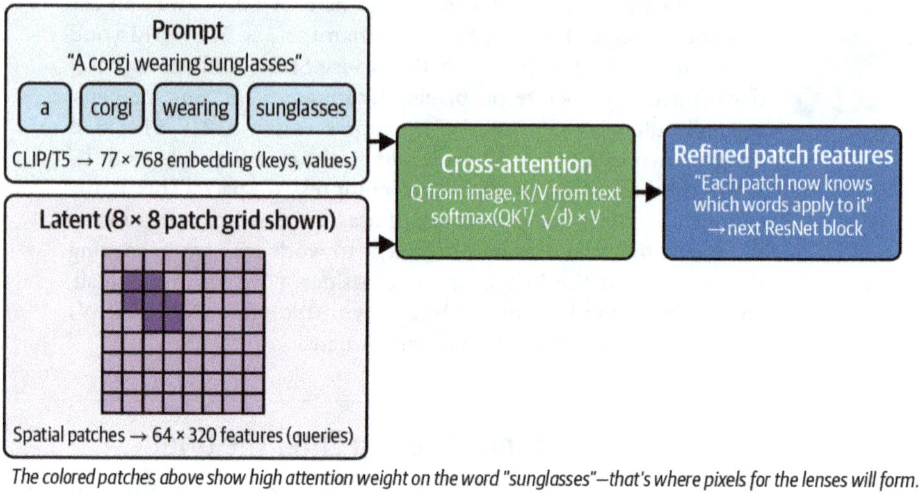

Figure 12-7. Cross-attention: how the prompt steers the pixels

It's the same cross-attention we saw earlier for vision language models (VLMs), but running in the opposite direction! We have a prompt ("a corgi wearing sunglasses"), and a set of latent space patches from the image. The idea here is to take the patches, one by one, as shown in the bottom left of Figure 12-7. The patch's feature vector will act as the query, which is scored against each of the embeddings from the prompt (aka the keys). For a patch sitting where the lenses will eventually appear, the goal is for the score to max on "sunglasses." The patch will then pull in a weighted blend of the token values (dominated by the one for "sunglasses") and add them to its own features. By the time the next block runs, the patch is now carrying the "essence" of sunglasses within it alongside whatever visual content it already had. Repeat this for every patch and every cross-attention layer, and the tokens from the prompt get "painted" into the latent space for that patch in the image. Then, during later inference, whenever that token appears in a prompt, the model knows to decode to something that looks like the patches that it learned have the "essence" of sunglasses within them.

The Latent Trick

Let's look a little more at the idea of latent spaces for the image patches. If everything we've looked at so far occurred in pixel space, then diffusion models would be far too slow for practical use. For example, a 512 × 512 × 3 image has 786,432 values. If each pixel had to be attended to 20 or more times to generate a single image, the memory and time cost of activations to train that would be brutal!

The breakthrough that made Stable Diffusion possible was the idea of running the process in a latent space instead. The idea is simple: use a small variational autoencoder (VAE). A VAE learns to compress images in a way that allows them to be decompressed with minimal loss. We've all seen compression utilities like ZIP or RAR, and likely understand a little about image compression like *.png* or *.jpeg* files. These are algorithmic compression, where a clever mathematician found out how to pack more information into less space with minimal loss. A VAE instead *learns* how to compress. If given a bunch of images, it can figure out a representation of those images that is smaller, but which when reinflated has minimal loss. To generalize, it has to be trained on lots of images. This compression is what we call a "latent."

In Stable Diffusion, a VAE was trained that reliably takes 512 × 512 × 3 images (with 786,432 values) and compresses them into 64 × 64 × 4 latents with 16,384 values. Now, if you do all the diffusion math on the latent, you're working with 48× less data, and thus it's more manageable for speed and memory.

So, the full inference pipeline with Stable Diffusion has three different forward passes per generation:

- The first is the text encoder taking your prompt and turning it into 77 vectors (one forward pass through CLIP).
- The second is the UNet denoising a random latent into a clean latent with 20 or so forward passes.
- The third is the VAE decoder that maps the clean latent into a 512 × 512 × 3 RGB image with one forward pass.

You can see this in Figure 12-8.

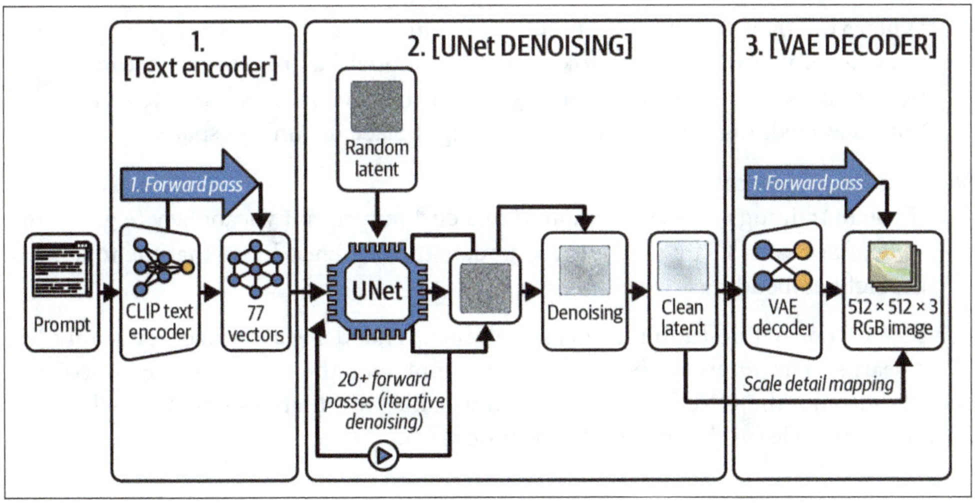

Figure 12-8. The inference pipeline in Stable Diffusion

As you work with or fine-tune different models, you'll see differences in these. You use the text encoder and the VAE off-the-shelf, and usually do fine-tuning on the UNet. So look out for differences in the specifics such as the size of the text encoder output (77 for SD 1.5, very different for others), as well as the latent and output sizes dictated by the VAE the model uses. These different sizes will ultimately impact the size of the prompt you can use to generate images with the model.

The Text Encoder

Earlier, we explored how the text becomes KV values for image patches, but let's just dig a little deeper into what it does. Ultimately, the text encoder is the part of the pipeline that turns "a corgi wearing sunglasses" into a numerical representation that the UNet can attend to.

For Stable Diffusion 1.5, this is the CLIP text encoder, specifically the ViT-L/14 variant trained on 400 million image-caption pairs by OpenAI. SDXL uses two text encoders in parallel (CLIP ViT-L plus OpenCLIP ViT-bigG). Some newer models use Google's T5 instead, which is much larger and produces noticeably better prompt adherence at the cost of higher VRAM.

The CLIP text encoder is, structurally, a vanilla transformer. It takes your tokenized prompt (padded or truncated to 77 tokens), runs it through 12 transformer blocks, and outputs 77 vectors of size 768. Those 77 vectors are what the UNet's cross-attention layers read.

When you fine-tune a diffusion model, you almost always leave the text encoder frozen. There are two main exceptions:

Rare-token training (DreamBooth, Textual Inversion)
: When you want to teach the model a specific subject (your dog, your product, your face), you bind it to a token that the model has never seen meaningfully before, like `<my-subject>`. The text encoder may need a small update so that this token's embedding actually points to the right place in concept space.

Style-specific prompt tokens
: If you're training a model to respond to a custom prompt vocabulary (e.g., "in the style of `arc-art`"), you may want to update the text encoder so that the token has the right embedding.

For 95% of LoRA fine-tuning use cases, the text encoder stays frozen and only the UNet learns. The interplay between the prompt and the image is then mediated entirely through the UNet's cross-attention weights, and that's exactly the right place for the model to learn the specifics of your domain.

The Scheduler: Managing Denoising

The scheduler is the simplest piece of the pipeline, and the one you won't touch in fine-tuning because it has no trainable parameters! It's still worth understanding because choosing the right scheduler can dramatically improve quality and speed.

A scheduler should address two issues:

Training time
: What's the noise schedule? Given a timestep `t`, how much noise was added to the image?

Inference time
: Given the current noisy image, the predicted noise, and the current timestep, how do I produce the slightly less noisy image at `t-1` (or some larger jump)?

The original DDPM scheduler uses 1,000 timesteps and follows the exact reverse process derived from the forward process. It works, but 1,000 forward passes through the UNet is painfully slow at inference time when you want to generate an image. Modern schedulers solve this by reformulating the reverse process with fewer steps, typically 20–50, using the following tactics:

DDIM (Denoising Diffusion Implicit Models)
: This was the first big speedup. It's deterministic and works well at 50 steps.

DPM-Solver/DPM++ (multistep)
: These are higher-order ODE solvers, usually optimal at 20–30 steps.

Euler and Euler Ancestral
: These are simple and stable; Ancestral injects fresh noise each step for more variation. These generally require 20–30 steps and 30–40 steps, respectively.

UniPC
: This is a recent solver that pushes the step count even lower (sometimes 10–15) with good quality.

For most fine-tuning work, the scheduler is something you pick once during inference. During *training*, I would encourage you to typically use the DPM scheduler (or DDIMScheduler in training mode) to sample noisy examples, because it's the cleanest theoretical fit for the noise-prediction objective. During *inference*, you swap to DPM++ or UniPC for speed.

In code, when using the diffusers library from Hugging Face, you'll notice that everything is treated as a pipeline. So, to load Stable Diffusion 1.5 as a pipeline, and specify the scheduler, you can do this:

```
from diffusers import StableDiffusionPipeline, DPMSolverMultistepScheduler
pipe = StableDiffusionPipeline.from_pretrained("runwayml/stable-diffusion-v1-5")
# Replace the slow default scheduler with a fast multistep solver
pipe.scheduler = DPMSolverMultistepScheduler.from_config(pipe.scheduler.config)
```

This little swap will turn a typical 50-step generation taking 12–15 seconds into a 25-step one taking 6–8 seconds with little quality difference for most prompts!

The Full Pipeline

In the previous section, we saw the term "pipe" used in code denoting a pipeline for inference. Let's look at that in a bit more detail now. The pipeline when you put all the pieces together, including the scheduler, will look like Figure 12-9.

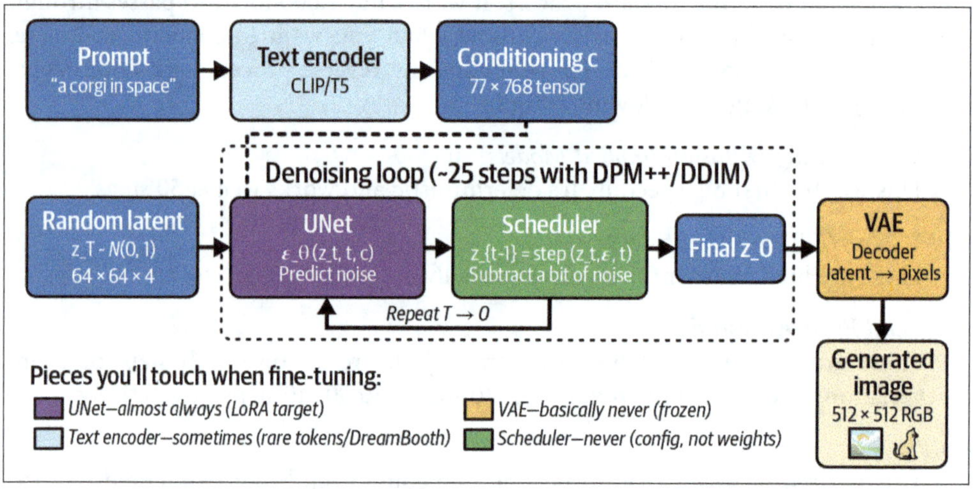

Figure 12-9. The Stable Diffusion pipeline

Step by step, it follows this process:

1. Tokenization: the prompt string is tokenized by CLIP into 77 tokens.
2. Encoding: the 77 tokens go through the CLIP text encoder, producing a [77, 768] tensor that we'll call "c" (for conditioning).
3. A random latent tensor is created from Gaussian noise, initialized with a random value. We'll call this z_T.
4. For 20–25 iterations (if using DPM++), the UNet predicts the noise in the current latent, and the scheduler will update the latent to denoise it.

5. The final latent, after all the iterations are done (called z_0), goes through the VAE decoder producing a [3, 512, 512] pixel tensor.
6. The pixel tensor is then clipped to [0, 1] and scaled up to [0, 255] to denormalize it, and saved as an image file.

In code, this looks like:

```
import torch
from diffusers import StableDiffusionPipeline, DPMSolverMultistepScheduler

pipe = StableDiffusionPipeline.from_pretrained(
    "runwayml/stable-diffusion-v1-5",
    torch_dtype=torch.float16,
)
pipe.scheduler = DPMSolverMultistepScheduler.from_config(pipe.scheduler.config)
pipe = pipe.to("cuda")

generator = torch.Generator(device="cuda").manual_seed(42)

image = pipe(
    prompt="a corgi wearing sunglasses",
    num_inference_steps=25,
    guidance_scale=7.5,
    generator=generator,
).images[0]

image.save("corgi.png")
```

I've provided this code in the book's download. It usually generates an image in less than 10 seconds depending on your hardware!

A few parameters worth understanding:

`num_inference_steps`
: This controls the number of denoising iterations. More steps means marginally better quality at the cost of linear inference time. For DPM++, 20–25 is the sweet spot.

`guidance_scale`
: This is the classifier-free guidance strength. Higher numbers (10+) force the model to adhere more strictly to the prompt at the cost of diversity and naturalness. Lower numbers (3–5) give more creative latitude, with 7.5 being the broadly accepted default.

`generator`
: This controls the random seed for the starting noise. Pin it for reproducibility; unpin it for variation. You see here, I used 42 as the seed. Change that and you'll see a different image despite the prompt staying the same!

Classifier-Free Guidance

The guidance scale parameter we mentioned in the previous section as a way to adhere to the prompt is actually quite fascinating in how it works. Let's take a closer look.

During training, the model is typically given a random empty prompt. Usually, this occurs about 5%–10% of the time, so it can learn to generate images both with and without text conditioning. So, at inference, you run the UNet twice per step on the same noisy latent: once with your real prompt, which gives you a conditional noise prediction `ε_cond`; and once with an empty prompt, which gives you an unconditional noise prediction `ε_uncond`. Both are just UNet outputs—vectors with the same shape as the latent.

The math behind it looks like this:

$$\varepsilon\_final = \varepsilon\_uncond + scale \cdot (\varepsilon\_cond - \varepsilon\_uncond)$$

If scale = 1, you just get the conditional prediction with no extra guidance applied! Basically, the model uses the standard conditional prediction (i.e., normal prompt without additional guidance).

If scale = 7.5 or greater, you increasingly exaggerate the difference between "with prompt" and "without prompt," steering the image more aggressively toward what the prompt describes. It costs you 2× compute per step because it's 2 UNet passes instead of 1, but it does dramatically improve prompt adherence!

When you fine-tune a model, this guidance will still work, as your LoRA learns to influence the conditional pass, while the unconditional pass continues to use the model's base behavior.

Negative Prompts

The unconditional path leads to a neat side effect. Instead of passing an empty string as the unconditional prompt, you can pass a *negative prompt*, which is a description of what you *do not* want to see. The math is the same, but now the guidance formula will push the generation away from the negative prompt (instead of away from an empty prompt) and toward the positive prompt. Let's take a look at a code example:

```
image = pipe(
    prompt="a corgi astronaut on Mars, cinematic lighting",
    negative_prompt="blurry, low quality, extra limbs, watermark, text",
    num_inference_steps=25,
    guidance_scale=7.5,
).images[0]
```

Negative prompts are one of the most underused tools in image generation. They're particularly powerful for cleaning up common failure modes. For example, "extra fingers, malformed hands" cleans up a lot of human generations; "blurry, jpeg artifacts" sharpens output noticeably; "text, watermark, signature" prevents the model from hallucinating fake captions onto the image. When you start evaluating a fine-tuned LoRA against the base model, controlling for the negative prompt is essential to make the comparison fair.

Fine-Tuning

Let's now take what we've learned about diffusion models and connect it back to fine-tuning. If you take nothing else away from this chapter, remember this: almost all diffusion fine-tuning attaches a LoRA to the UNet's attention layers.

Specifically, each attention block has four projection matrices:

`to_q`
: Projects features to the query

`to_k`
: Projects features to the key

`to_v`
: Projects features to the value

`to_out.0`
: Projects the attention output back to feature space

Both self-attention layers (where the image attends to itself) and cross-attention layers (where the image attends to the text) use these same four projection names. So a single LoRA configuration covers both, and that's exactly what you want, because both kinds of attention contribute to how the prompt shapes the image.

Here's the code, which looks just like LoRA configuration for language models:

```
from peft import LoraConfig

lora_config = LoraConfig(
    r=8,                  # rank: 8 to 32 is typical for image LoRAs
    lora_alpha=8,
    target_modules=["to_q", "to_k", "to_v", "to_out.0"],
    lora_dropout=0.0,
    bias="none",
)
```

> In the preceding code snippet, you might notice one big difference compared to the language-model LoRA we saw in earlier chapters. There's no `task_type`. That's because that parameter never actually changed the adapters; it just told PEFT which task-specific wrapper to use. The UNet isn't a language model, and matches none of PEFT's predefined tasks, so we just leave it out, and PEFT will fall back to its generic wrapper.

I've provided a script in the book's downloads that measures the total UNet parameters, and the LoRA trainable ones with this configuration, and you'll see from there that the UNet has 859.52M parameters for Stable DIffusion 1.5, while the LoRA has only 0.8M, which is a mere 0.09%.

So, with less than 1% of the UNet's weights, we have a set that is positioned at exactly the points where the image and text interact. That's where the new subjects (where you can draw a particular image, like "my dog") or styles (where you can define all images to follow a particular style, like "art nouveau") can be encoded. It's also why image LoRAs are so small (often 50–150 MB) and so easy to share.

Summary

That's the whole architecture of image generation with diffusion models. You've learned that a diffusion model is primarily a noise-prediction network that is called repeatedly to transform random static into a coherent image, guided by a text prompt. It has four main components:

Text encoder
: This is used to turn the prompt into a sequence of vectors. This is frozen for fine-tuning.

UNet
: This is the architecture used for denoising. It takes a noisy latent, a timestep, and the text embedding and predicts the noise for this timestep, if it can be removed. Here is where you attach your LoRA.

Scheduler
: This component controls the noise schedule at training time, and the denoising trajectory at inference time. It has no learned weights to tune; it's pure math.

VAE
: The variational autoencoder compresses and decompresses between pixels and latents. It's frozen during fine-tuning.

The training objective, then, becomes a simple one: minimize the MSE between predicted noise and actual noise. There's no preference data, reward model, RLHF complexity, or any other add-ons. It's simply paired image and caption data and a lot of gradient descent. (Just like the good old days!)

Inference flips that script. Start from random noise, and use the UNet to denoise it, before decoding the result through the VAE.

Everything you do from here on out will build upon that foundation. Fine-tuning the model to learn a new subject, a new artistic style, even a new vocabulary of prompt tokens to add a new style will be reduced to "attach a small set of trainable parameters at the right place in the UNet and run the same loop on your data."

The hard work is understanding *where* those places are and *why* they matter. Hopefully this chapter helped you with that!

In Chapter 13, you'll take this foundation and actually train something. We'll walk through the two canonical recipes for diffusion fine-tuning: *DreamBooth*, for teaching the model a specific subject (e.g., your dog, your product, your face), and *style LoRAs*, for injecting a visual style (e.g., anime line art, watercolor, your brand's photography) and run both, end to end, on a consumer GPU.

We'll also cover the practical side that always bites first-time fine-tuners: curating a small dataset, picking the right hyperparameters, evaluating whether the LoRA actually learned what you wanted, and the surprisingly nuanced problem of *brand consistency* in teaching a model your visual identity well enough that it can render new compositions in your style without mangling your trademarked subjects.

We'll explore all this with Stable Diffusion variations, and see how the patterns extend clearly to other models.

For now, you've made the conceptual leap from autoregressive token generation to iterative denoising. You should now understand the four components of a diffusion pipeline, so you can start to generate images from text.

CHAPTER 13

Fine-Tuning Diffusion Models

In Chapter 12, you saw how a diffusion model works from the inside: a frozen VAE, a frozen text encoder, a UNet that predicts noise, and a scheduler that turns predictions into pixels. You also saw, at the conceptual level, where the trainable knobs live. This chapter is where you actually turn and tune those knobs.

You're going to fine-tune diffusion models for two completely different outcomes. These will be to teach the model a specific *subject* and a specific *style*. You'll use the same model architecture and training loop for both, switching between them by changing only the training data.

The first (subject) teaches the model to draw one specific thing: your dog, your product, your face. The second (style) teaches it a visual vocabulary: your brand's photography, your illustrator's hand, an anime line-art look.

By the end of the chapter, you'll have walked through both recipes end-to-end on a single consumer GPU, you'll know how to compose multiple adapters at inference, and you'll have a quantitative evaluation harness that tells you whether your adapter actually learned what you wanted.

Two Recipes, One Architecture

A diffusion model can fail you in two main ways. It can refuse to draw the specific *thing* you want, such as your particular dog or your particular product. Or it can refuse to draw it in the *look* you want, such as your brand's photography style or your illustrator's hand. Both are fine-tuning problems, and both are solved by attaching a small LoRA to the UNet's attention layers and training it on a focused dataset. The skill you'll bring to the table to help fix this problem is in determining the shape of the dataset and the way you write the captions.

This is the single most important distinction in diffusion fine-tuning! Remember that *subject* training teaches the model *what* to draw. You feed it a number of pictures of one specific thing, all paired with a caption that includes a rare token (such as `sks dog`), and the model learns to bind that rare token to that thing.

Style training teaches the model *how* to draw. You feed it a number of pictures of *different* subjects, all rendered in the same visual idiom, and the model learns to bind a different rare token to the brushwork, palette, lighting, and composition that those pictures share. You can see this general idea in Figure 13-1.

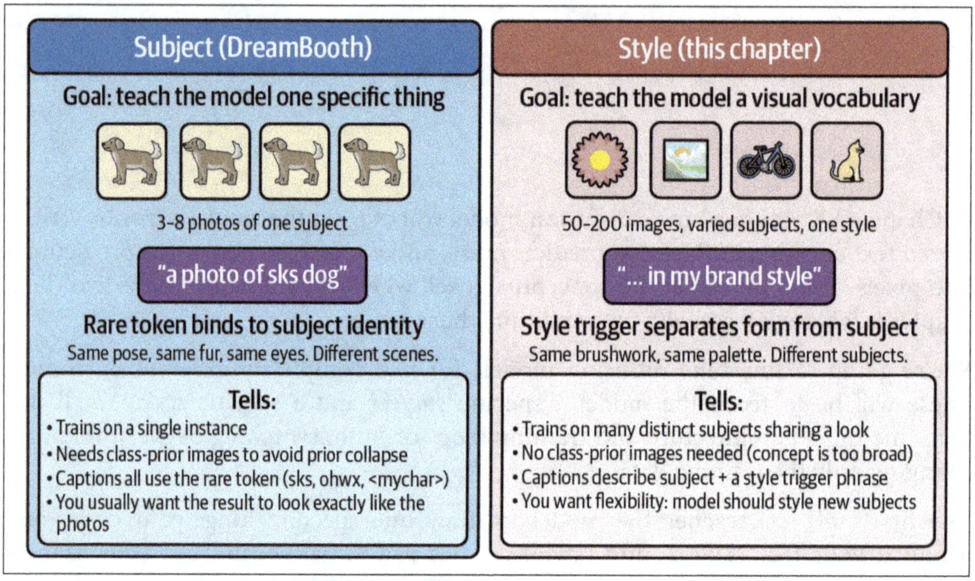

Figure 13-1. Subject versus style

If you remember nothing else from this chapter, remember the shape of those two datasets: subject training is many photos of one thing, while style training is many things that share a common look and feel.

The first wants narrow data and a class-prior set (I'll explain this more shortly) to prevent the model from forgetting what an ordinary dog looks like. The second wants broad data with no class prior at all, because the "class" of a style is the entire visual world rendered through that lens. The two problems share a single training script. You'll change the data, the captions, a few hyperparameters, and that's it.

You'll often want both at once, by the way. The flagship deliverable for most production use cases is a *brand image*: a specific subject (your product) rendered in a specific style (your brand's photography). You can sometimes get there with one LoRA, but in practice it's cleaner to train two separate adapters and compose them at inference.

We'll explore composition of multiple fine-tunes toward the end of the chapter, after we've built each kind of LoRA on its own.

> Again, where the LoRA goes is of utmost importance. We covered this in Chapter 12, but it's worth restating here because the rest of this chapter assumes it. In both DreamBooth and style training, you attach a LoRA to four projection matrices inside *every* attention block of the UNet: `to_q`, `to_k`, `to_v`, and `to_out.0`. These four points are where the model decides what each spatial location should pay attention to, and where the text prompt influences the image features. Less than 1% of the UNet's parameters live there, but those parameters carry the entire learning signal for "What does this new token mean?" The VAE and the text encoder stay frozen in both recipes. The scheduler has no learned weights to begin with.

DreamBooth: Teaching a Subject

The most common reason you might want to fine-tune a diffusion model isn't to teach it new general knowledge, but instead to teach it a *specific subject*; for example, your product, your pet, your company's mascot, or your own face. The technique for this is called *DreamBooth* (*https://oreil.ly/2nHUP*), originally proposed by researchers at Google in 2022 and rapidly adopted by the community.

The Core Ideas of DreamBooth

The concepts you need to learn in DreamBooth are twofold.

First, you need a way to refer to your subject in the prompt that doesn't fight with the model's existing knowledge. You can't just say "my dog" because the embedding for the words "my dog" already points at a strong general notion of "dog," and the fine-tuning gradient would effectively have to fight against that ingrained knowledge. Instead, you pick a token the model has almost never seen, like `sks`, `ohwx`, or a deliberately weird custom token like `<my-dog>`. During training, the model rapidly binds the visual concept of your specific dog to that rare token.

Second, you need to prevent the model from forgetting what a generic "dog" looks like in the process! This is called *prior preservation*. Without it, training on a few photos of your dog would tend to corrupt the model's general notion of "dog" so that *every* dog it generates starts to look like *your* dog. And while you love your little pooch, it's probably not a good idea to refactor the entire concept of a dog to look like yours. To prevent this, you also train on images of generic dogs (captioned `"a photo of a dog"`) alongside your subject images (captioned `"a photo of sks dog"`). The two losses get added together, with a small weight on the class-prior term.

> While the original technique required obscure, rare tokens (like `sks`) to prevent overwriting existing text encoder concepts, current personalization workflows like LoRA fine-tuning on SDXL or Flux have shifted away from this. The reason: modern text encoders can possess far richer language understanding. This allows trainers to pair high-quality natural language captions with clean tokenizer-friendly identifiers. Highly descriptive captions can handle the contextual separation, removing the need for rare tokens. But in order to learn the fundamentals, I'm working with the original DreamBooth technique for this chapter. It will set you up well for more advanced techniques.

The General Recipe

In modern practice, the DreamBooth recipe is almost always combined with LoRA. Here's the full workflow:

1. Collect 3–8 high-quality photos of your subject. Vary the background, pose, and lighting. It's not many, but it's often enough! Pick a rare token (like `sks`) and write your instance prompt: `"a photo of sks dog"`.
2. Autogenerate 200 or more class-prior images by asking the base model to produce `"a photo of a dog"` at least 200 times. In practice, I would recommend making many more and then hand-selecting 200 of the best ones. (This recommendation comes from the original DreamBooth paper.)
3. Attach a LoRA to the UNet's attention layers.
4. Train for 800–2,000 steps with a learning rate around 1e-4, batch size 1 per stream, gradient accumulation 4.
5. Save the LoRA adapter, which will weigh somewhere between 30 and 90 MB.
6. At inference, load the base SD pipeline, attach the LoRA, and prompt with your rare token: `"sks dog wearing a top hat in the Sistine Chapel"`.

That's it. There is no separate "class encoder" or "subject encoder" or anything else. The LoRA does all the work, and it lives in the same attention projections we've been looking at over the past few chapters.

Step 1: Getting images of your subject

Of course, if you want to get some of your own images to use, now's a good time. If you don't want to deal with that, don't worry; there's a very popular reference dataset that you can use from Hugging Face called *diffusers/dog-example*. It's five photos of a specific corgi dog, who's famous for being used in the original DreamBooth paper. It's the de facto "hello world" for diffusion fine-tuning. You can see an example of this cutie in Figure 13-2.

Figure 13-2. An example from the dataset

In the download for the book, there's a script that you can use to download and use the dog images, including labels. Here's a snippet that performs this:

```
from huggingface_hub import snapshot_download

REPO_ID = "diffusers/dog-example"
INSTANCE_PROMPT = "a photo of sks dog"

cached = snapshot_download(repo_id=REPO_ID, repo_type="dataset")
cached_path = Path(cached)

rows = []
for i, src in enumerate(images):
    dst = out / f"{i:02d}.jpg"
    shutil.copyfile(src, dst)
    rows.append({"file_name": dst.name, "text": args.instance_prompt})

with (out / "metadata.jsonl").open("w") as f:
    for row in rows:
        f.write(json.dumps(row) + "\n")
```

After running the helper, you'll have a *./dog_subject/* folder containing five *.jpg* photos of the same corgi taken from different angles, plus a *metadata.jsonl* file that pairs each photo with the caption `"a photo of sks dog"`. That's the entire subject side of the dataset. The corresponding class prompt is `"a photo of a dog"`, which is what we'll use to generate the prior set in the next section.

The dataset is small on purpose. DreamBooth's original paper (*https://oreil.ly/QGrvA*) showed that three to five images is enough when the subject is visually distinctive. Five photos of one corgi from five angles is *more* signal than the rare token needs to bind cleanly. If you're tempted to add more photos for "robustness," resist; what you actually want for a DreamBooth set is variety in pose and background, not raw count. Five well-chosen images beats fifty mediocre ones.

The reason every tutorial uses this exact dataset is that the results are predictable and comparable. If you train a LoRA on `dog-example` for 1,200 steps at learning rate 1e-4 with rank 8, you should get a model that reliably produces this corgi when prompted with `sks dog`, as opposed to a generic dog when prompted with `a dog`. Anything noticeably different from that means something in your setup is off. The dataset is your control variable, which is exactly what you want when you're still building intuition for the hyperparameters.

When you move on to training a LoRA for *your* product or pet, the workflow is identical. Drop your photos in a folder, write your *metadata.jsonl*, and point the training script at the new folder instead. The rest of this section uses *./dog_subject* because it's reproducible, but everything we cover applies unchanged to your own subject sets.

Step 2: Generating the class-prior set

A class-prior set is one that has images of the broader class that your subject belongs to. So, for example, if you're using the dog image from the previous section, that class would simply be `dog`. Its goal is to prevent you from polluting the original feature images with the one you're retraining. The good news is that it's easy to generate a dataset for this; you can just use the base model to generate images of the class.

It's easy to forget this dataset, and the results of your training might be pretty bad without it, so don't skip it! The rule of thumb is that you'll need about 200 images of the class. Here's the code to generate it with Stable Diffusion and a script I created for you that's available in the book's download:

```
python 00b_generate_class_prior.py \
    --class_prompt "a photo of a dog" \
    --out_dir ./class_dog \
    --count 200
```

It works like this:

```
pipe = StableDiffusionPipeline.from_pretrained(
    MODEL_ID, torch_dtype=torch.float16, safety_checker=None).to(device)
pipe.scheduler = DPMSolverMultistepScheduler.from_config(pipe.scheduler.config)

for i in range(start_idx, args.count):
    # Each image gets a different seed so we get variety, not 200 copies.
    gen = torch.Generator(device=device).manual_seed(args.seed + i)
    image = pipe(
        prompt=args.class_prompt,
        num_inference_steps=args.steps,
        guidance_scale=args.guidance,
        generator=gen,
    ).images[0]
    image.save(out / f"class_{i:04d}.png")
```

Let's go over some details worth calling out. The first is that I use a different seed for each image, so there'll be 200 images of different dogs instead of 200 copies of the same one. You'll also see that if the files exist, it will skip them; so if you cancel, you can just pick up where you left off. Finally, the 20 inference steps is enough for class-prior images. You'll see that they're not top quality; they just need to clearly depict the class, which they do.

Run this and it will take a few minutes. You'll need to do it only once per class, and subsequent training runs will reuse the same folder. The cost is very small relative to the rest of the training, and I believe it will give you the difference between a usable adapter and one that hallucinates your dog into every dog-shaped prompt!

So, after you've generated, take a quick look through the folder. The base model will produce some obvious failures like watermarked stock photos, missing dogs, multiple ones, etc. Delete these. You don't need to inspect everything in detail, just a quick scan. It will help your eventual model learn more effectively.

Step 3: The DreamBooth training step

Once you have your subject folder and your class folder, then training is pretty straightforward. Generally, the code can be achieved in about 30–40 lines, so it's worth covering the entire thing top to bottom.

The setup builds two separate dataloaders—one for each stream. Each dataloader bakes in its own caption: the the subject dataloader will pair every photo with `"a photo of sks dog"` (where `sks` is the rare token caption), and the priors dataloader pairs every photo with `"a photo of a dog"` (the generic caption). This way, the two streams stay distinguishable once they enter the same training step.

Let's take a look at the code:

```
# Two dataloaders, two different captions baked in at construction time.
subj_ds  = CaptionedFolderDataset(
    subject_dir, prompt="a photo of sks dog", tokenizer=tokenizer)
prior_ds = CaptionedFolderDataset(
    class_dir,   prompt="a photo of a dog",  tokenizer=tokenizer)

subj_loader  = DataLoader(subj_ds,  batch_size=1, shuffle=True)
prior_loader = DataLoader(prior_ds, batch_size=1, shuffle=True)
prior_iter = iter(prior_loader)
```

Now onto a training step itself. The goal is to pull one sample from each stream, concatenate them into a single batch size of 2, run them through the model together, and then split the batch back apart at the end so we can compute separate losses for the subject and for the prior. Here's the code:

```
for pixel_subj, ids_subj in subj_loader:
    # Pull one class-prior sample alongside this subject sample.
    # Wrap around if the prior loader runs out.
    try:
        pixel_prior, ids_prior = next(prior_iter)
    except StopIteration:
        prior_iter = iter(prior_loader)
        pixel_prior, ids_prior = next(prior_iter)

    # Concatenate the two streams into one batch of size 2.
    # Batch index 0 = subject image + rare-token caption ("sks dog").
    # Batch index 1 = class image + generic caption ("a dog").
    pixel = torch.cat([pixel_subj, pixel_prior]).to(device, dtype=dtype)
    ids = torch.cat([ids_subj,   ids_prior  ]).to(device)

    with torch.no_grad():
        latents =
          vae.encode(pixel).latent_dist.sample() *
                             vae.config.scaling_factor
        txt, pooled_output = text_encoder[ids]
        txt = output['last_hidden_state']

    # One random timestep and noise tensor per item in the batch.
    # Note that we have hardcoded a batch size of 2.
    # If you are using different batch sizes, this code would change.
    t = torch.randint(0,
                      scheduler.config.num_train_timesteps, (2,),
                                 device=device).long()
    noise = torch.randn_like(latents)
    noisy = scheduler.add_noise(latents, noise, t)

    pred = unet(noisy.float(), t, txt.float()).sample

    # Split the preds and targets back into subject + prior halves.
    pred_subj,  pred_prior  = pred.chunk(2, dim=0)
```

```
    noise_subj, noise_prior = noise.chunk(2, dim=0)

    # Two MSE terms, one per stream, summed with the prior weight.
    loss_subj  = F.mse_loss(pred_subj,  noise_subj)
    loss_prior = F.mse_loss(pred_prior, noise_prior)
    loss = loss_subj + prior_weight * loss_prior

    loss.backward()
    optimizer.step()
    optimizer.zero_grad()
```

The flow should look pretty familiar by now! The image is encoded into a latent representation using VAE, and the caption is encoded with CLIP. You then sample a random timestep and the corresponding noise. Ask the model to predict the noise and then work to minimize MSE against the ground truth.

The only DreamBooth-specific part is that the batch carries two streams: the rare-token caption travels with the subject image at batch index 0, while the generic caption travels with the class image at batch index 1. These will both pass through the UNet in the same forward call, and at the end they'll be split back apart so each stream can contribute its own loss. The `prior_weight` (typically 1.0) will control how strongly the class loss will pull back against the subject loss.

Typically, when you run this with a 4- to 8-photo subject, and around 200 class-prior images, training for 1,200 steps at 1e-4 learning rate, you would see your output looking something like this:

```
trainable params: 1.59M
built validation set of 32 fixed (image,t,noise) tuples
requested 1200 steps; subj samples/epoch=5; running 240 epoch(s)
step    0 | subj 0.1259 (avg  1 0.1259) | prior 0.0197 (avg  1 0.0197)
step   25 | subj 0.0517 (avg 26 0.1347) | prior 0.4841 (avg 26 0.1630)
step   50 | subj 0.0818 (avg 50 0.1290) | prior 0.0711 (avg 50 0.1720)
step   75 | subj 0.0243 (avg 50 0.1204) | prior 0.0891 (avg 50 0.1346)
  -> val_loss @ step 100: 0.0827
step  100 | subj 0.0306 (avg 50 0.1047) | prior 0.1784 (avg 50 0.1040)
...
step  275 | subj 0.1227 (avg 50 0.1068) | prior 0.0144 (avg 50 0.1291)
  -> val_loss @ step 300: 0.0797
  -> saved checkpoint to dog_lora/checkpoint-300
step  300 | subj 0.0056 (avg 50 0.1190) | prior 0.5976 (avg 50 0.1477)
...
step  575 | subj 0.0016 (avg 50 0.0540) | prior 0.2716 (avg 50 0.1698)
  -> val_loss @ step 600: 0.0775
  -> saved checkpoint to dog_lora/checkpoint-600
step  600 | subj 0.0083 (avg 50 0.0669) | prior 0.1386 (avg 50 0.1438)
...
step  875 | subj 0.0246 (avg 50 0.0803) | prior 0.1958 (avg 50 0.1611)
  -> val_loss @ step 900: 0.0756
  -> saved checkpoint to dog_lora/checkpoint-900
step  900 | subj 0.0584 (avg 50 0.1081) | prior 0.3029 (avg 50 0.1432)
```

```
...
step 1075 | subj 0.0345 (avg 50 0.1293) | prior 0.0027 (avg 50 0.1259)
  -> val_loss @ step 1100: 0.0753
step 1100 | subj 0.2096 (avg 50 0.1137) | prior 0.0171 (avg 50 0.1448)
step 1125 | subj 0.5768 (avg 50 0.1120) | prior 0.0273 (avg 50 0.1391)
step 1150 | subj 0.0183 (avg 50 0.0995) | prior 0.0239 (avg 50 0.1674)
step 1175 | subj 0.3383 (avg 50 0.0675) | prior 0.1580 (avg 50 0.1577)
  -> val_loss @ step 1200: 0.0741
Saved final LoRA adapter to ./dog_lora after 1200 steps
```

There are three important details in that log format, and they all exist because of an unintuitive property of diffusion training that the rest of this chapter will refer back to.

The first is that diffusion training loss is intrinsically noisy. Every training step samples a fresh random timestep t from U(0, 1000). Some timesteps are easy (low t, only a whisper of noise added; the model only has to predict a tiny correction). Others are very hard (high t, a heavily noised latent; the model has to predict a much larger noise tensor). Because the timestep is random at every step, each per-step loss is a sample from a very wide distribution. Look at the preceding log: at step `1075` the subject loss is a very low `0.0345`, but by step `1100` immediately after, it has ballooned to `0.2096`, and then to `0.5768` by step `1125`. Nothing went wrong between these three steps; the latter ones just drew an unlucky timestep on an unlucky image. This is fundamentally different from language-model training, where per-step loss is a much smoother signal.

To defend against this noise, the intuitive approach would be to use a moving average to smooth out any spikes. The script prints in parentheses; for example, `(avg 50 ...)`. It averages the last `--log_window` per-step losses. This helps, but it's not enough on its own. A 50-step window is dominated by however many high-`t` samples it happened to contain, which still varies a lot from window to window. The moving averages in the preceding log wander between roughly 0.05 and 0.14 with no clear trajectory; plot them and you mostly see noise. You can see this in Figure 13-3. Clearly, we need something stronger to determine whether the training is working!

So, a stronger way is to use a fixed validation set. At startup, the script samples `--val_size` (default 32) tuples of `(image, timestep, noise)` and freezes them. Every `--eval_every` steps (default 100), it runs the model on that frozen set and reports the mean MSE as `val_loss`. Because the timesteps and noise tensors never change between evaluations, the only thing that can change the validation loss is the model itself. The resulting curve is clean enough to plot and to use for early-stopping decisions (see Figure 13-4). The cost is minimal: 32 forward passes every 100 training steps is an overhead of about 1% processing power.

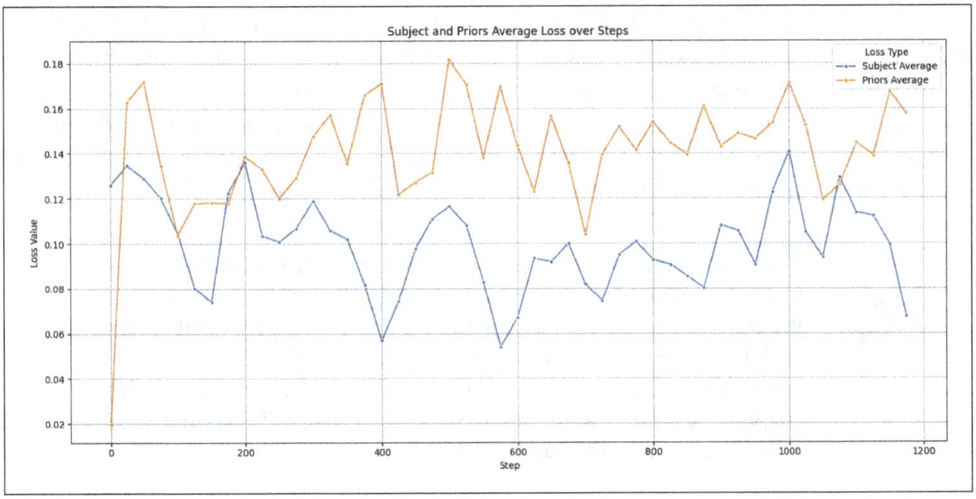

Figure 13-3. Subject and priors loss

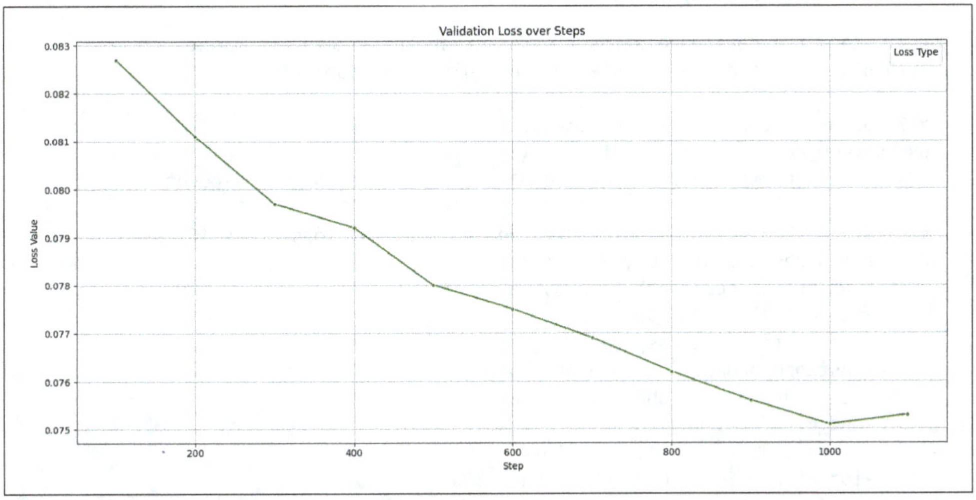

Figure 13-4. The `val_loss` for the DreamBooth fine-tune

In Figure 13-4, take a look at the the val_loss curve. It walks from 0.083 in the early epochs down to 0.075 in the later ones. That's a clean, almost monotonic descent of about 10% over the run. A healthy DreamBooth `val_loss` curve looks like this: a slow drift downward and a flattening tail. If yours instead bottoms out at step 600 and starts climbing back up, you're entering overtraining and you should reach for the checkpoint at the bottom of the curve. If it never drops meaningfully below its starting value, your learning rate is too low or your captions are wrong. Indeed, from looking at this, it's worth maybe training beyond 1,200 steps to find that flattening tail and see if you can get better results!

The script also saves intermediate adapters every `--checkpoint_every` steps (default 300) into `out_dir/checkpoint-NNN/`. It's important to remember that the final adapter isn't necessarily the best one. Five training images and 1,200 steps can put you right at the boundary of overtraining; the checkpoint at step 600 or 900 might actually look better than the one at 1,200. With the checkpoints on disk, you can compare them visually after the run finishes and pick the winner.

> Even validation loss is not the final word. Diffusion training loss tracks the task of predicting noise at random timesteps, not the property you actually care about (e.g., does the generated image look like your dog in a new pose?). A monotonic `val_loss` curve is necessary for a healthy run but not sufficient. A little later in this chapter, we'll cover a `strength-sweep` grid that will help, but your eyes will always be the best judge!

End to end, the workflow from the source code for this book to do this from the command line will look as follows:

```
# 1. Stage the reference dataset (5 corgi photos + metadata.jsonl)
python 00_download_dog_example.py --out_dir ./dog_subject

# 2. Generate the class-prior images
python 00b_generate_class_prior.py \
    --class_prompt "a photo of a dog" --out_dir ./class_dog --count 200

# 3. Train. The defaults below give you a clean val_loss every 100 steps
#    and a checkpoint every 300 steps.
python 03_train_dreambooth_lora.py \
    --subject_dir ./dog_subject \
    --class_dir   ./class_dog \
    --instance_prompt "a photo of sks dog" \
    --class_prompt  "a photo of a dog" \
    --out_dir     ./dog_lora \
    --steps 1200 --rank 16 --lr 1e-4 \
    --log_window 50 --checkpoint_every 300 \
    --val_size 32 --eval_every 100
```

Depending on your hardware, this can take anywhere from about 15 minutes up to a few hours if you're using a GPU. Colab is excellent for this, as you can upload the scripts and run them from within Colab's terminal. It doesn't have to be a notebook!

Using Your DreamBooth Adapter

Loading your adapter and getting a result is the same as with any other LoRA:

```
import torch
from diffusers import StableDiffusionPipeline, DPMSolverMultistepScheduler
```

```
pipe = StableDiffusionPipeline.from_pretrained(
    "runwayml/stable-diffusion-v1-5", torch_dtype=torch.float16
)
pipe.scheduler = DPMSolverMultistepScheduler.from_config(pipe.scheduler.config)

# Load the adapter with a specific name, or let it default to "default"
pipe.load_lora_weights("./dog_lora", adapter_name="dog")

# Set the adapter and its weight statefully on the pipeline
pipe.set_adapters(["dog"], adapter_weights=[1.0])

pipe = pipe.to("cuda")

gen = torch.Generator(device="cuda").manual_seed(42)
image = pipe(
    "sks dog wearing a top hat in front of the Eiffel Tower",
    num_inference_steps=25,
    guidance_scale=7.5,
    generator=gen,
).images[0]

image.save("dog_paris.png")
```

The `load_lora_weights` line is the workhorse here! It reads the LoRA adapters *.safetensors* file, finds the matching attention projection layers in the UNet, and injects the A and B matrices into the forward pass. The LoRA learned an association with the rare token during training, so from that point on, every time the model sees the token `sks dog`, the attention layers will route activations through both the original frozen weights and the LoRA delta you just trained.

You can sanity check this with the preceding code; note how the prompt uses the rare token. You could also prompt the same scene without it, such as `"a dog wearing a top hat in front of the Eiffel Tower"` to compare the results. If the second prompt also produces your dog, then you have a problem, for which you'll need to retrain with a greater class-prior weight or fewer steps.

The Training Hyperparameters That Matter

While many ML training scripts have too many hyperparameters to count, DreamBooth has relatively few that really matter. And in fact, I like to just think about the following three (described next) to simplify the workflow.

Rank

The first is *rank*. Subject training is a very *narrow* concept. While a small rank is often enough for some types of fine-tuning, I have found that for a recognizable subject like this specific dog, you probably have to start high at around 16. If you're short on time or capacity, try 8. Higher ranks will make the adapter bigger and prone to overfitting, so be careful!

Steps

The next is *steps*. This depends on your model. For SD 1.5, I have found 800 to 1,500 to be the right ballpark. For SDXL you need to go bigger, more like 1,200 to 2,000. Keep an eye on the subject loss; if it stops decreasing, that's when you stop training. If you see "prior collapse" (where the class loss creeps up), use fewer steps. This will vary by model and can only really be learned from experience. In this case, referring back to Figure 13-4, we trained for 1,200 steps, but as the loss was still decreasing, we might have been able to do some more! Do note that subject loss with diffusion fine-tuning is extremely noisy, and not the most reliable metric. Visual validation images or a fixed validation set can be much more reliable indicators. Still, decreasing loss isn't necessarily a bad thing!

Class-prior weight

Finally, there's *class-prior weight*. A weight of 1.0 gives you equal weighting between subject and class losses. It's usually fine. But if you start suffering from prior collapse where the class loss creeps up, you can raise this weight. If your subject is barely showing up, you can lower it. Don't go too low (lower than about 0.3) or you might lose it entirely!

For example, in Figure 13-5, you can see the inference for the dog in front of the Eiffel Tower where the model was trained with class-prior weight of 0.5 on the left, and 1.0 on the right.

Figure 13-5. Comparing class-prior weights

As you can see on the left, the dog looks more like a corgi, even if it's distorted. The dog on the right is a better image, but looks less like a corgi! These are some of the trade-offs you'll explore, and later in this chapter we'll look at the `strength-sweep` technique that will help you fine-tune this even more.

The class count itself isn't as sensitive as you might think. Start with 200 for the standard recipe. You might get away with 100, but don't go lower. Going above 400 will hit the law of diminishing returns!

> Sometimes, you'll run the inference code and the model produces a generic dog instead of your specific subject. I have found the usual suspect here is that the LoRA didn't actually load. The pipeline runs without errors, the image looks reasonable, but it's just the base model with a slightly nudged prompt embedding for the rare token. The training script I provided in the book's download will save in diffusers-native format (*pytorch_lora_weights.safetensors*) precisely to avoid this! Some code (particularly AI-generated code!) might call `unet.save_pretrained(out_dir)`, which will write PEFT-format adapter files (*adapter_config.json* + *adapter_model.safetensors*) whose key names diffusers' loader can sometimes misread.

Style LoRAs: Teaching a Visual Vocabulary

Style training is the second flavor. The architecture is the same, the training loop is the same, but the data design is different. There's a counterintuitive truth at the heart of style training: to teach a model *one specific style*, you need to show it *many different subjects* rendered in that style. If your training set is 100 photos of teacups in your brand style, the model will absolutely learn your brand style, but it will also learn that the style only applies to teacups. The first time you prompt it for `"a bicycle in mybrand style"`, the bicycle either won't show up, or it'll come out with some elements of teacups in it. That might look funny.

The reason is in the cross-attention layers. Cross-attention is where the text embedding talks to the image features. The model is learning, over and over, that the embedding for `mybrand style` should pull image features in some direction. If the only image features it ever sees during training are teacup features, the direction it learns is "shift toward looking like a teacup," instead of "shift toward looking like my brand." The remedy is to vary the *subject* as widely as you can while keeping the *style* narrow. People, food, landscapes, products, animals, abstract textures—the more diverse the subjects, the more the model is forced to factor the style in from the subjects.

This is also why captions matter more for style training than for subject training. In a DreamBooth caption, the rare token is the only thing the model needs to map to the visual concept. Everything else in the caption is just there to give the rare token a context. In a style caption, the rare token (the trigger) has to coexist with descriptions of many different subjects. Think of it like an adjective instead of a noun like you had with `sks dog`.

The style trigger has to learn to refer only to the visual treatment, while the rest of the caption tells the model what the visual treatment is being applied to.

Building a Style Dataset

A style dataset has four pieces: the images themselves, their captions, the metadata file that ties them all together, and a held-out evaluation set that you never train on. You can see this in Figure 13-6.

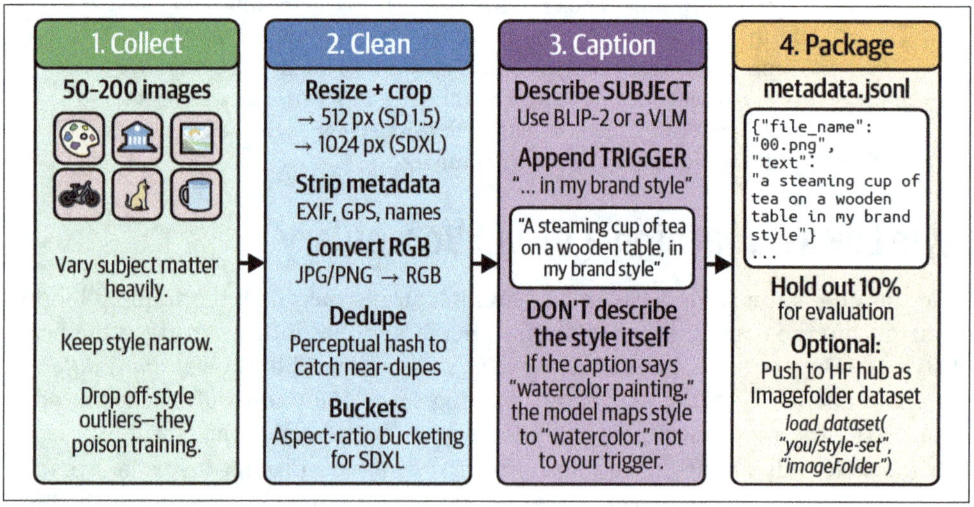

Figure 13-6. Curating a style dataset

For your first style LoRA, aim for 50 to 100 images. Fewer than 30 and the model will overfit, learning the textures and even the subjects of specific training images rather than the style itself. More than 200 and you're spending compute without buying yourself anything. Image quality matters more than image count. Drop the borderline examples. Drop the ones with text or watermarks. Drop anything that you'd hesitate to ship.

Once you have them, you need to clean them: make sure they are the right size for the model (e.g., 512 × 512 for SD 1.5, etc.), strip metadata from them, make sure you have no duplicates, etc.

You'll then need to caption them in detail without using the style of the image in the caption other than your keyword (e.g., "in mybrand style" instead of "an art deco poster in 1950s magazine cover style"). A verbose caption describing the contents is better, and a VLM can help with this.

Finally, a *metadata.jsonl* file with the details will be needed.

It's also important to vary the subjects deliberately. A well-balanced dataset of 80 images might look like 20 portraits, 20 products or still lifes, 20 interiors or environments, and 20 outdoors or landscape scenes. You don't have to hit those numbers exactly. What you're avoiding is a dataset that's 70% portraits and 30% everything else, because the resulting LoRA will silently overfit to portrait composition.

Style training is harder to ship a canonical example for, because most distinctive visual styles are either copyrighted or attached to a specific artist. It's not fair or recommended to replicate their style without their permission. So to that end, I have created a dataset with styles in it for you to use, and a script is available in the book's download that will make one for you with your own style description should you want it.

The choice of generator model matters. If you generate this dataset with SD 1.5 (the same model you'll fine-tune), the resulting LoRA is essentially learning to enforce a corner of the base model's existing output distribution, which ends up being somewhat circular and meta in nature! The script I provided used SDXL as the generator. SDXL has a larger UNet and two text encoders, was trained on different data, and produces visibly different output. An SD 1.5 LoRA trained on SDXL output is doing real cross-model style transfer, which is a meaningful exercise.

You can run the script like this. It will generate 80 images and the *metadata.jsonl* file:

```
python 01b_generate_style_dataset.py
--out_dir ./style_set
--style_suffix "art deco poster, bold geometric shapes, warm color palette"
--trigger "in artdecostyle"
```

You can see an example style image in Figure 13-7.

Figure 13-7. Generated Art Deco–style image[1]

When it comes to the captioning, you have to be very careful about how you create it. The job of the caption is twofold: simply to specify the subject of the image, and its style. Here's an example from the Art Deco ones in the download:

```
{"file_name": "000.png",
 "text": "a steaming cup of tea on a wooden table, in artdecostyle"}
```

Note that the captions are supposed to be a clear description of what's in the image, but without any kind of style information. You might see prompts that include wording like "shot on film," "golden hour," etc. Try to avoid these types of visual definitions when creating descriptions of images when you want to train for style, lest you confuse the process! Remember the whole point of using a rare trigger is to attach the style vocabulary to that token, and that token alone.

You can write captions by hand if you need, or use a model like BLIP-2 to automate the process. If you do this, though, you will need to read *every* caption. There will be hallucinations, missed objects, and occasional descriptions of style. A few minutes of cleanup will pay huge dividends!

1 This image was generated by Nano Banana in May 2026.

> Note the structure of the JSON we used. It had two columns, `file_name` and `text`. When using Hugging Face, you'll need to provide your metadata in that format.

Also, it's important to remember that the trigger phrase is not a *gate*; include it in the prompt and the style fires, omit it and the style stays off. That's not quite how a single-style LoRA actually behaves. Every image in your training set has the trigger in its caption, so the LoRA never sees an unstyled image paired with a nontrigger caption. There's nothing in the training data to teach the model that the trigger is the distinguishing signal. What the LoRA actually learns is "while I am loaded, apply this style."

When you load the adapter and generate at scale 1.0, the style will apply whether the trigger is in your prompt or not. The trigger pulls a little harder when it's present (the cross-attention math gives slightly more weight to embeddings the LoRA correlated with at training time), and this effect is most visible at low scales like 0.3–0.5, but it isn't a hard switch.

To get true gated behavior (i.e., style fires only when the trigger is in the prompt), you have to train on a *mixed* dataset: roughly half styled-and-triggered, half unstyled-and-untriggered. The LoRA then has both regimes to compare and the trigger becomes the actual signal. The chapter's synthetic generator doesn't do this for simplicity's sake, but it's a natural extension should you need it. For most production work, the soft-pull behavior is fine; you control style intensity with the inference scale, and the trigger word serves as a memorable label, a soft pull at low scale, and a way to disambiguate when composing multiple LoRAs.

Training

Training is very similar to the DreamBooth code that we saw earlier, except that you remove the prior-preservation pieces. The important part is this inner loop:

```
with torch.no_grad():
    latents = vae.encode(pixel).latent_dist.sample() * vae.config.scaling_factor
    encoder_hidden_states = text_encoder(input_ids)[0]

t = torch.randint(0, noise_sched.config.num_train_timesteps,
                  (bsz,), device=device).long()
noise = torch.randn_like(latents)
noisy = noise_sched.add_noise(latents, noise, t)

pred = unet(noisy.float(), t, encoder_hidden_states.float()).sample
loss = F.mse_loss(pred.float(), noise.float())
(loss / args.grad_accum).backward()
```

Reading that top to bottom, we can see that we first encode the image into a VAE latent space with the frozen encoder. The caption is encoded with CLIP. It then samples a random timestep `t`, with matching Gaussian noise, and works to minimize the MSE loss against the ground truth. The `(loss / args.grad_accum).backward()` line lets us accumulate several gradients over microbatches before calling the optimizer. This helps us fit it into a forward pass.

The only thing really being learned in this loop is the small LoRA delta on the UNet's attention projections. Every other tensor is frozen. You can see this in Figure 13-8.

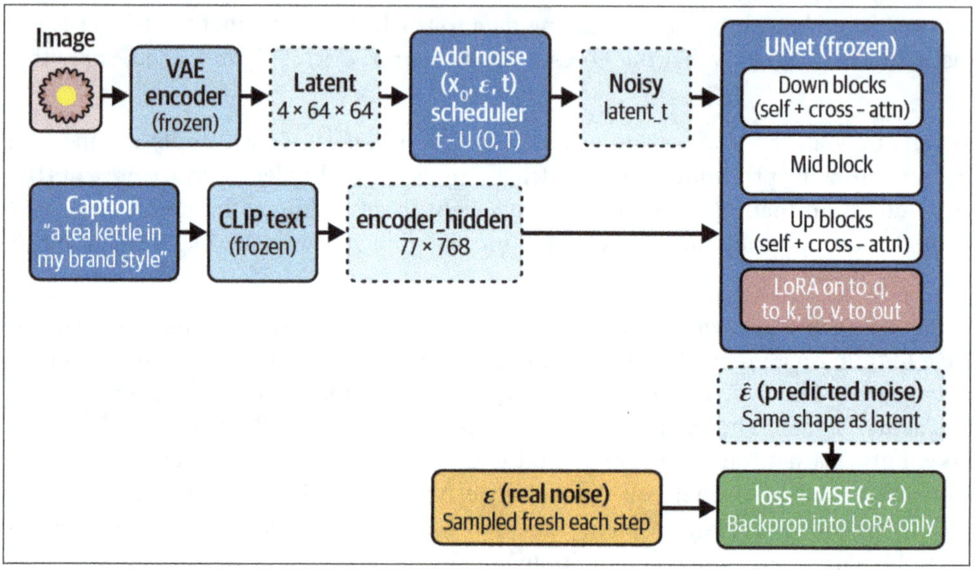

Figure 13-8. The style training loop

The diagram traces a single iteration of the loop you just read. The top row shows the image stream: a training image goes through the frozen VAE encoder to produce a 4 × 64 × 64 latent (the `vae.encode(...).latent_dist.sample() * scaling_factor` line in the code), then a random timestep t is sampled and the scheduler's `add_noise(latents, noise, t)` step mixes Gaussian noise ε into the latent at that noise level.

The bottom row shows the caption stream: the trigger-bearing text goes through the frozen CLIP text encoder to a 77 × 768 sequence of embeddings, which is exactly the `encoder_hidden_states` tensor the code constructs. Both streams meet at the UNet on the right, which receives the noisy latent, the timestep, and the text embeddings, and predicts ε̂, the noise it thinks was added. Compare ε̂ (predicted) against the original ε (real, the dashed blue box in the diagram) with MSE, and you have the single scalar loss that the script's `loss = F.mse_loss(pred.float(), noise.float())` line computes; the diagram's red box (LoRA on `to_q`, `to_k`, `to_v`, `to_out`) marks the only parameters that backpropagation actually updates.

The only difference from the DreamBooth loop is the absence of the class-prior term. The MSE between predicted noise and ground-truth noise is the entire learning signal, and the data variety inside the dataset is what teaches the trigger to refer to the style rather than to any specific subject.

In the downloadable script for the code in this book, I've added some logging to help trace the training:

- A moving average of per-microstep loss (window covers `log_window * grad_accum` microsteps by default, so 200 microsteps' worth of random timesteps).
- A *fixed validation set* of 32 frozen (image, timestep, noise) tuples, evaluated every `--eval_every` steps. This `val_loss` line is the clean signal you should plot and use for stopping decisions; the per-step "last" loss is too noisy to interpret directly. Both reasons are the same as in DreamBooth: diffusion training loss is intrinsically noisy because every step samples a random timestep.
- Intermediate checkpoints saved every `--checkpoint_every` steps into `out_dir/checkpoint-NNN/`. Style training often passes through a sweet spot before overfitting at higher step counts, so a step-1,000 adapter can sometimes look better than a step-1,500 one even when `val_loss` is still descending.

To use the provided script, you can call it like this, noting that the `--data_dir` parameter should point to the directory of your style images and *metadata.json*:

```
python 04_train_style_lora.py \
    --data_dir ./style_set \
    --out_dir  ./mybrand_lora \
    --steps    1500 \
    --lr       1e-4 \
    --rank     16 \
    --log_window 50 --checkpoint_every 300 \
    --val_size 32 --eval_every 100
```

When training, the output will look like this:

```
step  1025 | last 0.2706 (avg over 200 micro-steps: 0.1014)
step  1050 | last 0.1234 (avg over 200 micro-steps: 0.1034)
step  1075 | last 0.1673 (avg over 200 micro-steps: 0.1004)
step  1100 | last 0.4377 (avg over 200 micro-steps: 0.1115)
  -> val_loss @ step 1100: 0.0971
step  1125 | last 0.0318 (avg over 200 micro-steps: 0.1271)
step  1150 | last 0.2226 (avg over 200 micro-steps: 0.1247)
step  1175 | last 0.0393 (avg over 200 micro-steps: 0.1056)
step  1200 | last 0.1066 (avg over 200 micro-steps: 0.0953)
  -> val_loss @ step 1200: 0.0971
```

```
wrote 256 tensors to mybrand_lora/checkpoint-1200/pytorch_lora_weights
  key: unet.down_blocks.0.attentions.0.transformer_blocks.0.attn1.to_q.lora_A
  key: unet.down_blocks.0.attentions.0.transformer_blocks.0.attn1.to_q.lora_B
  key: unet.down_blocks.0.attentions.0.transformer_blocks.0.attn1.to_k.lora_A
-> saved checkpoint to mybrand_lora/checkpoint-1200
step  1225 | last 0.0031 (avg over 200 micro-steps: 0.1033)
step  1250 | last 0.3084 (avg over 200 micro-steps: 0.1082)
step  1275 | last 0.0753 (avg over 200 micro-steps: 0.1066)
step  1300 | last 0.0042 (avg over 200 micro-steps: 0.0952)
  -> val_loss @ step 1300: 0.0970
step  1325 | last 0.0411 (avg over 200 micro-steps: 0.0986)
step  1350 | last 0.1782 (avg over 200 micro-steps: 0.1087)
step  1375 | last 0.0785 (avg over 200 micro-steps: 0.1102)
step  1400 | last 0.1143 (avg over 200 micro-steps: 0.1095)
  -> val_loss @ step 1400: 0.0969
step  1425 | last 0.0092 (avg over 200 micro-steps: 0.0990)
step  1450 | last 0.1833 (avg over 200 micro-steps: 0.0961)
step  1475 | last 0.0880 (avg over 200 micro-steps: 0.1017)
step  1500 | last 0.0904 (avg over 200 micro-steps: 0.1054)
  -> val_loss @ step 1500: 0.0968
```

Read the `val_loss` line for convergence and use the moving average only to confirm whether anything is blowing up. If things go wrong, you'll see the microsteps values diverging wildly!

The per-step "last" loss is for completeness and should not be used to decide anything. We'll use the sweep technique I'll detail later to truly see whether this is working.

Using the Style Adapter

Running inference with an attached adapter is as simple as loading and applying the LoRA weights. Here's the code:

```python
import torch
from diffusers import StableDiffusionPipeline, DPMSolverMultistepScheduler

pipe = StableDiffusionPipeline.from_pretrained(
    "runwayml/stable-diffusion-v1-5", torch_dtype=torch.float16)
pipe.scheduler = DPMSolverMultistepScheduler.from_config(pipe.scheduler.config)
pipe.load_lora_weights("./mybrand_lora")
pipe = pipe.to("cuda")

gen = torch.Generator(device="cuda").manual_seed(42)
image = pipe(
    "an illustration of a beautiful woman elegantly sipping coffee, in mybrand",
    num_inference_steps=25,
    guidance_scale=7.5,
    cross_attention_kwargs={"scale": 1.0},
    generator=gen,
).images[0]
image.save("style_test.png")
```

Running this will produce something like Figure 13-9. The Art Deco style that `mybrand` was created to mimic clearly appears to be working!

Figure 13-9. Image with style LoRA applied[2]

Of course, older models like Stable Diffusion 1.5 struggled with anatomy, so it looks like the woman has at least three arms. But that's not the fault of the LoRA! Try using the techniques you learn in this chapter to train a model to produce a better image, or reprompt if you see issues like this.

Do note that the trigger phrase is optional. This is the most important practical fact about a single-style LoRA, and it's worth restating because it actively contradicts a lot of community guidance. When the LoRA is loaded, the style applies to every forward pass through the UNet, regardless of whether `in mystyle` is in your prompt. The exact same prompt with the trigger removed will still produce a styled image at scale 1.0. The trigger does pull a little harder at low scales (try comparing at scale 0.4 to see the effect clearly), and it acts as a useful disambiguator when you compose multiple LoRAs, but on its own it is not a switch. To turn the style off, use:

```
pipe.set_adapters(["mybrand"], adapter_weights=[0.0])
```

2 Image generated with the custom LoRA trained in this chapter, with SD 1.5, May 2026.

Alternatively, you can call `pipe.unload_lora_weights()`.

Understanding and Sweeping for Strength

To effectively use a LoRA, it's good to understand the scale parameter. Once a LoRA is loaded into a pipeline, you can scale its effect by passing a scale parameter to the cross-attention:

```
image = pipe(prompt=..., cross_attention_kwargs={"scale": 0.8}, ...).images[0]
```

Then, under the hood, every LoRA-wrapped layer computes as follows:

```
y = W_0 @ x + scale * (B @ A) @ x
```

Here, `W_0` is the base model's frozen weight matrix and `B @ A` is the LoRA's low-rank update. At scale 0, the LoRA contribution is zero and you get the base model exactly. At scale 1, you get what you trained. Higher values amplify the LoRA's influence beyond what training settled on, at the cost of artifacts; lower values dial the LoRA back without retraining. So the strength of the style will scale, as in Figure 13-10.

Figure 13-10. Sweeping for scale

In production, you almost never want exactly scale 1.0. Most well-trained LoRAs (subject *or* style) look best somewhere between 0.6 and 0.9. The exact sweet spot depends on the dataset, the rank, and how aggressively the captions tied the concept to the trigger. The way to find it is to sweep. I've provided a script to speed it up for you:

```
python 05_lora_strength_sweep.py
--lora ./mybrand_lora
--prompt "a steaming cup of tea on a wooden table, in mybrand style"
--scales 0.0 0.3 0.5 0.6 0.7 0.8 0.9 1.0 1.1 1.2 1.5 1.7
--seed 12345
--out grid.png
```

This generates the same prompt with the same seed at twelve strengths, tiles them into a grid, and saves it. Pin the seed; otherwise you're comparing two things at once. The grid will tell you a lot at a glance: At what scale does the concept become recognizable? At what scale does the model start producing artifacts? Where is the prompt fidelity still solid? You're looking for the highest scale that doesn't introduce visible artifacts.

You can see the output in Figure 13-11.

Figure 13-11. Multiple images created with different scales[3]

For me, looking at these images, I find the first three on the second row to be the most pleasing, and these correspond to strengths 0.7, 0.8, and 0.9, respectively.

The same sweep works for DreamBooth adapters. If your subject is barely recognizable at scale 1.0, the answer probably isn't more training; it's a slightly higher scale at inference. Conversely, if your subject is so dominant that you can't get it into varied scenes, sweep down. The strength knob is your single best tool for matching the model's behavior to a particular use case, and it's the first thing to reach for before retraining. This makes for a terrific tool for getting the most out of your LoRA.

3 Generated with Stable Diffusion and our custom style, May 2026.

Compositing Multiple LoRAs

A single LoRA is rarely the end state. In this chapter, we've shown both *subject* and *style* versions. Another option that we didn't show is a *lighting* LoRA. Each of them in isolation is okay, but it's when they get together that you can really build something special.

The diffusers library makes this easy; simply load and apply them with specified weights:

```
pipe.load_lora_weights("./mybrand_lora",      adapter_name="style")
pipe.load_lora_weights("./acme_mascot_lora", adapter_name="subject")
pipe.load_lora_weights("./studio_lora",       adapter_name="light")

pipe.set_adapters(
    ["style", "subject", "light"],
    adapter_weights=[0.8, 1.0, 0.4],
)
```

What this does, under the hood, is that in the attention layers, the LoRA deltas get summed:

```
y = W_0 @ x + 0.8 * (B_style @ A_style) @ x
            + 1.0 * (B_subject @ A_subject) @ x
            + 0.4 * (B_light @ A_light) @ x
```

The three adapters then all target the same `to_q`, `to_k`, `to_v`, and `to_out.0` projections, so the math ends up just being a straight addition!

The sweet spot and experimentation you need to do is in the relative weighting. Some guidelines from experience:

- When mixing, give the subject slightly more weight than the style. So, if you mix a subject and a style, the subject at 1.0, while the style is 0.7 or 0.8, could be a good starting point. Pushing the style weighting too high can distort the subject.
- If you train lighting or atmosphere LoRAs, they're generally something that adds to the rest of the image. So, if their weight is high (even 1.0), they can overwhelm the image. It's better to start them low.
- Your prompts should mention every trigger. They don't automatically load when the adapter is loaded; that happens through the cross-attention pathways. So, to control their weight, you should use their name (e.g., `"sks mascot, mycustom lighting, in mybrand style"`).
- The more LoRAs you add, the more difficult it is to cross-control them. Three is doable with care. Four or more, and your job can get difficult! If you need many of them at a time, it might be better to train on a combined dataset instead.

Going Beyond Stable Diffusion 1.5

For this chapter, I used the older Stable Diffusion 1.5 as the fine-tunable model because it's great for learning on. It's older and struggles with some types of images, but it's small, it's fast, the recipes are well known, and the LoRA tooling is very mature. For production work, you'll probably want to move beyond it, but everything you've learned here should still apply.

Here are a few other models to be aware of:

SDXL
: SDXL uses a larger UNet (around 2.6B parameters), two text encoders (so prompts can be longer and more nuanced), and operates at 1,024-pixel resolution. The LoRA target modules are the same (`to_q`, `to_k`, `to_v`, `to_out.0`). The training script is the same with the model ID swapped to `stabilityai/stable-diffusion-xl-base-1.0` and the resolution bumped to `1024`. Expect roughly 2× the training time and 2× the VRAM (so 20–24 GB at rank 16). The benefit is a much better, 1,024-resolution output and better prompt adherence out of the box. For brand work in 2026, SDXL is a really good practical model.

SD3 and Flux
: These moved away from the UNet architecture entirely. Instead of a U-shaped convolutional network with attention, they use a Diffusion Transformer (DiT), which is a stack of transformer blocks doing the same noise-prediction task. The training objective is unchanged. LoRA still works. The target module names change to things like `qkv`, `proj`, and the MLP layers. The diffusers library abstracts most of this away through `target_modules="all-linear"` configurations that find every attention projection automatically. The conceptual frame from this chapter transfers directly; you'll just be naming different modules. Code-generation models, when carefully steered, are your friends here.

Stable Video Diffusion and Sora
: Video diffusion models like Stable Video Diffusion and Sora apply the same noise-prediction objective to sequences of frames, with additional temporal attention layers to enforce frame-to-frame coherence. Fine-tuning these for a custom style or subject requires more data and more VRAM, but the recipe is the same.

ControlNet
: ControlNet is a different beast. It's not a LoRA at all. It's a parallel network that takes a conditioning image (a depth map, an edge map, a pose skeleton, a Canny edge detection) and feeds activations into the UNet to steer generation. ControlNets are heavier than LoRAs (often hundreds of MB) and need separate

training, but they pair beautifully with style LoRAs: use ControlNet to pin down the composition, use a style LoRA to control the visual treatment.

IP-Adapter
: This lightweight adapter is the answer to "I want this specific image to influence the output without training anything." It uses an image encoder to produce a conditioning vector that gets fed into the cross-attention layers alongside the prompt. You drop in a reference image, and the output borrows from it. IP-Adapters (*https://oreil.ly/0PRX_*) compose with style LoRAs cleanly, and they're often the right answer for one-shot brand work where you have a single reference image rather than a 100-image dataset.

The taxonomy at production scale, then, is to use a style LoRA for the visual treatment you'll use across many projects; use DreamBooth subject LoRA or IP-Adapter for the specific things you're rendering; use ControlNet for the composition; and finally, use a strong prompt to tie it all together. Each technique has its own training recipe, but you already understand the most fundamental one: train a small set of parameters on a small set of images at the points in the network where text meets pixels.

Preparing Adapters for Deployment

You've iterated, adapted, checked your strengths through sweeping, and you've got exactly what you want. Now, you'd like to ship a single model that doesn't require PEFT to be installed at inference time. Here's where `fuse_lora` is your friend. It bakes the deltas directly into the base UNet's weights and lets you save the result as a standalone artifact.

Here's an example:

```
pipe = StableDiffusionPipeline.from_pretrained(MODEL_ID,
                                               torch_dtype=torch.float16)
pipe.load_lora_weights("./mybrand_lora")
pipe.fuse_lora(lora_scale=0.8)          # bake in at the strength you settled on
pipe.save_pretrained("./mybrand_full")
```

There are trade-offs to be aware of. Once you've done the fusing, the `cross_attention_kwargs["scale"]` control knob is gone! It's effectively frozen at the values you baked in. But this is the right trade-off: you ship a single artifact, as the inference stack doesn't need PEFT or loading and adding LoRAs. Your inference will actually speed up slightly because you aren't loading and adding the new values!

Do note that the `torch_dtype` setting for float16 will save fused weights at that precision. It's always good to test if the image generator will work as you desire, lest this affect the behavior adversely.

Understanding Common Failure Modes

After you've trained a handful of diffusion LoRAs, you'll start recognizing the failure modes by sight. Here are the ones you're most likely to hit, and some ideas about how to approach them:

Loss is bouncing all over the place.
: This is *not* a failure mode, but it's the most common false alarm for first-time fine-tuners. Diffusion loss is intrinsically noisy because every step samples a random timestep `t`, and per-step loss is dominated by where in the noise schedule that sample landed, not by how well the model is learning. A value of 0.001 followed by 0.6 doesn't mean anything went wrong. Even the 50-step moving average will look noisy if you plot it. Read the `val_loss` line instead. It's computed on a fixed validation set whose timesteps and noise tensors never change, so the only thing that moves the number is the model itself. If that line is trending down or flat, training is fine. The honest final evaluation is to generate images from your checkpoints and look at them.

Style or subject doesn't show up.
: In this case, generations with and without the trigger look essentially the same. Likely causes: (1) learning rate is too low, (2) there are too few training steps, and (3) the trigger phrase is actually composed of common words. The fix order is to raise the learning rate to 2e-4, train for more steps, then if that still fails, pick a more unusual trigger.

Prior collapse (DreamBooth-specific) occurs.
: Every dog the model generates looks like your dog now, not just `sks dog`. Causes: you trained without enough class-prior images, you set the prior weight too low, or you trained too long. Fixes: regenerate 200 fresh class images, raise the prior weight to 1.5, and train for fewer steps, respectively. If the symptom persists, the LR is probably too high.

The style is overwhelming.
: Every output looks the same regardless of prompt, prompt fidelity has cratered, and the model can't draw a clean tea kettle anymore. Likely causes: overtraining, rank is too high for the dataset size, or captions don't vary subject information enough. Fix order: roll back to an earlier checkpoint, drop the rank, then reexamine your dataset for subject diversity.

Specific training images appear in outputs.
: You ask for `"a tea kettle"` and get something that looks suspiciously like image 0023 from your training set. This is straight-up memorization, and it happens when the dataset is too small or too repetitive. Fix: add more diverse images,

drop the rank, or train fewer steps. Light random crops and flips also make memorization harder.

The trigger works inconsistently.
: Some of the time the concept appears, some of the time it doesn't—even with the same prompt and different seeds. Likely cause: the captions didn't apply the trigger consistently during training. Audit your *metadata.jsonl* for captions that are missing the trigger or that include it in different forms.

Style applies even without the trigger in the prompt (style LoRAs).
: You load a style LoRA and generate `"a dog wearing a tuxedo"` without the trigger phrase. The output still comes out in your trained style. This is not a bug; it's the expected behavior of a LoRA trained on a single-style dataset where every caption included the trigger. With nothing in training to teach the model that the trigger is the distinguishing signal, the LoRA simply applies the style on every forward pass it participates in. The trigger does pull a bit harder when present (especially at low scales like 0.3–0.5), but it isn't a hard gate. To turn the style off, use `cross_attention_kwargs={"scale": 0.0}` or `pipe.unload_lora_weights()`. To get genuine trigger-gated behavior, you need a mixed training set: half styled-and-triggered images, half unstyled-and-untriggered images. The LoRA then has both regimes to compare and the trigger becomes the actual distinguishing signal.

The model has forgotten how to draw faces.
: Prompts that involve people produce melted, malformed faces. Cause: your training set is biased toward objects, environments, or abstract images, with few good faces. Fix: add 15–20 in-style portraits to the dataset, then retrain. This applies for style and lighting, of course.

Out of memory on a 12-GB card.
: SD 1.5 fits comfortably in 8 GB at inference and 10 GB during training. SDXL training really wants 16 GB minimum. If you're tight, enable `pipe.enable_attention_slicing()` and `pipe.enable_vae_tiling()` at inference, and use `gradient_checkpointing=True` during training. Drop training resolution to 512 for SD 1.5 or stay at 1024 for SDXL but reduce batch size to 1 with gradient accumulation 4–8.

Generated images look blurry or oversaturated.
: This is almost always a guidance scale issue, not a LoRA issue. Try lowering `guidance_scale` from 7.5 to 5.0. If everything looks too noisy, raise `num_inference_steps` from 20 to 30.

Pipeline produces different results on each run, despite a fixed seed.

Diffusers expect the `torch.Generator` on the same device as the tensors. So, check that you're using `torch.Generator(device="cuda").manual_seed(s)` rather than `torch.Generator().manual_seed(s)`. CPU- and GPU-based generators maintain different random number generator states, so using a CPU generator for GPU sampling will not produce deterministic results.

Slow first inference, fast subsequent ones.

The first run JIT-compiles CUDA kernels and warms up cuDNN's autotuner. This is normal. If you need consistent latency from request 1, run a single warm-up generation at startup.

Summary

In this chapter, we covered both *subject* and *style* LoRAs.

For subjects, collect just a few pictures with varied pose, lighting, and background. Pick a rare token and write your instance prompt. Get (or generate) a few hundred class-prior images so the model can tell the difference between your instance and the general one. Run the training script and, at inference time, try the object with the rare token. Sweep the strength to find the right balance.

For styles, collect a few hundred images that represent the target style. Vary them widely while keeping the style very narrow. Clean up the data, and caption it with an accurate description and your style trigger. After training, do inference on it, and don't forget to sweep the strength to find the right balance.

In production, use both; after you're happy with the results, fuse the adapter into the base model and ship.

That's the whole loop! It's very similar to language models except for the image-caption pairs instead of chat templates. And of course, the LoRA targets are UNet attention projections instead of transformer layers. But you can see that the DNA is the same.

So now, you can call yourself a diffusion fine-tuner. Congratulations!

CHAPTER 14

Optimization and Quantization

By now you have a fine-tuned model that works. Over the course of this book, you took a base Gemma model, fed it a curated medical Q&A dataset, trained a LoRA adapter, aligned it with DPO, and confirmed that it answers domain questions better than the stock model. That model lives as a base checkpoint plus a small LoRA adapter, and it runs comfortably on the GPU you trained it on.

The trouble is that the GPU you trained on is not the machine you ship on. Similarly with Stable Diffusion and subject/style tuning, you've created an adapter to shape its behavior.

This chapter is about closing the gap between "my model trains successfully" and "it deploys effectively." You're going to do three things to your model, each independent and each compounding: you'll merge the adapter back into the base so there's a single artifact to ship; you'll quantize the weights from 16 bits down to 4, cutting the model's footprint significantly with a loss in quality you can actually measure and control; and you'll tame the KV cache so the model stays fast and memory-bounded as conversations get long.

By the end, you'll have taken a 15-GB model that needs a data-center GPU and turned it into a 4.5-GB model that runs on a laptop, and you'll have the numbers to prove that its performance doesn't significantly degrade in the process.

The Deployment Gap

A fine-tuned model in float16 is a luxury object. Your medical Gemma-based model, merged and saved in 16-bit precision, is about 16–18 GB on disk and needs roughly the same amount of VRAM just to load—before you've even processed a single token. That's fine on the A100 or the rented L4 you trained on. However, it is not fine on a developer's laptop, a $200/month inference budget, a mobile NPU, or a hospital's air-gapped mini-PC. The whole promise of this book—owning a private expert model instead of renting a generalist—falls apart if the thing you own runs only on hardware you have to rent.

Optimization is how you collect on that promise. There are three levers, and it's worth being precise about what each one buys you, because they solve different problems and you'll often pull all three. Let's take a closer look at them:

Merging
: The first lever is *merging*. Right now, your model is composed of two files: the frozen base and the LoRA adapter. At inference time, PEFT computes the adapter's contribution on every forward pass and adds it to the base output. Every adapted layer runs two extra-small matrix multiplies (the input through A, then through B) on top of the normal one, on every token you generate. On an individual level, that's trivial, but multiplied across dozens of layers and thousands of tokens, it typically shaves a few percent off your throughput. That's a small but real overhead, and more importantly, it means your deployment target has to understand PEFT. Merging folds the adapter's math permanently into the base weights, leaving you a single standard model that any serving stack can load. Merging doesn't make the model smaller, but it's the precondition for most of what follows.

Quantization
: The second lever is *quantization*, and it's the big one. Quantization stores each weight using fewer bits. Going from 16-bit to 4-bit shrinks the model by about four times; thus, your 18-GB model becomes (roughly) a 4.5-GB model. It also speeds up inference, because on memory-bound workloads (which is most LLM inference) the bottleneck is moving weights from memory to the compute units, and smaller weights move faster. The catch is that quantization is lossy. The art is in losing precision where the model won't miss it.

KV-cache optimization
: The third lever is *KV-cache optimization*. As a conversation or document grows, the model caches the attention keys and values for every token it has already seen. That cache grows linearly with context length and can quietly become larger than the model weights themselves on long inputs. Shrinking and managing it is what keeps a long-context model from running out of memory halfway through its task.

You can see this in Figure 14-1.

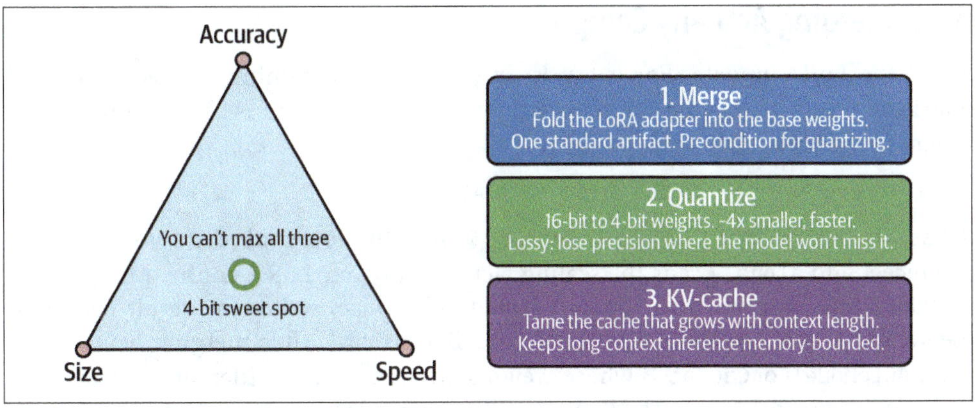

Figure 14-1. The optimization triangle

As you can see in the figure, these three levers move you around inside a triangle whose corners are size, speed, and accuracy. You can't max out all three at once. A 16-bit model is the most accurate and the largest; a 2-bit model is tiny and fast, but also noticeably degraded. Most of this chapter is about finding the spot on that triangle where you've taken almost all of the size-and-speed win while giving up as little of the accuracy as possible.

For most fine-tuned models, that spot turns out to be 4-bit. So a large part of this chapter is teaching you how to confirm that for your model rather than taking it on faith.

One piece of framing carries throughout the chapter: optimization is not a single irreversible button. Instead, it's a pipeline of reversible decisions, each of which you should measure. Merge, then check parity. Quantize, then measure perplexity and task accuracy. Pick a bit width, then confirm it's on the right side of the quality knee. The engineers who get burned by quantization are the ones who run quantize once, eyeball three outputs, and ship. The engineers who do it well treat every compression step as an experiment with a held-out test set, exactly the way you treated training.

Merging the Adapter into the Base

You met `merge_and_unload()` back in Chapter 9, where you used it to produce a standalone checkpoint for a quick sanity test. Here we're going to treat merging as a deliberate production step, because it's the foundation that quantization builds on, and because there are two precision traps that will silently corrupt your model if you get them wrong.

What Merging Actually Computes

Recall the LoRA update. For every layer you adapted, training learned two small matrices, `A` and `B`, and the effective weight at inference time is the original frozen weight plus a scaled low-rank product:

```
W_merged = W_base + (alpha / r) * (B @ A)
```

`W_base` is the original Gemma weight, `B @ A` is the low-rank delta your training produced, and `alpha / r` is the scaling factor from your LoRA config. Merging just evaluates this expression for every adapted layer once, writes the result back into the weight tensor, and discards the A and B matrices. After merging, you have a plain `AutoModelForCausalLM` whose weights are numerically different from the base model, with no adapter attached and no PEFT dependency at serve time. You can see this in Figure 14-2.

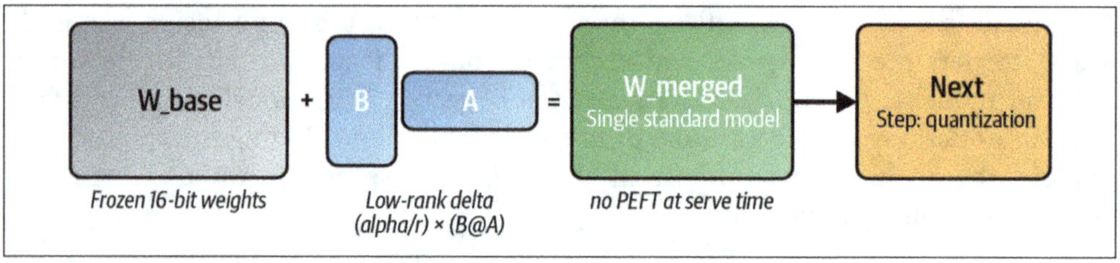

Figure 14-2. Folding the LoRA deltas into the base weights

All the mechanics for this are in a single line, which you've seen already:

```
merged = model.merge_and_unload()
```

This gives you the foundation for much of the rest of this chapter!

The 4-bit Merge Trap

As well as a terrific name for a heavy metal band, the 4-bit merge trap is something to watch out for, and a mistake that hits almost everybody early on in their journey. During QLoRA training, you loaded the base model in 4-bit via bitsandbytes NF4 in order to save VRAM. It's really tempting to keep that 4-bit base loaded, and then just call `merge_and_unload()` directly on it. That's the trap. When you merge into a 4-bit base, the adapter delta (which is typically 16-bit) gets added to the already compressed weights. The result is a model that is sloppily quantized, and the quality loss becomes apparent. But also avoidable!

The correct procedure is to merge in full precision, and *then* quantize, as a separate controlled step. So, you can load the base model fresh in bfloat16 or float16, attach your trained adapter, and then merge, like so:

```python
import torch
from transformers import AutoModelForCausalLM, AutoTokenizer
from peft import PeftModel

BASE = "google/gemma-4-e4b-it"                # the 4B-effective-parameter model
ADAPTER = "./medical-qa-v1-gemma4-lora"       # or the Hub repo id

# Load the base in HIGH precision, not 4-bit. This is the whole point.
base = AutoModelForCausalLM.from_pretrained(
    BASE,
    torch_dtype=torch.bfloat16,
    device_map="auto",
)

# Attach the trained adapter, then fold it in.
model = PeftModel.from_pretrained(base, ADAPTER)
merged = model.merge_and_unload()

# Save the merged model AND the tokenizer together.
tok = AutoTokenizer.from_pretrained(ADAPTER)   # picks up any custom tokens
merged.save_pretrained("./medical-gemma-merged", safe_serialization=True)
tok.save_pretrained("./medical-gemma-merged")
```

Notice two things. First, with `torch_dtype=torch.bfloat16`, you merge in the same precision the model was designed to run in, not in 4-bit. Second, you save the tokenizer alongside the weights, from the adapter directory, so that any special tokens or chat-template changes you made during fine-tuning travel *with* the model. It's important that the tokenizer matches the model, lest you end up with very subtle and hard-to-debug issues. For example, you'll have text generated, but it can be wrong, and not on par with the way you wanted the fine-tune to behave. Additionally, if you added special tokens, the tokenizer might split them into ordinary subwords, and your fine-tune won't behave the way you expected.

Verifying Parity

Merging is primarily a numerical operation, and things like that can go wrong quietly. So, before you build anything on top of the merged model, prove that it behaves like the adapter-attached model it's supposed to replace. Testing this is simple: run the same prompts through the PEFT model (i.e., the base + attached adapter) and the merged model, and then check the outputs. Then confirm that the outputs match. Here's an example:

```python
prompts = [
    "What are the first-line treatments for type 2 diabetes?",
    "Explain the mechanism of action of beta blockers.",
    "When is a CT scan preferred over an MRI?",
]

def next_token_logits(m, tok, text):
```

```
    msgs = [{"role": "user", "content": text}]
    inputs = tok.apply_chat_template(msgs,
                 add_generation_prompt=True,
                 return_tensors="pt", return_dict=True).to(m.device)
    with torch.no_grad():
        return m(**inputs).logits[0, -1].float().cpu()   # last-position logits

for p in prompts:
    a = next_token_logits(peft_model, tok, p)    # base + attached adapter
    b = next_token_logits(merged, tok, p)        # merged standalone
    same = int(a.argmax()) == int(b.argmax())
    print("MATCH" if same else "DRIFT",
              f"| max|Δlogit|={ (a-b).abs().max():.3f}", "|", p[:40])
```

It is tempting to instead compare with full greedy generations and check that the text matches token for token. Resist that! It can produce false alarms. When merging and adapting, you can have tiny rounding differences across a long decode and the transcripts can drift slightly apart, even if the merge is perfectly correct. The next-token prediction is more stable, where the merged model's `argmax` can match the adapter model's one, and the `logits` are nearly identical. So, the merge would be sound.

A genuinely broken merge would have wrong `dtype`, tokenizer mismatch, corrupted weights, and the like. Namely, the fine-tuning could be underapplied or overapplied rather than absent. This would show up immediately as a different predicted token with a large logit gap. In the book's download, I've provided a script (*01_merge_adapter.py*) which will handle this for you.

So, if you want to try this out for yourself, using the scripts available to you, you can run *00_finetune_gemma4.py* to get a LoRA on the medical Q&A set, if you don't have one already. Then, once you have that in hand, and in a directory named *medical-qa-v1-gemma4-lora*, you can run the adapter merging with this script:

```
python 01_merge_adapter.py \
    --base google/gemma-4-e4b-it \
    --adapter ./medical-qa-v1-gemma4-lora \
    --out ./medical-gemma-merged
```

In some environments, the dependencies pull in versions of TensorFlow that cause errors. If you are seeing protobuf errors when running this code, please use the environment variable `USE_TF=0` to get it to ignore TensorFlow and skip these issues.

When Not to Merge

Merging is right for the common use case—one model, one adapter. But it isn't free of trade-offs, and there's one scenario where you should keep the adapter separate.

If you serve many fine-tunes of the same base, say a different adapter per customer or per specialty, then merging multiplies your storage and memory by the number of adapters because each merged model is a full copy of the base. Typically, you can keep a single base in memory and hot swap small adapters per request.

You can see this general idea in Figure 14-3.

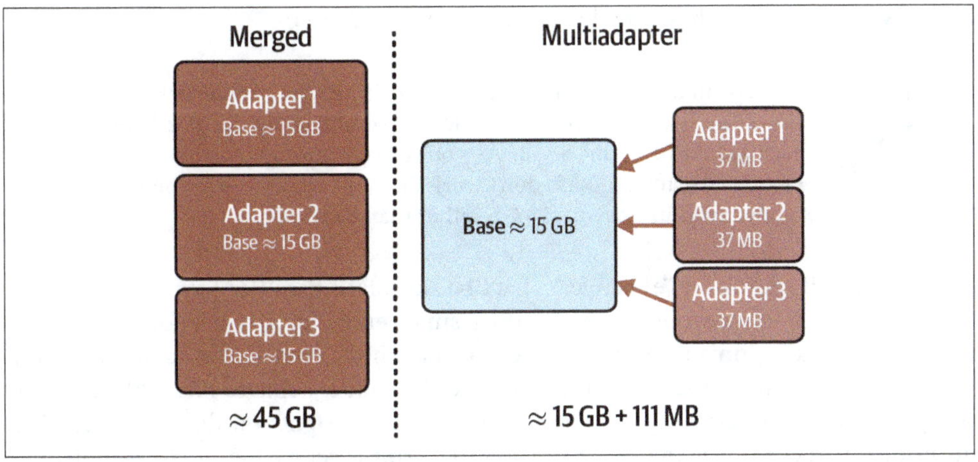

Figure 14-3. Merging versus hot swapping

Modern serving stacks, like vLLM, support exactly this multiadapter pattern, which you'll explore later. But for now, the goal is a single, deployable artifact, and merging is the right move. Everything downstream will assume you've done it.

How Quantization Actually Works

Before you do any quantization, it's good to understand how it actually works and what it's doing to your weights. Otherwise, it's a bit of a format zoo. When you picture the ways that a 16-bit number can become a 4-bit one, then the differences between GPT-Generated Unified Format (GGUF), Activation-aware Weight Quantization (AWQ), and Generative Pretrained Transformers Quantization (GPTQ) will stop being acronym soup and become engineering choices you can consider and reason about.

A Quick Refresher on Floating Point

A neural network weight is a number, like 0.0237 or –1.84. Stored as a 32-bit float (float32), each weight uses 4 bytes split into a sign bit, an 8-bit exponent, and a 23-bit mantissa. The exponent sets the scale (roughly, where the decimal point goes) and the mantissa sets the precision (how many significant digits you get).

Training and serving in 16-bit halves that to 2 bytes per weight. It generally comes in two flavors: float16 and bfloat16.

float16 keeps a 5-bit exponent and 10-bit mantissa; bfloat16 keeps the full 8-bit exponent of float32 but only a 7-bit mantissa, trading precision for the same dynamic range as float32, which is why it's the default for training large models.

Either way, 16-bit is the baseline this chapter compresses *from*.

> For a plain dense model the on-disk size is just the parameter count times the bytes per weight: a true 4B-parameter model at 2 bytes each would be about 8 GB. As you've seen throughout this book, Gemma 4's small models don't work that way, which is why the E4B model loads in closer to 18 GB rather than 8 GB.

The "E" in E4B stands for "effective." That's because E4B uses Per-Layer Embeddings (PLE),[1] giving every decoder layer its own small embedding table for each token instead of stacking on more transformer layers. Those embedding tables are large but cheap to use, since they're just lookups, so the model behaves like a 4B model at compute time while carrying far more than 4B static weights on disk. The practical upshot for this chapter is that your starting footprint is set by the *stored* weights, not the effective parameter count, and the stored weights are what quantization shrinks.

Ultimately, quantization asks: do we really need 16 bits per weight to serve a good model? For inference, the answer is almost always *no*. The weights have already been learned; we're not computing gradients anymore. We just need to represent them faithfully enough that the forward pass produces nearly the same activations. It turns out you can throw away most of the bits and still do that, if you're careful about *how* you throw them away.

From Floats to Integers: Scale and Zero-Point

The core trick is to stop storing each weight as an independent float, and instead store small integers plus a shared recipe for turning them back into floats. Take a group of weights, find their min and max, and then map *that* range onto a set of integers a 4-bit number can hold, which is 0–15. The recipe has two numbers: a *scale*, how much each step is worth; and a *zero-point* to determine which integer corresponds to a real zero.

1 PLE also means the embedding tables make up a big share of those weights, which is one reason the activation-aware methods later in the chapter (the ones that decide what to protect and what to crush) matter for this architecture.

Here is an example:

```
# Quantize a real weight w to a 4-bit integer q
scale      = (w_max - w_min) / 15
zero_point = round(-w_min / scale)
q          = clamp(round(w / scale) + zero_point, 0, 15)

# Dequantize back to an approximate float at inference time
w_approx   = (q - zero_point) * scale
```

Let's explore what that looks like, using Figure 14-4 as an example.

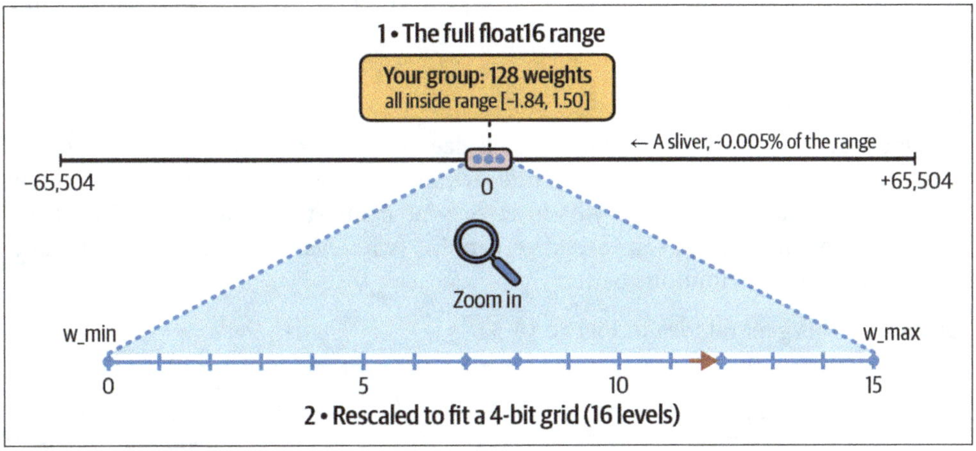

Figure 14-4. Quantization

As we can see in the figure, the upper number line has a 16-bit range, from roughly –65k to +65k. But you aren't using the full range. There's a small chunk in the middle that all of your data lives in. So, instead of compressing the full range (which is mostly empty), you can instead map your range to a smaller range. In this case, it goes to 4 bits, which only has 16 values. The idea of `w_min` is that it isn't 0 on the original line, but instead it's the start of your data range.

Why group size matters

It's not always that easy. In Figure 14-4, the range of data is buried in a small chunk of the first line. But data isn't always that sparse. It can be spread more evenly. When that happens, if you compute one scale and zero-point for an entire weight matrix (per-tensor quantization), a single huge outlier weight stretches the range so wide that all the ordinary weights get crammed into a few integer values, and you lose precision everywhere. If instead you compute a separate scale and zero-point for every small block of weights (per-group, commonly groups of 32, 64, or 128), each block gets a range tuned to its own values, so outliers only hurt their own immediate neighborhood. The cost is more bookkeeping: more scales and zero-points to store.

Smaller groups mean better fidelity and slightly larger files. Group size 128 is the common default, and the K-quants in GGUF and the group sizes in AWQ and GPTQ are all variations on this idea. (We'll talk more about K-quants in a bit.)

This is also why outliers get so much attention in the quantization literature. In transformer weights and especially activations, a small number of dimensions carry disproportionately large values, and they carry a lot of the model's signal. A naive quantizer that treats every weight equally will spend its precision budget accommodating those outliers and starve everything else. The smarter formats in the next section are, at heart, different strategies for protecting the weights that matter while aggressively compressing the ones that don't.

Symmetry and activations

Let's look at two more distinctions you'll see in tooling. *Symmetric* quantization forces zero-point to the *middle* of the integer range and assumes weights are roughly centered on zero (often true), which saves you from storing a zero-point at all. *Asymmetric* quantization keeps a real zero-point (wherever zero actually lands) and handles lopsided distributions better.

You can see this general idea in Figure 14-5.

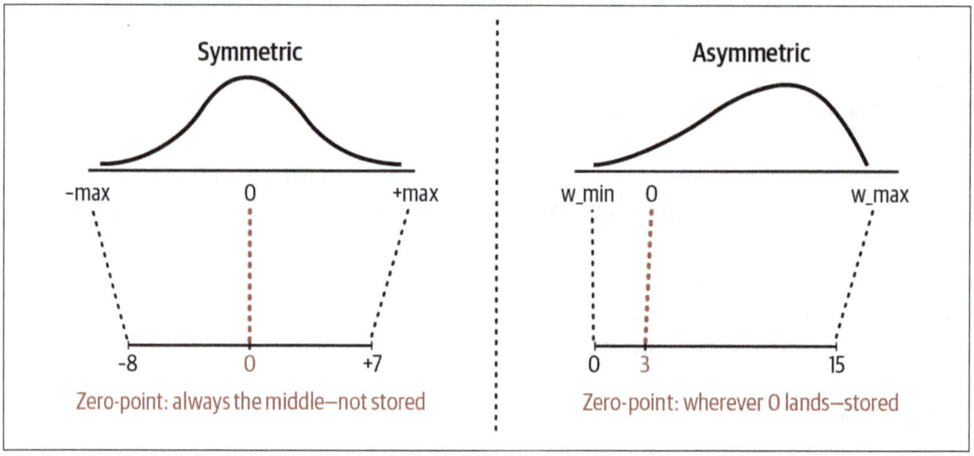

Figure 14-5. Symmetric versus asymmetric quantization

Most weight quantizers for LLMs use a symmetric or near-symmetric scheme per group.

The bigger distinction is weight-only versus weight-and-activation quantization. Everything we've discussed quantizes the static weights, which is safe because they don't change at runtime. Quantizing the *activations* (the values flowing through the network as it processes your prompt) is harder, because activations have nasty outliers that vary per input, and getting it wrong destroys quality. The formats most fine-tuners reach for, including the 4-bit GGUF and AWQ paths in this chapter, are weight-only; i.e., they shrink the weights and run the math in a higher precision. That gives you most of the size-and-speed benefit with a fraction of the risk. *Full-activation quantization* (int8 end-to-end) is a production optimization for high-throughput serving, and we'll note where it fits but won't make it the default, because at the small throughput requirements of running on your laptop, it's not necessary, and introduces unneeded complexity.

The Format Zoo

When you're just getting started, you might end up drowning in formats: GGUF, GPTQ, AWQ, EXL2, bitsandbytes, and likely a few new ones since I wrote this chapter! They're not interchangeable, and picking the wrong one will generally mean you have to redo everything. The good news is that they sort cleanly into a simple decision: determine where you need to run the model, and how much effort the quantization takes. Figure 14-6 shows this decision tree.

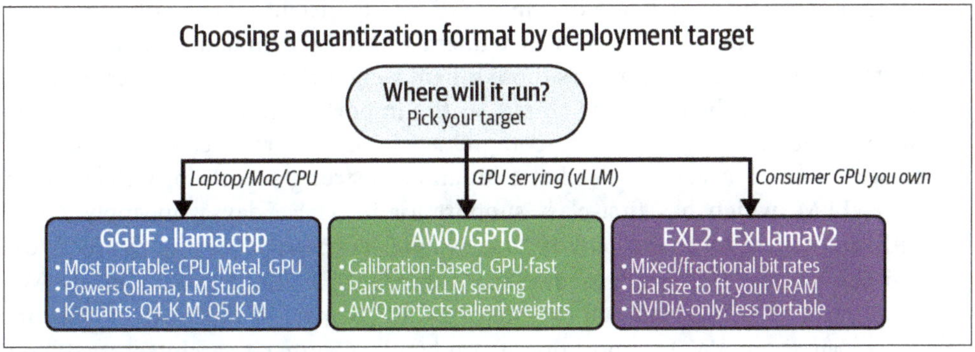

Figure 14-6. Choosing formats

Let's explore some of the options in this space:

bitsandbytes (NF4/int8)
: This is the one you already used in earlier chapters, probably without thinking of it as "a format." When you loaded the base model in 4-bit for QLoRA training, bitsandbytes quantized it on the fly with its NF4 scheme. It's fantastic for *training* because it's zero effort and integrates directly with the Transformers library loading path. It's a poor choice for *deployment*, though: it's slower at inference than the purpose-built formats, and it quantizes at load time rather than producing a compact file you can ship. Use it to train; reach for something else to serve.

GGUF (llama.cpp)
: GGUF is the format of the llama.cpp ecosystem, and it's the most portable option by a wide margin. A GGUF file runs on CPU, on Apple Silicon via

Metal, on NVIDIA and AMD GPUs, and it powers Ollama, LM Studio, and most local-AI desktop apps. Its quantization schemes are the K-quants with names like Q4_K_M and Q5_K_M, which mix bit widths intelligently across a model's layers. (We'll delve into K-quant naming in "Understanding the K-Quant Names" on page 325.) If your deployment target is a laptop, a Mac, a CPU server, or anything where you want one file that runs almost anywhere, GGUF is the default and it's where most of this chapter's hands-on work will live.

GPTQ
: GPTQ is a calibration-based, GPU-focused weight quantizer. It runs your model over a small sample of data and uses the resulting statistics to quantize each layer while compensating for the error introduced in the layers before it. The result is high-quality 4-bit (or 3-bit) weights for GPU inference, well supported by serving stacks. It needs a GPU and a calibration set, and the quantization itself takes a little while, but the output is fast and accurate on the hardware it targets.

AWQ
: AWQ is the activation-aware cousin of GPTQ. Its insight is that not all weights are equally important; the ones that interact with large-magnitude activations matter far more. AWQ identifies those salient weight channels from a calibration set and protects them, scaling things so the important weights survive quantization intact while the rest are compressed hard. In practice, AWQ tends to preserve task accuracy very well at 4-bit and is a strong default for GPU serving with vLLM, which has first-class support for it. These days you apply AWQ with the `llm-compressor` toolkit (the original `autoawq` library is deprecated), and the output is a `compressed-tensors` model that vLLM loads natively. We won't walk an AWQ run step by step in this chapter; at the time of writing, `llm-compressor` AWQ support doesn't yet handle Gemma 4's architecture. If you need a GPU-serving build today, GPTQ works through the same toolkit, and the official QAT w4a16 checkpoints, which we'll see later in this chapter, are the best route to consider.

EXL2 (ExLlamaV2)
: EXL2 is the enthusiast's format. It supports mixed and fractional bit rates (you can ask for an average of 4.65 bits per weight, say) and squeezes excellent quality-per-byte on NVIDIA GPUs. It's the format to know if you're running local models on consumer GPUs and want to dial the size to exactly fit your VRAM. It's GPU-only and tied to the ExLlamaV2 runtime, so it's less portable than GGUF, but for that specific use case it's hard to beat.

The decision, then, is mostly about the *target*:

- Shipping to laptops, Macs, CPUs, or desktop apps: use GGUF.
- Serving on GPUs at throughput with vLLM: use AWQ (or GPTQ).

- Packing a model tightly into a consumer GPU you own: use EXL2.
- Still training or experimenting: bitsandbytes is your friend and should stay where it is.

> Those are the defaults, but a few of the walls here are load-bearing rather than advisory. For example:
>
> - Quantized artifacts are one-way doors; you can't fine-tune a GGUF or GPTQ file, so the bfloat16 merged model is the asset you archive and the quants are outputs you can always regenerate.
> - GPTQ, AWQ, and EXL2 simply don't run on CPUs or Macs.
> - GGUF on a big GPU will load and run, but building a many-user serving deployment on it means fighting your own runtime; that's what the vLLM-native formats are for.
> - And bitsandbytes is never a deployment format at all; nothing gets smaller on disk, and its kernels are the slowest at inference.
>
> If you stay inside those walls, everything else in the zoo really is just preference and target hardware.

The medical model we've been working on through the book is meant to run privately and locally, possibly on a clinician's own machine, so our primary path is GGUF, with AWQ shown as the GPU-serving alternative. The next two sections walk through GGUF.

One more option sits above all of these for Gemma 4 *specifically*: the official Quantization-Aware Training checkpoints; however, it changes *when* you quantize rather than *how*, so we'll cover it a little later, after you've seen the post-training methods it improves on.

GPU Kernel Optimization: Why Fast Quantization Needs Fast Kernels

There's a puzzle hiding in everything we've just covered. Most GPUs don't have 4-bit math units; instead, the tensor cores that do the heavy lifting compute in 16-bit (or 8-bit on newer hardware). So when your Q4_K_M model runs, every weight still gets converted back to a higher precision before it's multiplied. If the weights have to be dequantized anyway, where does the speedup come from?

The answer is that LLM inference is memory-bound, not compute-bound. For every token generated, the entire model has to travel from GPU memory to the compute units, and that trip, not the arithmetic, is the bottleneck!

A 4-bit model moves a quarter of the bytes, so it can be nearly four times faster—but only if the software is smart about it. A naive implementation would dequantize the weights, write the full 16-bit copies back to memory, and then do the calculation. This will end up paying the memory cost it was supposed to avoid.

The trick is a fused kernel, which is a small, hand-tuned GPU program that loads the compressed weights, unpacks them in the GPU's on-chip memory, feeds them straight into the multiply, and throws them away. The 16-bit version of your model exists only for a fleeting moment, a tile at a time, in memory that's typically much faster than VRAM.

This is why the format zoo sorts by runtime as much as by format. A quantization scheme is only as fast as the kernels somebody wrote for it. GGUF is portable because the llama.cpp team hand-writes kernels for every K-quant on every backend (e.g., CUDA, Apple's Metal, plain CPU vector instructions). GPTQ and AWQ models fly on vLLM because of purpose-built kernels like Marlin (*https://oreil.ly/ALIEW*) that fuse dequantization into the matmul (matrix multiplication) at close to full memory bandwidth. And bitsandbytes is slower at inference precisely because its kernels were built for training-time convenience, not serving-time speed. The same file format with different kernels can differ in tokens-per-second by two or three times.

The practical upshot: you will almost certainly never write a GPU kernel, and you don't need to. You inherit them by choosing a serving stack, which is one more reason the question from Figure 14-6 ("Where will it run?") is the right question to ask first. Just remember, when you benchmark two quantized builds against each other, you're really benchmarking their kernels—so measure on the runtime you'll actually deploy.

Using GGUF with llama.cpp

This is likely where you'll spend most of your time as you explore deployment, because this format will run your private model on the hardware you own. It has two basic steps: first you'll convert your merged Hugging Face model into a GGUF file, and then you'll quantize that file to the bit width you want. Both steps will use tools from the llama.cpp repository.

Convert, Then Quantize

So, the first step will be to convert your merged model into a 16-bit GGUF. This step won't do any compression; it will just translate the model from the *.safetensors* layout into a single GGUF container, keeping the full float16 precision:

```
# One-time setup: clone and build llama.cpp's tooling.
git clone https://github.com/ggml-org/llama.cpp
pip install -r llama.cpp/requirements.txt

# Step 1: HF model -> 16-bit GGUF (no compression yet).
```

```
python llama.cpp/convert_hf_to_gguf.py \
    ./medical-gemma-merged \
    --outfile medical-gemma-f16.gguf \
    --outtype f16
```

Once you have the GGUF, you can then quantize that down to a K-quant. The `llama-quantize` tool takes the source file, the destination, and the quant type. Here's an example:

```
# Step 2: 16-bit GGUF -> 4-bit K-quant.
./llama.cpp/llama-quantize \
    medical-gemma-f16.gguf \
    medical-gemma-Q4_K_M.gguf \
    Q4_K_M
```

This second command is the one that will actually shrink the model, going from about 15 GB on disk to about 4.5 GB. The full sequence of code, including environment setup and verification, is captured in the *02_convert_to_gguf.sh* script in the download.

Having run the *01_merge_adapter.py* script from earlier in this chapter, you now only need to run the GGUF conversion script:

```
bash 02_convert_to_gguf.sh ./medical-gemma-merged
```

This will perform the conversion and launch an inference engine so you can try chatting with the model yourself!

Understanding the K-Quant Names

These GGUF quant types look very cryptic until you learn the pattern, after which they'll begin to make sense. Take the Q4_K_M that you saw in the previous section. The Q4 means that you'll have an average of 4 bits per weight. You'll see a variety there—usually Q2, Q3, Q5, Q6, or Q8. The K means it's a K-quant, which is a second-generation scheme that uses a block structure with per-block scaling rather than using one scale for a whole tensor. The trailing letter (in this case M) is the size tier within the bit width—S for small, M for medium, or L for large.

Ultimately, the tiers will differ based on how many of the model's most important tensors (typically the attention and feed-forward weights that carry the highest signal) are kept at a mostly higher bit width than the rest. Thus, Q4_K_M will keep the most important tensors at a little more precision than Q4_K_S, costing size for quality.

In practice, you don't really need to memorize the whole matrix of possibilities. The community has converged on a few sweet spots, and you can think of them like this:

- Q8_0 is 8-bit and essentially lossless. Use it when you want a safety reference to measure smaller quants against, but not typically for deployment.
- Q6_K is nearly indistinguishable from 16-bit, and a good choice when you have the space and want to be conservative.
- Q5_K_M is a strong middle ground.
- Q4_K_M is the workhorse, and the standard recommendation for most deployments. It's in the sweet spot of the quality versus size for the majority of models and where you should start.
- Q3_K_M and below will begin to show visible degradation, and it's for when you're really memory starved.
- Q2_K is the extreme end. The model will run and might sound good, but reasoning and reliability will degrade sharply. And for something like a medical model, that's a clear and unwanted showstopper.

Rule of thumb: start at Q4_K_M, measure, and only move if you need to!

The Importance Matrix

Another lever that you can use to improve your low-bit GGUF quants is called the *importance matrix*, or *imatrix*. It can be worth the extra steps for anything at 4-bit or below. It's the same idea behind the calibration-based quantizers from GPTQ and AWQ, but applied to GGUF. You run your model over a calibration set to measure which weights matter the most, save those statistics to a file, and then feed that file to `llama-quantize` so it protects those more important weights as it quantizes.

Here's an example:

```
# First, build the calibration text from your TRAINING pool (a few hundred
# in-domain Q&A pairs, never your test set):
python -c "
from datasets import load_dataset
ds = load_dataset('lmoroney/synthdata', split='train').select(range(300))
open('medical_calibration.txt','w').write(
    '\n\n'.join(ex['instruction'] + '\n' + ex['output'] for ex in ds))
"

# Measure weight importance on that in-domain text.
# Might change depending on how and where llama.cpp is built.
./llama.cpp/build/bin/llama-imatrix \
    -m medical-gemma-f16.gguf \
    -f medical_calibration.txt \
    -o medical.imatrix

# Quantize using the importance matrix for better low-bit fidelity.
./llama.cpp/build/bin/llama-quantize \
    --imatrix medical.imatrix \
```

```
        medical-gemma-f16.gguf \
        medical-gemma-Q4_K_M.gguf \
        Q4_K_M
```

At the end of running this, you'll end up with something like:

```
type =     f16, converting to q4_K .. size =      1.25 MiB ->      0.35 MiB
llama_model_quantize_impl: model size  = 14235.64 MiB (16.00 BPW)
llama_model_quantize_impl: quant size  =  5041.55 MiB (5.67 BPW)
```

That calibration text is where the imatrix earns its value, so treat it with the same care you'd generally give a training set. I like to follow two main rules here: the first is to make it *in-domain* where you fill the text file with representative medical Q&A, and not generic web text. This is because the imatrix will decide which weights to protect from the activations that are produced by the text. Calibrating on the wrong distribution will protect the wrong weights!

The second rule is to keep the three pools disjoint from each other. You have train, calibration, and test datasets. Draw the calibration one from the training distribution and never from the held-out test set! If the quantizer gets to peek at the data you'll later grade it on, your post-quantization scores will look artificially good and mean nothing. It's the same way that training on the test set gives a false sense of security. And there's a certain irony here: an honest imatrix only buys you a modest improvement in the first place, so contaminating your evaluation to flatter it is trading away the one thing that matters (numbers you can trust) for a gain that was never large.

One practical caveat: computing the imatrix runs the full-precision model over your calibration text, which is compute-heavy. On a GPU, it takes a few minutes; on CPU, it can take the better part of an hour, because a CPU-only build of llama.cpp crunches the 15 GB f16 model the slow way. If you have a GPU, build llama.cpp with CUDA (`cmake -B llama.cpp/build -S llama.cpp -DGGML_CUDA=ON`) and add `-ngl 99` to the `llama-imatrix` command to offload all layers to the GPU. If you don't, shrink the calibration set to around 100 samples, or simply skip the imatrix; a plain Q4_K_M build is already a solid, deployable model and the imatrix is optional polish.

Once you have the imatrix, you can pass it to the `llama-quantize` command as a parameter to get an optimized GGUF file. We'll explore how to serve that in Chapter 15.

A Better Way Forward: QAT

Everything we've looked at so far in this chapter is post-training quantization (PTQ). You took the *finished* model and compressed it when you were done. It's general. It will work on any model (with changes based on the quirks of particular models, of course) and the GGUF skills that you learned should apply to everything. But, it has a built-in ceiling. The weights were trained in full precision, and never asked to tolerate 4-bit rounding. So, when you compress them, some of the quality you lose is simply gone! Calibration and importance matrices can reduce that loss, but they won't eliminate it.

There's a second approach that attacks this problem from the other direction: Quantization Aware Training (QAT) simulates the rounding errors of low precision during training, so the model will learn weights that sit comfortably on the quantization grid during the process of overall learning. So, instead of compressing a model that wasn't designed for it, you train a model that expects to be 4-bit and compensates for that on the fly. The result: a 4-bit model that can perform really close to its 16-bit parent, recovering most of the gap that PTQ will leave on the table.

You can see this comparison in Figure 14-7.

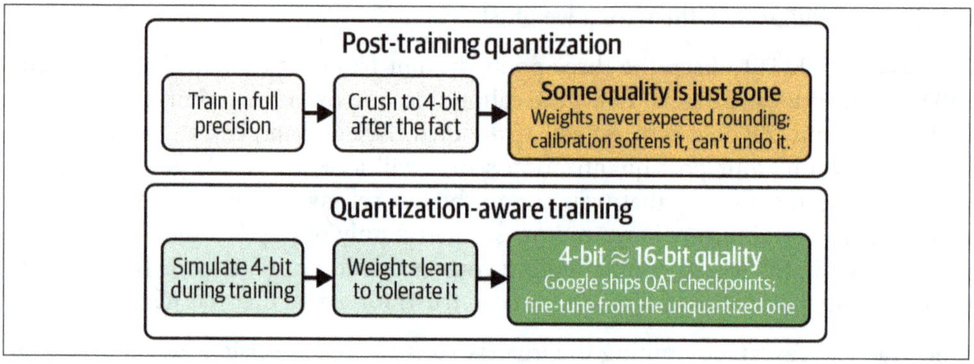

Figure 14-7. Comparing training types: PTQ versus QAT

Historically, QAT was a hard sell, because it would mean full expensive retraining that most teams couldn't justify. Train once at 16-bit, and then train again for 4-bit. What's changed is that some vendors *already do this for you*, and the Gemma 4 model we've been using throughout this book has official QAT checkpoints available for you to use. That turns QAT into an easy download instead of a full research project!

How to Get QAT Gemma

For each Gemma 4 size, including the E4B model, the official QAT collection provides a few flavors, each aimed at a different deployment target:

A q4_0 GGUF build—`{model}-qat-q4_0-gguf`
: For drop-in use across the llama.cpp ecosystem: LM Studio, Ollama, and anything else that reads GGUF, on CPU, Apple Silicon, or consumer GPUs. This is the QAT analog of what you built by hand earlier, except the quality loss is far smaller because the model was trained for it.

A w4a16 compressed-tensors build—`{model}-qat-w4a16-ct`
: For high-throughput GPU serving with vLLM or SGLang: 4-bit weights with 16-bit activations, in the `compressed-tensors` format those servers consume natively. This is the QAT counterpart to a post-training AWQ or GPTQ build, and on Gemma 4 it's the most reliable way to get that GPU-serving artifact today.

An unquantized QAT checkpoint—`{model}-qat-q4_0-unquantized`
: For half-precision weights pulled from the QAT pipeline before the final compression. This one is the important one for fine-tuners, and the next subsection explains why. There are also matching draft models (`-assistant`) for speculative decoding, and mobile-optimized variants for on-device use.

Using QAT for Fine-Tuning

Here's the subtlety. Google's QAT checkpoints are on the base model. However, you don't want the base model; you want your medical model. So the win isn't downloading the QAT GGUF and shipping it, because that throws away your fine-tuning. The win is to fine-tune on top of the unquantized QAT checkpoint instead of the vanilla base.

The workflow is the typical end-to-end pipeline: run a QLoRA fine-tune (you can use the *00_finetune_gemma4.py* script for this chapter, found in the book's download), followed by a merge, and the GGUF quantization. Nothing changes, except for the base model you load at the first step:

```
# Instead of fine-tuning from the vanilla base:
#   BASE = "google/gemma-4-e4b-it"
# start your LoRA run from the UNQUANTIZED QAT checkpoint:
BASE = "google/gemma-4-e4b-it-qat-q4_0-unquantized"
```

Train the LoRA adapter, and then merge it, as earlier in this chapter. When you quantize it to q4_0, the base weights are already quantization robust, and your fine-tuned version will inherit that robustness. The final 4-bit version should cost you far less accuracy than the PTQ on the vanilla model would. So you get most of QAT's benefit without ever running the expensive QAT pass yourself.

Let's look at a couple of caveats. First is that when you fine-tune on top of QAT weights and then requantize, you're not mathematically identical to Google's end-to-end QAT. Instead, you're inheriting quantization-friendly weights, and not rerunning through your own data. In practice, this will cover most of the gap, but "most" is why you'll need to do some measurement to be sure. The other caveat, of course, is that not every model will ship QAT checkpoints! So if you want to fine-tune a model, and there's no preexisting QAT, you're out of luck!

So, the decision is easy. If you're about to fine-tune a model that ships QAT weights, then use those. It's an easy and quick change that pays off on deployment. If you've already fine-tuned on the base model, and you're okay with that, you can quantize with the PTQ methods we've discussed in this chapter and measure the result. If the results are okay, based on your desired metrics, ship it! You can see this decision-making process in Figure 14-8.

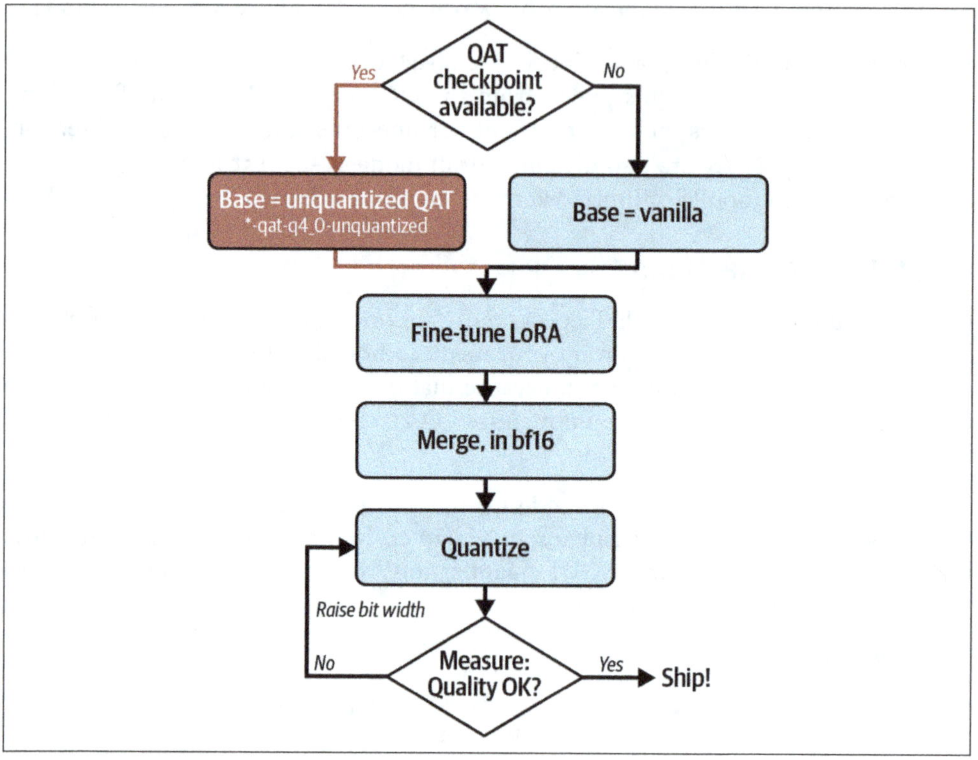

Figure 14-8. Your decision flowchart

Measuring Quantization Impact

There's several ways to compress your model, and of course, the big questions are how much does each method cost, and which ones are worth it? "It works and will answer questions" is one answer, but it's not a good one! Quantization degradation is real, and subtle. It's often invisible for some hand-picked test prompts. The discipline that separates a good deployment from a bad one is measuring the quality of every quant against the original using a hold-out test set—exactly the same as you did for the training run.

Two Metrics to Track

There are two main metrics to track:

Perplexity

The first is perplexity on a held-out set. *Perplexity* (see Chapter 9 for a detailed discussion) measures how surprised the model is by the text. It should find the text natural; lower is better. It's cheap to compute, it doesn't need a judge, and it's exquisitely sensitive to the kind of broad degradation quantization causes. Its weakness is that it measures language-modeling fidelity, not task correctness, so a model can keep a flat perplexity while still getting medical facts subtly wrong. Use perplexity as your early-warning tripwire; a perplexity jump between two quants is a red flag worth investigating, while a flat perplexity is necessary but not sufficient.

Task accuracy

The second is *task accuracy* on your domain test set, scored the way you score the real task. For the medical model that's the held-out medical Q&A set you've been carrying since Chapter 9, graded by whatever method you settled on (e.g., exact-match on structured answers or an LLM judge for open-ended ones). This is the number that actually matters, because it measures the thing the model is for. Perplexity tells you the model didn't break at the task; task accuracy tells you it's still good at its job.

The Bit-Width Sweep

The right way, of course, is not to pick one and hope, but to evaluate several models across the bit-width range and look at the curve. I've provided a script in the book's downloads (*03_perplexity_sweep.py*) that loads each model variant in turn, computes perplexity on a held-out set, and accuracy on the test set, printing a table of results:

```
variants = {
    "f16  (baseline)": "medical-gemma-f16.gguf",
    "Q6_K":            "medical-gemma-Q6_K.gguf",
    "Q5_K_M":          "medical-gemma-Q5_K_M.gguf",
    "Q4_K_M":          "medical-gemma-Q4_K_M.gguf",
    "Q3_K_M":          "medical-gemma-Q3_K_M.gguf",
}

rows = []
for name, path in variants.items():
    llm = load_gguf(path)
    ppl = perplexity(llm, heldout_text)          # lower is better
    acc = medical_accuracy(llm, test_set)        # higher is better
    size_gb = os.path.getsize(path) / 1e9
    rows.append((name, size_gb, ppl, acc))
    print(f"{name:18s} {size_gb:5.2f} GB  ppl={ppl:6.3f}  acc={acc:5.1%}")
```

One set of results I got looked like the following. Your numbers will differ, but the shape is what you want to watch out for:

```
variant             size       ppl    acc
f16  (baseline)     14.90 GB   6.41   84.2%
Q6_K                 6.28 GB   6.43   84.1%
Q5_K_M               5.42 GB   6.47   83.8%
Q4_K_M               4.68 GB   6.58   83.1%
Q3_K_M               3.79 GB   7.22   78.6%
```

Look how the accuracy and size are related. The drop-off from the baseline to Q4_K_M is only about 1%, but the model is one-third the size! Additionally, the perplexity only changed a little. Compare this with the numbers for Q3_K_M and you'll see why Q4_K_M is a good choice.

It's a good default to start from, but it's also worth testing your models to be sure!

KV-Cache Optimization

Quantizing the weights solves the static size problem and how much memory the model occupies at rest. But, there's a second, dynamic consumer of memory that grows with every token the model processes. On long inputs this can be very considerable. It's the KV cache, and managing it is an important lever.

What Is the KV Cache?

When a transformer generates text, each new token attends to every previous token. The keys (K) and values (V) for those previous tokens don't change as generation continues, so recomputing them for every new token would be enormously wasteful. Instead the model computes each token's key and value once and stores them in the *KV cache*, then reuses them for all subsequent tokens. This is the optimization that makes autoregressive generation practical. The cost is memory, and that memory grows linearly with the number of tokens in context.

You can size it exactly. The KV cache holds, for every layer and every key/value head, one vector per token:

```
kv_bytes = 2 * n_layers * n_kv_heads * head_dim * seq_len
             * batch * bytes_per_value
```

The leading `2` is for keys and values. Plug in a 4B-class model with, say, 34 layers, and a long 8,000-token context at 16-bit, and you're looking at well over a gigabyte of cache for a single sequence, on top of the weights. Serve several conversations at once and the cache, not the weights, becomes the thing that decides how much hardware you need.

You can see an example of how it might grow in Figure 14-9.

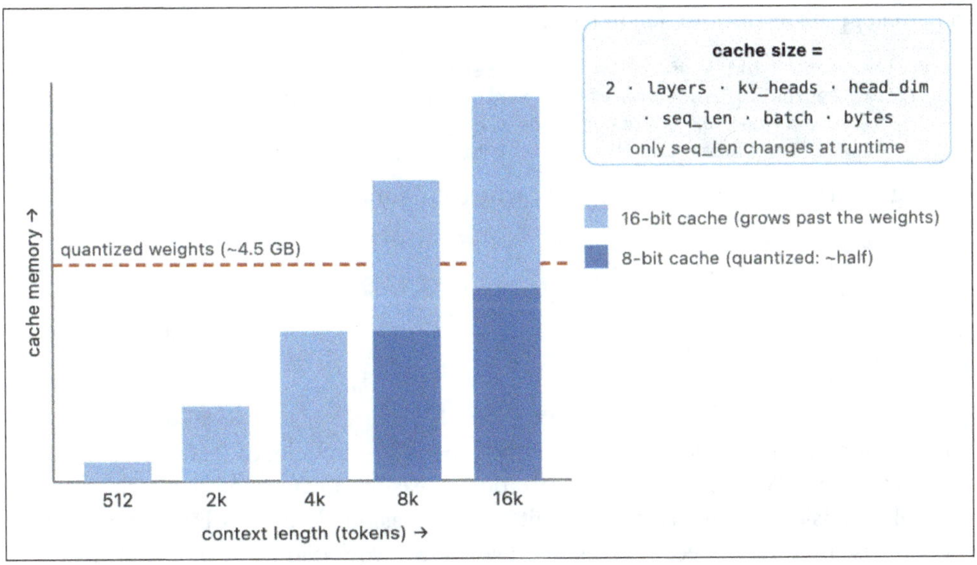

Figure 14-9. How the KV cache grows

So how do you get around this? Well, the good news is that the architecture innovations baked into the models already help with most of the work for this. Let's take a look at some in the next sections.

Grouped Query Attention

The first and biggest help is *grouped query attention* (GQA), which Gemma, Llama 3, and Mistral all use, and which you read about back in Chapter 2. GQA lets many query heads share a single key/value head, which directly shrinks `n_kv_heads` in the formula we just saw, often by a factor of four or eight. You get this for free simply by having chosen a modern architecture; there's nothing to configure. It's worth knowing that it's the reason your cache is as small as it is.

KV-Cache Quantization

The second lever is *KV-cache quantization*, the same idea you applied to the weights, now applied to the cache. The keys and values are just tensors, and you can store them in 8-bit or even 4-bit instead of 16-bit, halving or quartering the cache's footprint. Because the cache is read constantly during generation, quantizing it trades a little accuracy and a little compute for a lot of memory headroom, which is exactly the trade you want for long-context workloads.

In llama.cpp it's a runtime flag like this:

```
# llama.cpp: 8-bit keys and values at serve time.
./llama.cpp/build/bin/llama-cli -m medical-gemma-Q4_K_M.gguf \
    --cache-type-k q8_0 --cache-type-v q8_0 \
    -c 8192 -p "Summarize this patient history: ..."
```

If using the Transformers library, it's a cache configuration:

```
# transformers: store the KV cache in quantized form to fit longer context.
out = model.generate(
    input_ids,
    max_new_tokens=512,
    cache_implementation="quantized",
    cache_config={"backend": "quanto", "nbits": 4},
)
```

The runnable examples live in the book's downloads (*Chapter14/04kv_cache_quant.py*). As with weight quantization, measure. Quantizing the cache to 8-bit is usually invisible in quality, while 4-bit cache occasionally costs a little on tasks that need precise long-range recall, so test it on your own workload before committing.

PagedAttention

The third lever isn't something you configure on the model so much as something your *serving stack* does for you: `PagedAttention`, the technique behind vLLM. Naively, you'd allocate a contiguous block of memory for each sequence's cache that is sized to the maximum possible length, and this wastes enormous amounts of memory on sequences that turn out to be short.

`PagedAttention` manages the cache in small fixed-size pages, like virtual memory in an operating system, allocating them on demand and sharing identical pages (such as a common system prompt) across requests. The result is dramatically higher memory efficiency and throughput when serving many concurrent users. You don't *implement* it; you *get* it by serving with vLLM, which is the subject of Chapter 15. It's mentioned here because it's the production answer to the KV-cache problem, and because it informs *which* compressed artifact you build: if you're heading for vLLM, a `compressed-tensors` build (a GPTQ build, or the official QAT w4a16 checkpoints from earlier) pairs with `PagedAttention` to give you both small weights and an efficient cache.

Prefix Caching

A close cousin of `PagedAttention` is *prefix caching*. If every request to your medical model starts with the same 800-token system prompt, it's wasteful to recompute the keys and values for those 800 tokens on every single request because they're identical every time. Prefix caching keeps the KV entries for common prompt prefixes resident in memory and simply reuses them, so a new request only pays for computing the part that's actually new. On workloads with long shared instructions or few-shot examples in the prompt (which is most production deployments), this can cut TTFT dramatically. In vLLM, it's a flag (`--enable-prefix-caching`); llama.cpp does something similar automatically for a continuing conversation, reusing the cache from the previous turn rather than reprocessing the whole transcript.

Offloading

The last cache lever is offloading: when the cache outgrows GPU memory, spill the older portions to CPU RAM (or even disk) and pull them back on demand. It works because of the shape of attention access patterns. During generation, every new token technically attends to all previous tokens, but the serving stack can stream cache pages back in faster than naively recomputing them from scratch. The trade is latency for capacity: offloaded conversations respond a bit slower, but they respond, instead of failing with an out-of-memory error when a user pastes a massive amount of information. Think of it as the overflow safety valve behind the quantization and paging levers, rather than something you plan to rely on per-request.

Some Optimizations to Consider

Before we wire the pipeline together, two more optimizations deserve a mention. Neither changes your model artifact, as they're things a serving stack does at inference time. However, they will come up the moment you deploy, and one of them explains a file you may have noticed in the QAT collection (the `-assistant` draft models mentioned earlier).

The first is *speculative decoding*. Recall that generation is memory-bound; each new token requires hauling the entire model through memory for one forward pass, and most of that effort produces tokens that were, frankly, easy to predict (e.g., given "the patient should consult a...", even a tiny model knows "doctor" is coming). Speculative decoding exploits this by pairing your model with a much smaller draft model that races ahead and proposes several tokens cheaply, and then having the big model verify the whole batch in a single forward pass. Verifying k tokens costs barely more than generating one, because the bottleneck was always the memory trip, not the arithmetic. Accepted tokens are free speedup; rejected ones fall back to the big model's own prediction, so the output is probably identical to what the big model would have produced alone—a pure speed win, with no quality trade to measure. This is exactly what the `-assistant` draft models in the Gemma 4 QAT collection are for. Typical speedups are two to three times on predictable text, less on text that keeps the draft model guessing.

The second is *prefill/decode disaggregation*, and it matters once you're serving at scale. Processing a request has two very different phases: prefill, where the model ingests the whole prompt in one highly parallel, compute-bound pass; and decode, where it generates tokens one at a time in a memory-bound loop. Those two phases want different hardware: prefill loves raw compute, decode loves memory bandwidth. When both run on the same GPU, long prefills stall everyone else's token generation. Disaggregated serving splits them onto separate GPU pools, with the prefill workers handing the finished KV cache over to the decode workers. It's a data-center pattern, not a laptop one, and you won't configure it for the medical model, but it's why the big inference providers can keep latency flat under load. (You'll see the prefill/decode distinction again the moment you look at vLLM's metrics in Chapter 15.)

Putting It All Together: The Quantization Pipeline

You've now seen every step on its own. In practice, you want them wired into a single repeatable pipeline, because compression is something you'll redo every time you retrain, and a manual sequence of commands is a manual sequence of mistakes. The pipeline takes a base model and a freshly trained adapter and produces a measured, deployable artifact, gating on quality so you never accidentally ship a model that quantization broke.

The shape of the pipeline is a straight line with a checkpoint at the end. You can see it in Figure 14-10.

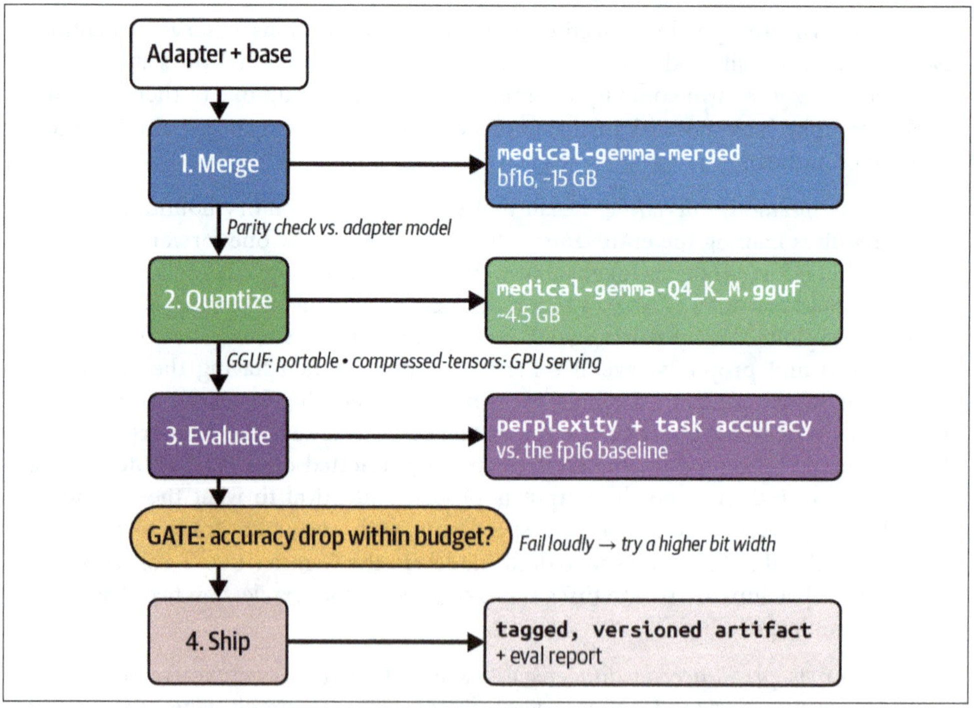

Figure 14-10. The compression and quantization pipeline

I've provided a script in the book's downloads (*Chapter14/05_compression_pipeline.py*) that implements this end to end. The orchestration is kind of boring, which ultimately is the point:

```
def compress(base, adapter, quant="Q4_K_M", max_acc_drop=0.02):
    merged = merge_adapter(base, adapter)
    assert parity_ok(merged, base, adapter)

    gguf_f16 = convert_to_gguf(merged)
    quantized = quantize_gguf(gguf_f16, quant)

    base_acc = task_accuracy(gguf_f16)
    quant_acc = task_accuracy(quantized)
    drop = base_acc - quant_acc

    if drop > max_acc_drop:
        raise QualityGateError(
            f"{quant} dropped accuracy by {drop:.1%} "
            f"(budget {max_acc_drop:.1%}). Try a higher bit width.")

    write_eval_report(quantized, base_acc, quant_acc, drop)
    return quantized
```

The `max_acc_drop` gate is the part to internalize. You decide up front how much accuracy you're willing to trade for size, encode it as a number, and let the pipeline enforce it. If Q4_K_M busts the budget, the pipeline fails loudly and tells you to step up to Q5_K_M, rather than quietly shipping a degraded model. This is the same philosophy as treating evaluation as a gate: compression is not done when the file is smaller, it's done when the file is smaller *and* you've proven it's still good enough.

After running the full pipeline on the medical model, the before-and-after tells the whole story of the chapter:

```
                  BEFORE               AFTER
artifact           base + adapter       medical-gemma-Q4_K_M.gguf
files              2 (base + 37 MB)     1
on-disk size       ~15 GB               ~4.5 GB
loads on           24 GB+ GPU           8 GB laptop / CPU
runtime dep        transformers+PEFT    llama.cpp / Ollama
task accuracy      84.2%                83.1%
```

To run this, you'll need to start with a fine-tuned LoRA of the medical Q&A. If you don't have one on hand, the *00_finetune_gemma4.py* script will create one for you.

Next, you'll install llama-cpp-python, and instruct the environment to ignore TensorFlow:

```
export USE_TF=0
pip install -q llama-cpp-python
```

The next step is to merge the fine-tuned adapter into the base model:

```
python 01_merge_adapter.py \
    --base google/gemma-4-e4b-it \
    --adapter ./medical-qa-v1-gemma4-lora \
    --out ./medical-gemma-merged
```

If the model won't fit into your GPU and VRAM, you can use a switch `--device cpu` at the end.

The next step is to convert and quantize to GGUF and use imatrix calibration. To do this, run the following code. First, create a python file called `format_data.py` with the code below:

```
from datasets import load_dataset
ds = load_dataset('lmoroney/synthdata', split='train').select(range(300))
open('medical_calibration.txt','w').write
    ('\n\n'.join(e['instruction']+'\n'+e['output'] for e in ds))
```

Then, run the following from the console:

```
python -c format_data.py
bash 02_convert_to_gguf.sh ./medical-gemma-merged medical_calibration.txt
```

Note that if you don't want to do the imatrix step, you can remove *medical_calibration.txt*.

When done, this will produce *medical-gemma-f16.gguf* and *medical-gemma-Q4_K_M.gguf*.

You can create other bit widths using `llama-quantize`, like this:

```
for q in Q6_K Q5_K_M Q3_K_M; do
  ./llama.cpp/build/bin/llama-quantize medical-gemma-f16.gguf
                                       medical-gemma-$q.gguf $q
done
```

Once you have this, you can perform the perplexity sweep to measure quality across the bit widths:

```
python 03_perplexity_sweep.py --test-set test_set.jsonl
```

This can take a few hours. When done, it will print the size/perplexity/F1 accuracy table, like this:

```
variant              size      ppl   ansF1
---------------------------------------------
f16  (baseline)    14.94GB    5.613  44.0%
Q6_K                6.17GB    5.654  43.4%
Q5_K_M              5.72GB    5.747  43.3%
Q4_K_M              5.30GB    6.177  42.1%
Q3_K_M              4.82GB    8.731  40.0%
```

The F1 scores might appear low, but they're actually quite healthy. The token-overlap F1 compares the words in the model's answer to those in the reference answer. For open-ended questions like this, two perfectly good answers to the same question would only share a fraction of their tokens because of paraphrasing, reordering, and varying in length. Two human doctors writing answers to the same question would also score well under 100%!

> Earlier in this chapter, I showed accuracy output instead of F1. The script gives you both options, and I thought for the purpose of this section, the F1 was a better output to use.

What matters is the shape of the column, where you can see the F1 answer is slowly sliding down from 44% to 42.1% as it gets to Q4_K_M. The steep drop happens between that and Q3_K_M. That's the "knee" that the code refers to, a sharp angle drop (like the knee on a leg). The quantization is behaving as expected.

Then, you can do the overall pipeline from Figure 14-10:

```
python 05_compression_pipeline.py \
    --base google/gemma-4-e4b-it \
    --adapter ./medical-qa-v1-gemma4-lora \
    --calib medical_calibration.txt \
    --test-set test_set.jsonl
```

You started with a model that needed a data-center GPU and a Python training stack to run. You finished with a single 4.5-GB file that runs on a laptop through Ollama. Through it all, you gave up only about a point of accuracy, and you now have a model that is genuinely yours to deploy anywhere. That's the deployment gap closed.

Avoiding Some Common Pitfalls

The same handful of mistakes account for most of the "my quantized model got dumb" complaints, and every one of them is avoidable once you know to look for it. Let's take a look at them:

Merging into a 4-bit base
: This is covered in "The 4-bit Merge Trap" on page 314 and is worth repeating because it's so common. If you keep the QLoRA training configuration and call `merge_and_unload()` on a model still loaded in 4-bit, you bake a double-quantization error into the merged weights before you've even started compressing. Always reload the base in bfloat16 or float16 for the merge, and quantize as a deliberate separate step.

Calibrating on the wrong data
: Calibrating on the wrong data (or worse, on your test set) could be a costly mistake. A medical model calibrated on generic web text quantizes worse on medical questions than one calibrated on medical Q&A, and a model calibrated on its own test set produces evaluation numbers that are simply fiction. Keep train, calibration, and test pools separate, and draw calibration from the training distribution.

Shipping without measuring
: Quantization degradation hides from casual inspection; three cherry-picked prompts will look fine right up until a user hits the case that breaks the model. Run the bit-width sweep, look at both perplexity and task accuracy, and make the decision from the table rather than from vibes.

Tokenizer or chat-template mismatch
: These are both mismatches between the compressed model and what you serve it with. If your fine-tune added special tokens or changed the chat template, those changes must travel with every artifact you produce, the merged model and the GGUF build alike. A mismatched template is the classic cause of a model that "loads fine but answers weirdly," and it's maddening to debug because nothing errors. Save the tokenizer alongside the weights at every step, and confirm the serving stack uses it.

Forgetting the KV cache in your memory budget
: Teams size their hardware for the quantized weights, deploy, and then run out of memory the first time a user pastes a long document, because the cache silently grows past the weights. Compute the cache size for your maximum supported context up front, and if it's large, quantize the cache or move to a paged-attention serving stack before it becomes a production incident. You can typically also set up alerts on threshold limits.

None of these are exotic. They're the ordinary friction of moving a model from the lab to the field, and a few minutes of measurement at each step is what separates a clean deployment from a confusing one.

Summary

Optimization is what turns a model that *trains* into a model that *ships*. In this chapter, you learned about the three most important levers you can manipulate for desired model optimization and quantization, and how their effects can positively compound.

First, you merged the LoRA adapter into the base to get a single standard artifact, taking care to merge in *full* precision, rather than into a quantized one. You verified parity against the adapter model before trusting the result. This merge didn't shrink the model, but it *is* the foundation that everything else is built on.

You learned how *quantization* works. Weights are stored as small integers plus a shared scale around a zero-point. That mental model hopefully helped demystify the format zoo that sorts by deployment target: GGUF for portable CPU, Apple Silicon, and desktop apps; AWQ or GPTQ for GPU serving; and EXL2 for packing consumer GPUs. We looked into the quantization of the medical model using GGUF through llama.cpp.

You also saw the difference between post-training quantization (PTQ) and Quantization-Aware Training (QAT), where the model is trained to tolerate lower precision from the start. With Gemma, Google ships QAT checkpoints for Gemma 4, so you can claim most of the benefit by fine-tuning on top of the QAT checkpoint by performing a single-line change at the start of training that pays dividends when you compress at the end. But, of course, QAT may not always be an option if the model creator doesn't provide you with one.

You also looked at the overall damage from quantization using perplexity and task accuracy. You saw that the common default for quantization is Q4_K_M, but also saw how to explore different schemes.

Next, you looked into the KV cache, and how it can be a major memory hog, and explored methods for quantization here, and how your serving stack's `Paged Attention` will help.

Ultimately, all of this territory covered is to show you that compression is a messy process. There are lots of steps, and lots of places where things can go wrong. But if you navigate your way through it effectively, you can really reap the rewards.

Next up, in Chapter 15, you're going to take the result of all this work and put it behind a real serving stack. You'll see vLLM for throughput, and Ollama for local edge deployment. You'll also see how it can be wrapped in an OpenAI-compatible API so the rest of your software can talk to it.

CHAPTER 15
Serving the Expert

You now have a private expert model that you can run! Over the past 14 chapters, you took a base Gemma 4 model, curated a medical Q&A dataset, trained a LoRA adapter, aligned it with DPO, merged it, and compressed it into a single GGUF file that loads on a laptop and still answers medical questions well. That file is the payoff of the whole book. But a file on disk is not a product. Nothing in your existing software can call it, no user can reach it, and it does nothing at all until a process loads it into memory and listens for requests.

That is just as true for the image models you built earlier. Back in Chapters 12 and 13, you left the language world entirely and fine-tuned diffusion models, teaching one a specific subject with DreamBooth and another a specific artistic style with a style LoRA.

All these models have the same problem: a trained checkpoint is not a service until something serves it. That is what this chapter is going to solve.

The serving principles here—wrapping a model in a standard API, thinking about throughput, and putting operational glue around it—will carry straight over to the diffusion model. Where they will differ is usually just the request shape (a prompt and image parameters in, image bytes out).

To keep this chapter concrete and focused, you will serve the language model you have been building all along, and the medical Gemma expert is the running example throughout.

This chapter closes the last gap from artifact to service. You will stand your model up two ways, because there are two very different jobs. You will use Ollama to run it locally for edge and single-user deployment, the case where privacy and simplicity matter most. You will use vLLM to serve it at high throughput on a GPU, the case where a real product needs to handle real concurrent traffic. Both of them expose your model through the same OpenAI-compatible API, which means the software you already wrote against a *paid* API can point at your own model by changing only two lines.

You will serve many experts from a single base, force structured output that downstream code can trust, and put a production gateway in front. By the end, you will own a running, callable, private expert, and you will be ready to think about what a world full of them looks like.

From Artifact to Service

Ultimately, your serving stack has one job: to keep your model loaded in memory and to turn incoming *requests* into *responses*—and to do it fast, correctly, and preferably without falling over under load. It sounds simple; and for one request at a time, it is simple. But the complexity comes with the words "under load."

A model that answers one developer in less than a second can collapse if a bunch of users hit it at once, because loading the weights, managing the growing KV cache, and scheduling overlapping requests are real engineering problems that a naive piece of code can easily get wrong.

There's no single right answer, because there's no single consistent serving job. Everything is different. The two ends of the spectrum, from high load to low load, pull in opposite directions, and optimizations for one will fail at the other.

At one end is the *edge* case: one user, one machine, and it's often offline. When you run your model on a laptop or a desktop application that wraps the model (such as a clinic with an air-gapped machine that cannot legally send patient data to the cloud), you're in this use case. Privacy and simplicity dominate. You'll also generally want the model to work on modest hardware with a simple user experience. Likely you'll want it to run on a CPU, a consumer GPU, or an Apple Silicon machine. It should not be like E.T.[1] and never want to phone home. Throughput isn't as important, because there's only one conversation at a time.

Here's where Ollama is a strong contender, because it's really easy to set up and use, handles many different models and can consume the GGUF files you worked on in Chapter 14.

The other end is the *throughput* use case: many users, shared infrastructure, a real product with real traffic (think Gemini, ChatGPT, or Claude). Here, you need to optimize for the number of users your infrastructure can handle at once. You need to think about the latency your *slowest* user encounters during a traffic spike. With

1 If you're not familiar with this adorable alien, check out the film, *E.T. the Extra-Terrestrial,* directed by Steven Spielberg (1982, Universal Pictures).

things like continuous batching, you fill the context window with multiple requests, or PagedAttention (see Chapter 14), so you keep the GPU saturated instead of idle. This is vLLM's territory. It generally prefers the merged 16-bit model or a GPU-friendly quantized build.

The good news: you don't have to choose a single ecosystem. Both stacks can speak the same OpenAI-compatible protocol, so the decision of *where* the model runs can be decoupled from *how* you access it. You can prototype at the edge with Ollama on your desktop, and then deploy to vLLM in production without changing your client code!

So let's start with that, and explore Ollama for local, edge serving.

Using Ollama

First, if you don't have it already, you can install Ollama using the instructions from Ollama (*https://ollama.com*). For the rest of this chapter, I'll assume you have it up and running. If you want some basic instructions on how to use it, especially with a Gemma model, check out the online course (*https://oreil.ly/nNBeT*) I teach about it.

Ollama is the fastest path from your GGUF file to a model that you can easily interact with. It manages models, loads them on demand, assigns them to the appropriate hardware, and even exposes them over a local HTTP API. If you're using a machine you control, like your laptop or a desktop, it's a great place to start. I use it with Gemma 4 on my laptop daily.

Ollama uses a concept called a Modelfile, which is roughly analogous to a Dockerfile. It defines everything you need to get a model running with a single line of code, including the model file, parameters, and other configurations. Sharing the Modelfile lets you move between machines while keeping an identical experience.

Here's the Modelfile for the *medical-gemma-Q4_K_M.gguf* you created in Chapter 14:

```
FROM ./medical-gemma-Q4_K_M.gguf

TEMPLATE """{{- if .System }}<|turn>system
{{.System }}<turn|>
{{ end }}
{{- range .Messages }}
{{- if eq .Role "user" }}<|turn>user
{{.Content }}<turn|>
{{ else if eq .Role "assistant" }}<|turn>model
{{.Content }}<turn|>
{{ end }}
{{- end }}<|turn>model
"""

PARAMETER temperature 0.3
```

```
PARAMETER top_p 0.9
PARAMETER top_k 40
PARAMETER num_ctx 8192
PARAMETER stop "<turn|>"

SYSTEM """You are a medical question-answering assistant..."""
```

Let's explore this. The `FROM` at the top will point to the *medical-gemma-Q4_K_M.gguf* file, so the model you serve will be the one you compressed and measured in Chapter 14.

The `TEMPLATE` command bakes in the Gemma 4 chat format, which is important because the model was fine-tuned using that exact format. Each turn opens with `<|turn>` followed by the role (system, user, or model) and closes with `<turn|>`. That's also why the stop parameter is set to <turn|>: the model stops generating when it closes its own turn. Keep a close eye on this, because template mismatches are often the cause of a model that loads fine but gives weird answers! Putting it into the Modelfile means that callers send plain messages and never have to hand-assemble the special tokens.

Understanding Template Mismatches

What does a template mismatch actually look like? It might not throw an error, and the model loads and responds! Instead, you'll see control tokens leaking into answers as literal text, generation that runs past its stop token or halts mid-sentence, a system prompt that's silently ignored, or a model that behaves like the base because your fine-tune's behavior is keyed to the exact token arrangement it was trained on. The fastest checks: compare `ollama show --template` output against what `apply_chat_template` produced during training (they should match exactly), send a system-prompt canary like `"only reply like a pirate"` to confirm instructions arrive, and test a multiturn exchange, which exercises role labels that one-shot prompts never touch. If quality still seems off with the template verified, rerun a slice of your held-out test set against the served model. If you see a systematic drop against the Chapter 14 numbers with identical weights, you can suspect the serving layer, not the model.

The `PARAMETER` commands set things like the temperature and context window size.

Finally, `SYSTEM` is used to specify the system prompt.

You can create an instance of your medical-gemma with this setup using a single command, where in this case the Modelfile is in the *Chapter15/00_Modelfile* directory:

```
ollama create medical-gemma -f Chapter15/00_Modelfile
```

This registers the model, reading your GGUF and configuration into Ollama's local store.

Once it exists, you can check if it's available using `ollama list`. And then you can run it like this to ask a specific question:

```
ollama run medical-gemma "What are first-line treatments for type 2 diabetes?"
```

You can also simply run `ollama run medical-gemma` to open a chat session. I'm writing this and testing on a Mac mini M4, and the medical-gemma outputs tokens faster than I can read them!

You can see this pipeline, namely starting with the GGUF, specifying a Modelfile, creating, and serving, in Figure 15-1.

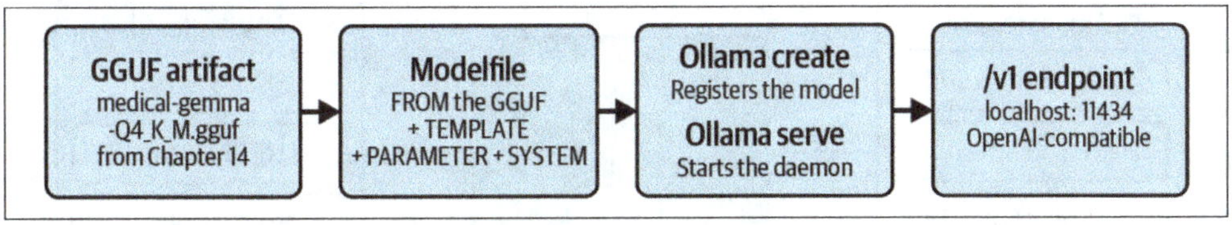

Figure 15-1. The GGUF-to-serving pipeline

When you run Ollama, you get a `/v1` endpoint at `http://localhost:11434`, and we'll explore how to hit that next. This is notable, because it provides the same endpoint syntax as the de facto standard OpenAI endpoints, making your life a lot easier when you build client code to interact with the model!

The OpenAI Endpoint Format

The OpenAI endpoint format has become a de facto standard for requests against a hosted API. It looks like this: a `POST` to `/v1/chat/completions` that carries a model name, a list of messages, and parameters like `temperature` or `stream`. That shape has become the standard way of talking to a language model. Ollama uses it too, so by running your GGUF on Ollama, your code to talk to your endpoint won't need to significantly change.

So, for example, if you want a client for the `medical-gemma` model you ran in the last section, your code can look like this:

```
from openai import OpenAI

# The api_key is required by the SDK but ignored by a local server.
client = OpenAI(base_url="http://localhost:11434/v1",
                api_key="not-needed-for-local")

resp = client.chat.completions.create(
    model="medical-gemma",
```

```
    messages=[{"role": "user",
               "content": "Explain the mechanism of beta blockers."}],
    temperature=0.3,
)
print(resp.choices[0].message.content)
```

The `base_url` here is configured for Ollama. Later, if you want to run the model on vLLM, you only need to change this. The rest of the code will work.

Figure 15-2 shows this basic idea. With the same endpoint structure, and the same JSON payload, your software and the backend are decoupled through a standard interface. So as long as each side understands that contract, they can change without breaking the application.

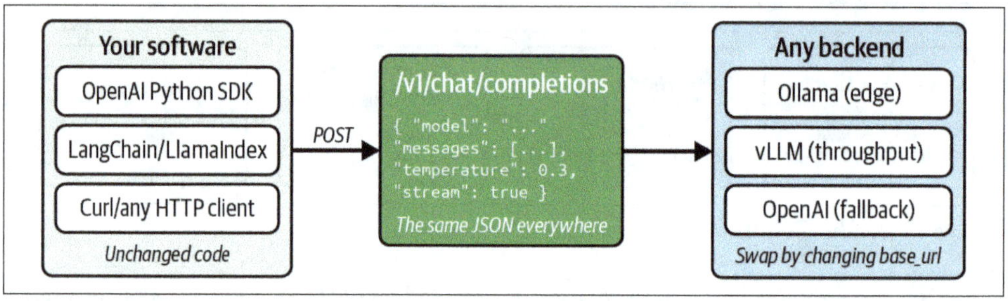

Figure 15-2. One contract, many backends

One feature that is important to call out for many scenarios, particularly chat ones, is streaming. Remember, a language model produces its output one token at a time. When chatting, users expect to *see* them appear one at a time, rather than a spinning wheel that is followed by the complete answer. The SDK supports this by providing `chat.completions.stream`.

You use it like this:

```
with client.chat.completions.stream(
    model="medical-gemma",
    messages=[{"role": "user", "content": "..."}],
) as s:
    for event in s:
        if event.type == "content.delta":
            print(event.delta, end="", flush=True)
```

It's interesting in that it doesn't *speed up* the response, and may in fact slow it down a little. But it *feels* faster because you're engaged reading token by token, instead of looking at a blank screen waiting for an answer. And because it's part of the contract, it will work with other backends, such as vLLM.

> **Streaming Responses**
>
> If you've seen streaming done differently, that's because there are two layers to it. The original mechanism, which still works on every version of the SDK, passed `stream=True` to `create()`.
>
> You would then get raw chunks and pull the text out of `chunk.choices[0].delta.content` yourself. The `chat.completions.stream()` helper used here is a newer convenience wrapper over exactly that: it adds typed events, handles cleanup via the `with` block, and can hand you the assembled final message when the stream ends.
>
> On older SDK releases, it lived at `client.beta.chat.completions.stream()`, so if the preceding code gives you an attribute error, either update the openai package or fall back to `stream=True`. The tokens arriving over the wire are identical either way.

Using vLLM

Ollama is built for one conversation at a time. Once you start dealing with concurrent users, the problem changes shape, and that's when it's probably good to start looking toward vLLM. This is an inference server that is built from the ground up for throughput, and is what many production open-model deployments will run on. It reads a standard Hugging Face model directory, so the merged bf16 model you produced in Chapter 14 will work well.

To install vLLM, it's recommended that you use an NVIDIA GPU. If you don't have one already, you can use Colab or any of the rental GPUs we discussed back in Chapter 3.

Generally, it's recommended that you run it in a virtual environment to keep dependencies clean, like this:

```
python3.12 -m venv .venv
source .venv/bin/activate
pip install --upgrade pip
pip install vllm
```

If you're running in Colab, with a machine you'll throw away at the end of the session, you might just want to use the last two lines. It's up to you! However, if you're doing this, you might need to be careful with dependencies, most notably the NVIDIA drivers to ensure that the ones vLLM is using match the ones that are already available in Colab.

When using vLLM, you generally use the named model from Hugging Face, or if you prefer, your own merged model having taken the base model and merged your LoRAs in. So, for example, if you used the merge model scripts from Chapter 14, you'll have a model directory called `medical-gemma-merged`, and you can serve it with:

```
vllm serve ./medical-gemma-merged \
    --served-model-name medical-gemma \
    --port 8000 \
    --max-model-len 8192 \
    --gpu-memory-utilization 0.90 \
    --dtype bfloat16
```

That command, wrapped with sensible defaults and found in the file *Chapter15/02_vllm_serve.sh* from the book's download, starts an OpenAI-compatible server on port 8000. The same client from earlier talks to it unchanged. So what are you buying by moving from Ollama to vLLM, given the interface is identical? The answer involves two techniques that you met in Chapter 14, now doing their real work.

The first is *continuous batching*. A naive server batches requests statically: it collects a group, runs them together, and waits for every request in the group to finish before starting the next group. Because requests finish at different times, the GPU sits idle waiting for the slowest one, and new requests wait for the whole batch to clear. vLLM instead schedules at the token level. The instant one sequence in the batch completes, its slot is refilled with a waiting request, so the GPU never idles and new work starts immediately. On realistic mixed traffic this is the difference between a GPU running at a fraction of its capacity and one running near full utilization. You can see this in Figure 15-3.

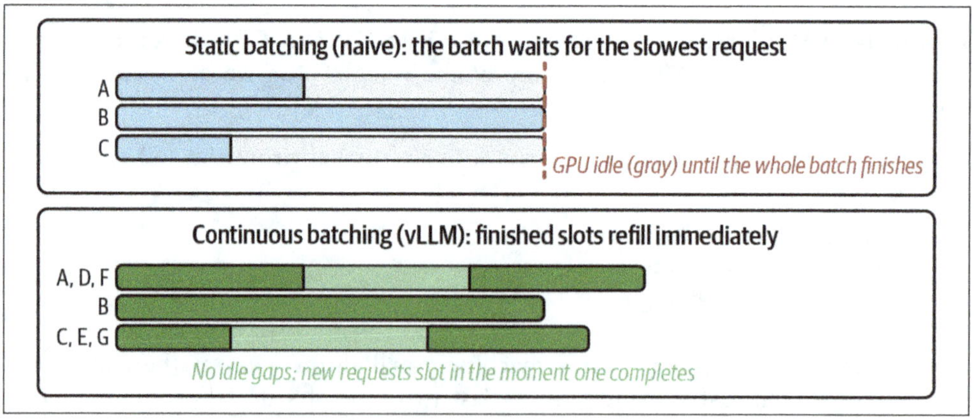

Figure 15-3. Static versus continuous batching

The second technique we're revisiting is `PagedAttention` for KV-cache management. Rather than reserving a contiguous block of memory per sequence sized to the maximum possible length, vLLM manages the cache in small, fixed-size pages allocated on demand (much like virtual memory in an operating system). It wastes almost no memory on short sequences and can share identical pages, such as a common system prompt, across requests. The result is that you fit far more concurrent conversations into the same GPU memory, which is the same thing as serving more users per dollar.

To help test this, I've provided a script in the book's download (*05_load_test.py*) that fires a configurable number of concurrent requests and will report both per-request latency and aggregate throughput, so you can measure how they perform with your hardware:

```
python code/05_load_test.py --base http://localhost:8000/v1 \
    --model medical-gemma --concurrency 16 --requests 64
```

Run it against Ollama at concurrency 1 and vLLM at concurrency 16, and the shape of the result will be clear: Ollama gives excellent single-user latency, and vLLM sustains far higher total throughput as concurrency climbs. That is the whole trade, quantified for your model instead of assumed.

A note on precision for GPU serving. Serving the merged bf16 model gives you maximum quality when the GPU has room. When it does not, point vLLM at a GPU-friendly quantized build. As you saw in Chapter 14, the format that pairs well with vLLM's `PagedAttention` is a `compressed-tensors` build such as GPTQ, or the official QAT w4a16 checkpoints, rather than the GGUF you built for Ollama. GGUF is the portable CPU and Apple Silicon format; for GPU serving, you want a format the GPU serving path is optimized for. The bit-width "knee" you found in Chapter 14 still governs the accuracy trade, so choose the quantized build the same way—from the table and not from vibes.

Your merged medical model serves on vLLM exactly the same way the stock Gemma 4 base does. It is the same architecture with the same tensor layout, so once vLLM can load the base, it can load your fine-tune; the client, the continuous batching, and the KV-cache handling all behave identically. There is nothing model-specific to configure.

Gemma 4 Considerations

As with any model, you'll find each has its own quirks that you might need to work around. In particular, Gemma 4 is a recent architecture, so let's look at some predeployment considerations.

The first consideration to be aware of is a possible error you could receive: *CUDA version mismatch at import time*. vLLM ships prebuilt CUDA binaries, and if the wheel you install was built for a different CUDA major version than your machine provides, the import fails with something like `ImportError: libcudart.so.13: cannot open shared object file`. This is common on managed environments like Colab, where the preinstalled PyTorch targets one CUDA line and the default vLLM wheel targets another.

The fix is to align them. Check the driver's CUDA version with `nvidia-smi`. The top-right number that you'll see is the highest CUDA the driver supports, not proof the runtime libraries are installed. Then, reinstall vLLM so its build matches (e.g., `uv pip install vllm --torch-backend=auto`) and restart the runtime so the old libraries unload before you try again.

The second consideration is the processor files. Because Gemma 4 is multimodal, vLLM resolves the checkpoint as `Gemma4ForConditionalGeneration` and expects *preprocessor_config.json* and *processor_config.json* alongside the weights, even though your medical model only ever handles text. The Chapter 14 merge script (*Chapter14/01_merge_adapter.py*) saves the full processor for exactly this reason, so if you used that, these files are already present.

Using Gemma 4 with vLLM

A version note on Gemma 4 support. Gemma 4 E4B uses cross-layer KV sharing (declared in the `config` as `num_kv_shared_layers`), where a block of later layers reuses the keys and values computed by earlier layers instead of projecting their own. That's a win for memory, but it means a serving stack has to implement the pattern explicitly. vLLM's support for it matured over several releases after Gemma 4 shipped. Early versions had gaps in both serving paths: some releases couldn't load a merged checkpoint (failing on the shared tail layers' missing `k_proj` and `v_proj` tensors—which are supposed to be absent, so your merge is correct), while others refused runtime LoRA for the Gemma 4 architecture—or worse, appeared to load the adapter but silently returned base-model answers.

So before you deploy, install the latest vLLM, try the path you want first, and, most importantly, run a slice of your held-out test set against whatever comes up. A server that starts cleanly is not evidence that your fine-tune is actually being served; your Chapter 14 accuracy numbers are the proof you should be looking at, and five minutes of retesting catches every one of these failure modes, including the silent one.

Serving the Unmerged Adapter

Merging isn't the only way to get your fine-tune behind an endpoint. vLLM can also load the unmodified base model and attach your adapter at runtime, applying its contribution on the fly, per request.

This is the same runtime-adapter mechanism you'll use to serve fleets of experts that you'll see in the next section, just applied to a single adapter. Here's an example:

```
vllm serve google/gemma-4-e4b-it \
    --enable-lora \
    --lora-modules medical-qa=./medical-qa-v1-gemma4-lora \
    --max-lora-rank 16 \
    --served-model-name gemma-base \
    --port 8000 --max-model-len 8192
```

Be sure to set the `max-lora-rank` parameter to at least the amount you trained your adapter for! The value of 16 should be safe here, but if you've done others, be sure to use them. For the model, you add a `--lora-modules` parameter, and list the models there. In this case, there's only one that you'll call `medical-qa` and point it at the LoRA directory.

Then, you can call the server to get this model by specifying that name (`medical-qa`) as the one you want, like so:

```
# the fine-tune
curl http://localhost:8000/v1/chat/completions
            -H "Content-Type: application/json" \
  -d '{"model":"medical-qa",
       "messages":[{"role":"user", "content":
       "First-line treatments for T2DM?"}]}'

# the unadapted base, for comparison
curl http://localhost:8000/v1/chat/completions -H
     "Content-Type: application/json" \
  -d '{"model":"gemma-base",
       "messages":[{"role":"user",
                    "content":"First-line treatments for T2DM?"}]}'
```

Run a few of your held-out questions through both, and the difference your fine-tuning made is visible side by side. This comparison is also your defense against the silent failure mode from the version consideration we just noted—if the two models give identical answers, your adapter isn't actually being applied, and you've caught it in one curl instead of in production.

So when do you serve unmerged versus merged? Runtime adapters cost a small per-request overhead (the adapter's matrices are applied on every forward pass), and they add a moving part. For a single expert in steady production, the merged artifact is still the cleaner ship: one file, no PEFT-shaped dependencies, nothing to configure. But the unmerged path wins during iteration—retrain the adapter, restart the server, and you're testing the new version without a merge-and-requantize cycle in between. It's the only path that scales to many experts, which is exactly where the next section goes.

This isn't optimal if you are only using a single fine-tune, as running merged is cleaner for that; however, it is the fastest way to iterate on an adapter, because it's the exact mechanism you'll use to scale up to a fleet of experts.

Serving Many Experts from One Base

Chapter 14 ended the merging discussion with a deliberate loose thread: if you serve many fine-tunes of the same base, one adapter per specialty or per customer, then merging and shipping a full model copy per expert multiplies your storage and memory by the number of experts. You now have everything you need to fix that! In fact, you already did it in the previous section, using `--enable-lora` with just one entry in the list. Scaling from one expert to a fleet is simply a case of adding lines to `--lora-modules`. Let's explore that.

The idea is to keep a single base model loaded in GPU memory and hot-swap the small LoRA adapters per request. The base weights (the expensive part) are loaded once. Each adapter is a few tens of megabytes, and vLLM applies the right one on the fly, based on which model the request names. Here's an example:

```
vllm serve google/gemma-4-e4b-it \
    --enable-lora \
    --max-loras 4 \
    --lora-modules \
        cardiology=./adapters/cardiology-lora \
        oncology=./adapters/oncology-lora \
        general-med=./medical-qa-v1-gemma4-lora \
    --port 8000 --max-model-len 8192
```

Here, a request routes to a specific expert simply by naming the adapter in the model field. Ask `cardiology` one question and `oncology` the next, and both run over the exact same base weights in memory, with no reload between them. The full launch script and example requests are in *Chapter15/03_vllm_multi_lora.sh*.

Serving multiple model adapters is illustrated in Figure 15-4.

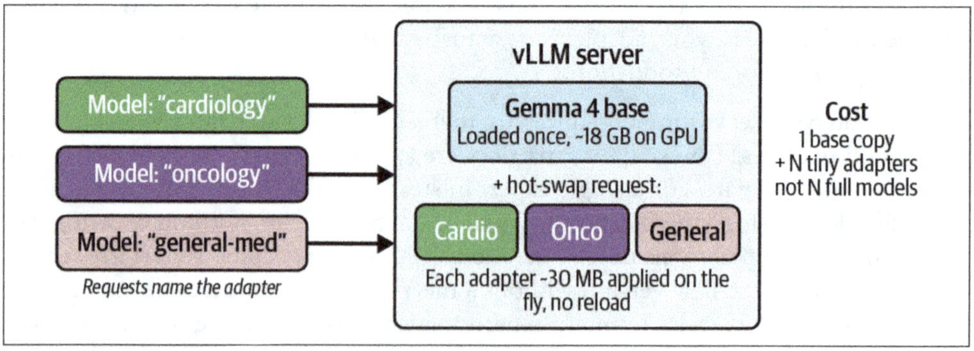

Figure 15-4. Serving multiple models

The economics are obvious. Ten merged models are ten full copies of the base, ten times the storage and, if you want them all hot, ten times the GPU memory. Ten adapters over one shared base are one base copy plus ten small deltas. For a business built on vertical AI, offering a different tuned expert to each customer is the difference between a deployment that scales and one that does not. The golden rule: merge and ship a standalone artifact when you serve one expert, and keep adapters separate when you need to serve a bunch of them.

Production Concerns

The difference between a demo and a service is having the operational glue that turns a running model into something you can safely expose. You want your code to parse the output reliably, so it needs to be structured; you want boundaries that control who can call the model and when. And of course, you need observability to know if things go wrong!

Structured Output

An expert model is only useful inside a pipeline if the software downstream can reliably parse its output. Asking the model politely to "respond in JSON" fails often enough—a stray sentence before the brace, a trailing comma, a hallucinated field—to break production at the worst time. Additionally, JSON is a format descriptor, and not a format itself. There's countless ways output could be expressed in JSON.

The fix is *guided decoding*, and it operates at the sampling level rather than the prompt level. The server constrains generation so that the only tokens the model is allowed to emit are ones that keep the output valid against a schema you supply. The output will parse far more reliably, because invalid output is made unrepresentable.

vLLM exposes this through a `guided_json` field. Here's an example:

```
TRIAGE_SCHEMA = {
    "type": "object",
    "properties": {
        "condition": {"type": "string"},
        "urgency": {"type": "string",
                    "enum": ["routine", "urgent", "emergency"]},
        "refer_to_specialist": {"type": "boolean"},
    },
    "required": ["condition", "urgency", "refer_to_specialist"],
}

resp = client.chat.completions.create(
    model="medical-gemma",
    messages=[{"role": "user",
               "content": "58yo, crushing chest pain, 20 min. Triage."}],
    extra_body={"guided_json": TRIAGE_SCHEMA},
)
data = json.loads(resp.choices[0].message.content)   # guaranteed to parse
```

Ollama also has the same capability through its `format` field. The goal is the same. For something like this, the `urgency` field is constrained to three different values, so you can reliably write code against it. When your model is a component in a larger system (rather than a chatbot, for example), this is essential!

A Gateway in Front

Both Ollama and vLLM already speak OpenAI, so why put anything in front of them? Because the model server's job is inference, and there are other concerns that you need to keep in mind when building a production system. For example, you'll need authentication so that not everyone who can reach the network can spend your GPU, a health check endpoint that your load balancer can poll and route traffic accordingly, a request timeout so one slow generation cannot pin a worker forever, and a single place to emit logs and enforce rate limits. You can also check other system metrics like queue sizes, GPU memory allocations, and so on.

The basic idea is shown in Figure 15-5.

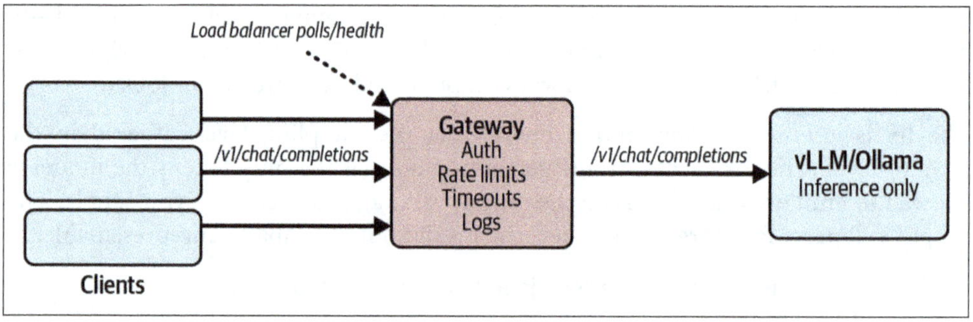

Figure 15-5. Adding a thin gateway

A thin gateway adds these without reimplementing inference, forwarding chat requests to the backend and wrapping them in operational discipline. The full version is in *Chapter15/06_fastapi_gateway.py* and its core is here:

```
@app.get("/health")
async def health():
    r = await _client.get("/models")      # cheap liveness poll of the backend
    return {"status": "ok" if r.status_code == 200 else "degraded"}

@app.post("/v1/chat/completions")
async def chat(request: Request, authorization: str = Header(default="")):
    if API_KEY and authorization != f"Bearer {API_KEY}":
        raise HTTPException(status_code=401, detail="invalid api key")
    try:
        resp = await _client.post("/chat/completions",
                                  content=await request.body())
    except httpx.TimeoutException:
```

```
        raise HTTPException(status_code=504, detail="model timed out")
    return resp.json()
```

> The version printed here is designed for simplicity. It buffers the complete response before returning it, which is fine for illustrating the auth and timeout pattern, but doesn't work if a client sends `"stream": true`. The full gateway in *Chapter15/06_fastapi_gateway.py* does it properly: it opens the backend request in streaming mode and returns a `StreamingResponse` that pipes bytes through as they arrive, so streaming and nonstreaming requests both pass through untouched.

The gateway will preserve the OpenAI contract, so your clients don't need to know what's behind it. That's ultimately the point. Every layer in the stack will keep the same interface, so you can insert operational elements without making breaking changes to callers.

Observability and Capacity

Two numbers can tell you whether or not a deployment is healthy. You should log these from day one: per-request latency and the TPS the server handles under real concurrency. The single structured log line the gateway emits per request is the seed of this. Keep an eye on the latency of your slowest 5% of users because just looking at averages can hide the spikes that make users abandon your product.

Capacity planning also brings back the KV-cache math from Chapter 14. Don't forget it! You should size hardware for the quantized weights, deploy them, and then find out that you run out of memory the first time a user pastes in a long document because of the rapid cache growth. Remember to compute the maximum supported context before you deploy, and adjust things like the cache quantization or the `PagedAttention` to manage it. Static weights are only a part of your memory budget.

Conclusion: The Future Is Specialized

Step back and look at what you've built across the pages of this book. You started at the API wall, paying per token to rent a generalist that knew a little about everything and next to nothing about your specialized domain. It seems so naive in hindsight!

Then you went under the hood. You learned how a transformer actually works. You explored tokens, embeddings, attention—the whole stack—not as trivia, but because every practical decision that followed depended on it! You saw what a LoRA attaches to, why a chat template matters, what a KV cache is and why it eats your memory. You picked a small open model, Gemma, and learned to read its architecture and understand it to optimize it.

Then came the part that actually makes an expert: the data. You curated and formatted a real medical Q&A dataset, learned why data quality beats data quantity, and ran the fine-tuning loop with LoRA and QLoRA where you trained a few million parameters instead of a few billion, on hardware you could actually afford. You learned to read loss curves, tune hyperparameters with a workflow, and evaluate the result with held-out test sets. And you went beyond imitation to preference—aligning the model with DPO so it didn't just know the right answers, but answered the right way.

Then you left pure language behind. You fine-tuned Gemma 4's vision side to reason about domain-specific images. You then crossed into an entirely different architecture: diffusion. There, you discovered that the playbook barely changed; it's the same LoRA, same data discipline, and same evaluate-then-iterate loop, whether teaching a model a dog with DreamBooth or your brand's style with a style LoRA. That was the quiet lesson of the middle of this book: fine-tuning is not a language-model trick, it's a general skill.

And finally, you made it real. You merged the adapter, quantized it while measuring exactly what it cost you, and served the result in two different ways: privately on a laptop with Ollama, and at production throughput with vLLM. These use the same standard API, with structured output you can build against.

That capability is the leading edge of a broad shift. The first era of LLM AI was defined by a handful of multibillion-dollar generalist models that were genuinely astonishing. But a single model that knows everything is rarely the right tool for a specific job. It's expensive, it's slow, it's hosted by somebody else so you must share your data, and your domain might be barely known to it.

The next leap forward is specialization—not one model that knows everything, but a swarm of specialists, each with deep expertise in a narrow area. For example, one model tuned on a hospital's protocols, another on a company's codebase, or one that catches an illustrator's style. Each of these examples, and countless others, should be small enough to run privately and cheap enough to retrain when the world changes.

The techniques in this book make that world buildable. The barrier to entry has been greatly lowered! The same laptop that runs your model could also be training the next adapter.

Therein lies an opportunity: take a domain that you understand better than any web crawl ever could. Gather the data. Train a model on it. Evaluate it. Compress it. Serve it.

You can now go build an expert, and help your customers own their AI!

Index

A

B

C

D

E

F

H

I

M

Q

R

S

T

U

V

W

X

Y

Z

About the Author

Laurence Moroney is an award-winning researcher and best-selling author. A veteran in the programming and machine learning industry, Laurence has authored over 20 books, including top-selling programming books, science fiction novels, and even movie-related comic books. He teaches popular AI specializations on Coursera with Andrew Ng of DeepLearning.AI. A recognized speaker all over the world, Laurence is passionate about demystifying AI and ML for software developers.

Colophon

The animal on the cover of *Fine-Tuning AI* is a Great Mormon swallowtail (*Papilio memnon*), a large butterfly found in South and Southeast Asia.

Great Mormon swallowtails are notable for their large wings, which can span up to nearly six inches for males. Females tend to be slightly smaller, with wingspans between three and five inches. Along with size, this species also shows a high degree of sexual dimorphism in color and pattern.

Males tend to have black wings decorated with light yellow or white bands. Females can have several different patterns, incorporating whites, blues, reds, and yellows on a black or dark brown base. Some of the female patterns imitate poisonous butterflies as a form of camouflage to deter predators.

The caterpillars are green with white spots and tend to be short and plump. They are commonly found on citrus trees, because the leaves are their preferred source of food. Both the caterpillars and the mature butterflies are a frequent sight in orchards and gardens.

Great Mormons have a large range and a stable population and are classified as being of least concern by the IUCN. Many of the animals on O'Reilly covers are endangered; all of them are important to the world.

The cover illustration is by Monica Kamsvaag and is based on an antique line engraving from *Insects Abroad*. The series design is by Edie Freedman, Ellie Volckhausen, and Karen Montgomery. The cover fonts are Gilroy Semibold and Guardian Sans. The text font is Adobe Minion Pro; the heading font is Adobe Myriad Condensed; and the code font is Dalton Maag's Ubuntu Mono.

www.ingramcontent.com/pod-product-compliance
Lightning Source LLC
LaVergne TN
LVHW061823241026
850939LV00028B/408